The

CICS

Programmer's
Desk
Reference

Doug Lowe

Mike Murach & Associates, Inc.

4697 West Jacquelyn Avenue
Fresno, California 93722
(209) 275-3335

Development team

Technical and production editor:	Anne Prince
Design and production consultant:	Steve Ehlers

Related books by Mike Murach & Associates, Inc.

CICS for the COBOL Programmer, Part 1: an Introductory Course by Doug Lowe
CICS for the COBOL Programmer, Part 2: an Advanced Course by Doug Lowe
CICS for the COBOL Programmer, Instructor's Guide by Doug Lowe

VSAM: Access Method Services and Application Programming by Doug Lowe
VSAM for the COBOL Programmer by Doug Lowe

MVS JCL by Doug Lowe
MVS TSO by Doug Lowe

DOS/VSE JCL by Steve Eckols
DOS/VSE ICCF by Steve Eckols

VM/CMS Commands and Concepts by Steve Eckols

20 19 18 17 16 15 14 13 12 11 10 9 8 7 6 5 4 3 2 1

Library of Congress Catalog Card Number: 87-72034

ISBN: 0-911625-43-7

Contents

Preface   iv

Section 1   CICS program design   1

Section 2   CICS programming fundamentals   17

Section 3   BMS mapset definition   35

Section 4   CICS commands   63

Section 5   Model CICS programs   235

Section 6   JCL procedures for CICS program development   315

Section 7   Resource definition   327

Section 8   Master Terminal and other operator transactions   335

Section 9   Testing and debugging   347

Section 10   AMS commands to define and manipulate VSAM files   359

Section 11   ISPF, ICCF, and CMS   391

Section 12   Reference tables   469

Index   475

Preface

If you're a CICS programmer, take a look at your desk. If you have more than three or four IBM manuals piled up along with one or two programming books, you need this book. If you have more than five or six IBM manuals piled up along with four or five programming books, you *desperately* need this book. This book has just one purpose: to combine all of the reference information you need as a CICS programmer into one handy, easy to use sourcebook. It's the only CICS book you should need on your desk; that's why I call it *The CICS Programmer's Desk Reference*.

What you'll find in this book

If you check the contents of this book, you'll find that it consists of twelve sections. Some of the sections are short, some are long. But I think you'll agree that these sections contain all the reference information you need as you develop CICS programs on a daily basis.

Section 1 summarizes the techniques of CICS program design as presented in my books, *CICS for the COBOL programmer, Part 1* and *Part 2*. In short, this section will help you create program structure charts that lead to simple, maintainable, and efficient programs.

Section 2 presents the basic techniques of command-level programming: how tasks and transactions are managed, how program storage is managed, and the Procedure Division requirements of a CICS program. Here, you'll find examples that show you how to code the top-level module of a pseudo-conversational program, how to handle exceptional conditions and AID keys, how to modify attribute bytes and edit input data, and more.

Sections 3 and 4 present detailed reference information for coding BMS mapsets and CICS commands. Here, you'll find detailed syntax diagrams along with explanations of parameters, options, and exceptional conditions. And you'll find lots of coding models that show you how to use each BMS macro or CICS command in the proper context.

Section 5 contains seven complete CICS programs, reprinted from *CICS for the COBOL Programmer, Part 1* and *Part 2*. You can use these programs as models for your own programs; although their specifications are simplified so they won't get unwieldy, the design and code of these programs can be applied to a wide range of production programs.

Sections 6 through 9 contain information you need to compile, test and debug a CICS program. In section 6, you'll find the JCL procedures you need to assemble BMS mapsets and translate and compile command-level programs, both for MVS and for DOS/VSE. In section 7, you'll find simple examples of the table entries you need to make to install a CICS application. In section 8, you'll find reference information that will help you use the master terminal transaction (CEMT) as well as several other CICS-supplied transactions. And section 9 provides reference information you'll need as you test and debug your programs, such as how to use CEDF and a description of the most common abend codes.

CICS and VSAM go hand in hand, so section 10 presents the details of using Access Method Services to define and manipulate VSAM files. And since you can't do many CICS programming activities without mastering your interactive system and its text editor, section 11 presents the details of the three most commonly used interactive systems: ISPF for MVS users, ICCF for DOS/VSE users, and CMS for VM users.

Finally, section 12 presents a variety of reference tables that come in handy during many phases of program development: hexadecimal conversion tables, the EBCDIC character set, and so on.

How to use this book

As its name implies, you'll probably use this book primarily as a desk reference, in much the same way as you use a dictionary. You don't open your dictionary every time you want to write something;

you use it only when you forget the spelling of a particular word or when you want to explore the nuances of a word's meaning. Likewise with this book: you won't need to refer to it for every line of code you write. But when you forget the syntax of a command, or when you want to explore the nuances of a command option, this book is the place to look.

That doesn't mean, however, that you'll turn to this book only when you're stuck. I suspect you'll find yourself constantly referring to certain sections of this book, such as the coding examples for CICS commands or the model programs. In fact, the coding examples and model programs may well be the most valuable part of this book. So borrow any of them that are relevant to the programs you're working on. If you do that for just a short while, you'll quickly develop a library of your own model programs. And that will significantly improve your productivity.

Although I wrote this book for experienced CICS programmers, that doesn't diminish its usefulness for beginning CICS programmers. In fact, one of the greatest frustrations of programmers new to the CICS environment is that there's so much to learn all at once: you have to learn not just CICS, but VSAM, JCL, and a text editor too. Any one of these topics is hard enough by itself; combined, its amazing any of us ever learned CICS programming. I know I would have learned CICS much faster if I had a book like this.

Conclusion

As far as I know, this book is unique. There are many CICS books, including two of my own, that strive to teach CICS programming to novices. But this is the only book I've seen that's designed specifically to assist the experienced CICS programmer on a daily basis. I'm confident that this book will help clear your desk. Of course, you'll want to keep your copies of *CICS for the COBOL Programmer, Part 1* and *Part 2* close at hand. But as for the pile of IBM manuals, they can safely go in the closet where they belong.

As always, I'm anxious to hear what you think about this book. If you have any comments, suggestions, criticisms, or questions, please use the postage-paid comment form at the back of this book. Your input will help us improve this product as well as future products.

Doug Lowe
Fresno, California
September, 1987

Section 1

CICS program design

This section describes techniques for designing CICS programs. It starts with a recommended development procedure. Then, it describes the various components of a complete CICS program specification. Next, it explains the pseudo-conversational programming technique. Finally, it shows you how to use top-down structured design techniques to design a CICS program.

A program development procedure

The preferred sequence for program development is given in figure 1-1. Although practical considerations may force a slightly different development sequence upon you, you should try to follow this sequence as much as possible. At the least, you should make sure that you analyze the programming problem before you design it and that you design the program before you start to implement it.

In figure 1-1, you can see that step 9 assumes top-down coding and testing. For short programs, you may code the entire program in one step and test it in another. In general, though, you should use top-down coding and testing on any program that takes longer than a day to code.

Within the analysis, design, and implementation tasks, you may rearrange the development steps somewhat. During the implementation phase, for instance, you obviously need to update the CICS tables, create the test data, and code at least a portion of the program so you can begin to test it. But to some extent it depends on the program you're writing and your personal preferences.

If you use walkthroughs in your shop, they should become part of your preferred development sequence. If, for example, design walkthroughs are required, the preferred development sequence becomes this:

1. Analyze the programming problem.
2. Conduct a specification walkthrough.
3. Design the program.
4. Conduct a design walkthrough.
5. Implement the program.

Analysis

1. Get complete specifications.
2. Get related programs, COPY members, and subprograms.

Design

3. Design the program using a structure chart.
4. If necessary, plan the modules of the program using pseudocode or HIPO diagrams.

Implementation

5. Plan the testing of the program by creating a test plan.
6. Make sure that the appropriate CICS tables are updated so you will be able to run your program later on.
7. Create the BMS mapsets required by your program. Create your own symbolic mapsets or use the ones generated by BMS.
8. If necesssary, create the test data for the test runs.
9. Code and test the program using top-down testing.
10. Document the program.

Figure 1-1   The preferred sequence of tasks for developing a CICS program

Developing program specifications

When you receive specifications for a program, they may already be complete. On the other hand, they may be quite sketchy. In any case, it's your job to make sure that the program specifications are complete.

A checklist for program specifications

Complete specifications consist of at least the components illustrated in the specifications for the model programs in this book. A checklist of basic components follows:

1. A program overview

2. A listing of COPY members for all files used by the program

3. Screen layouts for each entry or display screen in an interactive program

4. Screen flow diagrams for interactive programs that use more than one entry or display screen, but only when the flow from one screen to another isn't obvious

5. Print charts for all documents created by a program

In addition, your specifications may include decision tables, editing rules, and so on. Try to look beyond the obvious to make sure you have all the information you need to develop a program.

Program overviews

The program overview can be one or more pages, as illustrated by the overviews for the model programs. The top portion of the first overview page lists the files used by the program. The remainder of the form lists the major functions re-quired by the program. If necessary, you can use subsequent pages of this form to record details you feel are necessary for a complete understanding of the program's requirements.

Keep in mind that the overview is not supposed to indicate the sequence in which the functions of the program are to be performed. Instead, it is intended to specify the requirements of the program in enough detail so a professional programmer can design the program using only the overview and its supporting documents. In other words, the overview shows what the program is supposed to do, but not how the program is supposed to do it.

If you have access to a word processing system, it's best to develop the program overviews using this system. That way, you can make modifications and enhancements to the overviews as you develop the program with a minimum of effort. Figure 1-2, for example, shows the first overview page for the model edit program as prepared by a word processing system. In this case, the headings and rules in the overview are part of the word processing document so they print along with the specifications.

COPY members

COPY members should be available for all files that are used by a program on the assumption that any file is likely to be used by more than one program. So if COPY members have not yet been created for a file used by a program, you must either create them yourself or make sure that they get created.

Other candidates for COPY members are the Common Work Area (CWA), record layouts for temporary storage and transient data queues, data areas passed to programs via the START command, and so on. And, of course, the symbolic map descriptions for BMS mapsets should be available as COPY members, whether you code the descriptions yourself or use the ones automatically created by BMS.

```
-----------------------------------------------------------------
   Program:   MNT2100    Maintain customer file      Page: 1
   Designer:  Doug Lowe                               Date: 05-01-87
-----------------------------------------------------------------
   Input/output specifications
-----------------------------------------------------------------
   File       Description

   CUSTMAST   Customer master file


-----------------------------------------------------------------
   Process specifications
-----------------------------------------------------------------
   Until the operator indicates end of program by using the clear key
   in step 1:

   1.  Get a valid customer number from the KEY SCREEN and attempt to
       read the customer record.  If a record with the specified key
       exists, format its data and send it using the CUSTOMER SCREEN;
       if not, send the CUSTOMER SCREEN without data.

   2.  Get the data from the CUSTOMER SCREEN and determine the action
       to take: the clear key indicates that no action should be taken
       (just return to step 1); for an existing customer, PF1 indicates
       a delete operation and any other key (besides the clear key)
       indicates a change operation; for a new customer, any key other
       than the clear key indicates an addition.

   3.  For an addition, edit the customer data according to the rules
       given below.  If the data is valid, write the record to the
       customer file.

   4.  For a change, edit the customer data according to the rules
       given below.  If the data is valid, read and update the record
       in the customer file.

   5.  For a delete, delete the record from the customer file.

   6.  Implement this program using the pseudo-conversational
       programming technique.  For a change/delete operation, save
       the contents of the customer record in temporary storage
       between program executions; if the data in the record changes
       between executions, cancel the operation and notify the
       terminal user.
```

Figure 1-2   Specifications for a customer maintenance program (part 1 of 2)

```
------------------------------------------------------------------
    Program:    MNT2100    Maintain customer file        Page: 2
    Designer:   Doug Lowe                                Date: 05-01-87
------------------------------------------------------------------
    Editing rules:

    CM-CUSTOMER-NUMBER     Must be non-blank.
    CM-NAME                Must be non-blank.
    CM-ADDRESS             Must be non-blank.
    CM-CITY                Must be non-blank.
    CM-STATE               Must be a valid United States Postal
                           Service state code.  Use the installation
                           subprogram STATEDIT to validate the entry.
    CM-ZIP-CODE            Must be a valid United States Postal
                           Service zip code valid for CM-STATE.
                           Use the installation subprogram ZIPEDIT to
                           validate the entry.
```

Figure 1-2   Specifications for a customer maintenance program (part 2 of 2)

Screen layouts

If all screens in a system are formatted in a standard way, two benefits will result. First, the users will find that the interactive programs are easier to use. Second, it will be easier to create and maintain the mapsets that define these screens as well as the programs that process them. With this in mind, a list of suggestions for preparing screen layouts follows:

1. Divide your screens into three zones: the heading zone, the data zone, and the communication zone. The heading zone (usually, lines 1 and 2 of a screen) should be used to display information like the program name, the date, and the screen number. As much as possible, this should follow a standard format. The data zone should display all data relevant to the program. And, the communication zone (usually, lines 23 and 24 of a screen) should be used to display error messages and operator instructions.

2. As much as possible, the screens should be self-explanatory. In other words, the user shouldn't require an extensive user manual in order to use a program.

3. Whenever possible, data elements should be aligned vertically to make them easier to read.

4. Data elements should be grouped logically to make the screen easier to understand.

5. A screen shouldn't be unnecessarily crowded. If it is, consider using multiple screens.

6. If you use high intensity, color, or other highlighting techniques, use them consistently within the program and from one program to another.

7. Indicate errors in a useful and consistent way. At the least, an error message should identify the field in error and indicate what's wrong with it.

8. If an operator uses a dedicated source document for making entries to a program, the screen should be patterned after the source document.

9. When a data entry program doesn't have a dedicated source document, you should try to pattern the screen after a related output document or a primary input document.

Figure 1-3 shows a screen layout for an interactive program. The heading zone of this screen is just line 1; it displays the program function and the date. The communication zone is lines 23 and 24

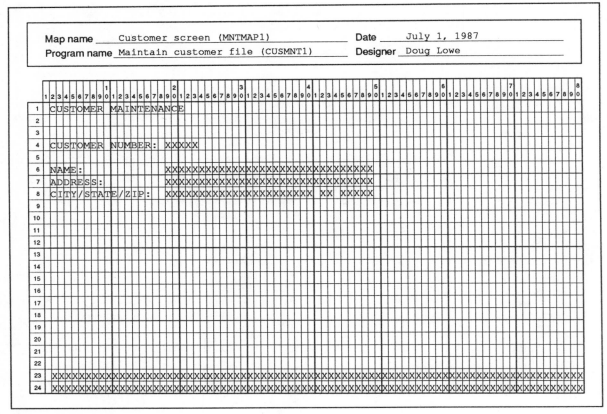

| Map name | Customer screen (MNTMAP1) | Date | July 1, 1987 |
| Program name | Maintain customer file (CUSMNT1) | Designer | Doug Lowe |

Figure 1-3   A screen layout

of the screen, with line 23 used for error messages and line 24 used for operator instructions.

Screen flow diagrams

If a program requires two or more screens, the program specifications should include a screen flow diagram that shows how the screens are to be used. In figure 1-4, for example, you can see a screen flow diagram for a program that uses two screens:

a key screen and a customer data screen. To relate this diagram to the screen layouts, the screen names used on the screen flow diagram should be the same as the names used on the screen layout forms.

The process boxes on the screen flow diagram represent the functions that must be performed to process the data from each operator entry. You can be as general or as specific as you wish when you list these functions; the screen flow diagram will serve only as a guide when you design your program.

Print charts

If your program produces output on a printer, you'll need a print chart that specifies the appearance of the printed data. Unless the data is printed on pre-printed forms (such as invoices), it should have a standard heading that gives the preparation date, the preparation time (if appropriate), and a serial number to uniquely identify the data.

Also, all reports should be as self-explanatory as possible. This means that all data items should be identified on the report itself; the user shouldn't be confused by codes that aren't fully explained or by data items that aren't identified. If you are forced to use codes to identify data items due to space limitations, make sure you use codes that are familiar to the user. Or, explain the codes on the bottom of each page of the report.

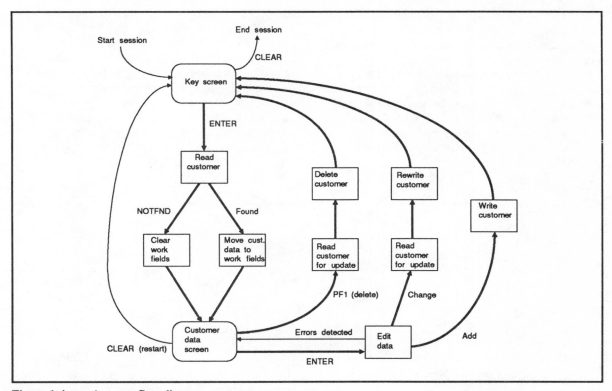

Figure 1-4   A screen flow diagram

Pseudo-conversational programming

Pseudo-conversational programming is a CICS program design technique that you should use for all your CICS programs. In a pseudo-conversational program, every SEND or SEND MAP command must be followed by a RETURN command. In other words, the program must end after it sends data to the terminal. On the RETURN command, the program specifies a trans-id so that when the operator presses the enter key (or any other AID key), the transaction is automatically restarted. Then, the program issues a RECEIVE or RECEIVE MAP command to receive the input data. The program can then process the data, issue another SEND or SEND MAP command, and end again.

The advantage of pseudo-conversational programming is that the program doesn't sit idle while the operator keys data at the terminal. In contrast, a *conversational program* (one that doesn't terminate itself after it sends data to the terminal) sits idle while it waits for the operator to enter input data. And that's inefficient because even though the program is idle, valuable CICS resources (such as main storage) are assigned to it.

Of all the techniques available to improve performance in a CICS system, pseudo-conversational programming probably has the greatest impact. As a result, most CICS shops require that *all* application programs be pseudo-conversational, even though pseudo-conversational programming makes your program's logic more complicated.

When you use pseudo-conversational programming, each operator entry is processed by a separate program execution. As a result, you must decide whether you want to package all of your application's functions into a single program that processes all of the application's screens, or whether you want to use several programs, one for each screen. I think it's usually best to code a single program. But if you decide to use several programs, you should indicate how you package the application's functions into programs by grouping them on the screen-flow diagram. For example, figure 1-5 shows the customer maintenance application's screen flow diagram with the functions packaged into two programs: one to process data from the key screen, the other to process data from the customer data screen.

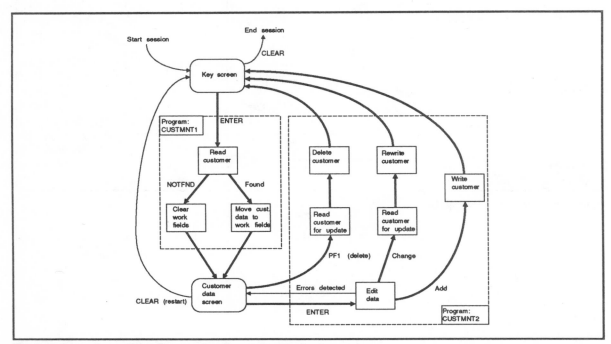

Figure 1-5   Screen flow diagram showing program packaging

Program design

You should use top-down design for the development of all programs. And, as documentation for your design, you should use a structure chart as shown in figure 1-6. This is the first page of the structure chart for the model order-entry program.

The basic principles of program design

1. Each module of a program should represent one and only one function.

2. The function of a called module must be logically contained in the function of its calling module.

3. You must be able to code each module in a single COBOL paragraph.

Four steps for creating structure charts

1. Create a rough draft of the structure chart.

2. Review and analyze the structure chart and revise it as necessary.

3. When you're satisfied with the structure chart, number the modules in it.

4. Draw a refined draft of the structure chart.

Level 0

This level should contain one module that represents the entire program. In a pseudo-conversational program, the program ends each time a map is sent to a terminal awaiting a response from the operator. Then, when the operator presses one of the AID keys (enter, clear, or a PF or PA key), CICS restarts the program. Basically, the function of the level-0 module in a CICS program is to determine what processing needs to be done during a particular execution of the program.

Level 1

In general, this level consists of one module for each screen used by the program. In addition, it should include one start-terminal-session module that properly formats the first screen. And it may include a send-termination-message module that's only executed at the end of the terminal session.

The structure chart in figure 1-6 uses all of these level-1 modules. From left to right, it has a start-terminal-session module, one module for each of the screens shown in the screen flow diagram, and a delete-TS-queue module.

Level 2 and below

For each screen your program processes, you must provide for at least three functions: (1) receiving the data from the screen, (2) processing the data, and (3) sending the next screen. As a result, most of your programs will have level-2 modules like those shown in the structure chart in figure 1-6. As you can see, each of the screen-handling modules calls a receive-screen module, a processing module, and a send-screen module. If necessary, however, a level-1 module can call more than one processing or send-screen module.

Below level-2, the structure of the program depends on the program specifications. Level 3 should contain the subordinates for each level-2 module. To make sure all subordinates are shown, you may want to list the functions that you feel make up each level-2 function. Then, make sure there's one module for each of these functions. Continue this idea for each level until none of the modules can be further divided.

Left-to-right module placement

In general, you place the subordinates at each level from left to right in the sequence in which you think they are likely to be executed. This does not mean, however, that they must be executed in that sequence; in many cases, they won't be executed in the implied sequence.

Module names

1. In most cases, module names should consist of one verb followed by one or two adjectives followed by one object. Occasionally, however, it is acceptable to name a module with only a verb and an object. For instance, "edit address" is acceptable as a module name if it is subordinate to a module named "edit customer data." In this case, it's obvious that the address is a customer address. But if the customer data provides for both a bill-to and a ship-to address, "edit address" is not an acceptable module name. In general, then, use an adjective whenever there's any chance for confusion. Remember that the module name should clearly indicate the function of the module.

2. Because the module number together with the module name will make up the paragraph name for the module in the COBOL program, the module name combined with the module number and separating hyphens must not exceed 30 characters. So you should try to keep your module names within these COBOL limitations.

    From a practical point of view, though, you often won't discover that a module name is too long until you code it in COBOL. Then, you can shorten the module name in your COBOL program, even though you leave it unchanged on your structure chart. For in-

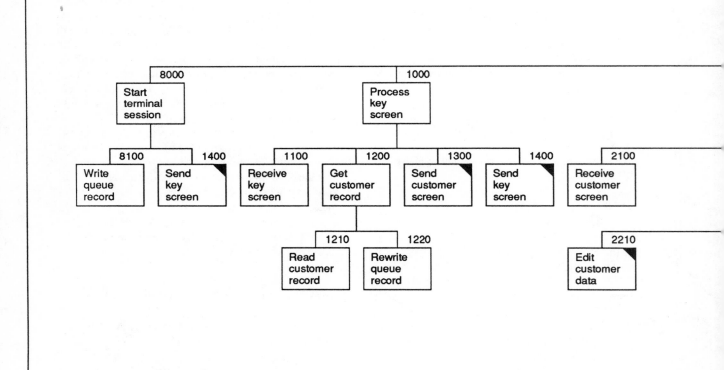

Figure 1-6   A structure chart

stance, a module named "edit inventory transaction" may become 300-EDIT-INVENTORY-TRAN in your COBOL code. But that shouldn't cause any confusion. On the other hand, if you want to shorten the name on your structure chart so it conforms to your COBOL code, that's okay too.

Verb list

Figure 1-7 is a list of module verbs broken down by function (input, output, or processing). We have suggested meanings for all of them; these meanings conform to the way the verbs are used in the programs presented in this handbook. If you add verbs to this list or modify the meaning of some of the verbs in the list, make sure the other program-

mers in your shop agree with your use of the verbs. In other words, all of the programmers in your shop should use the verbs in the same way.

Module numbers

1. All module numbers should be written outside of the module box on the structure chart at the upper righthand corner.

2. The top-level module should be given the number 000 or 0000.

3. The level-1 modules should be given numbers that are multiples of 100 or 1000. Start numbering with the left module and proceed to the right.

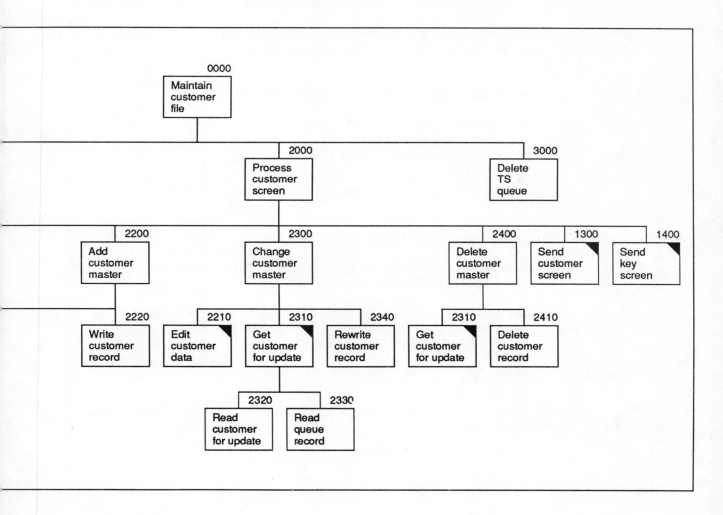

Input verbs	Suggested meaning
Get	Obtain an acceptable record or set of records. This can be used in a batch or an interactive program. Subordinate modules might read a record, edit a record, and dispose of an invalid record.
Read	Physically read records from a file, data base, or queue; count the record if required.
Receive	Receive mapped or unmapped data from a terminal.
Start	Establish positioning for subsequent read operations.

Output verbs

Delete	Remove a record from a file or data base.
Put	Two meanings: (1) Format an output record and call a module to physically write it on an output file; (2) Store an entry in a table and count entries if required.
Rewrite	Replace an existing record in a file, data base, or queue.
Send	Send mapped or unmapped data to a terminal.
Write	Write an output record to a file, data base, or queue.

Processing verbs

Accumulate	Develop totals by successive addition of intermediate totals.
Add	Add a record to a file. Subordinate modules might format the output record and physically write the record.
Apply	Apply a transaction to a record that is being updated or maintained without actually writing, rewriting, or deleting the record on the file. This verb is used in update and maintenance programs.
Calculate	Develop results by any combination of arithmetic operations.

Figure 1-7   A verb list (part 1 of 2)

Change	Modify a record in a file. Subordinate modules might format the changed record and physically write the record.
Compare	Compare two fields or records.
Convert	Change something from one form to another.
Create	Develop a record, table, or file.
Determine	Find out; may include arithmetic combination or file or data base retrieval.
Edit	Check one or more fields or records for validity.
Format	Prepare output records to be written but don't actually write them.
Load	(1) read and store entries in a table; (2) load a program into main storage for subsequent execution.
Maintain	Add records to, change records in, or delete records from a master file based on data maintenance transactions rather than operational transactions. (See update.)
Prepare	This is a general verb that should be used only in control modules. It means to prepare output by doing whatever needs to be done. Subordinate modules might read records, accumulate or calculate new dat fields, and prepare the output.
Process	This is a general verb that should be used only in control modules. It means to operate on input fields to do whatever needs to be done. Subordinate modules might receive terminal data, read file or data base records, accumulate or calculate new fields, and prepare output.
Produce	This is a general verb that should be used only in control modules. It means to produce output by doing whatever needs to be done. Subordinate modules might read records, accumulate or calculate new dat fields, and prepare the output.
Search	Look for in a table or file.
Store	Place entries in a table or fields in storage.
Update	The primary meaning is to change records in a master file based on data in operational transactions as opposed to data maintenance transactions.

Figure 1-7   A verb list (part 2 of 2)

4. From level 2 on down, the modules should be numbered by 10s or 100s. Often, it's most efficient to number down the legs by 10s. That way, all of the COBOL code for a leg will be found in consecutive paragraphs in the COBOL listing.

5. When a module is added to a structure chart after it's numbered, it should be given a number that indicates its logical placement in the structure chart. If, for example, you add a module to a chart that logically comes between modules 2330 and 2340, the new module should have a number between 2330 and 2340, like 2335.

6. Sometimes, you'll want to place a seldom-used module at the end of your program's Procedure Division. That way, you can keep your program's more heavily-used modules closer together so your program will execute more efficiently. To you do that, simply assign the module a high number (like 9500) and place it in numeric sequence near the end of the Procedure Division.

Isolate I/O functions

When you develop CICS programs, you should isolate both file and terminal I/O functions for two reasons. First, they have a significant effect on the structure of your programs. Second, in most cases, CICS requires you to use branching logic within an I/O module to process exceptional conditions. By following this guideline, your programs will be easier to design, develop, and maintain.

Shade common modules

1. A module that's called by more than one module is called a common module. Each common module should be shown as a subordinate to all modules that call it. And the upper righthand corner of each common module should be shaded as illustrated by modules 1300, 1400, 2210, and 2310 in figure 1-6.

2. If a common module has subordinates, the subordinates do not have to be shown each time the common module is drawn. If, for example, module 2480 is a common module with two subordinates, you don't have to repeat the subordinates the second time you show module 2480 on the structure chart. Obviously, module 2480 will call its subordinates every time it is executed.

Using more than one page for large charts

Most production programs will contain so many modules that they can't all be drawn on a single structure chart page. In this case, you use one page of a structure chart to refer to subsequent pages of the chart. Just be sure you clearly indicate how the pages relate to one another.

Checklist for review and analysis of a structure chart

1. Is the structure chart complete? (Does each module have all of its subfunctions represented by subordinate modules?)

2. Does each module name represent only one function? (Does the module name correspond to a single imperative sentence?)

3. Is proper subordination shown? (Is the function of each called module logically contained in the function of the calling module?)

4. Are the control spans reasonable? (Do some modules appear to have too many or too few subordinates?)

5. Are the modules independent? (Are control codes only passed to the calling module?)

6. Are the verbs consistent? (Do the same verbs always imply the same functions?)

Module planning

While you're creating a program structure chart, you often reach a point where you're not sure how a module or group of modules will work. When that happens, you can use either pseudocode or HIPO diagrams to plan the operation of individual program modules. In some shops, you may be required to precisely document the function of each program module using a detailed HIPO diagram. Usually, however, I find it more efficient to plan the key program modules using pseudocode, which is simply an English-language description of the processing a module will do.

Some general principles for module planning

Whether you use pseudocode or HIPO diagrams to plan your modules, here are some general principles you should keep in mind:

1. Keep the modules independent. When you're planning one module, it's okay to check your plans for other modules if you're just checking for trivial details: proper data names, whether a switch has been set, whether a field has been moved, and so on. But if you continually need to refer to processing steps in one module in order to plan a later module in the same program, something's wrong. Perhaps you should review your structure chart to make sure your modules are independent.

2. Document only the function specified by the module name. In some cases, you and other members of your programming group will agree that certain verbs will have conventional meanings in your shop; that is, the verbs will include certain subfunctions that aren't directly implied by their definitions. In the absence of such conventions, however, document only the function named by the module. If you find that a module needs to do more than is clearly implied by its name, you may need to change the module's name to clearly indicate its function, or you may need to add an additional module.

3. In general, move subfunctions down the line. Some subfunctions, like counting records or resetting total fields, are trivial enough that they don't require their own modules. Yet they're often hard to place in existing modules without violating the second principle (document only the named function). It's usually best to place these subfunction in the low-level module that's most closely related to the subfunction. For example, I suggest you count records in the modules that read the records. Often, however, there just isn't a low-level module that's appropriate for the subfunction. In that case, it's better to either create a separate module for the subfunction or place the subfunction in a higher-level module where it belongs.

4. In general, move control code up the line. Sometimes you can logically put certain elements of control code in more than one module of a program. For instance, the code that determines what action to take based on a PF key can be placed in the module that receives terminal data or in a higher-level control module. In this case, I recommend you move the control code up the line into the control module so the control module makes sense without referring to the lower-level modules. In many cases, this forces you to use switches that are set in lower-level work modules and tested in higher-level control modules. That's okay, as long as the switches have clearly-defined control functions and the control modules are easy to understand on their own.

Using pseudocode

When you use pseudocode to plan the modules of a program, you can record your pseudocode on any kind of paper you prefer; specialized forms aren't required. Figure 1-8 shows an example of pseudocode for a CICS program. Remember, pseudocode is your own planning code. It will normally not be subjected to any kind of formal review.

The language of pseudocode

Follow these general guidelines to improve the clarity of your pseudocode:

1.   Capatilize the control words, such as DO, UNTIL, IF, and ELSE.

2.   Use indentation to indicate your code's logical structure.

3.   Use simple English to express functions that don't require control constructs. Later on, you can worry about the coding details that will be required by COBOL.

How detailed should pseudocode be?

Since pseudocode is a personal language, we recommend this simple rule: Code as much detail as you need to convince yourself that you can code the module in COBOL. Avoid coding the program twice, once in pseudocode and again in COBOL.

Using HIPO diagrams

Some structured design methodologies have formalized techniques for recording the processing requirements of each program module. One technique is IBM's HIPO, which stands for Hierarchical Input-Processing-Output. HIPO uses extensive graphics to identify each module's inputs, outputs, and processing steps.

In my opinion, though, HIPO documentation, even with simplified graphics, is mostly a waste of time. After all, the module documentation should be nothing more than a tool to enable you to code your program. If it becomes more than that, it gets in the way of productivity. Nevertheless, if your shop requires HIPO diagrams, you'll have to create them according to your shop's standards.

```
DO 1100-RECEIVE-ENTRY-SCREEN.
IF not end of session
    DO 1200-EDIT-ORDER-DATA
    IF data is valid
        set up switch for verify screen
        DO 1300-SEND-ORDER-SCREEN
    ELSE
        set up switch for entry-screen with errors
        DO 1300-SEND-ORDER-SCREEN.
```

Figure 1-8   Pseudocode for a module of a command-level program

Section 2

CICS programming fundamentals

This section is a review of the fundamentals of coding command-level CICS programs in COBOL. It begins by describing how programs are executed under CICS. Then, it explains how your program can access main storage in various ways. And finally, it explains how to code the Procedure Division of a command-level program.

How programs execute under CICS

CICS is a *multitasking system*, which means that one of its principal functions is managing the concurrent execution of more than one task. Under CICS, a *task* is an execution of one or more programs which function together as a unit called a *transaction*. Depending on its requirements, a task may or may not be associated with a terminal device. If it is, the task can communicate with the terminal user.

When a transaction is invoked, a specified application program is loaded into storage (if it isn't already in storage) and a task is started. The difference between a task and a transaction is that while several users may invoke the same transaction, each execution of the transaction is treated as a separate task.

Each transaction is identified by a unique four-character code called a *transaction identifier*, or just *trans-id*. Most often, a transaction is invoked when an operator enters the transaction's trans-id at a terminal. For example, if an operator keys the characters ORD1 and presses the enter key, the transaction named ORD1 is invoked. And the terminal at which the trans-id was entered is automatically associated with the resulting task.

A special CICS table, called the *Program Control Table* (or just *PCT*), defines each transaction. Basically, the PCT contains a list of valid transaction identifiers. Each trans-id is paired with the name of the program CICS will load and execute when the transaction is invoked.

Another CICS table, called the *Processing Program Table* (or just *PPT*), contains a list of all valid program names. The PPT indicates each program's location: a storage address if the program has already been loaded or a disk location if the program hasn't been loaded. CICS uses the PPT to determine whether it will load a new copy of the program when the transaction is invoked.

To understand how a task is initiated under CICS, look at figure 2-1. Here, the operator starts a transaction by entering the trans-id ORD1. Then, CICS searces the PCT to find the program to be executed. As you can see, the program for transaction ORD1 is ORDPGM1. Next, CICS searches the PPT to determine the location of ORDPGM1. In this case, the program is on disk, so CICS locates it, loads it into storage, and initiates a task.

One final point about tasks, transactions, and programs: although a task is always the execution of a single transaction, it may result in the execution of more than one program. That's because although each transaction loads and executes a single program, that program may issue CICS commands (specifically, LINK or XCTL commands) to load and execute other programs, still within the context of the same task. And those programs may in turn execute still other programs. There's no limit to the number of programs that may be executed as a part of a single task.

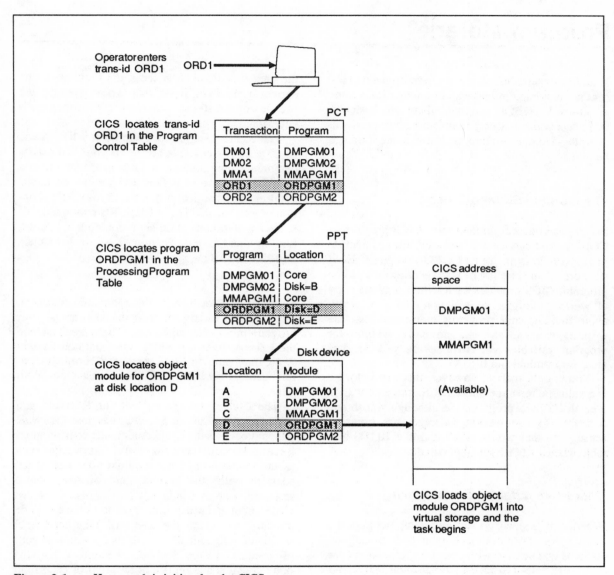

Figure 2-1   How a task is initiated under CICS

Program storage

With few exceptions, all CICS programs need to access main storage in one way or another. In a command-level COBOL program, there are basically two ways you can access main storage: through the Working-Storage Section or through the Linkage Section.

The Working-Storage Section

When you code a command-level CICS program in COBOL, you can use the Working-Storage Section just as you do in any other COBOL program. Even if more than one task is executing the same program, CICS provides each with a separate copy of working storage, so you don't have to worry about making your programs reentrant. Just use working storage as you normally would: for program variables and switches as well as data areas for terminal and file I/O.

You should realize, however, that main storage is a valuable resource under CICS...more so than in a batch COBOL program. So although you should feel free to use working storage, use common sense. In other words, don't define a 10,000-byte table when a 1,000 byte table will do.

Data areas outside your program

When CICS loads your program, it allocates storage for its Working-Storage Section and associates that storage with your program. However, you'll often need to access storage areas that are *not* associated with your task and, therefore, aren't accessable through your program's Working-Storage Section. There are three of these types of areas: the communication area, system areas, and user storage. You access these areas through entries coded in the Linkage Section.

The Communication Area The communication area is an area of main storage that's designed to let programs or tasks communicate with one another. In general, you'll use it in two ways: to communicate with a program you invoke via a LINK or XCTL command or to communicate with the next task invoked at the same terminal as the current task. (You'll do this when you use the pseudo-conversational programming technique, as I'll explain later in this section.)

The communication area can be any length you specify and its contents are up to you. To send a communication area to a task or program, you specify the name of a field (which can be in the Working-Storage Section) in the COMMAREA option of a LINK, XCTL, or RETURN command. To receive a communication area, you code its definition in the Linkage Section; it must be named DFHCOMMAREA.

System areas Besides the communication area, there are a variety of system data areas your program might need to access. These areas include the Execute Interface Block, the Common System Area, the Common Work Area, the Terminal Control Table User Area, and the Transaction Work Area.

The *Execute Interface Block* (or *EIB*) lets you communicate with the *Execute Interface Program*, which processes the CICS commands your program issues. The EIB contains useful information such as the terminal-id of the terminal your task is associated with, the current time of day, and a response code that indicates the results of the last CICS command processed. You don't have to code anything to access the EIB; the command-level translator automatically inserts its definition in your program's Linkage Section. Section 12 of this book contains a complete description of each field in the EIB.

The *Common System Area* (*CSA*) is a major CICS control block that contains important system information, including pointers to most of the other CICS control blocks. Although you can access this area in a command-level program, you ordinarily shouldn't.

The *Common Work Area* (*CWA*) is a storage area that can be accessed by any task in a CICS system. Its format is installation dependent; sometimes, it contains useful information such as the current date already converted to the form MM/DD/YY, your company's name, or other application-specific information.

The *Terminal Control Table User Area* (*TCTUA*) is a user-defined storage area that's unique to the terminal to which the current task is attached; this storage area is maintained even when no task is attached to the terminal. It's not used much in command-level programs.

The *Transaction Work Area* (*TWA*) is a storage area that's unique to the current task. It's deleted when the task ends. Like the TCTUA, the TWA isn't used much in command-level programs.

User storage Sometimes, you may want to allocate storage that's not part of your program's Working-Storage Section. To do that, you issue a GETMAIN command or an input command (such as READ or RECEIVE) using the SET option. These commands allocate storage for you and return the address of that storage to your program. Then, you can access that storage via the Linkage Section.

How to access storage outside your program

As I've already said, you access storage areas outside of your program via the Linkage Section. For the communication area, this is simple: you just code a field named DFHCOMMAREA in the Linkage Section. (It must be the first entry in the

Linkage Section.) For the EIB, it's simpler still: the command-level translator inserts the required coding automatically, so you don't need to code anything. To access other areas, however, you must include some special coding. And that coding depends on whether you're using the standard VS COBOL compiler or the newer VS COBOL II compiler.

Under the VS COBOL compiler, you code these storage areas in the Linkage Section and use a convention called *Base Locator for Linkage* (or *BLL*) to establish addressability to them. Figure 2-2 illustrates this convention. Quite simply, you must define an 01-level item in the Linkage Section following DFHCOMMAREA. In figure 2-2, I called this field BLL-CELLS, but the name doesn't matter. Each field in BLL-CELLS is a pointer that stores the address of a Linkage Section field. These pointers must be binary fullwords (PIC S9(8) COMP). The first pointer points to the BLL-CELLS item itself. Then, each subsequent pointer points to an 01-level item that follows in the Linkage Section. In figure 2-2, the pointer named BLL-FIELD-1 is used to address FIELD-1. Similarly, BLL-FIELD-2 is used for FIELD-2 and BLL-FIELD-3 is used for FIELD-3.

Remember that the names of the BLL cells don't matter. What does matter is the order in which they're coded. Within the BLL-CELLS group, the first pointer points to itself. The second pointer

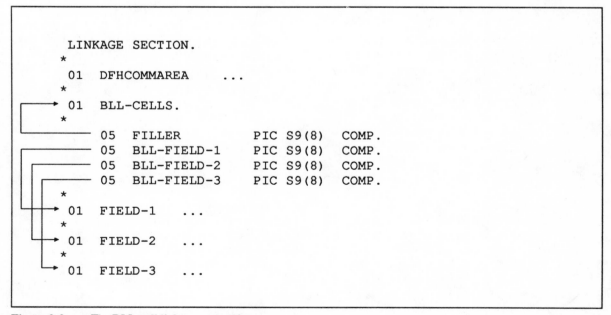

Figure 2-2   The BLL-cell linkage convention

first pointer points to itself. The second pointer points to the first subsequent 01 item, the third pointer points to the second subsequent 01 item, and so on.

Before you can access a Linkage Section field defined in this way, you must load the field's BLL cell with the proper address. Usually, you obtain the address of storage outside your program using the SET option of the various CICS commands that acquire the storage. For system areas like the CWA, you issue an ADDRESS command to obtain the appropriate address. In the SET option or AD-DRESS command, you specify the name of a BLL cell. When the command has completed, the Linkage Section field associated with the BLL cell is addressable.

Under the newer VS COBOL II compiler, the BLL cell convention isn't used. Instead, a special register called ADDRESS OF lets you reference the address of any Linkage Section field. So, instead of specifying BLL-FIELD-1 in a SET option or AD-DRESS command, you would specify ADDRESS OF FIELD-1 in the SET option. Using this technique, you don't have to code BLL cells at all. (Note that under VS COBOL II, you can *not* use BLL cells. So if you're converting a VS COBOL program to VS COBOL II, you'll have to remove all BLL cell definitions and replace any references to BLL cells with the ADDRESS OF special register.)

The Procedure Division

How to code program modules

The three principles that follow will improve the readability of a CICS program:

1. Each module in the structure chart is coded as a COBOL section.

2. The section name for each module consists of the module's number and name taken from the structure chart. The section name, of course, must be followed by the word SECTION.

3. The sections are placed in the program in the order specified by their module numbers.

How to code CICS commands

Each CICS command must begin with the words EXEC CICS and end with the word END-EXEC. I

recommend you separate options with spaces rather than commas and code each option on a separate line. So, your commands should follow this general format:

```
EXEC CICS
    command option-1(value)
             option-2(value)
             .
             .
END-EXEC.
```

How to code the top-level module

Figure 2-3 gives an example of the coding for the top level module of a typical pseudo-conversational program. The top level module of any pseudo-conversational program should begin by checking the length of the communication area (stored in the field EIBCALEN) to determine if it is the first time the program is being invoked within a given ter-

```
    0000-MAINTAIN-CUSTOMER-FILE SECTION.
*
    MOVE LOW-VALUE TO KEY-MAP
                      CUSTOMER-DATA-MAP.
    IF EIBCALEN = ZERO
        PERFORM 8000-START-TERMINAL-SESSION
    ELSE
        MOVE DFHCOMMAREA TO COMMUNICATION-AREA
        IF PROCESS-KEY-SCREEN
            PERFORM 1000-PROCESS-KEY-SCREEN
        ELSE
            PERFORM 2000-PROCESS-CUSTOMER-SCREEN.
    IF END-SESSION
        EXEC CICS
            XCTL PROGRAM('INVMENU')
        END-EXEC
    ELSE
        EXEC CICS
            RETURN TRANSID('MNT1')
                   COMMAREA(COMMUNICATION-AREA)
                   LENGTH(2)
        END-EXEC.
```

Figure 2-3   The top-level module of a pseudo-conversational program

minal session. If it is (EIBCALEN=ZERO), the module should call another module to start the terminal session; otherwise, it should check the value in the communication area to determine what processing needs to be done.

After the appropriate processing module has been executed, the program should end its current execution. If the operator has indicated that the terminal session should end, the program should invoke a module to display a termination message (this is optional) and transfer control to another program (most likely, a menu program). Otherwise, it should issue a RETURN command that specifies (1) the TRANSID option to cause the same transaction to be invoked the next time the operator presses ENTER or another AID key and (2) the communication area that should be passed to the next execution of the program.

```
      2100-READ-CUSTOMER-RECORD SECTION.
*
      EXEC CICS
          HANDLE CONDITION NOTFND(2100-NOTFND)
                           NOTAUTH(2100-NOTAUTH)
                           NOTOPEN(2100-NOTOPEN)
      END-EXEC.
      MOVE 'Y' TO CUSTOMER-FOUND-SW.
      EXEC CICS
          READ DATASET('CUSTMAS')
               INTO(CUSTOMER-RECORD)
               LENGTH(CUSTOMER-RECORD-LENGTH)
               RIDFLD(CR-CUSTOMER-NUMBER)
      END-EXEC.
      GO TO 2100-EXIT.
*
  2100-NOTFND.
*
      MOVE 'N' TO CUSTOMER-FOUND-SW.
      MOVE 'CUSTOMER RECORD NOT FOUND' TO OPERATOR-MESSAGE.
      GO TO 2100-EXIT.
*
  2100-NOTAUTH.
*
      MOVE 'N' TO CUSTOMER-FOUND-SW.
      MOVE 'YOU ARE NOT AUTHORIZED TO ACCESS THE CUSTOMER FILE'
          TO OPERATOR-MESSAGE.
      GO TO 2100-EXIT.
*
  2100-NOTOPEN.
*
      MOVE 'N' TO CUSTOMER-FOUND-SW.
      MOVE 'CUSTOMER FILE NOT AVAILABLE' TO OPERATOR-MESSAGE.
*
    2100-EXIT.
*
      EXIT.
```

Figure 2-4   Using the HANDLE CONDITION command

How to provide for exceptional conditions

Nearly all CICS commands can result in one or more unusual situations; CICS notifies you of these situations by raising *exceptional conditions*. In general, there are two quite different ways of providing for exceptional conditions in a CICS program. The method most commonly used is to issue HANDLE CONDITION commands, which name routines to be given control when a condition is detected. The second method, allowable only under CICS release 1.6 and later releases, is to code the NOHANDLE option on the CICS commands and test a response code following the command to see if any errors resulted. Because there are advantages and disadvantages to both approaches, I'll describe them both and let you decide which you'll use. (Of course, your shop's standards may well dictate one of the two approaches.)

Figure 2-4 shows the coding for a typical module that reads data from a file. Here, a HANDLE CONDITION command establishes processing routines for three error conditions: NOTFND, NOTAUTH, and NOTOPEN. Then, the READ command retrieves a record from the data set. If no error occurs, processing continues with the GO TO statement following the READ command. The GO TO statement transfers control to the exit paragraph, bypassing the error-processing routines. But, if the NOTFND, NOTAUTH, or NOTOPEN condition occurs, control is transferred immediately to the appropriate routine. In this example, each of the routines merely sets a switch; in an actual program, you might need more significant processing in the error routines. In any event, each error routine, except the last, ends with a GO TO statement that transfers control to the exit paragraph, bypassing the other error routines.

Figure 2-5 shows the same module using the NOHANDLE option under CICS release 1.7. Here, no HANDLE CONDITION command is issued; instead, the READ command includes the NOHANDLE option so that exceptional conditions don't cause the program to terminate abnormally. In addition, the READ command includes the RESP option, which names a variable into which a

```
       2100-READ-CUSTOMER-RECORD SECTION.
*
       EXEC CICS
           READ DATASET('CUSTMAS')
                INTO(CUSTOMER-RECORD)
                LENGTH(CUSTOMER-RECORD-LENGTH)
                RIDFLD(CR-CUSTOMER-NUMBER)
                NOHANDLE
                RESP(RESPONSE-CODE)
       END-EXEC.
       IF RESPONSE-CODE = DFHRESP(NORMAL)
           MOVE 'Y' TO CUSTOMER-FOUND-SW
       ELSE IF RESPONSE-CODE = DFHRESP(NOTFND)
           MOVE 'N' TO CUSTOMER-FOUND-SW
           MOVE 'CUSTOMER RECORD NOT FOUND' TO OPERATOR-MESSAGE
       ELSE IF RESPONSE-CODE = DFHRESP(NOTAUTH)
           MOVE 'N' TO CUSTOMER-FOUND-SW
           MOVE 'YOU ARE NOT AUTHORIZED TO ACCESS THE CUSTOMER FILE'
               TO OPERATOR-MESSAGE
       ELSE IF RESPONSE-CODE = DFHRESP(NOTOPEN)
           MOVE 'N' TO CUSTOMER-FOUND-SW
           MOVE 'THE CUSTOMER FILE IS NOT AVAILABLE'
               TO OPERATOR-MESSAGE
       ELSE
           PERFORM 9000-TERMINATE-PROGRAM.
```

Figure 2-5   Using the NOHANDLE and RESP options

response code is placed. After the READ command, a series of IF statements tests the response code field to see if the command executed normally or if it indicates a NOTFND, NOTAUTH, or NOTOPEN error. If the execution was not normal and the error wasn't NOTFND, NOTAUTH, or NOTOPEN, a termination module is invoked to abend the program.

The coding in figure 2-5 has several advantages over the coding in figure 2-4. To begin with, GO TO statements and paragraphs within sections are

eliminated. That makes the entire program easier to code and understand. In addition, the use of HANDLE CONDITION is inherently dangerous because it establishes exceptional condition handling not just for one CICS command, but for all CICS commands in the program. For example, the HANDLE CONDITION command in figure 2-4 establishes an error exit for the NOTAUTH condition. But you must remember that control will be transferred to 2100-NOTAUTH not just if the READ command in figure 2-4 raises the

```
    2100-RECEIVE-CUSTOMER-SCREEN SECTION.
*
    EXEC CICS
        HANDLE AID CLEAR(2100-CLEAR-KEY)
                   PF1(2100-PF1-KEY)
                   ANYKEY(2100-ANYKEY)
    END-EXEC.
    EXEC CICS
        RECEIVE MAP('MNTMAP2')
                MAPSET('MNTSET1')
                INTO(CUSTOMER-DATA-MAP)
    END-EXEC.
    GO TO 2100-EXIT.
*
 2100-CLEAR-KEY.
*
    MOVE 'Y' TO CANCEL-ENTRY-SW.
    GO TO 2100-EXIT.
*
 2100-PF1-KEY.
*
    IF CA-CUSTOMER-FOUND
        MOVE 'Y' TO PF-KEY-1-SW
    ELSE
        MOVE 'N' TO VALID-DATA-SW
        MOVE 'INVALID KEY PRESSED' TO CDM-D-ERROR-MESSAGE.
    GO TO 2100-EXIT.
*
 2100-ANYKEY.
*
    MOVE 'N' TO VALID-DATA-SW
    MOVE 'INVALID KEY PRESSED' TO CDM-D-ERROR-MESSAGE.
*
 2100-EXIT.
*
    EXIT.
```

Figure 2-6   Using the HANDLE AID command

NOTAUTH condition, but if any other subsequent CICS command raises NOTAUTH as well (and a lot of CICS commands can potentially raise NOTAUTH). With the NOHANDLE and RESP options, this isn't a problem; it's easy to isolate the error handling code for each command in the module that issues the command.

Because of these advantages, I suggest you use NOHANDLE and RESP if your shop is using CICS release 1.7 or a later release and if your shop's standards allow it. Under CICS release 1.6, you can code NOHANDLE but not RESP; you have to test the EIBRCODE field in the Execute Interface Block to determine what exceptional condition has been raised, if any. Because testing EIBRCODE can be as difficult as using HANDLE CONDITION commands, I recommend you don't use the NOHANDLE option under CICS 1.6.

How to detect the use of AID keys

When you issue a RECEIVE or RECEIVE MAP command to retrieve data from a terminal, you can detect which AID key the operator pressed to in-itiate the transmission. The AID keys are the enter key, the clear key, the PF keys, and the PA keys. The enter key and the PF keys transmit data from the terminal's buffer to the system, but the clear key and the PA keys transmit just an indication of which AID key was pressed; no other data is sent.

The usual technique for detecting the use of AID keys is to issue a HANDLE AID command before you issue a RECEIVE or RECEIVE MAP command, as shown in figure 2-6. As you can see, the structure of a module coded with a HANDLE AID command is similar to the structure of a module that includes a HANDLE CONDITION command.

Figure 2-7 shows an alternative to the HANDLE AID command; Here, the Execute Interface Block field EIBAID, which is updated after each RECEIVE or RECEIVE MAP command, is tested to see which AID key was pressed. (Actually, in a pseudo-conversational program, EIBAID is updated when the program is started. So you don't have to issue a RECEIVE or RECEIVE MAP command before you test EIBAID.)

To test EIBAID, you compare its value with one of the values in a CICS-supplied copy member named DFHAID. DFHAID consists of a series of

```
        2100-RECEIVE-CUSTOMER-SCREEN SECTION.
    *
        EXEC CICS
            RECEIVE MAP('MNTMAP2')
                    MAPSET('MNTSET1')
                    INTO(CUSTOMER-DATA-MAP)
                    NOHANDLE
                    RESP(RESPONSE-CODE)
        END-EXEC.
        IF         RESPONSE-CODE NOT = DFHRESP(NORMAL)
                AND RESPONSE-CODE NOT = DFHRESP(MAPFAIL)
            PERFORM 9000-TERMINATE-PROGRAM.
        IF EIBAID = DFHCLEAR
            MOVE 'Y' TO CANCEL-ENTRY-SW
        ELSE IF EIBAID = DFHPF1
            IF CA-CUSTOMER-FOUND
                MOVE 'Y' TO PF-KEY-1-SW
            ELSE
                MOVE 'N' TO VALID-DATA-SW
                MOVE 'INVALID KEY PRESSED' TO CDM-D-ERROR-MESSAGE
        ELSE
            MOVE 'N' TO VALID-DATA-SW
            MOVE 'INVALID KEY PRESSED' TO CDM-D-ERROR-MESSAGE.
```

Figure 2-7   Using EIBAID to detect AID keys

CICS programming fundamentals

one-byte fields named DFHENTER, DFHCLEAR, DFHPA1 - DFHPA3, and DFHPF1 - DFHPF24. Each field corresponds to one of the AID keys; so DFHENTER corresponds to the enter key, DFHPF5 corresponds to PF5, and so on.

When you provide for AID keys, be sure to consider the effect of exceptional conditions on your RECEIVE or RECEIVE MAP command. In particular, the RECEIVE MAP command will raise the MAPFAIL condition if the operator presses the clear key or a PA key; that's because data isn't actually transmitted from the terminal, so there's no data to map. If you use a HANDLE AID command to detect the use of the clear and PA keys (either explicitly or by specifying ANYKEY), the HANDLE AID command overrides the normal condition processing for MAPFAIL; control is given to the routine specified in the HANDLE AID command. However, if you test EIBAID rather than issue HANDLE AID commands, you must do one of three things: (1) issue a HANDLE CONDITION command for the MAPFAIL condition, (2) specify RESP and/or NOHANDLE on the RECEIVE MAP command, or (3) test EIBAID for the clear key or a PA key *before* you issue the RECEIVE MAP command. Otherwise, your program will abend when the operator presses the clear key or a PA key. In figure 2-7, I specified NOHANDLE and RESP on the RECEIVE MAP command and tested the response code to see if it's anything other than NORMAL or MAPFAIL.

The alternatives for processing AID keys are similar to the alternatives for processing exceptional conditions. As a result, I recommend you process both in a consistent way: either use HANDLE CONDITION and HANDLE AID commands exclusively, or use NOHANDLE and RESP to test for exceptional conditions and use EIBAID to test for AID keys. As long as you're consistent, both techniques have their advantages. So the choice is up to you.

How to control cursor positioning

Whenever your program issues a SEND MAP command, it should specify in one way or another where the cursor is to be placed on the screen. There are several ways that you can specify cursor positioning. The simplest is to specify the IC option in one of the fields in the BMS mapset defini-

tion. Then, unless you specify the CURSOR option on the SEND MAP command, CICS positions the cursor at that field. This technique is fine as long as you always want the cursor positioned at the same field. Usually, though, you'll want to use the SEND MAP command's CURSOR option so your program can specify different cursor locations as needed.

The CURSOR option of the SEND MAP command provides two basic techniques for positioning the cursor: direct and symbolic. In direct cursor positioning, you specify a buffer address that corresponds to the screen position at which you want the cursor displayed; buffer address 0 is the first column of the first row; address 80 is the first column of the second row, and so on. The drawback of direct cursor positioning is that it ties your program to specific screen locations. So if you change your mapset, you'll also have to change your program to indicate the new screen locations.

When you use symbolic cursor positioning, you specify which map field will contain the cursor. To place the cursor in a specific field, you move -1 to the corresponding length field in the symbolic map before you issue a SEND MAP command. Then, on the SEND MAP command, you specify the CURSOR option without a buffer address. If you move -1 to more than one length field, the cursor is positioned at the first field containing -1.

How to modify attribute bytes

When you define a BMS map, you specify attributes (such as normal or high intensity and protected or unprotected) for each field on the screen. When you issue a SEND MAP command, however, you can change those attributes by moving a value to the attribute byte field in the field's symbolic map description. For example, if an operator enters a field incorrectly, you could change that field's attribute byte to specify high intensity and then send the map (including an appropriate error message) back to the terminal. That way, the error will be more obvious.

IBM supplies a copy member named DFHBMSCA that includes many attribute bytes; it's shown in figure 2-8. Unfortunately, DFHBMSCA doesn't include all of the attribute byte values you need to use. Rather than use DFHBMSCA then, I suggest you code your own

```
01        DFHBMSCA.
   02     DFHBMPEM   PICTURE X    VALUE   IS   ' '.
   02     DFHBMPNL   PICTURE X    VALUE   IS   ' '.
   02     DFHBMASK   PICTURE X    VALUE   IS   '0'.
   02     DFHBMUNP   PICTURE X    VALUE   IS   ' '.
   02     DFHBMUNN   PICTURE X    VALUE   IS   '&'.
   02     DFHBMPRO   PICTURE X    VALUE   IS   '-'.
   02     DFHBMBRY   PICTURE X    VALUE   IS   'H'.
   02     DFHBMDAR   PICTURE X    VALUE   IS   '<'.
   02     DFHBMFSE   PICTURE X    VALUE   IS   'A'.
   02     DFHBMPRF   PICTURE X    VALUE   IS   '/'.
   02     DFHBMASF   PICTURE X    VALUE   IS   '1'.
   02     DFHBMASB   PICTURE X    VALUE   IS   '8'.
   02     DFHBMEOF   PICTURE X    VALUE   IS   ' '.
   02     DFHBMDET   PICTURE X    VALUE   IS   ' '.
   02     DFHSA      PICTURE X    VALUE   IS   ' '.
   02     DFHCOLOR   PICTURE X    VALUE   IS   ' '.
   02     DFHPS      PICTURE X    VALUE   IS   ' '.
   02     DFHHLT     PICTURE X    VALUE   IS   ' '.
   02     DFH3270    PICTURE X    VALUE   IS   ' '.
   02     DFHVAL     PICTURE X    VALUE   IS   'A'.
   02     DFHALL     PICTURE X    VALUE   IS   ' '.
   02     DFHERROR   PICTURE X    VALUE   IS   ' '.
   02     DFHDFT     PICTURE X    VALUE   IS   ' '.
   02     DFHDFCOL   PICTURE X    VALUE   IS   ' '.
   02     DFHBLUE    PICTURE X    VALUE   IS   '1'.
   02     DFHRED     PICTURE X    VALUE   IS   '2'.
   02     DFHPINK    PICTURE X    VALUE   IS   '3'.
   02     DFHGREEN   PICTURE X    VALUE   IS   '4'.
   02     DFHTURQ    PICTURE X    VALUE   IS   '5'.
   02     DFHYELLO   PICTURE X    VALUE   IS   '6'.
   02     DFHNEUT    PICTURE X    VALUE   IS   '7'.
   02     DFHBASE    PICTURE X    VALUE   IS   ' '.
   02     DFHDFHI    PICTURE X    VALUE   IS   ' '.
   02     DFHBLINK   PICTURE X    VALUE   IS   '1'.
   02     DFHREVRS   PICTURE X    VALUE   IS   '2'.
   02     DFHUNDLN   PICTURE X    VALUE   IS   '4'.
   02     DFHMFIL    PICTURE X    VALUE   IS   ' '.
   02     DFHMENT    PICTURE X    VALUE   IS   ' '.
   02     DFHMFE     PICTURE X    VALUE   IS   ' '.
   02     DFHMT      PICTURE X    VALUE   IS   ' '.
   02     DFHMFT     PICTURE X    VALUE   IS   ' '.
   02     DFHMET     PICTURE X    VALUE   IS   ' '.
   02     DFHMFET    PICTURE X    VALUE   IS   ' '.
```

Figure 2-8   The IBM-supplied COPY member DFHBMSCA

```
      01   FIELD-ATTRIBUTE-DEFINITIONS.
  *
          05   FAC-UNPROT                        PIC X     VALUE ' '.
          05   FAC-UNPROT-MDT                    PIC X     VALUE 'A'.
          05   FAC-UNPROT-BRT                    PIC X     VALUE 'H'.
          05   FAC-UNPROT-BRT-MDT                PIC X     VALUE 'I'.
          05   FAC-UNPROT-DARK                   PIC X     VALUE '<'.
          05   FAC-UNPROT-DARK-MDT               PIC X     VALUE '('.
          05   FAC-UNPROT-NUM                    PIC X     VALUE '&'.
          05   FAC-UNPROT-NUM-MDT                PIC X     VALUE 'J'.
          05   FAC-UNPROT-NUM-BRT                PIC X     VALUE 'Q'.
          05   FAC-UNPROT-NUM-BRT-MDT            PIC X     VALUE 'R'.
          05   FAC-UNPROT-NUM-DARK               PIC X     VALUE '*'.
          05   FAC-UNPROT-NUM-DARK-MDT           PIC X     VALUE ')'.
          05   FAC-PROT                          PIC X     VALUE '-'.
          05   FAC-PROT-MDT                      PIC X     VALUE '/'.
          05   FAC-PROT-BRT                      PIC X     VALUE 'Y'.
          05   FAC-PROT-BRT-MDT                  PIC X     VALUE 'Z'.
          05   FAC-PROT-DARK                     PIC X     VALUE '%'.
          05   FAC-PROT-DARK-MDT                 PIC X     VALUE ']'.
          05   FAC-PROT-NUM                      PIC X     VALUE '0'.
          05   FAC-PROT-NUM-MDT                  PIC X     VALUE '1'.
          05   FAC-PROT-NUM-BRT                  PIC X     VALUE '8'.
          05   FAC-PROT-NUM-BRT-MDT              PIC X     VALUE '9'.
          05   FAC-PROT-NUM-DARK                 PIC X     VALUE '@'.
          05   FAC-PROT-NUM-DARK-MDT             PIC X     VALUE QUOTE.
```

Figure 2-9   A better COPY member for attribute byte definitions

copy member, if your shop hasn't already done so. For example, figure 2-9 shows a copy member in which each attribute byte field has a meaningful name. So FAC-UNPROT-NUM-BRT specifies the unprotected, numeric, and bright attributes.

How to edit terminal input data

Most CICS programs you develop will require modules that edit input data entered by a terminal operator. These modules should insure that all data is entered in the correct format, that values are within the proper ranges, and so on. If any fields are found to be in error, an appropriate error message should be issued, the field in error should be visually highlighted, and the map should be sent back to the terminal.

Although there are many ways to edit input data, figure 2-10 shows the general structure I recom-

mend for edit modules. Basically, the module edits each field with a series of nested IF statements; each IF statement within the series tests for one of the field's required conditions.

When you detect an error, you do three things: (1) modify the attribute byte field so the error is highlighted, (2) move -1 to the length field so the cursor will be positioned in the field, and (3) move an appropriate error message to the error message field.

Although it's not apparent in figure 2-10, I edit the map fields from the bottom of the screen to the top. That way, all of the errors are highlighted, but the error message that's displayed refers to the first invalid field on the screen. If the program edited the fields from top to bottom, the error message would relate to the last invalid field on the screen.

The last statement in the edit module tests to see if an error message has been placed in the error message field. If so, a switch is set. Then, a higher-

```
IF error-condition-1 for field-1
    MOVE attribute-character TO attribute-field for field-1
    MOVE -1                  TO length-field for field-1
    MOVE error-message       TO error-message-field
ELSE IF error-condition-2 for field-1
    .
    .
    .
IF error-condition-1 for field-2
    .
    .
    .
IF error-message-field NOT = LOW-VALUE
    MOVE 'N' TO VALID-DATA-SW.
```

Figure 2-10 General structure of an edit module

level module can test that switch to determine what processing needs to be done. This assumes, of course, that LOW-VALUE is moved to the error-message field prior to the editing of the fields.

Although an edit module coded according to this pattern is straightforward, it can be long. For example, if a screen has 20 input fields, each requiring three field edits, the edit module will have 240 lines of code. Although you might be tempted to break this module down into several smaller ones, there's no need to. As long as the module's structure is straightforward, don't worry about its length. However, if some fields require complicated edits (like table or file look-ups), by all means create separate modules for them.

How to update file records

Many of the CICS programs you develop will require you to update records in one or more data sets. Although the coding for file updates is relatively straightfoward, there are two special considerations you need to be aware of: (1) avoiding deadlock when updating more than one record, and (2) assuring file integrity when updating records in a pseudo-conversational program.

Deadlock situations occur when two or more tasks are each waiting for a resource that the other is holding. In a program that updates more than one file record, this can be a problem if you don't take special precautions. For example, suppose one program attempts to update records 100 and 200,

and at the same time another program needs to update the same records, but in the reverse order. The first program reads and holds record 100, and the second program reads and holds record 200. Then, the first program attempts to read record 200, but can't because the second program is holding it for update. At the same time, the second program tries to read record 100, but can't because the first program is holding it. Each program is waiting for the other to release a record and neither program can progress until CICS intervenes and cancels one of them.

The simple way to avoid deadlock is to establish a standard order for file updates. Most shops simply say that all files should be updated in alphabetical order and, within the same file, records should be accessed in ascending key sequence. If you follow this simple guideline in all your programs, you'll avoid most deadlock situations.

You also need to know how to insure file integrity when you update a record in a pseudo-conversational program. That's because the READ UPDATE command holds a record only during execution of the program; between task executions, there's nothing to prevent another transaction from accessing the same record and changing it. And that can be disasterous.

There are two ways to deal with this problem in a pseudo-conversational program: you can *prevent* it or you can simply try to *detect* it. To prevent someone from accessing a record while a pseudo-conversational program is trying to update it, you must provide some way of indicating that the record is in the process of being updated. For example, you could designate the first byte of a file record as an "update in progress" switch; when a pseudo-conversational program first accesses the record, it turns this switch on. It turns the switch off again when the update is completed. All other programs that update the file must test the switch to see if the record is available.

There are two problems with this scheme. First, it will only work if all other programs that access the file follow it. Second, it's possible that the program that initially sets the switch will be unable to reset it. (The program may abend, the system may abend, or the terminal or network may go down.) If that happens, the record will be locked out indefinitely unless a special program is written to clear the "update in progress" switch.

A more common technique doesn't prevent integrity problems but detects them before they become problems. Rather than indicate that a record is being updated, each pseudo-conversational program that updates a record saves an image of the record between task executions, usually in a temporary storage queue that's uniquely identified by the terminal-id. Then, in the next execution, the program retrieves both the file record and the saved image and compares them; if they are different, it means that the record has been updated by another user, so the update attempt is denied. This is the technique that's used in the model programs in this book.

How to invoke other programs

If your program needs to invoke another program, there are three ways to do it: (1) invoke a subprogram with a COBOL CALL statement, (2) invoke another CICS program with a CICS LINK command, or (3) invoke another CICS program with a CICS XCTL command.

The use of COBOL subprograms invoked via the CALL statement is transparent to CICS; as far as CICS is concerned, the same program is being executed. That's because the programs are link-edited together to form a single load module. The one consideration you should be aware of is that the Execute Interface Block is not automatically acces-

sible in the called subprogram; to access it, you must define it in the subprogram's Linkage Section and issue an ADDRESS command to provide the required addressability.

The LINK command invokes a separate CICS program in a manner similar to a subprogram; when the invoked program ends by issuing a RETURN command, control returns to the invoking program at the point immediately after the LINK command. One way of thinking of programs within a CICS task is in terms of logical levels; a LINK command transfers control to a program at a lower logical level. When that program is finished, a RETURN command transfers control back up to the next higher logical level.

Like the LINK command, the XCTL command transfers control to another CICS program. But unlike the LINK command, the XCTL command provides no return mechanism. Instead, the program that issues the XCTL command is terminated and the specified program is invoked at the same logical level.

Figure 2-11 illustrates the distinction between LINK and XCTL. Here, CICS (which is always at the highest logical level) invokes program-A at level-1. Next, program-A issues a LINK command to invoke program-B at level-2. Then, program-B issues an XCTL command to invoke program-C at the same level. When program-C issues a RETURN command (without the TRANS-ID option), control is returned to the next higher level. So, execution continues with the statement in program-A following the LINK command that invoked program-B. When program-A issues a RETURN command, control returns to CICS.

COBOL features you can't use in a command-level CICS program

As you code your command-level program in COBOL, you must remember that many features of standard COBOL can't be used in a CICS program. Most, but not all, of those features are for functions that are performed using CICS commands instead of standard COBOL statements. Figure 2-12 lists the COBOL features you must avoid in a command-level program.

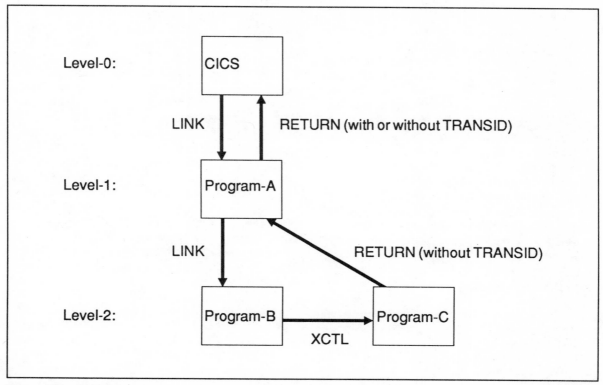

Figure 2-11   Logical levels

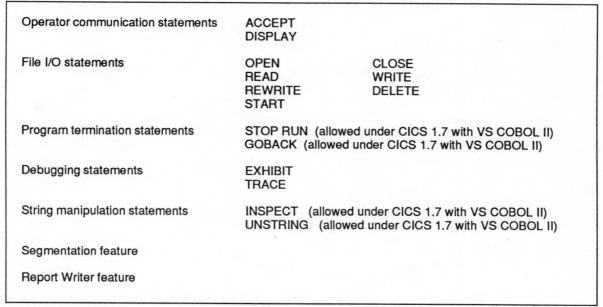

Figure 2-12   COBOL features that aren't allowed under CICS

Section 3

BMS mapset definition

Most CICS programs you develop will use Basic Mapping Support (BMS) to manage terminal input and output. To use BMS, you have to write an assembler language program called a mapset; the mapset defines the screens used by your program.

After you've coded your mapset, you must assemble it twice: once to create a physical mapset, and again to create a symbolic mapset. The physical mapset is a load module that BMS uses to map data between your program and the terminal your program is associated with. The symbolic mapset is a COPY member that you copy into your program; it defines the format of the screen data as it's processed by your program. The procedures for assembling BMS mapsets are found in Section 6.

Many shops use mapset generators to simplify BMS mapset creation. Simply put, a mapset generator is a program that lets you describe the final appearance of a map at a terminal by keying in data at the correct screen locations. The mapset generator then converts that into appropriate BMS macro instructions. If you have a mapset generator, by all means use it; it can save you a lot of work. On the other hand, you still need to know how to define your own BMS mapsets to use BMS effectively.

This section provides all the reference information you need to create BMS mapsets for 3270 terminals. First, it describes the various attributes that can be associated with data displayed on 3270 devices. Then, it describes the format of each BMS macro instruction in detail. Next, it shows you the format of the symbolic maps produced by BMS and tells you how to create your own symbolic maps in case you find the BMS symbolic maps to be inadequate. Finally, it provides a complete example of a BMS mapset that you can use as a model for your own mapsets.

Characteristics of 3270 display devices

Data displayed by BMS on a 3270 terminal is organized into fields, each of which is associated with specific attributes that control the field's appearance and operation. Since one of the basic functions of a BMS mapset is to specify the attributes of fields, it's important that you understand those attributes. So, I'll describe them now.

Field attributes for 3270s can be divided into two classes: standard attributes, which are available on all 3270 models, and extended attributes, which are available only on more advanced (and expensive) 3270 models.

Standard attributes

Standard 3270 field attributes are available on all 3270 terminal models. They are specified by a single byte, called an attribute byte, which occupies the character location on the screen that's immediately before the field to which it applies. On a 3270, fields have no explicit length; the end of one field is indicated by the presence of an attribute byte for the next field.

Figure 3-1 lists the three basic field characteristics specified by a standard attribute byte. The *protection attribute* specifies whether or not an operator can enter data into a field. The protection attribute can specify that a field is protected, unprotected, or auto-skip. If a field is protected, an operator cannot key data into it. However, the operator can enter data into an unprotected field. Generally, protected fields are used for captions and labels, while unprotected fields are used for data entry. An auto-skip field is like a protected field except that when the cursor moves to the auto-skip field's attribute byte, it automatically advances to the next unprotected field. Auto-skip attribute bytes are normally used to mark the end of unprotected data-entry fields. That way, the cursor moves automatically from one data-entry field to the next.

The *intensity attribute* specifies the display intensity for the field: normal, bright, or no-display. Normal and bright intensity are often used to distinguish captions and labels from variable data. At some installations, the captions are bright and the variable data is normal; at others, it's the other way around. So be consistent. If no-display is specified for a field, the data in the field isn't displayed on the screen.

The *shift attribute* specifies whether the keyboard is in numeric or alphanumeric shift. Don't be confused; the shift attribute has nothing to do with upper- or lower-case letters. Instead, it's designed to restrict a field to numeric data. When the numeric attribute is specified, the operator can enter only numeric data: numerals, a sign, and a decimal point. This doesn't ensure that the data is entered in a correct numeric format, but it helps.

Figure 3-2 shows the format of a standard 3270 attribute byte, indicating the bit positions that are responsible for each attribute setting. The last bit in an attribute byte, the *Modified Data Tag (MDT)*, doesn't control the appearance of the data in the field. Instead, it's used to indicate whether the field should be transmitted to the host system when the operator presses an AID key. If the MDT is on, the field is sent; otherwise, it's not. The MDT can be turned on by the application program when it sends data to the terminal. In addition, whenever an operator changes the data in a field, that field's MDT is turned on automatically.

Protection	Intensity	Shift
Protected	Normal	Alphanumeric
Unprotected	Bright	Numeric
Auto-skip (askip)	No-display	

Figure 3-1   Field attributes

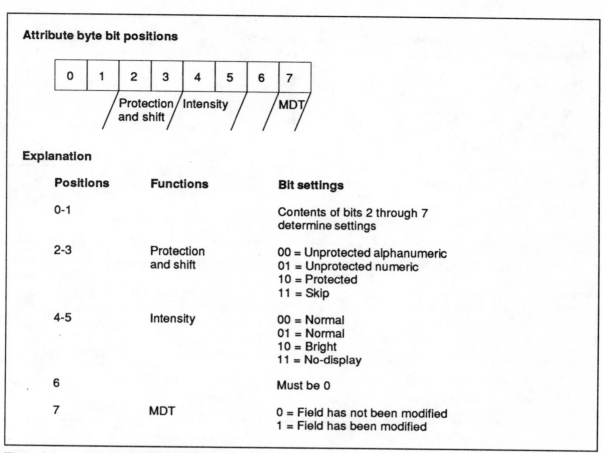

Figure 3-2   Format of the attribute byte

One more important function of the standard attribute byte is selecting the display color for inexpensive base color display terminals. A base color terminal can display data in one of four colors (blue, white, green, and red). The color for each field is determined by the combination of the field's protection and intensity attributes, as specified in figure 3-3.

Extended attributes

Advanced 3270 display models provide formatting options that aren't available with standard attribute bytes; these options are controlled by using *extended attribute bytes*. Unlike standard attribute bytes, extended attribute bytes do *not* occupy a position on the screen. Figure 3-4 lists the display attributes controlled by extended attributes bytes.

Terminals that support *extended color* let you specify one of seven colors for a field: blue, red, pink, green, turquoise, yellow, or white. These colors are independent of the field's protection and intensity attributes. Typically, you use extended color to draw attention to specific fields or to highlight relationships among fields that might otherwise appear unrelated.

Terminals that support *extended highlighting* provide three ways to highlight data besides bright intensity: blinking, reverse video (dark characters against a light background), and underlining. Like extended color and the standard intensity attribute, extended highlighting is normally used to draw attention to important data.

The *validation* feature lets you assign one of three special data entry properties to a field. In a *must-enter* field, the operator must enter at least one character of data into the field. In a *must-fill* field,

Protection attribute	Intensity attribute	Resulting color
Protected	Normal	Blue
Protected	Bright	White
Unprotected	Normal	Green
Unprotected	Bright	Red

Figure 3-3   How color is determined for a base-color terminal

Extended color	Extended highlighting	Validation	Programmed symbols
Blue	Blinking	Must fill	Up to six alternate
Red	Reverse video	Must enter	user-definable
Pink	Underline	Trigger	character sets
Green			
Turquoise			
Yellow			
White			

Figure 3-4   Extended attributes

the operator must enter data into each character position of the field. Data from a *trigger field* is transmitted to the CICS system as soon as the operator moves the cursor out of the field; no AID key needs to be pressed.

Terminals that support *programmed symbols* can display characters from any of up to six user-defined character sets. This feature is useful for engineering or other graphics applications. The alternate character sets are usually loaded into the terminal before the application program begins. Then, extended attributes are used to specify which character set should be used to display data.

How to code a BMS mapset

As you know, a BMS mapset is actually an assembler language program that consists of a number of macro instructions which are expanded by the assembler into a physical mapset and a symbolic mapset. Although you have to follow the assembler's coding rules in your mapset, you don't have to know how to write assembler language programs to develop a mapset; you just have to know how to code two assembler commands (PRINT and END) and three BMS macro instructions (DFHMSD, DFHMDI, and DFHMDF).

Figure 3-5 shows the general structure of the assembler commands and macro instructions you code in a mapset. The first command, PRINT NOGEN, causes the assembler to not print the statements generated by the BMS macro instructions. If you don't include PRINT NOGEN, the resulting assembler listing will contain hundreds of lines that aren't important to you. So always start your mapsets with PRINT NOGEN.

The last line of the mapset, END, is a required assembler command. It tells the assembler that there are no more source statements in the mapset.

The three BMS macro instructions you code for a mapset are DFHMSD, DFHMDI, and DFHMDF. Each mapset should contain one DFHMSD macro instruction; it supplies values that apply to the entire mapset. Then, each map within the mapset begins with a DFHMDI macro instruction; it supplies values that apply to a single map. For each field in the map, you code a DFHMDF macro instruction to define the field's attributes. (Actually, you code a DFHMDF macro for each attribute byte on the screen; some fields may require two DFHMDF macros because they need two attribute bytes: one to mark the beginning of the field, the other to mark the end.) If there's more than one map in the mapset, the next occurrence of a DFHMDI macro marks the end of one map and the beginning of the next. To mark the end of the entire mapset, however, you must code another DFHMSD macro instruction, this time specifying TYPE=FINAL.

All BMS macro instructions must follow the assembler's syntax rules. Those rules are summarized in figure 3-6.

Macro or command	Usage
PRINT NOGEN	Coded once at the beginning of the mapset; tells the assembler to not print the statements generated as a result of expanding the BMS macro instructions.
DFHMSD	Coded once; supplies values that apply to the entire mapset.
DFHMDI	Coded once for each map within the mapset; supplies values that apply to the map.
DFHMDF	Coded once for each field (or attribute byte) within the map; specifies the position, length, and attributes of each map field.
DFHMSD TYPE=FINAL	Coded after the last map in the mapset; tells BMS that the mapset is complete.
END	Must be the last statement in the input stream; tells the assembler that there are no more source statements.

Figure 3-5　BMS macros

Assembler language statement format:

label   op-code   parameters

Explanation

label	Supplies a symbolic name for the statement. Must be coded in column 1, begin with a letter, and may be up to seven characters long. (If you code an asterisk in column 1, the entire line is treated as a comment.)
op-code	Specifies the instruction to be executed; for a BMS macro, code DFHMSD, DFHMDI, or DFHMDF. Must begin in column 10.
parameters	Specifies one or more items of information required for the macro to work properly. Parameters should be separated by commas and the first parameter should follow the op-code after one space. If you need to continue the parameters to another line, code a non-blank character in column 72 and begin the next parameter in column 16 of the next line.

Figure 3-6   Rules for coding assembler language statements

The DFHMSD macro instruction

Function

The DFHMSD macro instruction has two formats. Format 1 defines a mapset. It supplies the mapset's name and other important information such as the type of terminal to which it applies, the source lan- guage it's used with, and whether or not it supports extended attributes. Format 2 marks the end of a mapset.

Syntax (format 1)

```
name  DFHMSD  TYPE= { &SYSPARM }
                    { DSECT    }
                    { MAP      }

            [, LANG= { COBOL }  ]
                     { ASM   }
                     { PLI   }

            [, MODE= { IN    }  ]
                     { OUT   }
                     { INOUT }

            [, TERM=terminal-type ]

            [, CTRL=(option,option...) ]

            [, STORAGE=AUTO ]

            [, TIOAPFX= { YES } ]
                        { NO  }

            [, EXTATT= { YES     } ]
                       { NO      }
                       { MAPONLY }

            [, DSATTS=(type,type...) ]          1.7 only

            [, MAPATTS=(type,type...) ]         1.7 only

            [, COLOR= { DEFAULT } ]
                      { color   }

            [, HILIGHT= { OFF       } ]
                        { BLINK     }
                        { REVERSE   }
                        { UNDERLINE }

            [, VALIDN= { MUSTENTER } ]
                       { MUSTFILL  }
                       { TRIGGER   }
```

Parameters (format 1)

TYPE

Specifies whether a physical map (TYPE=MAP) or a symbolic map (TYPE=DSECT) is to be generated. TYPE=&SYSPARM, which is the usual way to code this parameter, lets you specify this option at execution time via JCL.

LANG

Specifies the source language to be used for the symbolic map: COBOL, PL/I, or assembler (ASM). The default is ASM, so you should code LANG=COBOL if you're working in COBOL.

MODE

Specifies whether the mapset is used for input, output, or both. There's no performance advantage to specifying just input or output, so you'll usually code MODE=INOUT.

TERM

Specifies the type of terminal that can be used with this map. Common values are

ALL	This map may be used with any terminal.
3270	Same as ALL.
3270-1	This map may be used on a 3270 model-1 terminal (40 column display).
3270-2	This map may be used on a 3270 model-2 terminal (80 column display).

The IBM manual documents other values you can code for more obscure terminal types. Usually, you'll code TERM=3270-2.

CTRL

Specifes a list of control options in effect for each map in the mapset. Valid options are

FREEKB	Unlocks the terminal keyboard after each output operation.
FRSET	Turns off the MDT bit in each attribute byte in the terminal's buffer before each output operation. Use this option if you want the terminal only to transmit data that the operator modifies.
ALARM	Sounds the terminal's audible alarm during each output operation.
PRINT	Causes a 3270 printer to print the data in its buffer (after the output operation completes).
length	Specifies how line-endings are to be formatted for printed data; L40, L64, or L80 cause a new line to be formatted every 40, 64, or 80 characters and HONEOM honors the printer's default line length.

STORAGE

If STORAGE=AUTO is coded, the symbolic maps for each map in the mapset occupy separate storage locations; otherwise, they share the same storage (via a COBOL REDEFINES clause).

TIOAPFX

TIOAPFX generates a 12-byte FILLER item at the beginning of the symbolic map. It should always be specified for COBOL programs.

EXTATT

Specifies whether or not the maps in the mapset should support extended attributes. If you specify EXTATT=YES, provision is made in both the physical and symbolic maps for attributes for extended color, extended highlighting, programmed symbols, and validation. EXTATT is supported for compatibility with releases of CICS before 1.7; for new programs, you should specify DSATTS and MAPATTS instead.

DSATTS

(1.7 only) Specifies which extended attributes are to be supported in the symbolic map. You can specify any or all of the following attribute types:

COLOR	Extended color
HILIGHT	Extended highlighting
OUTLINE	Field outlining
PS	Programmed symbols
SOSI	Two-byte SO/SI characters
TRANSP	Background transparency
VALIDN	Validation

MAPATTS

(1.7 only) Specifies which extended attributes are to be supported in the physical map. You can specify any or all of the same types that are valid for the DSATTS parameter. You can specify physical map support for an attribute type that's not specified in the

DSATTS parameter, but not the other way around: any attribute type you specify in the DSATTS parameter should also be specified in the MAPATTS parameter.

COLOR

Specifies a default extended color for the mapset; you may specify DEFAULT for the terminal's default color, or you may specify BLUE, RED, PINK, GREEN, TURQUOISE, YELLOW, or NEUTRAL (white).

HILIGHT

Specifies a default extended highlighting for the mapset; you may specify OFF for no highlighting, or BLINK, REVERSE, or UNDERLINE.

VALIDN

Specifies a default field validation for the mapset; MUSTENTER means the operator must enter some data into each field; MUSTFILL means the operator must completely fill each field; and TRIGGER means that fields are transmitted from the terminal one at a time as data is entered into them.

Coding example (no extended attributes)

This example shows the basic parameters you should always code in a DFHMSD macro. You can use this as a model for your own mapsets if you don't need extended highlighting. (Note that this example doesn't show the non-blank character that's required in column 72 for continuation lines.)

```
TTRSET1   DFHMSD TYPE=&SYSPARM,
                 LANG=COBOL,
                 MODE=INOUT,
                 TERM=3270-2,
                 CTRL=FREEKB,
                 STORAGE=AUTO,
                 TIOAPFX=YES
```

Coding example (extended attributes under CICS 1.7)

This example shows how to provide for extended color attributes in both the physical and the symbolic mapsets under CICS release 1.7. For other attributes, you would simply code other attribute types. Under previous releases of CICS, you would code EXTATT=YES to generate support for extended color, extended highlighting, programmed symbols, and validation.

```
TTRSET1   DFHMSD TYPE=&SYSPARM,
                 LANG=COBOL,
                 MODE=INOUT,
                 TERM=3270-2,
                 CTRL=FREEKB,
                 STORAGE=AUTO,
                 TIOAPFX=YES,
                 DSATTS=COLOR,
                 MAPATTS=COLOR
```

Syntax (format 2)

```
DFHMSD TYPE=FINAL
```

Parameters (format 2)

TYPE

TYPE=FINAL indicates the end of the mapset.

The DFHMDI macro instruction

Function

The DFHMDI macro instruction defines a map within a mapset. It supplies the map's name and other important information such as the map's size and position. In addition, the DFHMDI macro can override defaults specified in a DFHMSD macro.

Syntax

```
name  DFHMDI SIZE=(lines,columns),

      [, LINE= {line-number      } ]
               {NEXT             }
               {SAME             }

      [, COLUMN= {column-number  } ]
                 {NEXT           }
                 {SAME           }

      [, JUSTIFY=( [ {LEFT } ] [, {FIRST} ] ) ]
                     {RIGHT}        {LAST }

      [, HEADER=YES ]

      [, TRAILER=YES ]

      [, CTRL=(option,option...) ]

      [, EXTATT= {YES     } ]
                 {NO      }
                 {MAPONLY }

      [, DSATTS=(type,type...) ]        1.7 only

      [, MAPATTS=(type,type...) ]       1.7 only

      [, COLOR= {DEFAULT} ]
                {color  }

      [, HILIGHT= {OFF       } ]
                  {BLINK     }
                  {REVERSE   }
                  {UNDERLINE }

      [, VALIDN= {MUSTENTER} ]
                 {MUSTFILL }
                 {TRIGGER  }
```

Parameters

SIZE

Specifies the size of the map in lines and columns. To fill an entire standard 3270 screen, code SIZE=(24,80).

LINE

Specifies the starting line number for the map. Usually coded LINE=1. LINE=NEXT tells BMS to place the map on the next available line on the screen. LINE=SAME tells BMS to place the map in the next available position on the same line as the last map sent to the terminal.

COLUMN

Specifies the starting column number for the map. Usually coded COLUMN=1. COLUMN=NEXT tells BMS to place the map in the next available screen column. COLUMN=SAME tells BMS to use the COLUMN specification from the most recently sent map that specifies the COLUMN parameter and the same combination of JUSTIFY options.

JUSTIFY

Specifies how the map should be aligned on the screen. The first set of JUSTIFY options (LEFT and RIGHT) specifies whether the COLUMN parameter refers to columns counted from the left or right edge of the screen. The second set of JUSTIFY options (FIRST and LAST) specifies whether the map should be placed at the top or bottom of the screen, allowing for header or trailer maps.

HEADER

If you code HEADER=YES, the map is treated as a header map.

TRAILER

If you code TRAILER=YES, the map is treated as a trailer map.

CTRL

Specifes a list of control options in effect for the map. Valid options are

FREEKB	Unlocks the terminal keyboard after each output operation.
FRSET	Turns off the MDT bit in each attribute byte in the terminal's buffer before each output operation. Use FRSET if you want the terminal only to transmit data that the operator modifies.
ALARM	Sounds the terminal's alarm.
PRINT	Causes a 3270 printer to start printing.
length	Specifies how line-endings are to be formatted for printed data; L40, L64, or L80 cause a new line to be formatted every 40, 64, or 80 characters and HONEOM honors the printer's default line length.

EXTATT

Specifies whether or not the map should support extended attributes. If you specify EXTATT=YES, both the physical and symbolic map support attributes for extended color, extended highlighting, programmed symbols, and validation. EXTATT is supported for compatibility with releases of CICS before 1.7; for new programs, you should specify DSATTS and MAPATTS instead.

DSATTS

(1.7 only)Specifies which extended attributes are to be supported in the symbolic map. You can specify any or all of the following attributes:

COLOR	Extended color
HILIGHT	Extended highlighting
OUTLINE	Field outlining
PS	Programmed symbols
SOSI	Two-byte SO/SI characters
TRANSP	Background transparency
VALIDN	Validation

MAPATTS

(1.7 only) Specifies which extended attributes are to be supported in the physical map. You can specify any or all of the same types that are valid for the DSATTS parameter. You can specify physical map support for an attribute type that's not specified in the DSATTS parameter, but not the other way around: any attribute type you specify in the DSATTS parameter should also be specified in the MAPATTS parameter.

COLOR

Specifies a default extended color for the map; you may specify DEFAULT for the terminal's default color, or you may specify BLUE, RED, PINK, GREEN, TURQUOISE, YELLOW, or NEUTRAL (white).

HILIGHT

Specifies a default extended highlighting for the map; you may specify OFF for no highlighting, or BLINK, REVERSE, or UNDERLINE.

VALIDN

Specifies a default field validation for the map; MUSTENTER means the operator must enter some data into each field; MUSTFILL means the operator must completely fill each field; and TRIGGER means that fields are transmitted from the terminal one at a time as data is entered into them.

Coding example (no extended attributes or message building)

This example shows you how to define a full-screen (24 by 80) map that doesn't require extended attributes or message building facilities. Just three parameters are specified: SIZE, LINE, and COLUMN.

```
MNTMAP1   DFHMDI SIZE=(24,80),
                 LINE=1,
                 COLUMN=1
```

Coding example (extended attributes under CICS 1.7)

This example shows how to provide for extended color attributes in both the physical and symbolic map under CICS release 1.7. For other attributes, you would simply code other attribute types. Under previous releases of CICS, you would code EXTATT=YES to generate support for extended color, extended highlighting, programmed symbols, and validation.

```
MNTMAP1   DFHMDI SIZE(24,80),
                 LINE=1,
                 COLUMN=1,
                 DSATTS=COLOR,
                 MAPATTS=COLOR
```

Coding example (message building)

This example shows three DFHMDI macros for a message building application. The first is for a header map, the second is for a one-line detail map, and the third is for a trailer map. The header map is positioned at the top of the screen; the detail map is positioned in the first column of the next available line; and the trailer map is positioned at the bottom of the screen.

```
LSTMAP1   DFHMDI SIZE=(5,80),
                 JUSTIFY=FIRST,
                 HEADER=YES
          .
          .
          .
LSTMAP2   DFHMDI SIZE=(1,80),
                 LINE=NEXT,
                 COLUMN=1
          .
          .
          .
LSTMAP3   DFHMDI SIZE=(2,80),
                 JUSTIFY=LAST,
                 TRAILER=YES
```

The DFHMDF macro instruction

Function

The DFHMDF macro instruction defines a map field by specifying its position, length, and attributes. Actually, DFHMDF defines an attribute byte. To define a protected field, you code one DFHMDF macro, since a protected field needs just one attribute byte. But to define an unprotected field, you code two DFHMDF macros: one to mark the beginning of the field and the other to mark the end.

Syntax

```
name      DFHMDF POS=(line,column)

          [, LENGTH=field-length ]

                        ⎧NORM⎫        ⎧PROT  ⎫
          [, ATTRB=( [ ⎨BRT ⎬ ] [, ⎨UNPROT⎬ ] [,NUM] [,IC] [,FSET] ) ]
                        ⎩DRK ⎭        ⎩ASKIP ⎭

             ⎧ INITIAL='literal' ⎫
          [, ⎨ XINIT=hex-value   ⎬ ]
             ⎩                   ⎭

          [, PICIN='picture-string' ]

          [, PICOUT='picture-string' ]

                      ⎧DEFAULT⎫
          [, COLOR=  ⎨color  ⎬ ]
                      ⎩       ⎭

                        ⎧OFF      ⎫
                        ⎪BLINK    ⎪
          [, HILIGHT= ⎨REVERSE  ⎬ ]
                        ⎩UNDERLINE⎭

                        ⎧MUSTENTER⎫
          [, VALIDN=  ⎨MUSTFILL ⎬ ]
                        ⎩TRIGGER  ⎭
```

Parameters

POS

Specifies the line and column position of the field's attribute byte.

LENGTH

Specifies the length of the field, not including the attribute byte. This length is used in the symbolic map, but doesn't imply any specific field length on the display. So the attributes specified for a particular field continue until the attribute byte for the next field is encountered.

ATTRB

Specifies the attribute byte settings for the field:

BRT	The field is displayed with high intensity.
NORM	The field is displayed with regular intensity.
DRK	The field is *not* displayed on the screen.
PROT	The field is protected; data may not be keyed into it.
ASKIP	The field is protected, and the cursor will automatically skip over it.
UNPROT	The field is unprotected; data may be keyed into it.
NUM	The field is numeric and is right-justified and zero-filled. If omitted, the field is assumed to be alphanumeric and is left-justified and space-filled.
IC	Specifies that the cursor should be located at the start of the data field.
FSET	Specifies that the MDT bit in the attribute byte should be turned on before the map is sent to the terminal.

INITIAL

Specifies the initial value of the field.

XINIT

Specifies a hexadecimal initial value for the field. The hex-value can be one or more two-character hex numbers, like XINIT=D0C1.

PICIN

Specifies a COBOL PICTURE string that defines the format of the data on input. Example: PICIN='999V99'. The length defined by PICIN must agree with the LENGTH parameter. If omitted, PICIN='X(n)' will be assumed where n is the value specified for the LENGTH parameter.

PICOUT

Specifies a COBOL PICTURE string defining the format of the data on output. Example: PICOUT='Z9.99'. The length defined by PICOUT must agree with the LENGTH parameter.

COLOR

Specifies an extended color for the field; you may specify DEFAULT for the terminal's default color, or you may specify BLUE, RED, PINK, GREEN, TURQUOISE, YELLOW, or NEUTRAL (white).

HILIGHT

Specifies extended highlighting for the field; you may specify OFF for no highlighting, or BLINK, REVERSE, or UNDERLINE.

VALIDN

Specifies field validation for the field; MUSTENTER means the operator must enter some data into each field; MUSTFILL means the operator must completely fill each field; and TRIGGER means that fields are transmitted from the terminal one at a time as data is entered into them.

Coding example (constant field)

This example shows how to define a constant field, used typically as a heading to identify the screen or an individual field on the screen. In this example, the constant is a screen heading beginning in column 2 of line 2 and containing the words MORTGAGE CALCULATION.

Screen layout

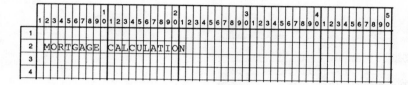

Map definition

```
DFHMDF POS=(2,1),
       LENGTH=20,
       ATTRB=(BRT,PROT),
       INITIAL='MORTGAGE CALCULATION'
```

Coding example (alphanumeric data-entry field)

This example shows how to code the DFHMDF macros necessary for an alphanumeric data entry field. Three DFHMDF macros are coded: one for the field's caption (a constant field), one to mark the start of the field, and one to mark the end of the field. The last DFHMDF macro specifies ATTRB=ASKIP, so the cursor will advance to the next screen field when it reaches the end of this field.

Screen layout

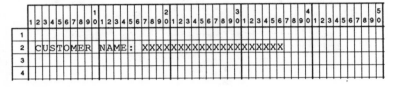

Map definition

```
          DFHMDF POS=(2,1),
                 LENGTH=14,
                 ATTRB=(BRT,PROT),
                 INITIAL='CUSTOMER NAME:'
NAME      DFHMDF POS=(2,16),
                 LENGTH=20,
                 ATTRB=UNPROT
          DFHMDF POS=(2,37),
                 LENGTH=1,
                 ATTRB=ASKIP
```

Coding example (numeric data-entry field)

This example shows how to code a numeric data entry field. Like the non-numeric data entry field, three DFHMDF macros are required: one to define the caption, one to define the start of the field, and one to define the end of the field. The ATTRB parameter of the second DFHMDF macro specifies the NUM option to enable numeric data entry. In addition, the PICIN parameter supplies a numeric picture.

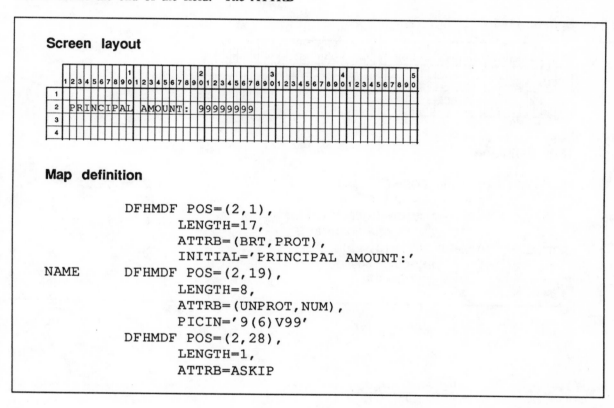

Screen layout

Map definition

```
        DFHMDF POS=(2,1),
               LENGTH=17,
               ATTRB=(BRT,PROT),
               INITIAL='PRINCIPAL AMOUNT:'
NAME    DFHMDF POS=(2,19),
               LENGTH=8,
               ATTRB=(UNPROT,NUM),
               PICIN='9(6)V99'
        DFHMDF POS=(2,28),
               LENGTH=1,
               ATTRB=ASKIP
```

Coding example (alphanumeric display-only field)

This example shows how to define an alphanumeric display-only field. Two DFHMDF macros are coded: one to define the field's caption, the other to define the field itself. The data to be displayed in this field will be supplied by the COBOL program via the symbolic map.

Screen layout

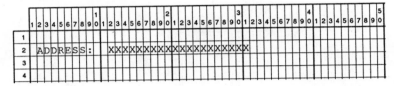

Map definition

```
        DFHMDF POS=(2,1),
               LENGTH=8,
               ATTRB=(BRT,PROT),
               INITIAL='ADDRESS:'
ADDRESS DFHMDF POS=(2,11),
               LENGTH=20,
               ATTRB=PROT
```

Coding example (numeric display-only field)

This example shows how to define a numeric display-only field. Two DFHMDF macros are coded: one to define the field's caption, the other to define the field itself. The data to be displayed in this field will be supplied by the COBOL program via the symbolic map.

Screen layout

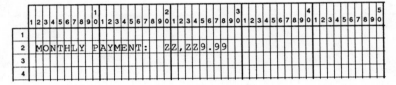

Map definition

```
           DFHMDF POS=(2,1),
                  LENGTH=16,
                  ATTRB=(BRT,PROT),
                  INITIAL='MONTHLY PAYMENT:'
ADDRESS    DFHMDF POS=(2,19),
                  LENGTH=9,
                  ATTRB=PROT,
                  PICOUT='ZZ,ZZ9.99'
```

Coding example (operator communication zone)

This example shows how to code the DFHMDF macro instructions to define a two-line operator communication zone: line 23 is used for operator instructions and line 24 is used to display error messages. Your installation may well have a standard format for this part of the screen; if so, find out what it is and follow it. (The third DFHMDF state-ment, labelled DUMMY, defines a one-byte field whose attributes are set to dark, protected, and FSET. This field serves one purpose: it prevents the MAPFAIL condition from being raised unless the operator uses the CLEAR key or a PA key. I suggest you include a field like this in all your maps.)

Screen layout

Map definition

```
MESSAGE    DFHMDF POS=(23,1),
                  LENGTH=79,
                  ATTRB=(BRT,PROT)
ERROR      DFHMDF POS=(24,1),
                  LENGTH=77,
                  ATTRB=(BRT,PROT)
DUMMY      DFHMDF POS=(24,79),
                  LENGTH=1,
                  ATTRB=(DRK,PROT,FSET),
                  INITIAL=' '
```

The symbolic map

You use a symbolic map in a COBOL program to access data sent to and received from a terminal screen. When you assemble a mapset, a symbolic map is created and placed in a COPY library. Then, you use a COPY statement to include the symbolic map in your COBOL program.

The symbolic map created by BMS isn't ideal for COBOL programming because it forces you to use eight-character data names. As a result, I often discard the BMS-generated symbolic map and create my own, using more meaningful data names. Whether you do that is up to you (and your shop's standards). In this section, I'll describe how to use BMS-generated symbolic maps and how to create your own.

BMS-generated symbolic maps

When BMS generates a symbolic map, it uses the seven-character names you supply in the mapset to form eight-character data names; a one-character suffix is added to the end of each name to identify the data-name's function. In the symbolic mapset, these names are coded in a specific order to match the data structure BMS requires. To use a BMS-generated symbolic mapset, however, you don't have to know the details of that structure; you just have to know how BMS generates its data names. (However, you do have to understand the symbolic map's structure if you want to create your own map. So I'll explain the symbolic map's structure when I show you how to code your own.)

BMS adds I and O to the end of the map name (coded on the DFHMDI macro) to form group names used to define the entire symbolic map. For example, if you specify MORMAP1 as the map name, BMS generates the names MORMAP1I and MORMAP1O. A REDEFINES clause is used so that both names refer to the same storage; thus, you can use them interchangeably.

For each named DFHMDF macro in the map, BMS generates several data names. Figure 3-7 shows the suffix associated with each data name, its

Suffix	Meaning	PICTURE	Option	Example
L	Length	S9(4) COMP		AMOUNTL
A	Attribute byte	X		AMOUNTA
F[1]	Flag	X		AMOUNTF
C	Color attribute	X	EXTATT=YES or DSATTS=COLOR	AMOUNTC
H	Highlight attribute	X	EXTATT=YES or DSATTS=HILIGHT	AMOUNTH
P	Programmed symbol attribute	X	EXTATT=YES or DSATTS=PS	AMOUNTP
V	Validation attribute	X	EXTATT=YES or DSATTS=VALIDN	AMOUNTV
M	SO/SI attribute	X	DSATTS=SOSI	AMOUNTM
T	Transparency attribute	X	DSATTS=TRANSP	AMOUNTT
U	Outlining attribute	X	DSATTS=OUTLINE	AMOUNTU
I	Input data	varies		AMOUNTI
O[2]	Output data	varies		AMOUNTO

Notes

1. The flag byte occupies the same storage as the attribute byte.
2. The output area occupies the same storage as the input area.

Figure 3-7   Symbolic map data names generated by BMS

meaning, which parameters cause it to be generated, its PICTURE, and an example of the complete data name for a map field named map as AMOUNT. Thus, the attribute byte for the AMOUNT field is AMOUNTA. You can use these data names in your COBOL program. So, to move the attribute byte constant FAC-UNPROT-NUM-BRT to the attribute byte for the AMOUNT field, you would code this COBOL statement:

```
MOVE FAC-UNPROT-NUM-BRT
    TO AMOUNTA.
```

Notice in figure 3-7 that the A and F fields define the same byte of the symbolic map data area. Thus, you can use those two data names interchangeably. Similarly, the I and O fields define the same storage, so you can interchange them as well.

How to create your own symbolic map

Because the symbolic maps generated by BMS aren't easy to read and use, I recommend you create your own symbolic map like the one shown in figure 3-8. Here are some simple rules to follow when you create a symbolic map:

1. Code one 01-level item for each map in your mapset, and choose a name for it that corresponds to the screen's function as described in the screen layout form for the screen. For example, a map named CUSTOMER-DATA-MAP corresponds to a layout form for a screen named *customer data screen.*

2. Don't forget to code a 12-byte FILLER item at the beginning of each map.

3. Start each data name with a two- or three-character prefix that's an abbreviation of the map name, like CDM for CUSTOMER-DATA-MAP. And include a one character code to identify the field's function, such as L for the length field. Follow that with a

description of the field. For example, CDM-L-CUSTOMER-NAME might be the name you create for the customer name length field in the customer data map.

4. If you don't use extended attributes, you'll need to define three data names for each map field, with these suffixes and in this order:

   L   Length field
   A   Attribute field
   D   Data field

5. If you use extended attributes, you'll have to code additional attribute fields. If you specify EXTATT=YES, you'll have to add four attribute byte fields between the basic attribute byte and the data field. As a result, you must define a total of seven fields, with these suffixes and in this order:

   L   Length field
   A   Attribute byte
   C   Color attribute
   P   Programmed symbols attribute
   H   Extended highlighting attribute
   V   Validation attribute
   D   Data

If you use the DSATTS parameter, the set of attribute bytes generated for the symbolic map depends on how you code the parameter. The easiest way to make sure your symbolic map is correct in this case is to check the symbolic map generated by BMS. To do that, change the BMS map assembly procedure so that the symbolic map is printed rather than saved in a data set. Section 6 shows you how to do that.

6. Separate each set of data names with a blank comment line.

7. Align the elements of the symbolic map so it's easy to read.

```
    01   INQUIRY-MAP.
*
         05   FILLER                        PIX X(12).
*
         05   IM-L-CUSTOMER-NUMBER          PIC S9(4)    COMP.
         05   IM-A-CUSTOMER-NUMBER          PIC X.
         05   IM-D-CUSTOMER-NUMBER          PIC X(5).
*
         05   IM-L-NAME                     PIC S9(4)    COMP.
         05   IM-A-NAME                     PIC X.
         05   IM-D-NAME                     PIC X(30).
*
         05   IM-L-ADDRESS                  PIC S9(4)    COMP.
         05   IM-A-ADDRESS                  PIC X.
         05   IM-D-ADDRESS                  PIC X(30).
*
         05   IM-L-CITY                     PIC S9(4)    COMP.
         05   IM-A-CITY                     PIC X.
         05   IM-D-CITY                     PIC X(21).
*
         05   IM-L-STATE                    PIC S9(4)    COMP.
         05   IM-A-STATE                    PIC X.
         05   IM-D-STATE                    PIC XX.
*
         05   IM-L-ZIP-CODE                 PIC S9(4)    COMP.
         05   IM-A-ZIP-CODE                 PIC X.
         05   IM-D-ZIP-CODE                 PIC X(5).
*
         05   IM-L-ERROR-MESSAGE            PIC S9(4)    COMP.
         05   IM-A-ERROR-MESSAGE            PIC X.
         05   IM-D-ERROR-MESSAGE            PIC X(77).
*
         05   IM-L-DUMMY                    PIC S9(4)    COMP.
         05   IM-A-DUMMY                    PIC X.
         05   IM-D-DUMMY                    PIC X.
```

Figure 3-8   A programmer-generated symbolic map

A complete BMS mapset

Figure 3-9 shows a screen layout for a customer inquiry program. To help you see how a BMS mapset relates to its screen layout, figure 3-10 shows the complete mapset for this screen. (The symbolic map I created for this screen was shown in figure 3-8.)

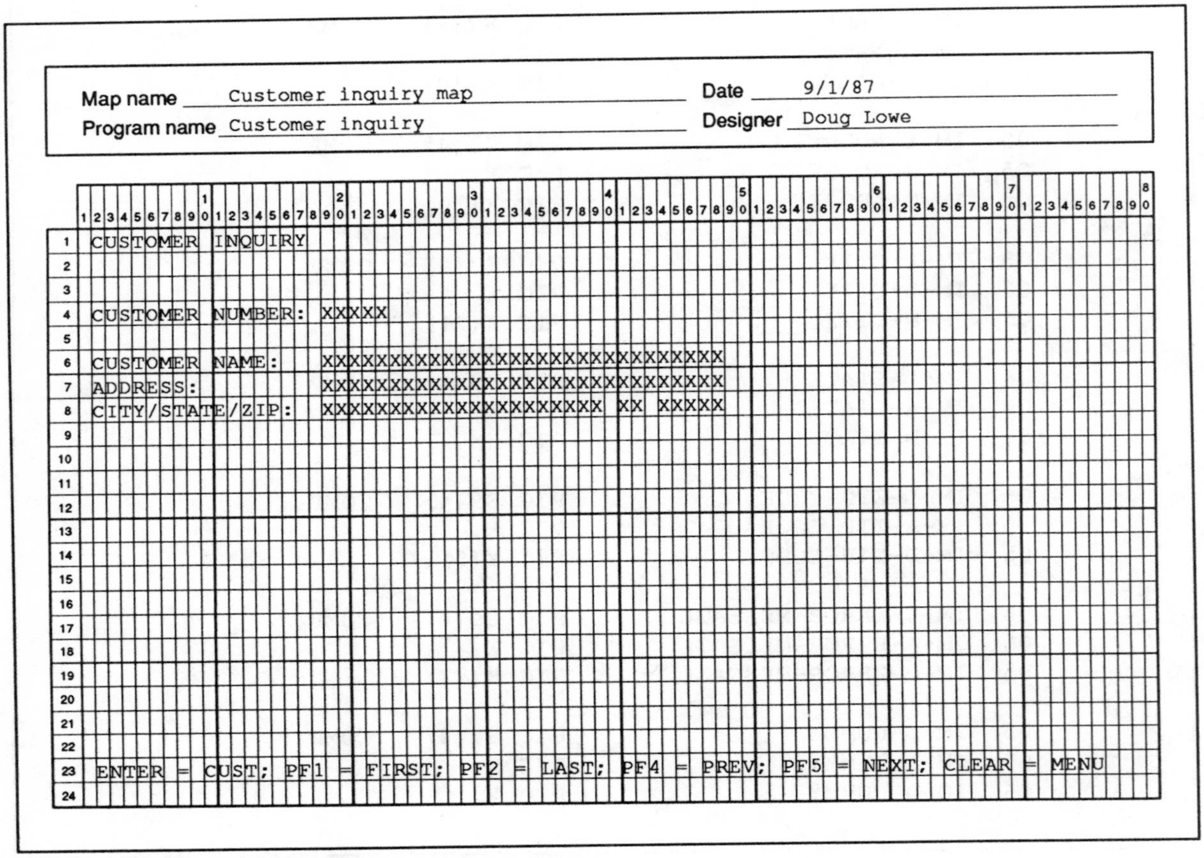

Figure 3-9   Screen layout for the mapset in figure 3-10

```
          PRINT NOGEN
INQSET1   DFHMSD TYPE=&SYSPARM,                                          X
                 LANG=COBOL,                                            X
                 MODE=INOUT,                                            X
                 TERM=3270-2,                                           X
                 CTRL=FREEKB,                                           X
                 STORAGE=AUTO,                                          X
                 TIOAPFX=YES
**************************************************************************
INQMAP1   DFHMDI SIZE=(24,80),                                          X
                 LINE=1,                                                X
                 COLUMN=1
**************************************************************************
          DFHMDF POS=(1,1),                                            X
                 LENGTH=16,                                            X
                 ATTRB=(BRT,PROT),                                     X
                 INITIAL='CUSTOMER INQUIRY'
**************************************************************************
          DFHMDF POS=(4,1),                                            X
                 LENGTH=16,                                            X
                 ATTRB=(BRT,PROT),                                     X
                 INITIAL='CUSTOMER NUMBER:'
NUMBER    DFHMDF POS=(4,18),                                           X
                 LENGTH=5,                                             X
                 ATTRB=(IC,UNPROT,FSET)
          DFHMDF POS=(4,24),                                           X
                 LENGTH=1,                                             X
                 ATTRB=ASKIP
**************************************************************************
          DFHMDF POS=(6,1),                                            X
                 LENGTH=14,                                            X
                 ATTRB=(BRT,PROT),                                     X
                 INITIAL='CUSTOMER NAME:'
NAME      DFHMDF POS=(6,18),                                           X
                 LENGTH=30,                                            X
                 ATTRB=PROT
**************************************************************************
          DFHMDF POS=(7,1),                                            X
                 LENGTH=8,                                             X
                 ATTRB=(BRT,PROT),                                     X
                 INITIAL='ADDRESS:'
ADDRESS   DFHMDF POS=(7,18),                                           X
                 LENGTH=30,                                            X
                 ATTRB=PROT
```

Figure 3-10   A complete BMS mapset (part 1 of 2)

```
************************************************************************
          DFHMDF POS=(8,1),                                           X
               LENGTH=15,                                             X
               ATTRB=(BRT,PROT),                                      X
               INITIAL='CITY/STATE/ZIP:'
CITY      DFHMDF POS=(8,18),                                          X
               LENGTH=21,                                             X
               ATTRB=PROT
STATE     DFHMDF POS=(8,40),                                          X
               LENGTH=2,                                              X
               ATTRB=PROT
ZIP       DFHMDF POS=(8,43),                                          X
               LENGTH=5,                                              X
               ATTRB=PROT
************************************************************************
MESSAGE   DFHMDF POS=(23,1),                                          X
               LENGTH=79,                                             X
               ATTRB=(BRT,PROT)
ERROR     DFHMDF POS=(24,1),                                          X
               LENGTH=77,                                             X
               ATTRB=(BRT,PROT)
DUMMY     DFHMDF POS=(24,79),                                         X
               LENGTH=1,                                              X
               ATTRB=(DRK,PROT,FSET)
************************************************************************
          DFHMSD TYPE=FINAL
          END
```

Figure 3-10   A complete BMS mapset (part 2 of 2)

Section 4

CICS commands

This section provides complete reference for all of the CICS commands you're likely to use in a command level program. The commands are listed in alphabetical order to make each entry easy to locate. For each command, you'll find

- a brief statement of the command's function

- the command's syntax

- an explanation of each of the command's options

- a listing and explanation of the exceptional conditions that can be raised by the command

- notes and tips which will help you better understand how the command works or help you use the command more effectively

- one or more real-life examples of how the command is used

Note that under CICS 1.6, you can code the NOHANDLE option on any command to suspend exceptional condition handling. And under 1.7, you can code NOHANDLE and RESP to make it easy to check for exceptional conditions. Those options are described in Section 2, but since they can be coded for any CICS command, I don't list them in the command syntax diagrams in this section.

Command arguments

Argument values

Most CICS commands require you to code one or more options. And most of the options require you to supply a value in parentheses. The syntax diagrams specify which of these types of values you can code for each option:

data-value
A COBOL data name coded in the Working-Storage or Linkage Section or a literal. The option may require a binary halfword, a binary fullword, or a character string.

data-area
A COBOL data name coded in the Working-Storage or Linkage Section. The option may require a binary halfword, a binary fullword, or a character string.

pointer-ref
The name of a BLL cell coded in the Linkage Section. A pointer-ref must be a binary fullword. (For the VS COBOL II compiler, you should use the ADDRESS OF special register rather than BLL cells.)

pointer-value
The name of a BLL cell coded in the Linkage Section or the name of a Working-Storage Section field that contains a BLL cell value. A pointer-value must be a binary fullword. (For the VS COBOL II compiler, you should use the ADDRESS OF special register rather than BLL cells.)

name
An alphanumeric literal (like 'CUSTMAST') or the name of a Working-Storage or Linkage Section field that contains the value to be used.

label
The name of a paragraph or section.

hhmmss
A numeric literal or the name of a 7-digit packed decimal field (PIC S9(7) COMP-3) defined in the Working-Storage or Linkage Section. *hh* represents hours, *mm* represents minutes, and *ss* represents seconds.

Data types

The value or data field you specify for an argument value must match the data type required by the option. Usually, one of three specific types is required:

binary halfword
PIC S9(4) COMP or PIC X(2).

binary fullword
PIC S9(8) COMP or PIC X(4).

character string
PIC X(*n*).

For binary halfwords and fullwords, don't use PIC X(2) or PIC X(4) if you need to perform arithmetic on the values the fields contain.

If an option doesn't specify a particular data type, you can use any group or elementary item.

The ABEND command

Function

Abnormal termination recovery. The ABEND command forces the current task to terminate abnormally. If a HANDLE ABEND command is in effect, control will be transferred to the routine it specifies. Otherwise, control is returned to CICS. An optional storage dump can be produced.

Syntax

```
EXEC CICS
    ABEND [ ABCODE(name) ]
          [ CANCEL ]
END-EXEC.
```

Options

ABCODE
Specifies that a storage dump should be produced and the one- to four-character value supplied should be used as the abend code. If you omit ABCODE, a storage dump is not produced.

CANCEL
Specifies that any active abend exit set up by a HANDLE ABEND command should be ignored.

Exceptional conditions

No exceptional conditions are raised as a result of the ABEND command.

Notes and tips

- Storage dumps are written to the CICS dump data sets; you'll have to determine your installation's procedures for printing dumps.

- Because the ABEND command causes your task to abend, Dynamic Transaction Backout is invoked. As a result, any changes your task made to recoverable resources will be reversed.

Coding example

This example shows how to issue an ABEND command, producing a storage dump identified by the abend code X100.

```
    9000-ABEND-PROGRAM SECTION.
*
    EXEC CICS
        ABEND ABCODE('X100')
    END-EXEC.
```

The ADDRESS command

Function

Execute interface program. The ADDRESS command lets you access system information that's maintained in storage outside of your program.

Syntax

```
EXEC CICS
    ADDRESS [ CSA(pointer-ref) ]
            [ CWA(pointer-ref) ]
            [ EIB(pointer-ref) ]          1.6 & 1.7 only
            [ TCTUA(pointer-ref) ]
            [ TWA(pointer-ref) ]
END-EXEC.
```

Options

CSA

Establishes addressability to the Common System Area, a major CICS system control block that contains important system information, including pointers to most of the other CICS control blocks.

CWA

Establishes addressability to the Common Work Area, a user-defined storage area common to all tasks in a CICS system.

EIB

(1.6 & 1.7 only) Establishes addressability to the Execute Interface Block. Normally, this addressability is automatically established when your

program is entered. However, if a called sub-program needs to access information in the EIB, it must issue an ADDRESS EIB command.

TCTUA

Establishes addressability to the Terminal Control Table Work Area, a user-defined storage area that's unique to the terminal to which the current task is attached.

TWA

Establishes addressability to the Transaction Work Area, a user-defined storage area that's unique to the current task. The TWA is deleted when the current task ends.

Exceptional conditions

No exceptional conditions are raised as a result of the ADDRESS command.

Notes and tips

- The ADDRESS command simply returns the address of one or more system areas; you must provide the linkage to access those areas. Using the VS COBOL compiler, you do that by coding BLL cells in the Linkage Section; with VS COBOL II, you use the ADDRESS OF special register instead.

- The CSA should be used only by systems programmers; accessing it incorrectly can lead to serious errors, which could bring down the entire CICS system.

- The format of the CWA is installation-dependent; sometimes, it contains useful information, such as the current date already converted to the form MM/DD/YY, a company name, and application-specific information.

- The TCTUA and TWA don't have much use in command-level programming; they're left-overs from the days of macro-level programming. In a command-level application, the function of both has been replaced by the communication area: the TCTUA was usually used to pass information from task to task in a pseudo-conversational application (that function is now done using the COMMAREA option on a RETURN command); and the TWA was used to pass information among programs within a task (that function is now done using the COMMAREA option on a LINK or XCTL command).

- The use of any of these options opens your program to the possibility of corrupting storage that's outside of your program's storage. And that can lead to serious problems. As a result, the ADDRESS command should be avoided whenever possible.

Coding example (VS COBOL)

This example shows how to access the Common Work Area using the VS COBOL compiler. The field BLL-CWA is used to provide linkage to the COMMON-WORK-AREA field, which defines the CWA.

```
        LINKAGE SECTION.
*
   01   BLL-CELLS.
*
        05   FILLER                    PIC S9(8) COMP.
        05   BLL-CWA                   PIC S9(8) COMP.
*
   01   COMMON-WORK-AREA.
              .
              .
              .
*
   PROCEDURE DIVISION.
*
              .
              .
              .
        EXEC CICS
              ADDRESS CWA(BLL-CWA)
        END-EXEC.
```

Coding example (VS COBOL II)

This example shows how to access the Common Work Area using the VS COBOL II compiler. The ADDRESS OF special register is used to provide linkage to the COMMON-WORK-AREA field, which defines the CWA.

```
    LINKAGE SECTION.
*
 01  COMMON-WORK-AREA.
        .
        .
        .
*
  PROCEDURE DIVISION.
*
        .
        .
        .
     EXEC CICS
         ADDRESS CWA(ADDRESS OF COMMON-WORK-AREA)
     END-EXEC.
```

The ASKTIME command

Function

Interval control. The ASKTIME command lets you obtain the current time and date. This information is stored in two Execute Interface Block fields: EIBTIME and EIBDATE. When a task is started, those fields are updated to reflect the starting time and date for the task. ASKTIME simply updates those fields. If you're using CICS 1.7, you can use the ABSTIME option to specify a field into which CICS places an "absolute time." You can then use this field in a FORMATTIME command to format the time in one of several ways.

Syntax

```
EXEC CICS
    ASKTIME [ ABSTIME(data-area) ]          1.7 only
END-EXEC.
```

Options

ABSTIME

(1.7 only) Specifies a binary doubleword item (PIC S9(16) COMP). The value returned represents the number of milliseconds that have elapsed since midnight, January 1, 1900. The value is suitable for timing operations or for conversion (using FORMATTIME) to other formats.

Exceptional conditions

No exceptional conditions are raised as a result of the ASKTIME command.

Notes and tips

- The time values stored in EIBTIME and EIBDATE are precise enough for most uses, such as time-stamping data or displaying the current time and date on the terminal screen. So use the ASKTIME command only when you need an absolutely precise time value.

- EIBDATE is a 7-digit packed decimal field (PIC S9(7) COMP-3). The date is stored in the form 00yyddd, where *yy* is the last two digits of the year and *ddd* is the current date's number within the year. January 1, 1990 is 0090001; December 31, 1990 is 0090365.

- EIBTIME is also a 7-digit packed decimal field (PIC S9(7) COMP-3). The time is stored in the form 0hhmmss, where *hh* represents hours (24-hour clock), *mm* represents minutes, and *ss* represents seconds. Midnight is stored as 0000000; one second before midnight is 0235959.

- ABSTIME is an eight-byte binary value that represents the number of milliseconds that have elapsed since midnight, January 1, 1900.

Coding example

This example shows how to obtain an absolute time and, using a FORMATTIME command, get the current day-of-week. ABSOLUTE-TIME is a double-word (PIC S9(16) COMP), and DAY-OF-WEEK if a fullword (PIC S9(8) COMP).

```
  0500-GET-DAY-OF-WEEK SECTION.
*
      EXEC CICS
          ASKTIME ABSTIME(ABSOLUTE-TIME)
      END-EXEC.
      EXEC CICS
          FORMATTIME ABSTIME(ABSOLUTE-TIME)
                     DAYOFWEEK(DAY-OF-WEEK)
      END-EXEC.
```

The ASSIGN command

Function

Execute interface program. The ASSIGN command lets you obtain information from various system control areas. Although most application programs don't need to use any of this information, it can be useful at times.

Syntax

```
EXEC CICS
    ASSIGN option(data-area)...
END-EXEC.
```

Options

Note: You can specify up to 16 of the following options on a single ASSIGN command. Each must specify a data area, but the format of the data area depends on the option you specify.

ABCODE

4-byte alphanumeric field: returns the abend code if an abend has occurred; otherwise, returns spaces.

APPLID

8-byte alphanumeric field: returns the name used to identify the CICS system to other CICS systems or to a batch system.

BTRANS

(1.7 only) 1-byte alphanumeric field: returns a flag indicating whether the terminal supports background transparency (an advanced graphics display feature); HIGH-VALUE (hex FF) indicates that background transparency is supported; LOW-VALUE (hex 00) indicates it is not.

COLOR

1-byte alphanumeric field: returns a flag indicating whether the terminal supports extended color; HIGH-VALUE (hex FF) indicates that extended color is supported; LOW-VALUE (hex 00) indicates it is not.

CWALENG

Halfword binary field (PIC S9(4) COMP): returns the length of the Common Work Area.

DESTCOUNT

Halfword binary field (PIC S9(4) COMP): used with BMS overflow processing; following a ROUTE command, returns the number of different terminal types specified in the route list; during overflow processing, returns a number indicating which type of terminal caused the overflow.

DESTID

8-byte alphanumeric field: returns the destination identifier when batch data interchange is used.

DESTIDLENG

Halfword binary field (PIC S9(4) COMP): returns the length of the DESTID field.

EXTDS

1-byte alphanumeric field: returns a flag that indicates whether the terminal supports extended data streams; HIGH-VALUE (hex FF) indicates that extended data streams are supported; LOW-VALUE (hex 00) indicates they are not.

FACILITY
4-byte alphanumeric field: returns the identifier of the facility, such as a terminal or destination, that initiated the task.

FCI
1-byte alphanumeric field: returns a hex value that indicates the type of facility that initiated the task: interval control (hex 00), a terminal (hex 01), or a destination (hex 08).

HILIGHT
1-byte alphanumeric field: returns a flag indicating whether the terminal supports extended highlighting; HIGH- VALUE (hex FF) indicates that extended highlighting is supported; LOW-VALUE (hex 00) indicates it is not.

MAPCOLUMN
(1.6 & 1.7 only) Halfword binary field (PIC S9(4) COMP): returns the number of the column in which the current output map is positioned.

MAPHEIGHT
(1.6 & 1.7 only) Halfword binary field (PIC S9(4) COMP): returns the height (in lines) of the current output map.

MAPLINE
(1.6 & 1.7 only) Halfword binary field (PIC S9(4) COMP): returns the number of the line in which the current output map is positioned.

MAPWIDTH
(1.6 & 1.7 only) Halfword binary field (PIC S9(4) COMP): returns the width (in columns) of the current output map.

NETNAME
(1.7 only) 8-byte alphanumeric field: returns the name of the SNA logical unit that originated the task.

NUMTAB
1-byte alphanumeric field: used for 2980 terminals to position the passbook printer.

OPCLASS
3-byte alphanumeric field: returns the operator's class.

OPERKEYS
(1.6 & 1.7 only) 8-byte alphanumeric field: returns the operator's complete 8-byte security key.

OPID
3-byte alphanumeric field: returns the operator's ID number.

OPSECURITY
3-byte alphanumeric field: returns the first 3 bytes of the operator's security key.

OUTLINE
(1.7 only) 1-byte alphanumeric field: returns a flag that indicates whether the terminal supports outlining; HIGH-VALUE (hex FF) indicates that outlining is supported; LOW-VALUE (hex 00) indicates it is not.

PAGENUM
Halfword binary field (PIC S9(4) COMP): used for BMS overflow processing; returns the current page number for the destination that caused the overflow.

PS
1-byte alphanumeric field: returns a flag that indicates whether the terminal supports programmed symbols; HIGH-VALUE (hex FF) indicates that programmed symbols are supported; LOW-VALUE (hex 00) indicates they are not.

QNAME
(1.7 only) 4-byte alphanumeric field: returns the name of the transient data destination that caused the task to be initiated.

RESTART
1-byte alphanumeric field: returns a flag that indicates whether a task has been restarted; HIGH-VALUE (hex FF) indicates that a restart has occurred; LOW-VALUE (hex 00) indicates that the task has been started normally.

SCRNHT
Halfword binary field (PIC S9(4) COMP): returns the height in lines of the 3270 terminal.

SCRNWD

Halfword binary field (PIC S9(4) COMP): returns the width in columns of the 3270 terminal.

STARTCODE

2-byte alphanumeric field: returns a code that indicates how the current task was started. Possible codes are: transient data ATI (QD); interval control START command without data (S); interval control START command with data (SD); terminal input (TD); other task attached by user (U).

SYSID

4-byte alphanumeric field: returns the name of the CICS system.

TCTUALENG

Halfword binary field (PIC S9(4) COMP): returns the length of the Terminal Control Table User Area.

Exceptional condition

Note: unless you provide for this condition with a HANDLE CONDITION command, the task will be terminated if it occurs.

INVREQ

Indicates that the type of information you requested is not available or isn't valid.

Notes and tips

- The following ASSIGN command options are useful for programs that need to use advanced capabilities of 3270 devices:

BTRANS	OUTLINE
COLOR	PS
EXTDS	SCRNHT
HILIGHT	SCRNWD
VALIDATION	

TERMCODE

2-byte alphanumeric field: returns a code indicating the terminal type and model.

TWALENG

Halfword binary field (PIC S9(4) COMP): returns the length of the Transaction Work Area.

USERID

(1.7 only) 8-byte alphanumeric field: returns the user-id of the currently signed on user.

VALIDATION

1-byte alphanumeric field: returns a flag indicating whether the terminal supports field validation; HIGH-VALUE (hex FF) indicates that validation is supported; LOW-VALUE (hex 00) indicates it is not.

- There are several ASSIGN options I've omitted here because they apply to non-3270 terminals or to other obscure CICS functions.

- The following ASSIGN command options are useful for programs that need to use advanced BMS facilities:

DESTCOUNT	MAPLINE
MAPCOLUMN	MAPWIDTH
MAPHEIGHT	PAGENUM

Coding example

This example shows how to obtain four terminal characteristics: screen height, screen width, color support, and field outlining support. This informa-tion can then be used to determine how data should be sent to the terminal.

```
EXEC CICS
    ASSIGN  SCRNHT(SCREEN-HEIGHT)
            SCRNWD(SCREEN-WIDTH)
            COLOR(TERMINAL-COLOR-SW)
            OUTLINE(TERMINAL-OUTLINE-SW)
END-EXEC.
```

The BIF DEEDIT command

Function

Built-in function. The BIF DEEDIT command formats alphanumeric data into numeric data: non-numeric characters are removed; the remaining data is right-justified and padded on the left with zeros.

Syntax

```
EXEC CICS
    BIF DEEDIT FIELD(data-area)
               LENGTH(data-value)
END-EXEC.
```

Options

FIELD
Specifies the data area that contains the data to be de-edited.

LENGTH
Specifies the length of the data area specified in the FIELD option.

Exceptional conditions

No exceptional conditions are raised as a result of the BIF DEEDIT command.

Notes and tips

- The BIF DEEDIT command doesn't really provide all the functions needed to properly process free-form input data. For example, it ignores decimal points; so 10.0 yields a different result than 10.00.

- Future support for the BIF DEEDIT is questionable. In later releases of CICS, there's a system parameter that disables the BIF DEEDIT function altogether. As a result, I suggest you don't use it.

Coding example

This example shows how to de-edit a 10-byte field.

```
EXEC CICS
    BIF DEEDIT FIELD(NUMERIC-TEXT-ENTRY-FIELD)
               LENGTH(10)
END-EXEC.
```

The CANCEL command

Function

Interval control. The CANCEL command cancels the effect of a DELAY, POST, or START command.

Syntax

```
EXEC CICS
    CANCEL [ REQID (name) ]
           [ TRANSID (name) ]
           [ SYSID (name) ]
END-EXEC.
```

Options

REQID
Specifies an eight-character request-id that was associated with the command you want cancelled. The only case in which REQID isn't required is when you're cancelling a POST command you issued earlier from within the same task. In that case, don't code any options on the CANCEL command. REQID is required if you code TRANSID or SYSID.

TRANSID
Specifies a four-character transaction identifier for the transaction you want cancelled. TRANSID isn't normally used, since REQID is required to uniquely identify the START command, and thus the transaction, to be cancelled.

SYSID
Specifies the one- to four-character name of a remote system on which a DELAY, POST, or START command is to be cancelled.

Exceptional conditions

Note: unless you provide for these conditions with a HANDLE CONDITION command, the task will be terminated if any of them occur.

INVREQ
The CANCEL command is not allowed.

ISCINVREQ
An undeterminable error occurred on the remote system (specified in the SYSID option).

NOTAUTH
(1.7 only) The transaction's PCT entry specified that resource security checking should be done and the operator is not authorized to cancel the requested interval control function.

NOTFND

There is no unexpired interval control command associated with the request identifier you specified.

SYSIDERR

The system identified by SYSID could not be located or accessed.

Notes and tips

- To cancel an interval control request, you must usually supply the request-id of the command you want to cancel. There are two ways to get the request-id. The first is to retrieve it from EIBREQID immediately after the DELAY, POST, or START command and store it in a variable for later use. The second is to assign your own request-id by coding the REQID option on the DELAY, POST, or START command. Usually, it's easier to let CICS assign the request-id and just move it from EIBREQID if you need to use it later.

- The CANCEL command won't work if the interval command you want to cancel has already expired. For example, if you issue a START command to start a task in 10 minutes, you can't cancel it with a CANCEL command once the 10-minute period has elapsed and the task has started. If you issue a CANCEL command for an interval command that has expired, the NOTFND condition is raised.

- You don't usually need to handle any of the conditions that can be raised by the CANCEL command. They represent errors from which your program can't generally recover.

Coding example

This example shows how to cancel a command whose request-id is stored in a field named START-REQUEST-ID.

```
EXEC CICS
    CANCEL REQID(START-REQUEST-ID)
END-EXEC.
```

The DELAY command

Function

Interval control. The DELAY command lets you suspend your task until a specified time interval has elapsed or a specified time of day has arrived.

Syntax

```
EXEC CICS
    DELAY [ { INTERVAL(hhmmss) } ]
          {   TIME(hhmmss)    }
          [ REQID(name) ]

END-EXEC.
```

Options

INTERVAL

Specifies how long the task should be suspended. You can code a literal in the form hhmmss; leading zeros can be omitted. Or, you can code a data name; the data area must be a 7-digit packed decimal field (PIC S9(7) COMP-3); its value must be in the form 0hhmmss. If both INTERVAL and TIME are omitted, INTERVAL(0) is assumed.

TIME

Specifies the time of day until which the task should be suspended. You can code a literal in the form hhmmss; leading zeros can be omitted. Or, you can code a data name; the data area must be a 7-digit packed decimal field (PIC S9(7) COMP-3); its value must be in the form 0hhmmss.

REQID

Specifies a one- to eight-character request identifier that's associated with the DELAY command.

Exceptional conditions

Note: INVREQ causes your task to terminate unless you provide for it with a HANDLE CONDITION command; if the EXPIRED condition occurs, it is simply ignored.

EXPIRED

The time specified in the TIME option has already expired.

INVREQ

The DELAY command is not allowed.

Notes and tips

- There aren't many good uses for the DELAY command; most installations are more concerned with speeding up CICS response time than with delaying it. For some projects, it might be appropriate to force a minimum response time on terminal transactions. To do that with a DELAY command, get the time from EIBTIME or ASKTIME when the task first starts; add a fixed amount to this time, and then, just before issuing the SEND MAP command, issue a DELAY command specifying the calculated time in the TIME option. A better alternative is to use the POST and WAIT EVENT commands.

- One possible use for the DELAY command is when your program needs to retry an operation after a failure, allowing time for an operator to correct the problem that caused the failure. In this case, you might delay your task 15 seconds before retrying the operation. Be sure, though, to limit the number of retries so that your task doesn't wait indefinitely.

- You don't usually need to handle either of the exceptional conditions that result from the DELAY command. They represent errors from which your program can't generally recover.

Coding example

This example shows how to delay a task for 15 seconds.

```
EXEC CICS
    DELAY INTERVAL(15)
END-EXEC.
```

The DELETE command

Function

File control. The DELETE command removes a record from a file. The record may have been previously read by a READ command with the UPDATE option, or the record may be retrieved and deleted in a single operation by the DELETE command. In addition, you can specify a generic key to delete more than one record. The file can be a VSAM KSDS, ESDS, RRDS, or path. (CICS also supports BDAM, and earlier releases supported ISAM. Those uncommonly used access methods aren't covered.)

Syntax

```
EXEC CICS
    DELETE DATASET(name)
          [ RIDFLD(data-area) ]
          [ KEYLENGTH(data-value) ]
          [ GENERIC ]
          [ NUMREC(data-area) ]
          [ RBA|RRN ]
          [ SYSID(name) ]
END-EXEC.
```

Options

DATASET

Specifies the one- to eight-character name of the data set that contains the record to be deleted.

RIDFLD

Specifies a data area that identifies the record to be deleted. If omitted, the record must have been previously retrieved using a READ command with the UPDATE option. The contents of the RIDFLD field depends on whether RBA or RRN is specified; if neither is specified, the RIDFLD field contains a key for a VSAM KSDS or path or an ISAM file. For a generic delete (see the KEYLENGTH and GENERIC options, below), the RIDFLD must still be as long as the file's defined key length.

KEYLENGTH

Specifies a binary halfword (PIC S9(4) COMP) or literal value that contains the length of the key. Used only for a generic delete along with the GENERIC option. Must be less than the file's defined key length. Not valid if RBA or RRN is specified.

GENERIC

Specifies that only a part of the key in the RIDFLD field should be used, as indicated by the KEYLENGTH option. All records with a key whose leftmost character positions (as specified by KEYLENGTH) match the RIDFLD field are deleted.

NUMREC

Specifies a data area that CICS sets to the number of records deleted by a generic delete. Valid only when GENERIC and KEYLENGTH are specified.

RBA

Specifies that the RIDFLD field is a Relative Byte Address (RBA) for a VSAM KSDS or ESDS. An RBA is a binary fullword (PIC S9(8) COMP).

RRN

Specifies that the RIDFLD is a Relative Record Number (RRN) for a VSAM RRDS. An RRN is a binary fullword (PIC S9(8) COMP). The RRN of the first record in an RRDS is 1.

SYSID

Specifies the one- to four-character name of a remote system that contains the file.

Exceptional conditions

Note: unless you provide for these conditions with a HANDLE CONDITION command, the task will be terminated if any of them occur.

DISABLED

(1.7 only) The data set is disabled, probably as a result of the master terminal operator explicitly disabling the file using CEMT SET DISABLE.

DSIDERR

The data set name specified in the DATASET option isn't defined in the File Control Table.

DUPKEY

(1.7 only) Occurs only when deleting via an alternate index path that allows duplicate keys; indicates that more than one record with the specified key exists. The DELETE command deletes only the first.

ILLOGIC

A serious VSAM error occurred.

INVREQ

The DELETE request is prohibited by the file's FCT entry. Can also occur if the record was not previously retrieved by a READ command with the UPDATE option and the DELETE command doesn't specify RIDFLD or if a READ UPDATE command was issued for the file and the DELETE command does specify RIDFLD.

IOERR

An I/O error occurred.

ISCINVREQ

An undeterminable error occurred on the remote system (specified in the SYSID option).

NOTAUTH

(1.7 only) The transaction's PCT entry specified that resource security checking should be done and the operator is not authorized to access the data set.

NOTFND

The specified record could not be located.

NOTOPEN

The file is not open.

SYSIDERR

The system identified by SYSID could not be located or accessed.

Notes and tips

- The DELETE command causes your task to hold the control interval that contains the record; the CI is held until your task ends. While it is held, no other task can update any of the records in that CI.

- To prevent deadlock situations, follow two rules: (1) update files in alphabetical order and (2) update records in ascending key sequence.

- The only exceptional condition you normally need to handle for the DELETE command is NOTFND. If you're deleting records via a path that allows nonunique keys, you should also handle DUPKEY. The other exceptional conditions represent errors from which your program can't generally recover.

Coding example (READ UPDATE and DELETE VSAM KSDS records)

This example retrieves and deletes a VSAM KSDS record. Two separate program modules are involved; after module 3500 is invoked to read the record, the program determines if module 3600 should be invoked to delete the record. (If the read and delete operations were always performed together, it would be better to combine them as in the next example.)

```
        PERFORM 3500-READ-ACCOUNT-RECORD.
        IF RECORD-FOUND
            PERFORM 3600-DELETE-ACCOUNT-RECORD.
        .
        .
        .
*
  3500-READ-ACCOUNT-RECORD SECTION.
*
        EXEC CICS
            HANDLE CONDITION NOTFND(3500-NOTFND)
        END-EXEC.
        EXEC CICS
            READ DATASET('ACCOUNT')
                INTO(ACCOUNT-RECORD)
                RIDFLD(AR-ACCOUNT-NUMBER)
                UPDATE
        END-EXEC.
        MOVE 'Y' TO RECORD-FOUND-SW.
        GO TO 3500-EXIT.
*
  3500-NOTFND.
*
        MOVE 'N' TO RECORD-FOUND-SW.
*
  3500-EXIT.
*
        EXIT.
*
  3600-DELETE-ACCOUNT-RECORD SECTION.
*
        EXEC CICS
            DELETE DATASET('ACCOUNT')
        END-EXEC.
```

Coding example (DELETE VSAM KSDS records)

This example retrieves and deletes a VSAM KSDS record with a single DELETE command; no READ UPDATE command is involved. The NOTFND condition is provided in case the record to be deleted doesn't exist.

```
    3500-DELETE-ACCOUNT-RECORD SECTION.
*
        EXEC CICS
            HANDLE CONDITION NOTFND(3500-NOTFND)
        END-EXEC.
        EXEC CICS
            DELETE DATASET('ACCOUNT')
                   RIDFLD(AR-ACCOUNT-NUMBER)
        END-EXEC.
        MOVE 'Y' TO RECORD-FOUND-SW.
        GO TO 3500-EXIT.
*
    3500-NOTFND.
*
        MOVE 'N' TO RECORD-FOUND-SW.
*
    3500-EXIT.
*
        EXIT.
```

The DELETEQ TD command

Function

Transient data control. The DELETEQ TD command deletes the records in a transient data destina tion, reclaiming the space occupied by its records and removing any records that haven't been read.

Syntax

```
EXEC CICS
    DELETEQ TD QUEUE(name)
              [ SYSID(name) ]
END-EXEC.
```

Options

QUEUE

Specifies the one- to four-character name of the destination to be deleted.

SYSID

Specifies the one- to four-character name of a remote system that contains the queue.

Exceptional conditions

Note: unless you provide for these conditions with a HANDLE CONDITION command, the task will be terminated if any of them occur.

ISCINVREQ

An undeterminable error occurred on the remote system (specified in the SYSID option).

NOTAUTH

(1.7 only) The transaction's PCT entry specifies that resource security checking should be done and the operator is not authorized to access the destination.

QIDERR

The destination specified in the QUEUE option isn't defined in the Destination Control Table.

SYSIDERR

The system identified by SYSID could not be located or accessed.

Notes and tips

- You should always delete a transient data destination once its records have been processed. Although you can't retrieve records once they've been processed, the space they occupy is still allocated to the destination. So, unless you issue a DELETEQ TD command, that space isn't available for other uses.

- It's important to realize that the DELETEQ TD command deletes the records in a destination but doesn't delete the destination itself. Since destinations are defined in the Destination Control Table (DCT), they can't be created or deleted while CICS is running.

- You don't usually need to handle any of the exceptional conditions that result from the DELETEQ TD command. They represent errors from which your program can't generally recover.

Coding example

This example shows how to issue a DELETEQ TD command to delete a transient data destination. No exceptional conditions are handled. The name of the destination is stored in the four-character alphanumeric field named DESTINATION-ID.

```
    5400-DELETE-TRANSIENT-DATA SECTION.
*
     EXEC CICS
         DELETEQ TD QUEUE(DESTINATION-ID)
     END-EXEC.
```

The DELETEQ TS command

Function

Temporary storage control. The DELETEQ TS command deletes a temporary storage queue, delet- ing any records remaining in the queue and reclaim- ing the space used by the queue.

Syntax

```
EXEC CICS
    DELETEQ TS QUEUE(name)
               [ SYSID(name) ]
END-EXEC.
```

Options

QUEUE
Specifies the one- to eight-character name of the temporary storage queue to be deleted.

SYSID
Specifies the one- to four-character name of a remote system that contains the queue.

Exceptional conditions

Note: unless you provide for these conditions with a HANDLE CONDITION command, the task will be terminated if any of them occur.

ISCINVREQ
An undeterminable error occurred on the remote system (specified in the SYSID op- tion).

NOTAUTH
(1.7 only) The transaction's PCT entry specified that resource security checking should be done and the operator is not authorized to access the destination.

QIDERR
The queue specified in the QUEUE option doesn't exist.

SYSIDERR
The system identified by SYSID could not be located or accessed.

Notes and tips

- Temporary storage queues are created dynamically: whenever a program writes a record to a queue that doesn't exist, the queue is created. Once created, however, a queue must be explicitly deleted. No special table entries are required for temporary storage queues, unless they are to be made recoverable.

- There are two ways to delete a temporary storage queue: an application program can issue a DELETEQ TS command or an operator with the proper authority can invoke the CEBR transaction and issue a PURGE command (CEBR is the temporary storage browse transaction.) Because a queue can be deleted at any time, you should handle or ignore the QIDERR condition whenever you issue a DELETEQ TS command.

- You don't generally need to handle any of the exceptional conditions that result from the DELETEQ TS command. They represent errors from which your program can't generally recover.

Coding example

This example shows how to issue a DELETEQ TS command to delete a temporary storage queue. The QIDERR condition is ignored so that if the queue does not exist, the task won't be terminated. The temporary storage queue name is stored in a field named TS-QUEUE-ID.

```
    5500-DELETE-TEMPORARY-STORAGE SECTION.
*
        EXEC CICS
            IGNORE CONDITION QIDERR
        END-EXEC.
        EXEC CICS
            DELETEQ TS QUEUE(TS-QUEUE-ID)
        END-EXEC.
```

The DEQ command

Function

Task control. The DEQ command releases a user-defined resource that was reserved for exclusive use by an ENQ command issued by your task. Any other task that has issued an ENQ command for the same resource will then be allowed to continue.

Syntax

```
EXEC CICS
    DEQ RESOURCE(data-area)
        [ LENGTH(data-value) ]
END-EXEC.
```

Options

RESOURCE

Identifies the resource to be released. If LENGTH is also specified, the character string (up to 255 bytes) contained in the data area is used to identify the resource; if LENGTH is omitted, the address of the data area identifies the resource.

LENGTH

Specifies a binary halfword (PIC S9(4) COMP) or literal value that indicates the length (up to 255) of the character string specified in the RESOURCE option.

Exceptional conditions

No exceptional conditions are raised as a result of the DEQ command.

Notes and tips

- The ENQ/DEQ facility is useful for single threading access to resources that you don't want to be shared: printers, destinations, temporary storage queues, etc.

- The ENQ/DEQ facility will work properly only if all tasks that use a particular resource issue ENQ commands and identify the resource in the same way. The ENQ/DEQ facility does nothing to prevent programs that don't issue an ENQ command from accessing the resource.

- Most installations have a standard that specifies how resources are named; find out that standard and be sure to follow it.

Coding example

This example shows how to issue a DEQ command to release a printer that was reserved by an ENQ command so the program could send output to it.

The printer's terminal-id is used as the character string in the RESOURCE option.

```
          .
          .
          .
 *
   01   PRINTER-ID                 PIC X(4)        VALUE 'L86P'.
 *
          .
          .
          .
 *
   PROCEDURE DIVISION.
 *
   0000-PRODUCE-INVENTORY-LISTING SECTION.
 *
          .
          .
          .
       EXEC CICS
           ENQ RESOURCE(PRINTER-ID)
               LENGTH(4)
       END-EXEC.
       PERFORM 2000-PRINT-INVENTORY-LINE
           UNTIL END-OF-REPORT.
       PERFORM 3000-PRINT-TOTAL-LINE.
       EXEC CICS
           DEQ RESOURCE(PRINTER-ID)
               LENGTH(4)
       END-EXEC.
          .
          .
          .
```

The DUMP command

Function

Dump control. The DUMP command forces a storage dump; it can be useful in certain debugging situations, although better tools are usually available.

Syntax

```
EXEC CICS
    DUMP DUMPCODE(name)
        [ FROM(data-area) ]
        [{ LENGTH(data-value)
           FLENGTH(data-value) }]      1.6 & 1.7 only
        [ COMPLETE ]
        [ TASK ]
        [ STORAGE ]
        [ PROGRAM ]
        [ TERMINAL ]
        [ TABLES ]
        [ DCT ]
        [ FCT ]
        [ PCT ]
        [ PPT ]
        [ SIT ]
        [ TCT ]
END-EXEC.
```

Options

Note: if you don't code any options on the DUMP command, the output produced is similar to that produced if you code the TASK option, except that DL/I control blocks aren't included.

DUMPCODE
Specifies a one- to four-character name that identifies the dump.

FROM
Specifies a data area that's dumped; the storage dump begins at the specified data area and continues for the length specified in the LENGTH or FLENGTH option.

LENGTH
Specifies a binary halfword (PIC S9(4) COMP) or literal value that indicates the length of the FROM area to be dumped.

FLENGTH
(1.6 & 1.7 only) Specifies a binary fullword (PIC S9(8) COMP) that contains the length of the FROM area to be dumped.

COMPLETE
Specifies that all available task information is to be dumped, including all CICS tables and DL/I control blocks.

TASK
Specifies that task information is to be dumped, including programs and certain control blocks (including DL/I control blocks).

STORAGE
Specifies that task storage areas and certain control blocks should be dumped.

PROGRAM
Specifies that task program areas and certain control blocks should be dumped.

TABLES
Specifies that CICS tables should be dumped.

DCT
Specifies that the Destination Control Table should be dumped.

FCT
Specifies that the File Control Table should be dumped.

PCT
Specifies that the Program Control Table should be dumped.

PPT
Specifies that the Processing Program Table should be dumped.

SIT
Specifies that the System Initialization Table should be dumped.

TCT
Specifies that the Terminal Control Table should be dumped.

Exceptional conditions

There are no exceptional conditions raised as a result of the DUMP command.

Notes and tips

- Storage dumps are written to the CICS dump data sets; you'll have to determine your installation's procedures for printing dumps.

- Usually, a transaction dump is produced automatically when a task abends. So you need to code a DUMP command only in unusual situations.

- Some of the DUMP options produce excessive amounts of information that are useful only for debugging CICS system problems. For application program debugging, specify TASK, PROGRAM, or STORAGE or code the DUMP command with no options.

Coding example

This example shows how to force a storage dump of all task-related information.

```
EXEC CICS
    DUMP TASK
END-EXEC.
```

The ENDBR command

Function

File control. The ENDBR command terminates a browse operation. All browse operations should be terminated by an ENDBR command; tasks which terminate without ending browse operations may result in errors.

Syntax

```
EXEC CICS
    ENDBR DATASET(name)
          REQID(data-value)
        [ SYSID(name) ]
END-EXEC.
```

Options

DATASET
Specifies the one- to eight-character name of the data set from which a record is to be read.

REQID
Specifies a binary halfword (PIC S9(4) COMP) or literal value that identifies the browse operation; used only when your program controls two or more browse operations at the same time. For each I/O command that's part of the same browse operation, specify the same REQID value.

SYSID
Specifies the one- to four-character name of a remote system that contains the file.

Exceptional conditions

Note: unless you provide for these conditions with a HANDLE CONDITION command, the task will be terminated if any of them occur.

DISABLED
(1.7 only) The data set is disabled, probably as a result of the master terminal operator explicitly dis-abling the file using CEMT.

DSIDERR
The data set name specified in the DATASET option isn't defined in the File Control Table.

ILLOGIC
A serious VSAM error occurred.

INVREQ
A browse operation has not been properly started by a STARTBR command.

IOERR
An I/O error occurred.

ISCINVREQ
An undeterminable error occurred on the remote system (specified in the SYSID option).

NOTAUTH
> (1.7 only) The transaction's PCT entry specified that resource security checking should be done and the operator is not authorized to access the data set.

NOTOPEN
> (1.6 & 1.7 only) The file is not open.

SYSIDERR
> The system identified by SYSID could not be located or accessed.

Notes and tips

- Do *not* issue a READ/UPDATE, WRITE, or DELETE command for a data set while you have an active browse for the same data set: that can lead to a deadlock situation. Instead, issue an ENDBR command before you issue a READ/UPDATE, WRITE, or DELETE command. Then, you can resume your browse operation by issuing a STARTBR command.

- You don't usually need to handle any of the exceptional conditions that result from the ENDBR command. They represent errors from which your program can't generally recover.

Coding example

This example terminates a browse operation for a file named ACCOUNT.

```
    9100-END-ACCOUNT-BROWSE SECTION.
*
        EXEC CICS
            ENDBR DATASET('ACCOUNT')
        END-EXEC.
```

The ENQ command

Function

Task control. The ENQ command reserves a user-defined resource for exclusive use by your task; any other task that issues an ENQ command for the same resource will be suspended until your task ends or issues a DEQ command for the resource.

Syntax

```
EXEC CICS
    ENQ RESOURCE(data-area)
      [ LENGTH(data-value) ]
      [ NOSUSPEND ]
END-EXEC.
```

1.7 only

Options

RESOURCE
Identifies the resource to be reserved. If LENGTH is also specified, the character string (up to 255 bytes) contained in the data area is used to identify the resource; if LENGTH is omitted, the address of the data area identifies the resource.

LENGTH
Specifies a binary halfword (PIC S9(4) COMP) or literal value that indicates the length (up to 255) of the character string specified in the RESOURCE option.

NOSUSPEND
(1.7 only) Indicates that if the resource is already reserved, control is returned immediately to your program at the point following the ENQ command.

Exceptional conditions

ENQBUSY

Indicates that another task has already issued an ENQ command naming the resource you specified. ENQBUSY is one of the few exceptional conditions that does not cause your task to be terminated. Instead, its action depends on whether you issue a HANDLE CONDITION command for the ENQBUSY condition and whether you specify NOSUSPEND on the ENQ command. If you do neither, ENQBUSY simply causes your task to be suspended until the resource becomes available; then, control returns to your program at the first statement following the ENQ command. If you issue a HANDLE CONDITION command for the ENQBUSY condition, control is transferred to the label you specify; your program can do additional work, but to reserve the resource, it must issue the ENQ command again. If you specify NOSUSPEND on the ENQ command, control is returned to the statement following the ENQ command if the resource is unavailable; again, you'll have to issue another ENQ command to reserve the resource later.

Notes and tips

- The ENQ/DEQ facility is useful for single threading access to resources that you don't want to be shared: printers, destinations, temporary storage queues, etc.

- The ENQ/DEQ facility will work properly only if all tasks that use a particular resource issue ENQ commands and identify the resource in the same way. The ENQ/DEQ facility does nothing to prevent programs that don't issue an ENQ command from accessing the resource.

- Most installations have a standard that specifies how resources are named; find out that standard and be sure to follow it.

Coding example

This example shows how to issue an ENQ command to reserve a printer so the program can send output to it. The character string in the RESOURCE option is the printer-id. Thus, any other task that issues an ENQ command using the same printer terminal-id will be suspended until this program issues the DEQ command.

```
         .
         .
         .
 *
  01   PRINTER-ID                 PIC X(4)        VALUE 'L86P'.
 *
         .
         .
         .
 *
  PROCEDURE DIVISION.
 *
  0000-PRODUCE-INVENTORY-LISTING SECTION.
 *
         .
         .
         .
     EXEC CICS
         ENQ RESOURCE(PRINTER-ID)
             LENGTH(4)
     END-EXEC.
     PERFORM 2000-PRINT-INVENTORY-LINE
         UNTIL END-OF-REPORT.
     PERFORM 3000-PRINT-TOTAL-LINE.
     EXEC CICS
         DEQ RESOURCE(PRINTER-ID)
             LENGTH(4)
     END-EXEC.
         .
         .
         .
```

The ENTER command

Function

Trace control. The ENTER command writes a user trace entry in the CICS trace table, which is printed when a transaction dump is produced. (The ENTER command has an additional function: writing Event Monitor Points for user monitoring. That function isn't covered here.)

Syntax

```
EXEC CICS
    ENTER TRACEID(data-value)
        [ FROM(data-area) ]
        [ RESOURCE(data-area) ]          1.6 & 1.7 only
END-EXEC.
```

Options

TRACEID
Specifies a binary halfword (PIC S9(4) COMP) that contains the trace identifier that will be associated with the user trace entry. The value must be 0-199.

FROM
Specifies an eight-byte alphanumeric field; the contents of this field are placed in the data field of the user trace entry.

RESOURCE
(1.6 & 1.7 only) Specifies an eight-byte alphanumeric field; the contents of this field are placed in the resource field of the user trace entry.

Exceptional condition

Note: unless you provide for this condition with a HANDLE CONDITION command, the task will be terminated if it occurs.

INVREQ
(1.6 & 1.7 only) The TRACEID value is greater than 199.

Notes and tips

- For the ENTER command to work, the trace facility must be activated by a TRACE ON command issued from a command-level program. Alternatively, a terminal operator can use the CEMT transaction to activate the trace facility.

- You probably won't use the ENTER command often. Although its main function is for program debugging, there are better debugging facilities available. There are few cases where a user trace entry really helps.

- You don't usually need to handle the INVREQ condition that results from the ENTER command. It represents an error from which your program generally can't recover.

Coding example

This example shows how to create a user trace entry using 100 as the trace identifier.

```
EXEC CICS
    ENTER TRACEID(100)
END-EXEC.
```

The FORMATTIME command

Function

Interval control. The FORMATTIME command accepts a time value in the absolute time format and returns a time value in any of several formats. Valid for CICS release 1.7 only.

Syntax

```
                                                    ┌──────────┐
                                                    │ 1.7 only │
                                                    └──────────┘
    EXEC CICS
        FORMATTIME ABSTIME(data-value)
                   [ YYDDD(data-area) ]
                   [ YYMMDD(data-area) ]
                   [ YYDDMM(data-area) ]
                   [ DDMMYY(data-area) ]
                   [ MMDDYY(data-area) ]
                   [ DATE(data-area) ]
                   [ DATEFORM(data-area) ]
                   [ DATESEP [(data-value)] ]
                   [ DAYCOUNT(data-area) ]
                   [ DAYOFWEEK(data-area) ]
                   [ DAYOFMONTH(data-area) ]
                   [ MONTHOFYEAR(data-area) ]
                   [ YEAR(data-area) ]
                   [ TIME(data-area) ]
                   [ TIMESEP [(data-value)] ]
    END-EXEC.
```

Options

*Note: in the descriptions that follow, **yy** represents a two-digit year (like 90 for 1990); **yyyy** represents a four-digit year (like 1990); **mm** represents a two-digit month (like 04 for April); **dd** represents a two-digit day within the current month; **ddd** represents a three-digit day within the current year, and / or : represent optional separator characters.*

ABSTIME

Specifies a binary doubleword item (PIC S9(16) COMP) that represents the number of milliseconds that have elapsed since midnight, January 1, 1900. Usually, the value is obtained with an ASKTIME command.

YYDDD

Specifies a six-byte field; CICS returns the year and day within the year in the form yy/ddd.

YYMMDD

Specifies an eight-byte field; CICS returns the year, month, and day in the form yy/mm/dd.

YYDDMM

Specifies an eight-byte field; CICS returns the year, day, and month in the form yy/dd/mm.

DDMMYY

Specifies an eight-byte field; CICS returns the day, month, and year in the form dd/mm/yy.

MMDDYY

Specifies an eight-byte field; CICS returns the month, day, and year in the form mm/dd/yy.

DATE

Specifies an eight-byte field; CICS returns the date in the installation's standard date format, specified in the System Initialization Table (SIT).

DATEFORM

Specifies a six-byte field; CICS returns YYMMDD, DDMMYY, or MMDDYY to indicate the installation's standard date format.

DATESEP

Specifies a single character value to be used as a separator between the month, day, and year components of a date value. If you omit DATESEP, no separator is used; if you specify DATESEP but don't provide a value, a slash (/) is used.

DAYCOUNT

Specifies a binary fullword (PIC S9(8) COMP); CICS returns the number of days that have passed since January 1, 1900. (January 1, 1900 is day 0).

DAYOFWEEK

Specifies a binary fullword (PIC S9(8) COMP); CICS returns a number that corresponds to the current day of the week: Sunday is 0, Monday is 1, and so on.

DAYOFMONTH

Specifies a binary fullword (PIC S9(8) COMP); CICS returns the day within the current month.

MONTHOFYEAR

Specifies a binary fullword (PIC S9(8) COMP); CICS returns a number that corresponds to the current month: January = 1, February = 2, and so on.

YEAR

Specifies a binary fullword (PIC S9(8) COMP); CICS returns the four-digit year (such as 1990).

TIME

Specifies an eight-byte field; CICS returns the time in the form hh:mm:ss.

TIMESEP

Specifies a single character value to be used as a separator between the hours, minutes, and seconds components of a time value. If you omit DATESEP, no separator is used; if you specify DATESEP but don't provide a value, a colon (:) is used.

Exceptional conditions

No exceptional conditions are raised as a result of the FORMATTIME command.

Notes and tips

- The FORMATTIME command is usually used in combination with the ASKTIME command to simplify the process of formatting time and date values for output. To ensure that dates are formatted consistently, use the DATE option, which obtains the format and separator character from the System Initialization Table.

- Some of the formatting options might be useful in applications that require date calculations or comparisons. For example, a dunning application might use the DAYCOUNT option to determine how old (in days) a customer's account is. And the DAYOFMONTH and DAYOFWEEK options might be used in payroll applications.

Coding example

This example shows how to get the current day-of-week (a number that ranges from 0 to 6). The absolute time is first obtained using an ASKTIME command. ABSOLUTE-TIME is a doubleword (PIC S9(16) COMP), and DAY-OF-WEEK is a fullword (PIC S9(8) COMP).

```
    0500-GET-DAY-OF-WEEK SECTION.
*
    EXEC CICS
        ASKTIME(ABSOLUTE-TIME)
    END-EXEC.
    EXEC CICS
        FORMATTIME ABSTIME(ABSOLUTE-TIME)
                   DAYOFWEEK(DAY-OF-WEEK)
    END-EXEC.
```

The FREEMAIN command

Function

Storage control. The FREEMAIN command releases virtual storage that was previously acquired with a GETMAIN command so that CICS can use it for other purposes.

Syntax

```
EXEC CICS
    FREEMAIN DATA(data-area)
END-EXEC.
```

Options

DATA

Specifies the name of the Linkage Section field that overlays the storage area you want freed.

Exceptional conditions

There are no exceptional conditions for the FREEMAIN command.

Notes and tips

• Note that in the DATA option, you specify the Linkage Section field that's linked to the storage you want freed; you do *not* specify the address of the field. In other words, specify the Linkage Section description of the field itself, not the BLL cell (VS COBOL) or ADDRESS special register (VS COBOL II).

• You don't need to specify the length of the storage area to be freed. CICS uses control information that immediately precedes the storage to determine how much to release.

Coding example

This example shows how to release virtual storage that was previously acquired by a GETMAIN command; the storage is addressed by a Linkage Section field named INVENTORY-RECORD. See the coding examples for the GETMAIN command to see how the storage was originally acquired.

```
EXEC CICS
    FREEMAIN DATA(INVENTORY-RECORD)
END-EXEC.
```

The GETMAIN command

Function

Storage control. The GETMAIN command acquires a specified amount of virtual storage; that storage is held until a FREEMAIN command is issued or the task ends.

Syntax

```
EXEC CICS
    GETMAIN SET(pointer-ref)
           {LENGTH(data-value) }
           {FLENGTH(data-value)}        1.6 & 1.7 only
           [ INITIMG(data-value) ]
           [ NOSUSPEND ]                1.7 only
END-EXEC.
```

Options

SET
Establishes addressability to the storage to be acquired. For the VS COBOL compiler, this should be a BLL cell that's associated with the Linkage Section description of the storage; for the VS COBOL II compiler, use the ADDRESS special register for the Linkage Section storage description.

LENGTH
Specifies a binary halfword (PIC S9(4) COMP) or literal value that indicates the length of the storage to be acquired.

FLENGTH
(1.6 & 1.7 only) Specifies a binary fullword (PIC S9(8) COMP) that contains the length of the storage to be acquired.

INITIMG
Specifies a one-byte field whose value is used to initialize the storage acquired. If omitted, the storage is *not* initialized.

NOSUSPEND
(1.7 only) Indicates that if storage is not available, control is returned immediately to your program at the point following the GETMAIN command. If omitted, your program is suspended until storage can be acquired, unless you've issued a HANDLE CONDITION command for the NOSTG condition.

Exceptional conditions

LENGERR

(1.6 & 1.7 only) Occurs only when FLENGTH is specified; you requested too much storage. Under MVS/XA, the limit is about 64K in 24-bit mode and about 1G in 31-bit mode. If you don't issue a HANDLE CONDITION command for the LENGERR condition, your task is abnormally terminated if it occurs.

NOSTG

The amount of storage you requested is not immediately available. Normally, your task is suspended until the storage can be acquired. But if you issue a HANDLE CONDITION command for the NOSTG condition, control will return to your program if the storage isn't available.

Notes and tips

- Frankly, there aren't many uses for the GETMAIN or FREEMAIN commands. They're most useful when you use *locate-mode I/O* rather than *move-mode I/O*. With locate-mode I/O, you use the SET option to specify the address of an I/O area. For input operations, CICS obtains the required storage and returns its address to you; for output operations, you must first obtain the storage (usually with a GETMAIN command) and provide its address to CICS. With move-mode I/O, you use data areas in your program's Working Storage Section for I/O areas, and you identify those areas with the INTO and FROM options. Locate-mode I/O is dangerous, however, because it's too easy to access and can accidentally damage important system information. And that can terminate not only your task but the entire CICS system as well. So use move-mode I/O and avoid the GETMAIN and FREEMAIN commands.

Coding example (VS COBOL)

This example shows how to acquire 2,048 bytes of virtual storage; the storage is initialized to HEX-00 (a working-storage field defined with a value of LOW-VALUE) and addressed via a BLL cell named BLL-INVENTORY-RECORD. After the GETMAIN command executes, INVENTORY-RECORD (and any data names defined subordinate to it) can be used.

```
       LINKAGE SECTION.
*
   01   BLL-CELLS.
*
       05   FILLER                      PIC S9(8)   COMP.
       05   BLL-INVENTORY-RECORD        PIC S9(8)   COMP.
*
   01   INVENTORY-RECORD.
   .
   .
   .
   PROCEDURE DIVISION.
   .
   .
   .
       EXEC CICS
           GETMAIN SET(BLL-INVENTORY-RECORD)
                   LENGTH(2048)
                   INITIMG(HEX-00)
       END-EXEC.
   .
   .
   .
```

Coding example (VS COBOL II)

This example shows how to acquire 2,048 bytes of virtual storage using the VS COBOL II compiler; the storage is initialized to HEX-00 (a working-storage field defined with a value of LOW-VALUE) and addressed via the ADDRESS special register. After the GETMAIN command executes, INVENTORY-RECORD (and any data names defined subordinate to it) can be used.

```
     LINKAGE SECTION.
*
     01   INVENTORY-RECORD.
     .
     .
     .
     PROCEDURE DIVISION.
     .
     .
     .

         EXEC CICS
              GETMAIN SET(ADDRESS OF INVENTORY-RECORD)
                      LENGTH(2048)
                      INITIMG(HEX-00)
         END-EXEC.
     .
     .
     .
```

The HANDLE ABEND command

Function

Abnormal termination recovery. The HANDLE ABEND command lets you establish an abend exit; this exit receives control whenever an abend occurs.

Syntax

```
EXEC CICS

                  { PROGRAM(name)
                  { LABEL(label)
    HANDLE ABEND  { CANCEL
                  { RESET

END-EXEC.
```

Options

PROGRAM
Specifies the one- to eight-character name of a program that should be invoked (via a LINK command) if the current program abends.

LABEL
Specifies the COBOL paragraph or section name of a routine within the current program that should be invoked (via GO TO) if the program abends.

CANCEL
Specifies that the effect of a previous HANDLE ABEND command at the same program level is to be cancelled.

RESET
Specifies that a previously cancelled abend exit should be reestablished.

Exceptional condition

Note: unless you provide for this condition with a HANDLE CONDITION command, the task will be terminated if it occurs.

PGMIDERR
Occurs only when you specify the PROGRAM option; the program you specified isn't defined in the Processing Program Table (PPT).

Notes and tips

- The HANDLE ABEND command is usually used to extend the normal CICS abend facilities. For example, you might want to display a terminal message that's more useful than the standard CICS abend message. Or, you might want to record detailed abend information in a log. You might also want to try to recover from certain types of errors, but that's not usually an easy matter. The usual way to provide a standardized abend processing routine is to use the PROGRAM option; all programs simply issue a HANDLE ABEND command to establish the specified program as the abend exit.

- A task can establish more than one abend exit at various program levels (that is, for programs invoked via LINK commands). Whenever an abend occurs, CICS invokes the abend exit that was established by the last HANDLE ABEND command your task issued at the current program level or at a higher level.

- If the program you specify as an abend exit can't be located, your application program probably shouldn't continue processing. As a result, there's little point in handling the PGMIDERR condition for this command.

Coding example

This example shows how to establish a program named ABEND1 as an abend exit.

```
EXEC CICS
    HANDLE ABEND PROGRAM('ABEND1')
END-EXEC.
```

The HANDLE AID command

Function

Basic Mapping Support. The HANDLE AID command lets you establish routines that are invoked when an AID key (such as the enter key or a PF or PA key) is detected by a RECEIVE MAP command.

Syntax

```
EXEC CICS
     HANDLE AID option [(label)]
END-EXEC.
```

Options

option

Specifies the name of the AID key to be handled. You can code up to 16 options in a single HANDLE AID command. If you need to handle more than 16 AID keys at once, just issue more than one HANDLE AID command. If you specify a label, control is transferred to that label when the specified key is detected; if you omit the label, no action is taken when the specified key is pressed. You can specify the following options:

ENTER	The enter key
CLEAR	The clear key
PA1-PA3	Program attention keys
PF1-PF24	Program function keys
ANYKEY	Any PA key, PF key, or the clear key

Exceptional conditions

There are no exceptional conditions for the HANDLE AID command.

Notes and tips

- There are several ways to provide for AID key processing in a CICS program; they are described in detail in Section 2 of this book. Using the HANDLE AID command forces you to take careful control of the execution flow of your program, since control can be transferred to the exit from any RECEIVE or RECEIVE MAP command in your program. As a result, if you use the HANDLE AID command, I suggest you follow the guidelines presented in Section 2.

- The Execute Interface Block field, EIBAID, contains a flag that indicates which AID key was pressed; you can test this field whether or not you provide a HANDLE AID command. For pseudo-conversational programs, EIBAID is updated at the start of each task. So you can test EIBAID *before* you issue a RECEIVE or RECEIVE MAP command.

Coding example

This example shows how to use the HANDLE AID command in a module that receives mapped input from a terminal. Here, the clear key causes control to branch to 2100-CLEAR-KEY, where CANCEL-ENTRY-SW is set to 'Y'; PF1 causes control to branch to 2100-PF1-KEY, where 'Y' is moved to PF-KEY-1-SW; and any other key (other than the enter key) causes control to branch to 2100-ANYKEY, where VALID-DATA-SW is set to 'N'. These switches are tested elsewhere in the program.

```
      2100-RECEIVE-KEY-SCREEN SECTION.
 *
          EXEC CICS
              HANDLE AID CLEAR(2100-CLEAR-KEY)
                         PF1(2100-PF1-KEY)
                         ANYKEY(2100-ANYKEY)
          END-EXEC.
          EXEC CICS
              RECEIVE MAP('MNTMAP2')
                      MAPSET('MNTSET1')
                      INTO(CUSTOMER-DATA-MAP)
          END-EXEC.
          GO TO 2100-EXIT.
 *
      2100-CLEAR-KEY.
 *
          MOVE 'Y' TO CANCEL-ENTRY-SW.
          GO TO 2100-EXIT.
 *
      2100-PF1-KEY.
 *
          MOVE 'Y' TO PF-KEY-1-SW.
          GO TO 2100-EXIT.
 *
      2100-ANYKEY.
 *
          MOVE 'N' TO VALID-DATA-SW.
          MOVE 'INVALID KEY PRESSED' TO CDM-D-ERROR-MESSAGE.
 *
      2100-EXIT.
 *
          EXIT.
```

The HANDLE CONDITION command

Function

Execute interface program. The HANDLE CONDITION command specifies how certain exceptional conditions should be processed.

Syntax

```
EXEC CICS
     HANDLE CONDITION condition-name [(label)] ...
END-EXEC.
```

Options

condition-name

The exceptional condition whose processing is specified. If a label is included, control is transferred to the label when the condition is raised. If a label is *not* included, the default action for the condition is restored; usually, the default action is to terminate the task. Up to 16 conditions can be specified in a single HANDLE CONDITION command; if you need to handle more than 16 conditions, just issue more than one HANDLE CONDITION command.

Exceptional conditions

No exceptional conditions are raised by the HANDLE CONDITION command.

Notes and tips

- There are several ways to provide for exceptional condition processing in a CICS program; they are described in detail in Section 2 of this book. Using the HANDLE CONDITION command forces you to take careful control over the execution flow of your program, since control can be transferred to the exit from any CICS command in your program. As a result, if you use the HANDLE CONDITION command, I suggest you follow the guidelines presented in Section 2.

- An exceptional condition handling routine established by a HANDLE CONDITION can be disabled permanently or temporarily in one of several ways. If you issue a HANDLE CONDITION command specifying the condition name but no label, the default processing action is restored for the command. If you issue an IGNORE CONDITION command for the condition, the condition is simply ignored; in that case, you can test the Execute Interface Block to see if the command executed correctly. If you issue a PUSH HANDLE command, all HANDLE CONDITION exits you've established are ignored until you issue a subsequent POP HANDLE command. Finally, you can code NOHANDLE or RESP on *any* CICS command to temporarily disable any exceptional condition processing.

- You can use the catch-all condition name ERROR to provide a common error-handling exit for errors that aren't specified elsewhere in a HANDLE CONDITION command.

- Most of the exceptional conditions represent error conditions from which your program cannot recover. Usually, you should not handle those conditions; instead, let CICS abnormally terminate the task. If you want to extend the standard abend processing facilities of CICS, use the HANDLE ABEND command to establish an abend exit.

Coding example

This example shows how to establish a routine to process the NOTFND condition in a module that reads a record from a data set. When the module has completed, CUSTOMER-FOUND-SW will contain 'Y' if the record was found or 'N' if the record was not found.

```
    1200-READ-CUSTOMER-RECORD SECTION.
*
        MOVE 'Y' TO CUSTOMER-FOUND-SW.
        EXEC CICS
            HANDLE CONDITION NOTFND(1200-NOTFND)
        END-EXEC.
        EXEC CICS
            READ DATASET('CUSTMAS')
                INTO(CUSTOMER-MASTER-RECORD)
                RIDFLD(CM-CUSTOMER-NUMBER)
        END-EXEC.
        GO TO 1200-EXIT.
*
    1200-NOTFND.
*
        MOVE 'N' TO CUSTOMER-FOUND-SW.
*
    1200-EXIT.
*
        EXIT.
```

The IGNORE CONDITION command

Function

Execute interface program. The IGNORE CONDITION command lets you specify that one or more exceptional conditions should be ignored; if the specified conditions are raised, processing continues with the next statement in the program.

Syntax

```
EXEC CICS
    IGNORE CONDITION condition-name ...
END-EXEC.
```

Options

condition-name
The exceptional condition that is to be ignored. Up to 16 conditions can be specified in a single IGNORE CONDITION command; if you need to ignore more than 16 conditions, just issue more than one IGNORE CONDITION command.

Exceptional conditions

No exceptional conditions are raised by the IGNORE CONDITION command.

Notes and tips

- With the IGNORE CONDITION command, you can selectively disable exceptional conditions. Then, you test for those conditions after each command by examining fields in the Execute Interface Block instead of using HANDLE CONDITION commands. If you use this technique, however, realize that most of the conditions can be raised by more than one command. For example, the LENGERR condition can be raised by any of 18 different commands, including READ, RECEIVE, WRITEQ TD, and GETMAIN. The point is this: if you issue an IGNORE CONDITION command for a particular condition, you'll have to test the EIB for that condition after *every* command that can possibly raise that condition. Otherwise, the results could be disasterous.

- An alternative to the IGNORE CONDITION command is the NOHANDLE and RESP options. These options, which can be coded on *any* CICS command, suspend exceptional condition handling for a single command. Following the command, you must properly test for exceptional conditions. NOHANDLE and RESP are described in Section 2.

Coding example

This example shows how to suspend condition handling for three conditions: NOTFND, DUPREC, and DUPKEY.

```
EXEC CICS
     IGNORE CONDITION NOTFND
                      DUPREC
                      DUPKEY
END-EXEC.
```

The ISSUE commands

Function

Terminal control. The ISSUE commands initiate various control operations for terminal devices. They are not normally used.

Syntax

```
EXEC CICS
    ISSUE COPY TERMID(name)
            [ CTLCHAR(data-value) ]
            [ WAIT ]
END-EXEC.
```

```
EXEC CICS
    ISSUE DISCONNECT
END-EXEC.
```

```
EXEC CICS
    ISSUE ERASEAUP [ WAIT ]
END-EXEC.
```

```
EXEC CICS
    ISSUE PRINT
END-EXEC.
```

```
EXEC CICS
    ISSUE RESET
END-EXEC.
```

Options

COPY

Specifies that the contents of a specified terminal's screen buffer are to be copied into the current terminal's screen buffer. The terminals must be attached to the same control unit.

TERMID

Specifies the one- to four-character name of the terminal whose buffer contents are to be copied. This name must appear in the Terminal Control Table (TCT).

CTLCHAR

Specifies a one-byte copy control character; usually omitted.

WAIT

Specifies that CICS is to wait until the operation has completed before returning control to the application program.

DISCONNECT

Breaks the connection between the terminal and the processor.

ERASEAUP

Erases all unprotected fields on the terminal screen.

PRINT

Specifies that the contents of the current terminal's screen buffer are to be copied to a printer; how the printer is selected depends on the terminal type and the how the network is defined. For 3270 terminals attached to the same control unit, the print key gives you the same function without the use of CICS resources.

Exceptional conditions

Note: unless you issue a HANDLE CONDITION command for this condition, the task wil be terminated if it occurs.

TERMIDERR

ISSUE COPY only; the terminal you specified in the TERMID option isn't in the Terminal Control Table (TCT).

Notes and tips

- These are seldom used commands, for good reason: in a modern telecommunications network, terminal device control operations should not be managed by application programs. Instead, the network itself provides that control. So avoid these commands whenever possible.

THE JOURNAL COMMAND

Function

Journal control. The JOURNAL command writes a record to a journal file.

Syntax

```
EXEC CICS
    JOURNAL JFILEID(data-value)
            JTYPEID(data-value)
            FROM(data-area)
            LENGTH(data-value)
          [ PREFIX(data-value) ]
          [ PFXLENG(data-value) ]
          [ REQID(data-area) ]
          [ WAIT ]
          [ STARTIO ]
          [ NOSUSPEND ]            1.7 only
END-EXEC.
```

Options

JFILEID
Specifies a binary halfword (PIC S9(4) COMP) that indicates the journal to which the record is written. Its value must be 1 to 99 and must be defined in the Journal Control Table (JCT).

JTYPEID
Specifies a two-character code that's placed in the journal record to identify the record.

FROM
Specifies the data area that contains the record to be written.

LENGTH
Specifies a binary halfword (PIC S9(4) COMP) or literal value that indicates the length of the record to be written.

PREFIX
Specifies the data area that contains the user prefix that's to be included in the journal record.

PFXLENG
Specifies a binary halfword (PIC S9(4) COMP) that contains the length of the PREFIX field. Required if PREFIX is specified.

REQID
Specifies a binary fullword (PIC S9(8) COMP); CICS will place a unique value in

this field to identify the journal record; you can use this value later in a WAIT JOURNAL command.

WAIT

Specifies that the journal record is to be written synchronously; that is, control is not returned to your task until the journal record has been sucessfully written. If WAIT is omitted, the journal record is written asynchronously; control is returned to your program immediately.

STARTIO

Specifies that the journal buffer should be written to the journal file immediately.

NOSUSPEND

(1.7 only) Specifies that if there's not enough room in the journal buffer, control should be returned immediately to the program. If NOSUSPEND is omitted and you don't issue a HANDLE CONDITION command for the NOJBUFSP condition, the program is suspended until enough journal buffer space is available to contain the record.

Exceptional conditions

Note: unless you provide for these conditions with a HANDLE CONDITION command, the task will be terminated if any of them except NOJBUFSP occur.

IOERR

An I/O error occurred.

JIDERR

The journal identifier you specified in the JFILEID option isn't defined in the Journal Control Table (JCT).

LENGERR

The journal record is larger than the journal buffer.

NOJBUFSP

There isn't enough room in the buffer to hold the journal record; normally, this causes the ask to be suspended until the buffer is written to the file. However, you can override this action by specifying NOSUSPEND on the JOURNAL command or by issuing a HANDLE CONDITION command for the NOBUFSP condition.

NOTAUTH

(1.7 only) The transaction's PCT entry specified that resource security checking should be done and the operator is not authorized to access the journal.

NOTOPEN

The journal data set is not open.

Notes and tips

- A CICS system can have up to 99 journal files, each identified by a unique number. Journal 1 is called the *system log*; it's used by CICS recovery facilities. The other journals are called *user journals*.

- Journal records have a standardized format that includes several prefix areas. The *common prefix* identifies the journal record type: whether it was written automatically by CICS or by a user program. The *system prefix* contains information about the task that wrote the journal record: its task number, transaction id, terminal id, and a time stamp. These prefixes, which are generated automatically by CICS, are followed by an optional *user prefix* that can contain similar information. Finally, the user prefix is followed by *user data*.

- Journal records can be written in one of two ways: *synchronously* or *asynchronously*. When you write a journal record synchronously, your task waits until the record has been written to disk. When you write a journal record asynchronously, control returns to your task as soon as the record has been placed in a buffer; the record will be written to disk later (usually within one second). If necessary, you can issue a WAIT JOURNAL command to suspend your task until a previously written journal record is actually written to disk. Asynchronous journal output is more efficient and should be used whenever possible.

- Normally, you won't handle any exceptional conditions for the JOURNAL command. Other than NOJBUFSP, they represent conditions from which your program probably can't recover. And for NOJBUFSP, it's usually best to let CICS suspend your task until buffer space becomes available.

Coding example (synchronous journal output)

This example shows how to delete a data set record after first recording the record in a journal. Synchronous journal output is used, so the data set record isn't deleted until the journal record is written to disk.

```
    3100-DELETE-CUSTOMER-RECORD SECTION.
*
        EXEC CICS
            JOURNAL JFILEID(7)
                    JTYPEID('CD')
                    FROM(CUSTOMER-MASTER-RECORD)
                    LENGTH(97)
                    WAIT
        END-EXEC.
        EXEC CICS
            DELETE FILE('CUSTMAS')
                   RIDFLD(CM-CUSTOMER-NUMBER)
        END-EXEC.
```

Coding example (asynchronous journal output)

This example shows how to delete a data set record after first recording the record in a journal. Asynchronous journal output is used, so the program does not wait for the journal record to be written to disk before it deletes the data set record.

However, a WAIT JOURNAL command is issued so that the program will not continue beyond the DELETE commad before the journal record is written to disk.

```
     3100-DELETE-CUSTOMER-RECORD SECTION.
*
         EXEC CICS
             JOURNAL JFILEID(7)
                     JTYPEID('CD')
                     FROM(CUSTOMER-MASTER-RECORD)
                     LENGTH(97)
                     REQID(WS-REQID)
         END-EXEC.
         EXEC CICS
             DELETE FILE('CUSTMAS')
                    RIDFLD(CM-CUSTOMER-NUMBER)
         END-EXEC.
         EXEC CICS
             WAIT JOURNAL JFILEID(7)
                          REQID(WS-REQID)
         END-EXEC.
```

THE LINK COMMAND

Function

Program control. The LINK command invokes a program, which causes the program to be loaded into storage if necessary. Data can be passed to the invoked program. When the invoked program ends, control is returned to the statement following the LINK command in the invoking program.

Syntax

```
EXEC CICS
    LINK PROGRAM(name)
        [ COMMAREA(data-area) ]
        [ LENGTH(data-value) ]
END-EXEC.
```

Options

PROGRAM
Specifies the one- to eight-character name of the program to be invoked. This name must be defined in the Processing Program Table (PPT).

COMMAREA
Specifies a data area that's passed to the invoked program as a communication area. The invoked program accesses the communication area via its DFHCOMMAREA field, which is addressed to the data area specified in the invoking program. In other words, the invoked program accesses the communication area in the same storage locations as the invoking program; the communication area is not copied to another area of storage. (This works differently than it does for an XCTL or RETURN command; see the descriptions of those commands for details.)

LENGTH
Specifies a binary halfword (PIC S9(4) COMP) or literal value that indicates the length of the data area specified in the COMMAREA option; this option is required if you code COMMAREA.

Exceptional conditions

Note: unless you provide for these conditions with a HANDLE CONDITION command, the task will be terminated if either of them occur.

NOTAUTH
(1.7 only) The transaction's PCT entry specified that resource security checking should be done and the operator is not authorized to access the program.

PGMIDERR
The program is not defined in the Processing Program Table (PPT).

Notes and tips

- The LINK command invokes a CICS program as if it were a subprogram. You can achieve a similar result by using a COBOL CALL statement. Although the CALL statement is faster (because CICS isn't involved), the LINK command has some distinct advantages: it automatically provides addressability to the EIB and you don't have to link-edit the subprogram together with the invoking program. (Under CICS 1.7 and the VS COBOL II compiler, you can dynamically invoke a subprogram that's not link edited to the main program. In this case, LINK and CALL have almost the same function.)

- The XCTL command also transfers control to another program, but no return mechanism is set up. As a result, as soon as a program issues an XCTL command, CICS is free to reclaim the storage occupied by that program and use it for other purposes. Because that's a performance benefit, you should use XCTL rather than LINK whenever possible.

- If application processing can continue without the linked program, you should handle the PGMIDERR and NOTAUTH conditions; if the program is critical to the application, though, there's little point in handling those conditions.

Coding example

This example invokes a program named MMIN2010, passing it a five-byte communication area named NEXT-INVOICE-NUMBER. No exceptional conditions are provided for, since both NOTAUTH and PGMIDERR represent errors from which the program can't recover.

```
    5000-GET-NEXT-INVOICE-NUMBER SECTION.
*
        EXEC CICS
            LINK PROGRAM('MMIN2010')
                  COMMAREA(NEXT-INVOICE-NUMBER)
                  LENGTH(5)
        END-EXEC.
```

The LOAD command

Function

Program control. The LOAD command retrieves an object module, loads it into virtual storage, and returns its length and address to the program that issued the LOAD command.

Syntax

```
EXEC CICS
    LOAD PROGRAM(name)
        [ SET(pointer-ref) ]
        ⎰ LENGTH(data-area)  ⎱
        ⎱ FLENGTH(data-area) ⎰        1.6 & 1.7 only
        [ ENTRY(pointer-ref) ]
        [ HOLD ]
END-EXEC.
```

Options

PROGRAM

Specifies the one- to eight-character name of the object module to be loaded. This name must be defined in the Processing Program Table (PPT).

SET

Specifies a binary fullword (PIC S9(8) COMP) into which CICS returns the address where the object module was loaded. For the VS COBOL compiler, you can specify a BLL cell in the SET option to establish addressability to the object module. For the VS COBOL II compiler, you can do the same thing by specifying the ADDRESS OF special register in the SET option.

LENGTH

Specifies a data area (binary halfword) that's set to the length of the object module retrieved.

FLENGTH

(1.6 & 1.7 only) Specifies a data area (binary fullword) that's set to the length of the object module retrieved.

ENTRY

Specifies a data area that's set to the virtual storage address where the object module was loaded.

HOLD

Specifies that the object module should remain in storage after the current task finishes. If specified, the object module can be removed later by a RELEASE command; if omitted, the object module is automatically removed when the task ends.

Exceptional conditions

Note: unless you issue a HANDLE CONDITION command for these conditions, the task will be terminated if either of them occur.

NOTAUTH

(1.7 only) The transaction's PCT entry specified that resource security checking should be done and the operator is not authorized to access the specified object module.

PGMIDERR

The object module is not defined in the Processing Program Table (PPT).

Notes and tips

• The LOAD command actually loads a program into storage if the program isn't already loaded. If the program is already in virtual storage, the LOAD command simply returns the address of the program.

• Although the load module can be an executable program which you can invoke via a LINK or XCTL command, it's often a table which is addressed via the Linkage Section. Any table whose entries rarely change, such as state or zip codes, is a good candidate for this technique.

• Depending on the application, you may or may not need to provide for the NOTAUTH and PGMIDERR conditions.

Coding example (loading a constant table using VS COBOL)

This example shows the Linkage Section and the Procedure Division code required to load and address a table stored as an object module. The table is held after the task ends, so it can be released only by a RELEASE command.

```
    LINKAGE SECTION.
*
  01   BLL-CELLS.
*
      05  FILLER                 PIC S9(8)   COMP.
      05  BLL-STATE-TABLE        PIC S9(8)   COMP.
*
  01   STATE-TABLE.
*
      05  STATE-CODE             OCCURS 52  PIC XX.
*
  PROCEDURE DIVISION.
*
  0000-ACCEPT-CUSTOMER-ORDERS SECTION.
*
      EXEC CICS
          LOAD PROGRAM('STATABL')
               SET(BLL-STATE-TABLE)
               HOLD
      END-EXEC.
          .
          .
          .
```

Coding example (assembler-language source code for constant table)

This example shows the assembler-language coding required to create a constant table that can be loaded and addressed as shown in the previous ex- ample. After the initial comments, the program consists simply of DC statements that define literal values. There are no executable statements.

```
STATABL   START 0
* * * * * * * * * * * * * * * * * * * * * * * * * * * * * * * * * * * * * * * * * * * * * * * * * * * * * *
*                                                                          *
*      THIS CONSTANT TABLE CONTAINS 52 TWO-BYTE ENTRIES                    *
*      CORRESPONDING TO THE FIFTY STATES PLUS PUERTO RICO                  *
*      AND THE DISTRICT OF COLUMBIA                                        *
*                                                                          *
* * * * * * * * * * * * * * * * * * * * * * * * * * * * * * * * * * * * * * * * * * * * * * * * * * * * * *
          DC    CL10'AKALARAZCA'
          DC    CL10'COCTDCDEFL'
          DC    CL10'GAHIIAIDIL'
          DC    CL10'INKSKYLAMA'
          DC    CL10'MDMEMIMNMO'
          DC    CL10'MSMTNCNDNE'
          DC    CL10'NHNJNMNVNY'
          DC    CL10'OHOKORPAPR'
          DC    CL10'RISCSDTNTX'
          DC    CL10'UTVAVTWAWV'
          DC    CL4'WIWY'
          END
```

The POP HANDLE command

Function

Execute interface program. The POP HANDLE command restores HANDLE ABEND, HANDLE AID, and HANDLE CONDITION commands that were temporarily suspended by a PUSH HANDLE command. Valid for releases 1.6 and 1.7 only.

Syntax

```
EXEC CICS                    ┌─────────────┐
     POP HANDLE              │ 1.6 & 1.7 only │
END-EXEC.                    └─────────────┘
```

Options

The POP HANDLE command has no options.

Exceptional conditions

There are no exceptional conditions for the POP HANDLE command.

Notes and tips

- You can think of the PUSH and POP HANDLE commands as implementing a push-down stack for the settings established by HANDLE ABEND, HANDLE AID, and HANDLE CONDITION commands. Each time you issue a PUSH HANDLE command, the current HANDLE settings are pushed on top of the stack and all current settings are restored to system defaults. Then, when you issue a POP HANDLE command, the HANDLE settings on top of the stack are removed from the stack and made current.

- PUSH and POP HANDLE are most useful when you use called subprograms. A called subprogram can begin by issuing a PUSH HANDLE command; that saves the current HANDLE settings. Then, the called subprogram can issue whatever HANDLE commands it needs; before it returns to the calling program, it issues a POP HANDLE command to restore the HANDLE settings to their original status. Note that this isn't required when you invoke a program via LINK; in that case, CICS automatically deactivates the HANDLE AID and HANDLE CONDITION settings of the caller. (Any abend exits established by HANDLE ABEND commands, however, remain active.)

Coding example

This example shows how you might use PUSH and POP HANDLE commands in a called subprogram. When used this way, the called subprogram can es- tablish its own HANDLE settings without altering the settings of the calling program.

```
    PROCEDURE DIVISION USING CUSTOMER-KEY
                             CUSTOMER-RECORD.
 *
    0000-GET-CUSTOMER-RECORD SECTION.
 *
        EXEC CICS
            PUSH HANDLE
        END-EXEC.
        EXEC CICS
            HANDLE CONDITION NOTFND(1100-NOTFND)
        END-EXEC.
            .
            .
            .
        EXEC CICS
            POP HANDLE
        END-EXEC.
 *
    0000-EXIT-PROGRAM.
 *
        EXIT PROGRAM.
```

The POST command

Function

Interval control. The POST command creates a Timer Event Control Block that expires when a specified time interval has elapsed. You can then use a WAIT EVENT command to suspend your task until the posted event expires.

Syntax

```
EXEC CICS
    POST [ { INTERVAL(hhmmss) } ]
         {   TIME(hhmmss)    }
         SET(pointer-ref)
         [ REQID(name) ]
    END-EXEC.
```

Options

INTERVAL

Specifies a time interval. You can code a literal in the form hhmmss; leading zeros can be omitted. Or, you can code a data name; the data area must be a 7-digit packed decimal field (PIC S9(7) COMP-3); its value must be in the form 0hhmmss. If both INTERVAL and TIME are omitted, INTERVAL(0) is assumed.

TIME

Specifies a time of day. You can code a literal in the form hhmmss; leading zeros can be omitted. Or, you can code a data name; the data area must be a 7-digit packed decimal field (PIC S9(7) COMP-3); its value must be in the form 0hhmmss. If both INTERVAL and TIME are omitted, INTERVAL(0) is assumed.

SET

Specifies a binary fullword (PIC S9(8) COMP) into which CICS places the address of the Timer Event Control Area. If you need to access the Timer Event Control Area directly, you should provide the proper linkage using BLL cells (VS COBOL) or the ADDRESS OF special register (VS COBOL II). Otherwise, this can be a simple working storage section field.

REQID

Specifies a one- to eight-character request identifier that's associated with the Timer Event Control Area. If you issue a CANCEL command specifying the same request identifier, the Timer Event Control Area is cancelled. If you omit REQID, CICS generates a unique request identifier and places it in the EIBREQID field in the Execute Interface Block.

Exceptional conditions

Note: unless you provide for the INVREQ condition with a HANDLE CONDITION command, the task will be terminated if it occurs.

EXPIRED

The time you specified in the INTERVAL or TIME option has already arrived. If you do not issue a HANDLE CONDITION command for this condition, the condition is ignored and the event is considered to be expired immediately.

INVREQ

The interval control request is invalid.

Notes and tips

- One possible, though unlikely, use for the POST and WAIT EVENT commands is to force a minimum response time for terminal transactions. To do that, issue a POST command at the start of the task, specifying the minimum response time (perhaps 3 seconds) in the INTERVAL option. Then, before you issue the final SEND MAP command, issue a WAIT EVENT command. That way, the terminal won't receive output faster than the minimum response time will allow. Of course, this doesn't account for data transmission time, which is often the largest component of total response time.

- You don't usually need to handle any of the exceptional conditions that result from the POST command. They represent error conditions from which your program can't generally recover.

Coding example

This example shows how to issue POST and WAIT EVENT commands to ensure a minimum 3 second response time. Because this type of function affects the high-level coding of the program, I've included all of the program's top level module and parts of several subordinate modules. WS-ECA-POINTER is a working storage field defined as PIC S9(8) COMP.

```
    0000-PROCESS-CUSTOMER-INQUIRY SECTION.
*
    IF EIBCALEN = ZERO
        PERFORM 8000-START-TERMINAL-SESSION
    ELSE
        MOVE DFHCOMMAREA TO COMMUNICATION-AREA
        EXEC CICS
            POST EVENT INTERVAL(3)
                      SET(WS-ECA-POINTER)
        END-EXEC
        PERFORM 1000-PROCESS-INQUIRY-SCREEN.
    IF END-SESSION
        EXEC CICS
            XCTL PROGRAM('MENU1')
        END-EXEC
    ELSE
        EXEC CICS
            RETURN TRANSID('INQ1')
                   COMMAREA(COMMUNICATION-AREA)
                   LENGTH(1)
        END-EXEC.
*
  1000-PROCESS-INQUIRY-SCREEN SECTION.
*
    PERFORM 1100-RECEIVE-INQUIRY-SCREEN.
    IF NOT END-SESSION
        PERFORM 1200-GET-CUSTOMER-DATA
        PERFORM 1300-SEND-INQUIRY-SCREEN.
        .
        .
        .
  1300-SEND-INQUIRY-SCREEN SECTION.
*
    EXEC CICS
        WAIT EVENT ECADDR(WS-ECA-POINTER)
    END-EXEC.
    EXEC CICS
        SEND MAP ...
    END-EXEC.
```

The PURGE MESSAGE command

Function

Basic Mapping Support. The PURGE MESSAGE command lets you delete a logical message before your task terminates.

Syntax

```
EXEC CICS
    PURGE MESSAGE
END-EXEC.
```

Options

The PURGE MESSAGE command has no options.

Exceptional condition

Note: unless you provide for this condition with a HANDLE CONDITION command, the task will be terminated if it occurs.

TSIOERR

An I/O error has occurred on the temporary storage data set.

Notes and tips

- The PURGE MESSAGE command is useful if, while your program is building a message, it encounters an error which won't let it complete the message. In that case, the program should issue a PURGE MESSAGE command so that all of the CICS resources—especially the temporary storage space occupied by the message—are released.

- You don't usually need to provide for the TSIOERR condition. It represents an error from which your program can't generally recover.

Coding example

This example shows how to issue a PURGE MESSAGE command. Here, module 1000 is first invoked to build a message; this module is invoked repeatedly until MESSAGE-COMPLETE-SW is turned on. If a situation arises that prevents the message from being created, MESSAGE-CAN-CELED-SW is turned on. After module 1000 completes, that switch is tested; if it's on, a PURGE MESSAGE command is issued to delete the portion of the message that was created before the error condition occurred.

```
        .
        .
        .
    PERFORM 1000-BUILD-INQUIRY-MESSAGE
        UNTIL MESSAGE-COMPLETE.
    IF MESSAGE-CANCELED
        EXEC CICS
            PURGE MESSAGE
        END-EXEC.
        .
        .
        .
```

The PUSH HANDLE command

Function

Execute interface program. The PUSH HANDLE command suspends HANDLE ABEND, HANDLE AID, and HANDLE CONDITION commands; a POP HANDLE command can be used to restore the saved settings. Valid for release 1.6 and 1.7 only.

Syntax

```
EXEC CICS                    1.6 & 1.7 only
    PUSH HANDLE
END-EXEC.
```

Options

The PUSH HANDLE command has no options.

Exceptional conditions

There are no exceptional conditions for the PUSH HANDLE command.

Notes and tips

- You can think of the PUSH and POP HANDLE commands as implementing a push-down stack for the settings established by HANDLE ABEND, HANDLE AID, and HANDLE CONDITION commands. Each time you issue a PUSH HANDLE command, the current HANDLE settings are pushed on top of the stack and all current settings are restored to system defaults. Then, when you issue a POP HANDLE command, the HANDLE settings on top of the stack are removed from the stack and made current.

- PUSH and POP HANDLE are most useful when you use called subprograms. A called subprogram can begin by issuing a PUSH HANDLE command; that saves the current HANDLE settings. Then, the called subprogram can issue whatever HANDLE commands it needs; before it returns to the calling program, it issues a POP HANDLE command to restore the HANDLE settings to their original status. Note that this isn't required when you invoke a program via LINK; in that case, CICS automatically deactivates the HANDLE AID and HANDLE CONDITION settings of the caller. (Any abend exits established by HANDLE ABEND commands, however, remain active.)

Coding example

This example shows how you might use PUSH and POP HANDLE commands in a called subprogram. When used this way, the called subprogram can establish its own HANDLE settings without altering the settings of the calling program.

```
      PROCEDURE DIVISION USING CUSTOMER-KEY
                               CUSTOMER-RECORD.
 *
  0000-GET-CUSTOMER-RECORD SECTION.
 *
      EXEC CICS
          PUSH HANDLE
      END-EXEC.
      EXEC CICS
          HANDLE CONDITION NOTFND(1100-NOTFND)
      END-EXEC.
          .
          .
          .
      EXEC CICS
          POP HANDLE
      END-EXEC.
 *
  0000-EXIT-PROGRAM.
 *
      EXIT PROGRAM.
```

THE READ COMMAND

Function

File control. The READ command retrieves one record from a file. The file can be a VSAM KSDS, ESDS, RRDS, or path. (CICS also supports BDAM and earlier releases support ISAM. Those uncommonly used access methods aren't covered here.)

Syntax

```
EXEC CICS
    READ DATASET(name)
        { INTO(data-area)  }
        { SET(pointer-ref) }
        [ LENGTH(data-area) ]
          RIDFLD(data-area)
        [ KEYLENGTH(data-value) ]
        [ GENERIC ]
        [ SYSID(name) ]
        [ RBA|RRN ]
        [ GTEQ|EQUAL ]
        [ UPDATE ]
END-EXEC.
```

Options

DATASET
Specifies the one- to eight-character name of the data set from which a record is to be read.

INTO
Specifies the name of a data area into which the data record is moved.

SET
Specifies the name of a data area into which the address of the retrieved record is placed.

LENGTH
Specifies a binary halfword data area (PIC S9(4) COMP) that contains the length of the record. On entry, the data area indicates the size of the INTO data area, if INTO is specified. On exit, the data area contains the size of the record retrieved. Required if INTO is specified, unless the file has fixed-length records; optional for SET.

RIDFLD
Specifies a data area that identifies the record to be retrieved. The contents of the RIDFLD field depends on whether RBA or RRN is specified; if neither is specified, the RIDFLD field contains a key for VSAM KSDS or path retrieval. For a generic read (see the KEYLENGTH and GENERIC options below), the RIDFLD must still be as long as the file's defined key length.

KEYLENGTH
Specifies a binary halfword (PIC S9(4) COMP) or literal value that indicates the length of the key, which must be less than the file's defined key length. Used only for a generic read along with the GENERIC option. Not valid if RBA or RRN is specified.

GENERIC
Specifies that only a part of the key in the RIDFLD field should be used, as indicated by the KEYLENGTH option. The first record with a key whose leftmost character positions (as specified by KEYLENGTH) match the RIDFLD field is retrieved.

SYSID
Specifies the one- to four-character name of a remote system that contains the file.

RBA
Specifies that the RIDFLD field is a Relative Byte Address (RBA) for a VSAM KSDS or ESDS. An RBA is a binary fullword (PIC S9(8) COMP).

RRN
Specifies that the RIDFLD is a Relative Record Number (RRN) for a VSAM RRDS. An RRN is a binary fullword (PIC S9(8) COMP). The RRN of the first record in an RRDS is 1.

GTEQ
Specifies that the first record whose key value is greater than or equal to the key specified in the RIDFLD field is to be retrieved. This will always retrieve a record from the file unless the specified key is greater than the largest key in the file.

EQUAL
Specifies that only a record whose key matches the RIDFLD field exactly will be retrieved. If you omit GTEQ and EQUAL, EQUAL is assumed.

UPDATE
Specifies that you intend to update the record by rewriting or deleting it; the entire control interval containing the record is held under exclusive control by your task. No other task can access any record in the control interval until: (1) you issue a REWRITE, DELETE, or UNLOCK command to release the record or (2) your task ends. If the file is recoverable, the control interval is held until the task ends even if you issue a REWRITE, DELETE, or UNLOCK command.

Exceptional conditions

Note: unless you provide for these conditions with a HANDLE CONDITION command, the task will be terminated if any of them occur.

DISABLED
(1.7 only) The data set is disabled, probably as a result of the master terminal operator explicitly dis-abling the file using CEMT SET DISABLE.

DSIDERR
The data set name specified in the DATASET option isn't defined in the File Control Table.

DUPKEY
Occurs only when retrieving via an alternate index (path) that allows duplicate keys; indicates that more than one record with the specified key exists. The READ command retrieves only the first record with the specified key.

ILLOGIC
A serious VSAM error occurred.

INVREQ
The READ request is prohibited by the file's FCT entry. Can also occur if the KEYLENGTH value is incorrect.

IOERR
An I/O error occurred.

ISCINVREQ
An undeterminable error occurred on the remote system (specified in the SYSID option).

LENGERR

The length of the record retrieved exceeds the length specified in the LENGTH option.

NOTAUTH

(1.7 only) The transaction's PCT entry specified that resource security checking should be done and the operator is not authorized to access the data set.

NOTFND

The specified record could not be located.

NOTOPEN

The file is not open.

SYSIDERR

The system identified by SYSID could not be located or accessed.

Notes and tips

- To read a record via an alternate index, simply specify a path name in the DATASET option. If the alternate index allows duplicate keys, only the first record for each alternate key value can be retrieved by the READ command; to retrieve more than one record with the same alternate key value, use the READ-NEXT command. If the alternate key does allow duplicates, don't forget to handle the DUPREC condition.

- When you issue a READ command with the UPDATE option, CICS holds the entire control interval that contains the record until you issue an UNLOCK command, a SYNC-POINT command, or until your task ends. While the control interval is held, no other task can access any record in it.

- The only exceptional condition you should usually handle for the READ command is NOTFND. If you're retrieving records via a path that allows duplicate keys, you should also handle DUPKEY. The other conditions, however, represent errors from which your program can't generally recover.

Coding example (fixed-length VSAM KSDS records)

This example retrieves a fixed length record from a VSAM KSDS. The record, identified by the key value in ACCOUNT-NUMBER, is placed in the field named ACCOUNT-RECORD. The NOTFND condition is handled to provide for invalid key values.

```
    2100-READ-ACCOUNT-RECORD SECTION.
*
    EXEC CICS
        HANDLE CONDITION NOTFND(2100-NOTFND)
    END-EXEC.
    EXEC CICS
        READ DATASET('ACCOUNT')
            INTO(ACCOUNT-RECORD)
            RIDFLD(ACCOUNT-NUMBER)
    END-EXEC.
    MOVE 'Y' TO RECORD-FOUND-SW.
    GO TO 2100-EXIT.
*
  2100-NOTFND.
*
    MOVE 'N' TO RECORD-FOUND-SW.
*
  2100-EXIT.
*
    EXIT.
```

Coding example (variable-length VSAM ESDS records)

This example retrieves a record from a variable-length VSAM ESDS. The record is identified by the RBA value in ACCOUNT-MASTER-RBA. The LENGTH field initially contains the maximum record length the program will accept; after the READ command, it contains the length of the record that was read. NOTFND provides for records that can't be located.

```
    2100-READ-ACCOUNT-RECORD SECTION.
*
        EXEC CICS
            HANDLE CONDITION NOTFND(2100-NOTFND)
        END-EXEC.
        EXEC CICS
            READ DATASET('ACCOUNT')
                INTO(ACCOUNT-RECORD)
                LENGTH(ACCOUNT-RECORD-LENGTH)
                RIDFLD(ACCOUNT-MASTER-RBA)
                RBA
        END-EXEC.
        MOVE 'Y' TO RECORD-FOUND-SW.
        GO TO 2100-EXIT.
*
    2100-NOTFND.
*
        MOVE 'N' TO RECORD-FOUND-SW.
*
    2100-EXIT.
*
        EXIT.
```

THE READNEXT COMMAND

Function

File control. The READNEXT command retrieves the next sequential record from a file during a browse operation. The file can be a VSAM KSDS, ESDS, RRDS, or path. (Earlier releases of CICS also supported ISAM, but that's not covered here.)

Syntax

```
EXEC CICS
    READNEXT DATASET(name)
             { INTO(data-area)    }
             { SET(pointer-ref)   }
             [ LENGTH(data-area) ]
               RIDFLD(data-area)
             [ KEYLENGTH(data-value ]
             [ RBA|RRN ]
             [ REQID(data-value) ]
             [ SYSID(name) ]
END-EXEC.
```

Options

DATASET
Specifies the one- to eight-character name of the data set from which a record is to be read.

INTO
Specifies the name of a data area into which the data record is moved.

SET
Specifies the name of a data area into which the address of the retrieved record is placed.

LENGTH
Specifies a binary halfword data area (PIC S9(4) COMP) that contains the length of the record. On entry, the data area indicates the size of the INTO data area, if INTO is specified. On exit, the data area contains the size of the record retrieved. Required if INTO is specified, unless the file has fixed-length records; optional for SET.

RIDFLD
Specifies a data area that identifies the record to be retrieved. The contents of the RIDFLD field depends on whether RBA or RRN is specified; if neither is specified, the RIDFLD field contains a key for VSAM KSDS or path or ISAM file retrieval. For a generic browse, the RIDFLD field must still be as long as the file's defined key length; when the READ-NEXT command finishes, CICS puts the complete key value in the RIDFLD field.

Normally, you should leave the contents of the RIDFLD field unchanged during a browse operation. If you change the field before you issue a READNEXT command, the browse is restarted from the new location.

KEYLENGTH

Specifies a binary halfword (PIC S9(4) COMP) or literal value that indicates the length of the key, which must be less than the file's defined key length. If you specify KEYLENGTH, the browse is restarted at the key location indicated by the RIDFLD field. Not valid if RBA or RRN is specified.

RBA

Specifies that the RIDFLD field is a Relative Byte Address (RBA) for a VSAM KSDS or ESDS. An RBA is a binary fullword (PIC S9(8) COMP).

RRN

Specifies that the RIDFLD is a Relative Record Number (RRN) for a VSAM RRDS. An RRN is a binary fullword (PIC S9(8) COMP). The RRN of the first record in an RRDS is 1.

REQID

Specifies a binary halfword (PIC S9(4) COMP) or literal value that identifies the browse operation; used only when your program controls two or more browse operations at the same time. For each I/O command that's part of the same browse operation, specify the same REQID value.

SYSID

Specifies the one- to four-character name of a remote system that contains the file.

Exceptional conditions

Note: unless you provide for these conditions with a HANDLE CONDITION command, the task will be terminated if any of them occur.

DISABLED

(1.7 only)The data set is disabled, probably as a result of the master terminal operator explicitly dis-abling the file using CEMT SET DISABLE.

DSIDERR

The data set name specified in the DATASET option isn't defined in the File Control Table.

DUPKEY

Occurs only when retrieving via an alternate index (path) that allows duplicate keys; indicates that at least one more record with the specified key exists. To retrieve all of the records with the same key value, issue successive READNEXT commands; DUPKEY will be raised for each except the last, indicating that the next READNEXT command will retrieve a record with a different key value.

ENDFILE

Occurs when there are no more records to be retrieved.

ILLOGIC

A serious VSAM error occurred.

INVREQ

The READNEXT request is prohibited by the file's FCT entry. Can also occur if a browse operation has not been properly started by a STARTBR command, if you change the meaning of the RIDFLD option (key, RBA, or RRN) during the browse, or if the KEYLENGTH value is incorrect.

IOERR

An I/O error occurred.

ISCINVREQ

An undeterminable error occurred on the remote system (specified in the SYSID option).

LENGERR

The length of the record retrieved exceeds the length specified in the LENGTH option.

NOTAUTH

(1.7 only) The transaction's PCT entry specified that resource security checking should be done and the operator is not authorized to access the data set.

NOTFND
The specified record could not be located.

NOTOPEN
The file is not open.

SYSIDERR
The system identified by SYSID could not be located or accessed.

Notes and tips

- Before you can issue a READNEXT command, you must begin a browse operation by issuing a STARTBR command. Browsing is relatively inefficient because a VSAM string is held for the duration of the browse. (A string is required for each concurrent access to a VSAM file; so if 10 strings are specified for a file, 10 simultaneous accesses are permitted.) Because of this inefficiency, try to avoid browsing if possible.

- Notice that the READNEXT command does not have an UPDATE option. You can't update (or delete) a record that you've retrieved during a browse operation until you end the browse by issuing an ENDBR command.

- To browse a file via an alternate path, specify the path name in the DATASET option. Be aware that if the alternate index allows duplicate keys, the DUPKEY condition will be raised if there's more than one record with the same alternate key value. So be sure to handle the DUPKEY condition.

- When you retrieve records with duplicate keys, the records are presented in the sequence in which they were created. If the alternate indexes were recently rebuilt, that will be in prime key sequence. But don't count on it. (Actually, if the alternate index isn't upgradable, any duplicates will always be in prime key sequence since the alternate index entries can be created only by rebuilding the index.)

- The only exceptional condition you normally need to handle for the READNEXT command is ENDFILE. If you're browsing via a path that allows duplicate keys, you should also specify DUPKEY. The other exceptional conditions represent errors from which your program can't generally recover.

Coding example (base cluster)

This example shows how to retrieve records during a browse operation. The records are retrieved directly from a base cluster via the primary key. Several program modules are shown to indicate the program logic necessary to invoke the browse module repeatedly. (The code for module 1100-START-ACCOUNT-BROWSE is shown in the coding example for the STARTBR command later in this section.)

```
          .
          .
          .
      MOVE LOW-VALUE TO AR-ACCOUNT-NUMBER.
      PERFORM 1100-START-ACCOUNT-BROWSE.
      EXEC CICS
          HANDLE CONDITION ENDFILE(2100-ENDFILE)
      END-EXEC.
      PERFORM 2000-PROCESS-ACCOUNT-RECORD
          UNTIL END-OF-BROWSE.
          .
          .
          .
  *
   2000-PROCESS-ACCOUNT-RECORD SECTION.
  *
      PERFORM 2100-READ-NEXT-ACCOUNT-RECORD.
      IF NOT END-OF-BROWSE
          .
          .
          .
  *
   2100-READ-NEXT-ACCOUNT-RECORD SECTION.
  *
      EXEC CICS
          READNEXT DATASET('ACCOUNT')
                   INTO(ACCOUNT-RECORD)
                   RIDFLD(AR-ACCOUNT-NUMBER)
      END-EXEC.
      GO TO 2100-EXIT.
  *
   2100-ENDFILE.
  *
      MOVE 'Y' TO END-OF-BROWSE-SW.
  *
   2100-EXIT.
  *
      EXIT.
```

Coding example (alternate index)

This example shows how to retrieve duplicate key records via an alternate index. Here, module 1800 retrieves up to 10 invoice records with a given alternate key value. (The alternate key is a customer number, which indicates the customer to which an invoice is related.) The DUPKEY condition indicates if more invoices are available for the customer; as soon as DUPKEY is not detected, 'N' is moved to MORE-INVOICES-SW. Notice that there's no GO TO statement following the READ-NEXT command in module 1820. When the last of a set of duplicate records is read, the DUPKEY condition is not raised. To process this record properly, control falls into 1820-DUPKEY. So the only purpose for the 1820-DUPKEY label is to branch around the MOVE statement that sets the switch.

```
 1800-GET-INVOICE-RECORDS SECTION.
*
     PERFORM 1810-START-INVOICE-BROWSE.
     EXEC CICS
         HANDLE CONDITION DUPKEY(1820-DUPKEY)
     END-EXEC.
     PERFORM 1820-READ-INVOICE-RECORD
         VARYING INVOICE-SUB FROM 1 BY 1
         UNTIL   INVOICE-SUB > 10
                 OR NOT MORE-INVOICES.
*
     .
     .
     .
*
 1820-READ-INVOICE-RECORD SECTION.
*
     EXEC CICS
         READNEXT DATASET('INVPATH')
                  INTO(INVOICE-RECORD)
                  RIDFLD(CM-CUSTOMER-NUMBER)
     END-EXEC.
     MOVE 'N' TO MORE-INVOICES-SW.
*
 1820-DUPKEY.
*
     MOVE INV-INVOICE-NUMBER
         TO IM-D-INVOICE-NUMBER(INVOICE-SUB).
     MOVE INV-PO-NUMBER      TO IM-D-PO-NUMBER(INVOICE-SUB).
     MOVE INV-INVOICE-DATE   TO IM-D-INVOICE-DATE(INVOICE-SUB).
     MOVE INV-INVOICE-TOTAL
         TO IM-D-INVOICE-TOTAL(INVOICE-SUB).
*
 1820-EXIT.
*
     EXIT.
```

THE READPREV COMMAND

Function

File control. The READPREV command retrieves the previous sequential record from a file during a browse operation. In other words, READPREV reads records backwards. The file can be a VSAM KSDS, ESDS, RRDS, or path. (Earlier releases of CICS also support ISAM, but that's not covered here.)

Syntax

```
EXEC CICS
    READPREV DATASET(name)
            { INTO(data-area)  }
            { SET(pointer-ref) }
            [ LENGTH(data-area) ]
              RIDFLD(data-area)
            [ KEYLENGTH(data-value ]
            [ RBA|RRN ]
            [ REQID(data-value) ]
            [ SYSID(name) ]
END-EXEC.
```

Options

DATASET
Specifies the one- to eight-character name of the data set from which a record is to be read.

INTO
Specifies the name of a data area into which the data record is moved.

SET
Specifies the name of a data area into which the address of the retrieved record is placed.

LENGTH
Specifies a binary halfword data area (PIC S9(4) COMP) that contains the length of the record. On entry, the data area indicates the size of the INTO data area, if INTO is specified. On exit, the data area contains the size of the record retrieved. Required if INTO is specified, unless the file has fixed-length records; optional for SET.

RIDFLD
Specifies a data area that identifies the record to be retrieved. The contents of the RIDFLD field depends on whether RBA or RRN is specified; if neither is specified, the RIDFLD field contains a key for VSAM KSDS or path or ISAM file retrieval. For a generic browse, the RIDFLD field must still be as long as the file's defined key length; when the READNEXT command finishes, CICS puts the complete key value in the RIDFLD field.

Normally, you should leave the contents of the RIDFLD field unchanged during a browse operation. If you change the field before you issue a READPREV command, the browse is restarted from the new location.

KEYLENGTH

Specifies a binary halfword (PIC S9(4) COMP) or literal value that indicates the length of the key, which must be less than the file's defined key length. If you specify KEYLENGTH, the browse is restarted at the key location indicated by the RIDFLD field. Not valid if RBA or RRN is specified.

RBA

Specifies that the RIDFLD field is a Relative Byte Address (RBA) for a VSAM KSDS or ESDS. An RBA is a binary fullword (PIC S9(8) COMP).

RRN

Specifies that the RIDFLD is a Relative Record Number (RRN) for a VSAM RRDS. An RRN is a binary fullword (PIC S9(8) COMP). The RRN of the first record in an RRDS is 1.

REQID

Specifies a binary halfword (PIC S9(4) COMP) or literal value that identifies the browse operation; used only when your program controls two or more browse operations at the same time. For each I/O command that's part of the same browse operation, specify the same REQID value.

SYSID

Specifies the one- to four-character name of a remote system that contains the file.

Exceptional conditions

Note: unless you provide for these conditions with a HANDLE CONDITION command, the task will be terminated if any of them occur.

DISABLED

(1.7 only) The data set is disabled, probably as a result of the master terminal operator explicitly dis-abling the file using CEMT SET DISABLE.

DSIDERR

The data set name specified in the DATASET option isn't defined in the File Control Table.

DUPKEY

Occurs only when retrieving via an alternate index (path) that allows duplicate keys; indicates that at least one more record with the specified key exists. To retrieve all of the records with the same key value, issue successive READPREV commands; DUPKEY will be raised for each except the last, indicating that the next READPREV command will retrieve a record with a different key value.

ENDFILE

Occurs when there are no more records to be retrieved (the beginning of the file has been reached).

ILLOGIC

A serious VSAM error occurred.

INVREQ

The READPREV request is prohibited by the file's FCT entry. Can also occur if a browse operation has not been properly started by a STARTBR command, if you change the meaning of the RIDFLD option (key, RBA, or RRN) during the browse, or if the KEYLENGTH value is incorrect.

IOERR

An I/O error occurred.

ISCINVREQ

An undeterminable error occurred on the remote system (specified in the SYSID option).

LENGERR

The length of the record retrieved exceeds the length specified in the LENGTH option.

NOTAUTH

(1.7 only) The transaction's PCT entry specified that resource security checking should be done and the operator is not authorized to access the data set.

NOTFND

The specified record could not be located. This can occur if a READPREV command immediately follows a STARTBR command and the STARTBR command refers to a record that's not in the file (even if the STARTBR command specified GTEQ).

Notes and tips

- Before you can issue a READNEXT command, you must begin a browse operation by issuing a STARTBR command. Browsing is relatively inefficient because a VSAM string is held for the duration of the browse. (A string is required for each concurrent access to a VSAM file; so if 10 strings are specified for a file, 10 simultaneous accesses are permitted.) Because of this inefficiency, try to avoid browsing if possible.

- Notice that the READPREV command does not have an UPDATE option. You can't update (or delete) a record that you've retrieved during a browse operation until you end the browse by issuing an ENDBR command.

- To browse a file via an alternate path, specify the path name in the DATASET option. Be aware that if the alternate index allows duplicate keys, the DUPKEY condition will be raised if there's more than one record with the same alternate key value. So be sure to handle the DUPKEY condition.

NOTOPEN

The file is not open.

SYSIDERR

The system identified by SYSID could not be located or accessed.

- If you issue a READPREV command immediately following a READNEXT command, the same record is retrieved again. And, because of a peculiarity in the way READPREV works, you should not issue it immediately after a STARTBR command unless the STARTBR command established positioning at the end of the file by specifying hex FF (HIGH-VALUE) in the RIDFLD field; instead, issue READNEXT followed by two READPREV commands.

- The only exceptional condition you normally should handle for the READPREV command is ENDFILE. If you're browsing via a path that allows duplicate keys, you should also specify DUPKEY. The other exceptional conditions represent errors from which your program can't generally recover.

Coding example (browse backwards)

This example shows how to retrieve records backwards during a browse operation. Several program modules are shown to indicate the program logic necessary to invoke the browse module repeatedly.

(The code for module 1100-START-ACCOUNT-BROWSE is shown in the coding example for the STARTBR command later in this section.)

```
          .
          .
          .
      MOVE HIGH-VALUE TO AR-ACCOUNT-NUMBER.
      PERFORM 1100-START-ACCOUNT-BROWSE.
      EXEC CICS
          HANDLE CONDITION ENDFILE(2100-ENDFILE)
      END-EXEC.
      PERFORM 2000-PROCESS-ACCOUNT-RECORD
          UNTIL END-OF-BROWSE.
          .
          .
          .
 *
  2000-PROCESS-ACCOUNT-RECORD SECTION.
 *
      PERFORM 2100-READ-PREV-ACCOUNT-RECORD.
      IF NOT END-OF-BROWSE
          .
          .
          .
 *
  2100-READ-PREV-ACCOUNT-RECORD SECTION.
 *
      EXEC CICS
          READPREV DATASET('ACCOUNT')
                   INTO(ACCOUNT-RECORD)
                   RIDFLD(AR-ACCOUNT-NUMBER)
      END-EXEC.
      GO TO 2100-EXIT.
 *
  2100-ENDFILE.
 *
      MOVE 'Y' TO END-OF-BROWSE-SW.
 *
  2100-EXIT.
 *
      EXIT.
```

Coding example (retrieve previous record after STARTBR)

This example shows how to retrieve the record immediately preceding the record at which positioning is established by a STARTBR command. Four browse commands are issued: STARTBR, READNEXT, READPREV, and READPREV. (Module 1100-START-ACCOUNT-BROWSE is shown in

the description of the STARTBR command.) This elaborate coding is not required if the STARTBR command establishes positioning at the end of the file by specifying HIGH-VALUE in the RIDFLD field.

```
    3000-GET-PREV-ACCOUNT-RECORD SECTION.
*
        MOVE WS-ACCOUNT-NUMBER TO AR-ACCOUNT-NUMBER.
        PERFORM 1100-START-ACCOUNT-BROWSE.
        IF NOT END-OF-BROWSE
            PERFORM 3100-READ-NEXT-ACCOUNT-RECORD
            PERFORM 3200-READ-PREV-ACCOUNT-RECORD
            PERFORM 3200-READ-PREV-ACCOUNT-RECORD.
*
    3100-READ-NEXT-ACCOUNT-RECORD SECTION.
*
        EXEC CICS
            HANDLE CONDITION ENDFILE(3100-ENDFILE)
        END-EXEC.
        EXEC CICS
            READNEXT DATASET('ACCOUNT')
                     INTO(ACCOUNT-RECORD)
                     RIDFLD(AR-ACCOUNT-NUMBER)
        END-EXEC.
        GO TO 3100-EXIT.
*
    3100-ENDFILE.
*
        MOVE 'Y' TO END-OF-BROWSE-SW.
*
    3100-EXIT.
*
        EXIT.
*
```

```
    3200-READ-PREV-ACCOUNT-RECORD SECTION.
*
      EXEC CICS
            HANDLE CONDITION ENDFILE(3200-ENDFILE)
      END-EXEC.
      EXEC CICS
            READPREV DATASET('ACCOUNT')
                     INTO(ACCOUNT-RECORD)
                     RIDFLD(AR-ACCOUNT-NUMBER)
      END-EXEC.
      GO TO 3200-EXIT.
*
    3200-ENDFILE.
*
      MOVE 'Y' TO END-OF-BROWSE-SW.
*
    3200-EXIT.
*
      EXIT.
```

THE READQ TD COMMAND

Function

Transient data control. The READQ TD command reads a record from a specified transient data queue (also called a destination).

Syntax

```
EXEC CICS
     READQ TD QUEUE(name)
              { INTO(data-area) }
              { SET(pointer-ref) }
              [ LENGTH(data-area) ]
              [ SYSID(name) ]
              [ NOSUSPEND ]            1.7 only
     END-EXEC.
```

Options

QUEUE

Specifies the one- to four-character name of the transient data queue from which data is retrieved.

INTO

Specifies the name of a data area into which the data record is moved.

SET

Specifies the name of a data area into which the address of the retrieved record is placed.

LENGTH

Specifies a binary halfword data area (PIC S9(4) COMP) that contains the length of the record. On entry, the data area indicates the size of the INTO data area, if INTO is specified. On exit, the data area contains the size of the record retrieved. Required if INTO is specified, unless the destination is extrapartition and has fixed-length records; optional for SET.

SYSID

Specifies the one- to four-character name of a remote system that contains the destination.

NOSUSPEND

(1.7 Only) Specifies that if the QBUSY condition is raised, control is to return immediately to the program; execution continues with the statement following the READQ TD command. If you omit NOSUSPEND, the processing that occurs when QBUSY is raised depends on whether you specify a HANDLE CONDITION command for the QBUSY condition. If you do, control is transferred to the label you specify in the HANDLE CONDITION command; if you don't, your task is simply suspended until the queue is available; then, the record is read.

Exceptional conditions

Note: unless you provide for these conditions (other than QBUSY) with a HANDLE CONDITION command, the task will be terminated if any of them occur.

IOERR

An I/O error occurred.

ISCINVREQ

An undeterminable error occurred on the remote system.

LENGERR

The length of the record retrieved exceeds the length specified in the LENGTH option.

NOTAUTH

(1.7 only) The transaction's PCT entry specified that resource security checking should be done and the operator is not authorized to access the queue.

NOTOPEN

The queue is not open.

QBUSY

Another task is writing or deleting a record in the queue. If you don't specify this condition in a HANDLE CONDITION command, CICS simply suspends your task until the queue is available.

QIDERR

The specified destination doesn't exist.

QZERO

There are no records in the destination.

SYSIDERR

The system identified by SYSID could not be located or accessed.

Notes and tips

- There are two types of transient data destinations: intrapartition and extrapartition. All intrapartition destinations are stored in a VSAM file called DFHNTRA; access to these destinations is efficient. Extrapartition destinations, however, are QSAM files (on disk or a other sequential device like a tape drive or a printer) managed not by CICS, but by the operating system. Because of the way CICS interacts with QSAM, extrapartition destinations are relatively inefficient. So avoid using them. (The syntax of the READQ TD command is the same for both types of destinations.)

- An intrapartition destination can be used with automatic transaction initiation (ATI) so that a transaction is started as soon as the number of records in the destination reaches a specified trigger level. Because of this feature, intrapartition destinations are often used for applications in which data from one program needs to be temporarily gathered so it can be processed by another program.

- One common use of ATI is for printer applications: an ATI transaction uses a READQ TD command to retrieve records from a destination; then, the transaction formats the data properly and sends it to a printer. This technique removes detailed printer considerations from the application program that creates the data to be printed; all that program has to do is write records to the proper destination.

- Records are always retrieved from a destination in the order in which they were written. And each record can be read only once; when you read a record, the record is effectively deleted from the destination.

- The transient data facility provides no mechanism for holding a destination for exclusive use. If you need to write several uninterrupted records to a destination, use the ENQ and DEQ commands.

- The only exceptional condition you should normally handle for the READQ TD command is QZERO. The others represent errors from which your program can't generally recover.

Coding example

The following example shows how to retrieve a record from a transient data destination. The QZERO condition is handled to terminate the processing loop when no more records are available. LENGERR isn't handled; if a record with an incorrect length is read, the task is terminated.

```
          .
          .
          .
      EXEC CICS
          HANDLE CONDITION QZERO(2100-QZERO)
      END-EXEC.
      PERFORM 2000-PROCESS-ACCOUNT-RECORD
          UNTIL QUEUE-EMPTY.
          .
          .
          .
 *
  2000-PROCESS-ACCOUNT-RECORD SECTION.
 *
      PERFORM 2100-READ-ACCOUNT-RECORD.
      IF NOT QUEUE-EMPTY
          .
          .
          .
 *
  2100-READ-ACCOUNT-RECORD SECTION.
 *
      EXEC CICS
          READQ TD QUEUE('ACCT')
                   INTO(ACCOUNT-RECORD)
                   LENGTH(ACCOUNT-RECORD-LENGTH)
      END-EXEC.
      GO TO 2100-EXIT.
 *
  2100-QZERO.
 *
      MOVE 'Y' TO QUEUE-ZERO-SW.
 *
  2100-EXIT.
 *
      EXIT.
```

THE READQ TS COMMAND

Function

Temporary storage control. The READQ TS command reads a record from a specified temporary storage queue.

Syntax

```
EXEC CICS
    READQ TS QUEUE(name)
            { INTO(data-area)   }
            { SET(pointer-ref)  }
            LENGTH(data-area)
            [ NUMITEMS(data-area) ]
            [ ITEM(data-value)|NEXT ]
            [ SYSID(name) ]
END-EXEC.
```

1.6 & 1.7 only

Options

QUEUE

Specifies the one- to eight-character name of the temporary storage queue from which data is retrieved.

INTO

Specifies the name of a data area into which the data record is moved.

SET

Specifies the name of a data area into which the address of the retrieved record is placed.

LENGTH

Specifies a binary halfword data area (PIC S9(4) COMP) that contains the length of the record. On entry, the data area indicates the size of the INTO data area, if INTO is specified. On exit, the data area contains the size of the record retrieved.

NUMITEMS

(1.6 & 1.7 only) Specifies a binary halfword data area (PIC S9(4) COMP); CICS places the total number of records in the queue in this field.

ITEM

Specifies the item number of the record to be retrieved.

NEXT

Specifies that the next queue record in sequence should be read. Any task in a CICS system can affect the positioning of a READQ TS NEXT command by issuing a READQ TS command for the same queue; CICS does *not* maintain a separate position within the queue for each task.

SYSID

Specifies the one- to four-character name of a remote system that contains the destination.

Exceptional conditions

Note: unless you provide for these conditions with a HANDLE CONDITION command, the task will be terminated if any of them occur.

INVREQ
The READQ TS command is attempting to retrieve a record created by a macro-level program using the DFHTS TYPE=PUT macro. Records created in that way can't be retrieved by command-level programs.

IOERR
An I/O error occurred.

ISCINVREQ
An undeterminable error occurred on the remote system (specified in the SYSID option).

ITEMERR
No record exists for the item number specified by the ITEM option.

LENGERR
The length of the record retrieved exceeds the length specified in the LENGTH option.

NOTAUTH
(1.7 only) The transaction's PCT entry specified that resource security checking should be done and the operator is not authorized to access the queue.

QIDERR
The specified queue does not exist.

SYSIDERR
The system identified by SYSID could not be located or accessed.

Notes and tips

- All temporary storage queues are held in one of two places: in virtual storage or in a VSAM file called DFHTEMP. As a result, access to data in temporary storage is efficient.

- To create a unique temporary storage queue name, incorporate the terminal-id that's in the Execute Interface Block.

- The READQ TS command provides both direct and sequential access to temporary storage records. For direct access, specify the number of the record you want to retrieve in the ITEM option; for sequential access, specify NEXT. Note, however, that any task that accesses the same temporary storage queue affects the positioning for a READQ TS NEXT command. To safely process the records in sequence, use unique queue names or reserve the queue for exclusive access using the ENQ and DEQ commands.

- Because temporary storage queues are created and deleted dynamically, you should always handle the QIDERR condition. If you specify the ITEM option, you should also handle the ITEMERR condition. The other conditions represent errors from which your program can't generally recover.

Coding example

This example shows how to read the first record from a temporary storage queue. ITEM is specified to be sure the first record is retrieved; if NEXT were used, another task could affect positioning within the queue.

```
3000-READ-QUEUE-RECORD SECTION.
*
    EXEC CICS
        HANDLE CONDITION ITEMERR(3000-ITEMERR)
                         QIDERR(3000-QIDERR)
    END-EXEC.
    EXEC CICS
        READQ TS QUEUE(TS-QUEUE-NAME)
                 INTO(TS-QUEUE-AREA)
                 LENGTH(TS-QUEUE-LENGTH)
                 ITEM(1)
    END-EXEC.
    MOVE 'Y' TO TS-RECORD-FOUND-SW.
    GO TO 3000-EXIT.
*
3000-ITEMERR.
*
    MOVE 'N' TO TS-RECORD-FOUND-SW.
*
3000-QIDERR.
*
    MOVE 'N' TO TS-RECORD-FOUND-SW.
*
3000-EXIT.
*
    EXIT.
```

THE RECEIVE COMMAND

Function

Terminal control. The RECEIVE command retrieves input data sent from a terminal device.

Basic Mapping Support is not used, so the format of the received data depends on the terminal type.

Syntax

```
EXEC CICS
     RECEIVE   { INTO(data-area)  }
               { SET(pointer-ref) }
             [ LENGTH(data-area)
             [ MAXLENGTH(data-value) ]        1.6 & 1.7 only
             [ NOTRUNCATE ]                   1.6 & 1.7 only
             [ ASIS ]
             [ BUFFER ]
     END-EXEC.
```

Options

INTO

Specifies the name of a data area into which the received data is moved.

SET

Specifies a binary fullword (PIC S9(8) COMP) into which the address of the received data is placed.

LENGTH

Specifies a binary halfword (PIC S9(4) COMP) that indicates the length of the received data. If you specify INTO, the initial value of this field is used to indicate the maximum length of the data that can be received, unless you code MAXLENGTH. For INTO or SET, CICS updates the LENGTH field to indicate the actual length of the data that was received.

MAXLENGTH

(1.6 & 1.7 only) Specifies a binary halfword (PIC S9(4) COMP) or literal value that indicates the maximum length of the data that can be received.

NOTRUNCATE

(1.6 & 1.7 only) Specifies that if the length of the data sent from the terminal excedes the maximum length specified by LENGTH or MAXLENGTH, the excess data is to be retained and presented to the program when it issues subsequent RECEIVE commands. If you omit NOTRUNCATE, the excess data is discarded and the LENGERR condition is raised. In either case, the LENGTH field is updated to reflect the actual amount of data received, including any excess.

ASIS

Specifies that lower case characters are *not* to be translated to upper case. In certain cases, ASIS has no effect. For example, ASIS has no effect for the first RECEIVE command issued by a transaction.

BUFFER

Specifies that the entire 3270 terminal buffer should be retrieved, including null characters and other control sequences. If you omit BUFFER, the received data is a standard 3270 data stream.

Exceptional conditions

Note: unless you provide for these conditions with a HANDLE CONDITION command, the task will be terminated if any of them occur.

LENGERR

The length of the data received excedes the length specified in the LENGTH option. CICS discards the excess data.

TERMERR

(1.7 only) A terminal I/O error occurred (VTAM only).

Notes and tips

- Frankly, the programming requirements for processing terminal input using the RECEIVE command are complicated. As a result, it's unreasonable to use basic terminal control commands for full-screen interactive programs; use BMS instead. Use basic terminal control commands only in special situations where the format of terminal input data is simple.

- One common use for the RECEIVE command is to retrieve the "command line" the operator entered to initiate the transaction. Normally, that data is entered on an unfor-

matted screen (one without fields defined by attribute bytes), so the format of the data is simple; the data entered by the operator is presented to the program exactly as it was entered. Usually, the first four characters of the data will be the trans-id entered by the operator to start the transaction. The trans-id is then followed by any additional data entered by the operator.

- You should usually handle the LENGERR condition for the RECEIVE command. But the TERMERR condition represents an error from which your program can't recover.

Coding example

This example shows how to use a RECEIVE command to retrieve the command line entered by the operator to start a transaction. In this case, the command line should consist of the trans-id followed by a space and a one- to five-character customer number. If the customer number is missing, an AID key is pressed (detected by a HANDLE AID command) or, if too much data is entered, an appropriate error message is formatted and 'N' is moved to VALID-DATA-SW.

```
      WORKING-STORAGE SECTION.
*
      .
      .
      .
 01   COMMAND-LINE.
*
      05   CL-TRANS-ID              PIC X(4).
      05   FILLER                   PIC X.
      05   CL-CUSTOMER-NUMBER       PIC X(5).
*
 01   COMMAND-LENGTH               PIC S9(4)    VALUE +10   COMP.
*
      .
      .
      .
 PROCEDURE DIVISION.
*
 0000-PROCESS-CUSTOMER-INQUIRY SECTION.
*
      PERFORM 1000-RECEIVE-INQUIRY-DATA.
      .
      .
      .
```

```
*
 1000-RECEIVE-INQUIRY-DATA SECTION.
*
      EXEC CICS
          HANDLE AID ANYKEY(1000-ANYKEY)
      END-EXEC.
      EXEC CICS
          HANDLE CONDITION LENGERR(1000-LENGERR)
      END-EXEC.
      EXEC CICS
          RECEIVE INTO(COMMAND-LINE)
                  LENGTH(COMMAND-LENGTH)
      END-EXEC.
      IF CL-CUSTOMER-NUMBER = SPACE OR LOW-VALUE
          MOVE 'N' TO VALID-DATA-SW
          MOVE 'YOU MUST SUPPLY A CUSTOMER NUMBER'
              TO ERROR-MESSAGE.
      GO TO 1000-EXIT.
*
 1000-ANYKEY.
*
      MOVE 'N' TO VALID-DATA-SW.
      MOVE 'WRONG KEY PRESSED' TO ERROR-MESSAGE.
      GO TO 1000-EXIT.
*
 1000-LENGERR.
*
      MOVE 'N' TO VALID-DATA-SW.
      MOVE 'TOO MUCH DATA ENTERED' TO ERROR-MESSAGE.
*
 1000-EXIT.
*
      EXIT.
```

THE RECEIVE MAP COMMAND

Function

Basic Mapping Support. Receives data from a terminal and formats it using a BMS map definition.

Syntax

```
EXEC CICS
     RECEIVE MAP(name)
             [ MAPSET(name) ]
             { INTO(data-area)  }
             { SET(pointer-ref) }
             [ ASIS ]
END-EXEC.
```

Options

MAP

Specifies the one- to seven-character name of the map to be used to map the input data.

MAPSET

Specifies the one- to seven-character name of the mapset that contains the specified map. This name must be defined in the Processing Program Table (PPT). If omitted, the name specified in the MAP option is used.

INTO

Specifies the data area into which the mapped input data will be placed.

SET

Specifies a binary halfword field (PIC S9(4) COMP) that will be set to the address of the mapped input data.

ASIS

Specifies that lower-case characters are *not* to be converted to upper-case.

Exceptional conditions

Note: unless you provide for these conditions with a HANDLE CONDITION command, the task will be terminated if any of them occur.

INVMPSZ

The line width specified in the map is larger than the line width supported by the terminal.

MAPFAIL

The data cannot be formatted; this happens if a SEND MAP command was not issued before the operator entered data, if the operator presses the ENTER key without entering any data, or if the operator presses the CLEAR key or a PA key.

Notes and tips

- If you omit the INTO and SET options, BMS adds the letter I to the end of the map name you specify to determine the name of the input data area. So, if the map is named CUSTMAP, the input data area is CUSTMAPI. BMS uses the same convention when it assembles the symbolic map, so if you copy the BMS-generated symbolic mapset into your program, the names will match up. However, you must code INTO (or SET) if (1) you want to use your own version of the symbolic map or (2) you specify a data name rather than a literal value in the MAP option.

- You can avoid the MAPFAIL condition altogether by doing two things: (1) issuing a HANDLE AID command to process the PA or CLEAR keys (HANDLE AID has precedence over HANDLE CONDITION) and (2) including in the mapset a one-byte dummy field with FSET specified so at least one byte of data is sent to the program whenever the operator presses ENTER or a PF key.

Coding example

This example shows a typical module that receives input data from a terminal. The data is mapped into a data area called MENU-MAP, a symbolic map created by the programmer.

```
    110-RECEIVE-MENU-SCREEN SECTION.
*
        EXEC CICS
            HANDLE AID CLEAR(110-CLEAR-KEY)
                       ANYKEY(110-ANYKEY)
        END-EXEC.
        EXEC CICS
            RECEIVE MAP('MENUMAP')
                    MAPSET('MENUSET')
                    INTO(MENU-MAP)
        END-EXEC.
        GO TO 110-EXIT.
*
    110-CLEAR-KEY.
*
        MOVE 'Y' TO END-SESSION-SW.
        GO TO 110-EXIT.
*
    110-ANYKEY.
*
        MOVE 'N' TO VALID-DATA-SW.
        MOVE 'INVALID KEY PRESSED' TO MM-D-ERROR-MESSAGE.
*
    110-EXIT.
*
        EXIT.
```

THE RELEASE COMMAND

Function

Program control. The RELEASE command frees the virtual storage occupied by an object module previously loaded by a LOAD command. A RELEASE command is required only if the LOAD command specified the HOLD option.

Syntax

```
EXEC CICS
     RELEASE PROGRAM(name)
END-EXEC.
```

Option

PROGRAM

Specifies the one- to eight-character name of the load module to be released.

Exceptional conditions.

Note: unless you provide for these conditions with a HANDLE CONDITION command, the task will be terminated if any of them occur.

NOTAUTH

(1.7 only) The transaction's PCT entry specified that resource security checking should be done and the operator is not authorized to access the specified object module.

PGMIDERR

The object module is not defined in the Processing Program Table (PPT).

Notes and tips

• If you specify the HOLD option on a LOAD command, you should release the program using a RELEASE command unless you want the program to remain in virtual storage indefinitely. If the program is needed only by a particular application, make sure you release it when that application is no longer active.

• As a general rule, provide for exceptional conditions in the same way as you do for the LOAD command that loads the program you're releasing.

Coding example

This example shows how to release an object
module originally retrieved by a LOAD command.

```
 0500-RELEASE-STATE-TABLE SECTION.
*
     EXEC CICS
         RELEASE PROGRAM('STATABLE')
     END-EXEC.
```

THE RESETBR COMMAND

Function

File control. The RESETBR command resets the current position of a browse operation. The RESETBR command itself does not retrieve a record; it just establishes position for subsequent retrieval. The browse operation should always end with an ENDBR command.

Syntax

```
EXEC CICS
    RESETBR DATASET(name)
            RIDFLD(data-area)
          [ KEYLENGTH(data-value) ]
          [ GENERIC ]
          [ RBA|RRN ]
          [ GTEQ|EQUAL ]
          [ REQID(data-value) ]
          [ SYSID(name) ]
    END-EXEC.
```

Options

DATASET

Specifies the one- to eight-character name of the data set for which a browse operation is to be started.

RIDFLD

Specifies a data area that identifies the record at which the browse operation is to continue. The contents of the RIDFLD field depends on whether RBA or RRN is specified; if neither is specified, the RIDFLD field contains a key for VSAM KSDS or path or ISAM file retrieval. For generic positioning (see the KEYLENGTH and GENERIC options below), the RIDFLD field must still be as long as the file's defined key length.

To begin a browse operation at the first record in the file, place hexadecimal zeros (LOW-VALUE) in the RIDFLD field. To begin a browse operation at the last record in the file, place hexadecimal FFs (HIGH-VALUE) in the RIDFLD field.

KEYLENGTH

Specifies a binary halfword (PIC S9(4) COMP) or literal value that indicates the length of the key, which must be less than the file's defined key length. Used only for a generic read along with the GENERIC option. Not valid if RBA or RRN is specified.

GENERIC

Specifies that only a part of the key in the RIDFLD field should be used, as indicated by the KEYLENGTH option. Positioning is established at the first record with a key whose leftmost character positions (as specified by KEYLENGTH) match the RIDFLD field.

RBA

Specifies that the RIDFLD field is a Relative Byte Address (RBA) for a VSAM KSDS or ESDS. An RBA is a binary fullword (PIC S9(8) COMP).

RRN
> Specifies that the RIDFLD is a Relative Record Number (RRN) for a VSAM RRDS. An RRN is a binary fullword (PIC S9(8) COMP). The RRN of the first record in an RRDS is 1.

GTEQ
> Specifies that positioning is to be established at the first record whose key value is greater than or equal to the key specified in the RIDFLD field. This will always establish positioning in the file unless the specified key is greater than the largest key in the file. If you omit GTEQ and EQUAL, GTEQ is assumed.

EQUAL
> Specifies that positioning will be established

at the record whose key matches the RIDFLD field exactly. If no such record exists, the NOTFND condition is raised and the browse operation is not started.

REQID
> Specifies a binary halfword (PIC S 9(4) COMP) or literal value that identifies the browse operation; used only when your program controls two or more browse operations at the same time. For each I/O command that's part of the same browse operation, specify the same REQID value.

SYSID
> Specifies the one- to four-character name of a remote system that contains the file.

Exceptional conditions

Note: unless you provide for these conditions with a HANDLE CONDITION command, the task will be terminated if any of them occur.

DISABLED
> (1.6 & 1.7 only) The data set is disabled, probably as a result of the master terminal operator explicitly dis abling the file using CEMT SET DISABLE.

DSIDERR
> (1.7 only) The data set name specified in the DATASET option isn't defined in the File Control Table.

ILLOGIC
> A serious VSAM error occurred.

INVREQ
> The STARTBR request is prohibited by the file's FCT entry. Can also occur if you specify a REQID value that's already used for another browse operation within the same task.

IOERR
> An I/O error occurred.

ISCINVREQ
> An undeterminable error occurred on the remote system (specified in the SYSID option).

NOTAUTH
> (1.7 only) The transaction's PCT entry specified that resource security checking should be done and the operator is not authorized to access the data set.

NOTFND
> The specified record could not be located.

NOTOPEN
> The file is not open.

SYSIDERR
> The system identified by SYSID could not be located or accessed.

Notes and tips

- Before you can issue a RESETBR command, you must begin a browse operation by issuing a STARTBR command. Browsing is relatively inefficient because a VSAM string is held for the duration of the browse. (A string is required for each concurrent access to a VSAM file; so if 10 strings are specified for a file, 10 simultaneous accesses are permitted.) Because of this inefficiency, try to avoid browsing if possible.

- To browse a file via an alternate path, specify the path name in the DATASET option.

- Another way to change the position during a browse is to simply change the value of the RIDFLD specified in the READNEXT or READPREV command; the new key value you supply becomes the new browse position. This technique, called *skip-sequential processing*, is more efficient than RESETBR because it changes position and retrieves a record in a single operation. As a result, I suggest you use it instead of the RESETBR command.

- The only exceptional condition you should normally handle for the RESETBR command is NOTFND. The others represent errors from which your program can't generally recover.

Coding example

This example resets a browse operation for a file named ACCOUNT. The browse operation will continue at the record indicated by AR-ACCOUNT-NUMBER: if this field contains hex zeros (LOW-VALUE), the browse starts at the beginning of the file; if it contains hex FFs (HIGH-VALUE), the browse starts at the end of the file; otherwise, the browse starts at the indicated record.

```
    4500-RESET-ACCOUNT-BROWSE SECTION.
*
    EXEC CICS
        HANDLE CONDITION NOTFND(4500-NOTFND)
    END-EXEC.
    EXEC CICS
        RESETBR DATASET('ACCOUNT')
                RIDFLD(AR-ACCOUNT-NUMBER)
    END-EXEC.
    MOVE 'N' TO END-OF-BROWSE-SW.
    GO TO 4500-EXIT.
*
    4500-NOTFND.
*
        MOVE 'Y' TO END-OF-BROWSE-SW.
*
    4500-EXIT.
*
        EXIT.
```

THE RETRIEVE COMMAND

Function

Interval control. The RETRIEVE command is used in transactions that were invoked via a START command; it retrieves data passed to the program via the START command's FROM option.

Syntax

```
EXEC CICS
      RETRIEVE  { INTO(data-area)   }
                { SET(pointer-ref)  }
                [ LENGTH(data-area) ]
                [ RTRANSID(data-area) ]
                [ RTERMID(data-area) ]
                [ QUEUE(data-area) ]
                [ WAIT ]
      END-EXEC.
```

Options

INTO

Specifies the name of the data area into which the data specified in the FROM or SET option of the START command that started the task will be placed.

SET

Specifies a binary halfword field (PIC S9(4) COMP) that will be set to the address of the data specified in the FROM or SET option of the START command that started the task.

LENGTH

Specifies a binary halfword field (PIC S9(4) COMP) that indicates the length of the received data. When you specify INTO, the initial value of the LENGTH field indicates the maximum length that can be retrieved; if the input data exceeds this length, it is truncated and the LENGERR condition is raised. Whether you specify INTO or SET, CICS updates the LENGTH field to indicate the actual length of the retrieved data.

RTRANSID

Specifies a four-character field into which the data specified in the RTRANSID option of the START command that started the task is placed.

RTERMID

Specifies a four-character field into which the data specified in the RTERMID option of the START command that started the task is placed.

QUEUE

Specifies an eight-character field into which the data specified in the QUEUE option of the START command that started the task is placed.

WAIT

Specifies that if no data is currently available, the task is to be suspended until more data is made available; that is, when an unexpired START command expires.

Exceptional conditions

*Note: unless you provide for these conditions with
a HANDLE CONDITION command, the task will
be terminated if any of them occur.*

ENDDATA
No data is available for the started task.

ENVDEFERR
The RETRIEVE command specified a
FROM, SET, RTRANSID, RTERMID, or
QUEUE option and no corresponding option
was specified in the START command.

INVREQ
The interval control request is invalid.

INVTSREQ
Temporary storage facilities are not available;
interval control requires temporary storage
for data passed to started tasks.

IOERR
An I/O error occurred.

LENGERR
The length specified in the LENGTH option
is less than the length of the data retrieved.

NOTAUTH
(1.7 only) The transaction's PCT entry
specified that resource security checking
should be done and the operator is not
authorized to access the data.

NOTFND
The data has been deleted by another task.

Notes and tips

• When more than one START command is issued for the same trans-id specifying the
same expiration time and each START command passes data to the task to be started, a
single execution of the transaction can
process all of the data sent by each START
command. To do that, the program should
issue RETRIEVE commands repeatedly until
the ENDDATA condition is raised. You
don't have to code your programs in this way,
though. If you code the program so that just
one RETRIEVE command is issued, each
START command will result in a separate in-
vocation of the program.

• The RTRANSID, RTERMID, and QUEUE
options are designed to let you pass specific
types of information to a started task:
RTRANSID passes a transaction identifier,
RTERMID passes a terminal identifier, and
QUEUE passes the name of a transient data
destination. If your application requires you
to pass this information to a started task, you

might consider using these options. However,
there's no reason you can't pass that same
data using the FROM/INTO options. And, as
a matter of fact, you can pass any information
you wish in the RTRANSID, RTERMID, or
QUEUE fields; CICS doesn't make any as-
sumptions about the contents of those fields
other than their lengths.

• The WAIT option can be used for applications that make heavy use of data passed via
START commands; it causes the task to
remain active even if there isn't currently any
data to process. Because the task remains active, however, it consumes CICS resources
even when it's idle. So don't specify WAIT
unless your application uses data passed via
interval control almost constantly.

• You should always handle the ENDDATA
condition. The other conditions represent errors from which your program can't generally
recover.

Coding example

This example shows the top-level modules of a program that processes data sent to it from START commands. For efficiency, the program processes as many data items as are available before it terminates. Notice that the HANDLE CONDITION command for the ENDDATA condition is placed in module 0000. That way, it will be executed only once, no matter how many data items are retrieved.

```
    0000-PROCESS-ORDERS SECTION.
*
        EXEC CICS
             HANDLE CONDITION ENDDATA(1100-ENDDATA)
        END-EXEC.
        PERFORM 1000-PROCESS-ORDER
            UNTIL END-OF-DATA.
        EXEC CICS
             RETURN
        END-EXEC.
*
     1000-PROCESS-ORDER SECTION.
*
        PERFORM 1100-RETRIEVE-ORDER-DATA.
        IF NOT END-OF-DATA

            .
            .
            .
*
     1100-RETRIEVE-ORDER-DATA SECTION.
*
        EXEC CICS
             RETRIEVE INTO(CUSTOMER-ORDER)
                      LENGTH(CUSTOMER-ORDER-LENGTH)
        END-EXEC.
        GO TO 1100-EXIT.
*
     1100-ENDDATA.
*
        MOVE 'Y' TO END-OF-DATA-SW.
*
     1100-EXIT.
*
        EXIT.
```

THE RETURN COMMAND

Function

Program control. The RETURN command terminates program execution, returning control to the invoking program.

Syntax

```
EXEC CICS
    RETURN [ TRANSID(name) ]
           [ COMMAREA(data-area) ]
           [ LENGTH(data-value) ]
END-EXEC.
```

Options

TRANSID

Specifies the one- to four-character name of the transaction to be invoked when the terminal operator presses an attention key. The trans-id must be defined in the Program Control Table (PCT). TRANSID is valid only for programs that are invoked by terminal users.

COMMAREA

Specifies a data area that's passed to the next execution of a pseudo-conversational program. The next program execution accesses the communication area via its DFHCOMMAREA field, which addresses a

copy of the communication area specified in the RETURN command. (This works differently than it does for a LINK command; see the descriptions of that command for details.) COMMAREA is valid only when TRANSID is specified.

LENGTH

Specifies a binary halfword (PIC S9(4) COMP) or literal value that indicates the length of the data area specified in the COMMAREA option; this option is required if you code COMMAREA.

Exceptional conditions

Note: unless you provide for these conditions with a HANDLE CONDITION command, the task will be terminated if any of them occur.

INVREQ

Indicates one of two errors: (1) you specified the COMMAREA option in a program that was invoked from another program by a LINK command; (2) you specified the TRANSID option for a task that's not attached to a terminal.

NOTAUTH

(1.7 only) The current transaction's PCT entry specified that resource security checking should be done and the operator is not authorized to access the transaction specified in the TRANSID option.

Notes and tips

- You use the RETURN command to implement a pseudo-conversational program by specifying both the TRANSID option and the COMMAREA option. In the TRANSID option, you specify the trans-id that will be used to restart the program when the operator presses an AID key (enter, clear, or a PA/PF key). The COMMAREA option passes data forward to the next program execution; even if you don't need to pass data, you can use the presence of a communication area to determine whether or not a program is being executed for the first time.

- You don't usually need to handle either of the exceptional conditions that occur for the RETURN command; they both represent errors from which your program can't generally recover.

Coding example

This example shows the complete high-level module of a pseudo-conversational program. EIB-CALEN is a CICS-defined field that indicates the length of the communication area, which is used as a switch to trigger first-time processing. On all executions of the program but the first in a terminal session, a one-byte communication area is passed.

```
    0000-DISPLAY-CUSTOMER-RECORD SECTION.
*
        MOVE LOW-VALUE TO INQUIRY-MAP.
        IF EIBCALEN = ZERO
            PERFORM 8000-START-TERMINAL-SESSION
        ELSE
            PERFORM 1000-PROCESS-CUSTOMER-SCREEN.
        IF END-SESSION
            EXEC CICS
                XCTL PROGRAM('INVMENU')
            END-EXEC
        ELSE
            EXEC CICS
                RETURN TRANSID('INQ1')
                       COMMAREA(COMMUNICATION-AREA)
                       LENGTH(1)
            END-EXEC.
```

THE REWRITE COMMAND

Function

File control. The REWRITE command updates a record in a file. The record must have been previously read by a READ command with the UPDATE option. The file can be a VSAM KSDS, ESDS, RRDS, or path. (CICS also supports BDAM, and earlier releases support ISAM. Those uncommonly used access methods aren't covered here.)

Syntax

```
EXEC CICS
     REWRITE DATASET(name)
             FROM(data-area)
           [ LENGTH(data-area) ]
           [ SYSID(name) ]
END-EXEC.
```

Options

DATASET
Specifies the one- to eight-character name of the data set that contains the record to be updated.

FROM
Specifies the name of a data area from which the data record is moved.

LENGTH
Specifies a binary halfword data area (PIC S9(4) COMP) that contains the length of the record to be updated. Not required if the file has fixed-length records.

SYSID
Specifies the one- to four-character name of a remote system that contains the file.

Exceptional conditions

Note: unless you provide for these conditions with a HANDLE CONDITION command, the task will be terminated if any of them occur.

DISABLED
(1.7 only) The data set is disabled, probably as a result of the master terminal operator explicitly dis-abling the file using CEMT SET DISABLE.

DSIDERR
The data set name specified in the DATASET option isn't defined in the File Control Table.

DUPREC
The record contains an alternate key value that already exists, the alternate index does not allow duplicate keys, and the alternate index is a part of the file's upgrade set or access is via the path.

ILLOGIC
A serious VSAM error occurred.

INVREQ
The REWRITE request is prohibited by the file's FCT entry. Can also occur if the record was not previously retrieved by a READ command with the UPDATE option.

IOERR
An I/O error occurred.

ISCINVREQ
An undeterminable error occurred on the remote system (specified in the SYSID option).

LENGERR
The length specified in the LENGTH option exceeds the maximum record length allowed for the file.

NOSPACE
There is not enough space allocated to the data set to contain the record.

NOTAUTH
(1.7 only) The transaction's PCT entry specified that resource security checking should be done and the operator is not authorized to access the data set.

NOTOPEN
The file is not open.

SYSIDERR
The system identified by SYSID could not be located or accessed.

Notes and tips

- To rewrite a record, you must first read the record with the UPDATE option. This places a lock on the control interval that contains the record so that other CICS tasks can't access it. If the file is recoverable, that lock is held until the task ends. Otherwise, it's released when a REWRITE or RELEASE command is issued for the file.

- When you rewrite a record, you can change any data within the record except the file's primary key. You can also change the record's length.

- You don't usually need to handle any of the exceptional conditions that result from the REWRITE command. They represent error conditions from which your program can't generally recover.

Coding example (READ UPDATE and REWRITE VSAM KSDS records)

This example retrieves and updates a VSAM KSDS record. AR-ACCOUNT-NUMBER identifies the record to be read and NEW-ACCOUNT-RECORD contains the data that's to replace the current record. The NOTFND condition is handled in case the READ command can't locate the record.

```
    4100-UPDATE-ACCOUNT-RECORD SECTION.
*
        EXEC CICS
            HANDLE CONDITION NOTFND(4100-NOTFND)
        END-EXEC.
        EXEC CICS
            READ DATASET('ACCOUNT')
                INTO(ACCOUNT-RECORD)
                RIDFLD(AR-ACCOUNT-NUMBER)
                UPDATE
        END-EXEC.
        MOVE 'Y' TO RECORD-FOUND-SW.
        EXEC CICS
            REWRITE DATASET('ACCOUNT')
                FROM(NEW-ACCOUNT-RECORD)
        END-EXEC.
        GO TO 4100-EXIT.
*
    4100-NOTFND.
*
        MOVE 'N' TO RECORD-FOUND-SW.
*
    4100-EXIT.
*
        EXIT.
```

THE ROUTE COMMAND

Function

Basic Mapping Support. The ROUTE command lets you specify one or more terminals to which a BMS message is to be routed.

Syntax

```
EXEC CICS
     ROUTE [ LIST(data-area) ]
           [ OPCLASS(data-area) ]
           { INTERVAL(hhmmss) }
           { TIME(hhmmss)     }
           [ ERRTERM[(name)] ]
           [ TITLE(data-area) ]
           [ LDC(name) ]
           [ REQID(name) ]
           [ NLEOM ]
```

Options

LIST
Specifies a list of terminals to which the logical message should be routed. The route list is a data area consisting of one or more 16-byte entries, each identifying one terminal or operator. I'll describe the format of each under *Notes and tips*.

OPCLASS
Specifies a three-byte field that indicates which classes of operators the message should be delivered to. Each bit in the three-byte field corresponds to one of the 24 allowable operator classes; the first bit corresponds to operator class 24, and the last bit corresponds to operator class 1. If a bit position is on, the message is delivered to operators of the corresponding class; if a bit position is off, the message is *not* delivered to operators of that class.

INTERVAL
Specifies how long BMS should wait before BMS should deliver the logical message. You can code a literal in the form hhmmss; leading zeros can be omitted. Or, you can code a data name; the data area must be a 7-digit packed decimal field (PIC S9(7) COMP-3); its value must be in the form 0hhmmss. If both INTERVAL and TIME are omitted, INTERVAL(0) is assumed.

TIME
Specifies the time of day at which BMS should deliver the logical message. You can code a literal in the form hhmmss; leading zeros can be omitted. Or, you can code a data name; the data area must be a 7-digit packed decimal field (PIC S9(7) COMP-3); its value must be in the form 0hhmmss. If both INTERVAL and TIME are omitted, INTERVAL(0) is assumed.

ERRTERM

Specifies the one- to four-character terminal-id of a terminal that should be notified if the message can't be delivered. If you specify ERRTERM without a name, the terminal attached to the task that originated the message is assumed.

TITLE

Specifies a data area that includes the title used to identify the message during page retrieval. The title field must begin with a binary halfword field (PIC S9(4) COMP) that indicates the length of the entire title field, including the two bytes occupied by the length field.

LDC

Specifies a two-character name that's associated with the Logical Device Code to be used to format the message. Valid only for logical units that support Logical Device Codes.

REQID

Specifies a two-character name that's used for message recovery. If omitted, '**' is assumed.

NLEOM

Specifies that BMS should use new-line (NL) and end-of-margin (EOM) print orders as it builds the logical message. If you specify NLEOM on the ROUTE command, you should also specify it on the SEND MAP/SEND TEXT commands that build the message.

Exceptional conditions

Note: unless you provide for these conditions (other than RTEFAIL or RTESOME) with a HANDLE CONDITION command, the task will be terminated if any of them occur.

INVERRTERM

The terminal identifier specified in the ERRTERM option isn't defined in the Terminal Control Table (TCT).

INVLDC

The LDC name specified in the LDC option isn't valid for the logical unit.

INVREQ

(1.6 & 1.7 only) There is a format error in the route list.

RTEFAIL

The ROUTE command does not specify any terminals other than the one attached to the current task. If this condition is raised, the task is not terminated; instead, control returns directly to the application program.

RTESOME

BMS is able to route the message to some, but not all, of the specified terminals.

Notes and tips

- To route a logical message, you must issue a ROUTE command *before* you issue the SEND MAP, SEND TEXT, or SEND CONTROL commands to build the message. To properly build the message, each of these commands should specify the ACCUM and PAGING options. To complete the message so it can be delivered, issue a SEND PAGE command.

- Routed logical messages are held in temporary storage until they can be delivered. A parameter in the System Initialization Table (SIT) lets an installation specify how long undelivered messages are kept; if this time is exceeded, the undelivered message is automatically deleted.

- Each entry in a route list is 16 bytes long and contains the following information:

  Bytes 0-3   The terminal identifier of a terminal to which you want the message sent.

  Bytes 4-5   An LDC name for logical units that support LDC.

  Bytes 6-8   The operator identifier of an operator to whom you want the message sent.

  Byte 9   A status value that CICS updates to indicate whether or not the message was sucessfully routed to the terminal or operator specified in this entry; any value other than hex zeros (LOW-VALUE) indicates that the message wasn't routed to this terminal or operator.

  Bytes 10-15 Must be spaces.

  After the last entry in the list, code a binary halfword field (PIC S9(4) COMP) initialized to -1.

- If you're routing a message to a printer terminal, you should code the NLEOM option to control printer line spacing. That reduces the number of bytes that must be sent to the printer.

- You don't usually need to handle any exceptional conditions that result from the ROUTE command. They represent errors from which your program can't generally recover.

Coding example

This example shows portions of a program that builds a logical message and routes it to two printer terminals. The terminal-ids for the printers are L1P1 and L2P5.

```
01   ROUTE-LIST.
*
     05   LIST-ENTRY-1.
          10   LE1-TERMINAL-ID     PIC X(4)    VALUE 'L1P1'.
          10   FILLER             PIC X(12)   VALUE SPACE.
     05   LIST-ENTRY-2.
          10   LE2-TERMINAL-ID     PIC X(4)    VALUE 'L2P5'.
          10   FILLER             PIC X(12)   VALUE SPACE.
     05   FILLER                  PIC S9(4)   VALUE SPACE   COMP.
*
     .
     .
     .

 PROCEDURE DIVISION.
*
 0000-PRODUCE-INVENTORY-LISTING SECTION.
*
     EXEC CICS
         ROUTE LIST(ROUTE-LIST)
                NLEOM
     END-EXEC.
     .
     .
     .
     EXEC CICS
         SEND PAGE
     END-EXEC.
     .
     .
     .
```

THE SEND COMMAND

Function

Terminal control. The SEND command transmits
data to a terminal without using BMS services to
format the data.

Syntax

```
EXEC CICS
     SEND FROM(data-area)
          LENGTH(data-value)
        [ DEST(name) ]
        [ WAIT ]
        [ INVITE|LAST ]
        [ DEFRESP ]
        [ STRFIELD ]
        [ ERASE ]
        [ CTLCHAR(data-area) ]
END-EXEC.
```

Options

FROM
Specifies the data area that contains the output data.

LENGTH
Specifies a binary halfword (PIC S9(4)
COMP) or literal value that indicates the
length of the FROM area.

DEST
Specifies the four-character name of the ter-
minal to which the output data should be sent.
Valid only under TCAM.

WAIT
Specifies that the application program should
be suspended until the output operation has
completed.

INVITE
Specifies that the next terminal control operation will be a RECEIVE command. Valid
only under VTAM.

LAST
Specifies that this is the last terminal output
operation for the transaction. Valid only
under VTAM.

DEFRESP
Specifies that the terminal must issue a
response to the output message whether the
operation was successful or not; normally, a
response is required only when an error occurs. Valid only under VTAM.

STRFIELD

Specifies that the output data contains structured fields. If you code STRFIELD, you cannot code ERASE or CTLCHAR.

ERASE

Specifies that the terminal's display screen is to be erased before data is sent. If you code ERASE, you cannot code STRFIELD.

CTLCHAR

Specifies a one-byte field that contains a write- control-character. If you code CTLCHAR, you cannot code STRFIELD.

Exceptional conditions

Note: unless you provide for this condition with a HANDLE CONDITION command, the task will be terminated if it occurs. Note that TERMERR occurs only under VTAM; for BTAM or TCAM, no exceptional conditions are raised as a result of the SEND command.

TERMERR

(1.7 only) A terminal I/O error has occurred. Occurs only under VTAM.

Notes and tips

- The SEND command is best used to send small amounts of unformatted data to a terminal. If any but the simplest formatting is required, you're better off using BMS to handle the formatting.

- Under VTAM, you can improve performance by coordinating SEND and RECEIVE commands using the INVITE and LAST options. When you issue a SEND command, code INVITE if the next operation will be RECEIVE. For the transaction's last SEND command, code LAST.

SEND

Coding example

This program segment shows how data can be sent to a 3270 terminal without using BMS. Here, the output data consists of three display lines; the lines are padded with spaces so they are each 80 characters long. As a result, the display will be correct only for standard 80-column displays. Module 3000 begins by moving data from a customer record to the output area; then, it issues the SEND command. The ERASE option is specified so that the previous contents of the terminal screen are erased.

```
    WORKING-STORAGE SECTION.
*
    .
    .
    .
*
    01  CUSTOMER-DATA-LINES.
*
        05  CDL-LINE-1.
            10  FILLER            PIC X(10)   VALUE 'CUSTOMER: '.
            10  CDL-CUSTOMER-NO    PIC X(5).
            10  FILLER            PIC X(5)    VALUE SPACE.
            10  CDL-NAME           PIC X(30).
            10  FILLER            PIC X(30)   VALUE SPACE.
        05  CDL-LINE-2.
            10  FILLER            PIC X(20)   VALUE SPACE.
            10  CDL-ADDRESS        PIC X(30).
            10  FILLER            PIC X(30)   VALUE SPACE.
        05  CDL-LINE-3.
            10  FILLER            PIC X(20)   VALUE SPACE.
            10  CDL-CITY           PIC X(21).
            10  FILLER            PIC X       VALUE SPACE.
            10  CDL-STATE          PIC XX.
            10  FILLER            PIC X       VALUE SPACE.
            10  CDL-ZIP-CODE       PIC X(5).
            10  FILLER            PIC X(30)   VALUE SPACE.
    .
    .
    .
```

```
*
  PROCEDURE DIVISION.
*
  0000-PROCESS-CUSTOMER-INQUIRY SECTION.
*
      PERFORM 1000-RECEIVE-INQUIRY-DATA.
      IF VALID-DATA
          PERFORM 2000-READ-CUSTOMER-RECORD
          IF CUSTOMER-FOUND
              PERFORM 3000-SEND-CUSTOMER-DATA.
*
   .
   .
   .
*
  3000-SEND-CUSTOMER-DATA SECTION.
*
      MOVE CM-CUSTOMER-NO TO CDL-CUSTOMER-NO.
      MOVE CM-NAME        TO CDL-NAME.
      MOVE CM-ADDRESS     TO CDL-ADDRESS.
      MOVE CM-CITY        TO CDL-CITY.
      MOVE CM-STATE       TO CDL-STATE.
      MOVE CM-ZIP-CODE    TO CDL-ZIP-CODE.
      EXEC CICS
          SEND FROM(CUSTOMER-DATA-LINES)
               LENGTH(240)
               ERASE
      END-EXEC.
```

THE SEND CONTROL COMMAND

Function

Basic Mapping Support. The SEND CONTROL command lets you send device control instructions to a terminal. No mapped data is sent. Valid for release 1.6 and 1.7 only.

Syntax

```
                                                   1.6 & 1.7 only

    EXEC CICS
        SEND CONTROL  [ ERASEAUP | ERASE ]
                      [ ALARM ]
                      [ FREEKB ]
                      [ FRSET ]
                      [ CURSOR [(data-value)] ]
                      [ PRINT ]
                      [ FORMFEED ]
                      [ ACCUM ]
                        ┌ PAGING                    ┐
                      [ { TERMINAL [WAIT] [LAST] }  ]
                        └                           ┘
                      [ REQID (name)
                        ┌ L40    ┐
                      [ { L64    } ]
                        { L80    }
                        └ HONEOM  ┘

    END-EXEC.
```

Options

ERASEAUP
Erases all of the unprotected fields on the screen.

ERASE
Erases the entire display screen.

ALARM
Sounds the terminal's alarm.

FREEKB
Unlocks the terminal's keyboard.

FRSET
Resets the Modified Data Tag (MDT) bit of each attribute character to zero.

CURSOR
Specifies a binary halfword field (PIC S9(4) COMP) whose value indicates the screen position at which the cursor is to be placed. The row and column corresponding to a given cursor position value depends on the number of columns in each line; for a standard 80-column display, column 1 of row 1 is cursor position 0; column 1 of row 2 is cursor position 80, and so on.

PRINT
When used with a printer, specifies that the data is to be printed; if PRINT is omitted, the data is sent to the printer but not printed.

FORMFEED

Causes the printer to advance to the top of the next page.

ACCUM

Specifies that this command is a part of a message building operation.

PAGING

Specifies that output should be held in temporary storage until it can be delivered to its final destination.

TERMINAL

Specifies that output should be sent directly to the terminal.

WAIT

Specifies that the task should be suspended until the output operation has completed.

LAST

For logical units only, specifies the last terminal output operation for the task.

Exceptional conditions

Note: unless you provide for these conditions with a HANDLE CONDITION command, the task will be terminated if any of them other than RETPAGE occur.

IGREQCD

A VTAM error has occurred.

IGREQID

You changed the REQID value for a logical message.

REQID

Specifies a two-character name that's used for message recovery. If omitted, '**' is assumed. All BMS commands for the same logical message must specify the same REQID value.

L40

Specifies that the maximum line length for printed output is 40 characters.

L64

Specifies that the maximum line length for printed output is 64 characters.

L80

Specifies that the maximum line length for printed output is 80 characters.

HONEOM

Specifies that CICS should honor the printer's default end-of-margin setting when determining the maximum print line length.

INVREQ

The request is invalid; this often means that during the creation of a message, you changed an option—such as PAGING or TERMINAL—that must remain constant for the message.

TSIOERR

A temporary storage I/O error has occurred.

Notes and tips

- You should use the SEND CONTROL command only when you need to send control information to a terminal without sending data; all of the options you can specify on a SEND CONTROL command can also be specified on a SEND MAP or SEND TEXT command. As a result, coding a SEND CONTROL comand is equivalent to moving hex zeros (LOW-VALUE) to a symbolic map and issuing a SEND MAP command with the DATAONLY option; in both cases, control information is sent without any data.

- Although the CURSOR option lets you place the cursor at any screen location, you'll usually want to use the symbolic cursor positioning technique instead. Symbolic cursor positioning is described in Section 2.

- Several SEND CONTROL options are particularly useful when sending data to a printer. In particular, the FORMFEED option causes the printer to advance to the next page; the L40, L64, L80, and HONEOM commands let you specify print line lengths (usually, you'll specify HONEOM); and the PRINT option instructs the printer to begin printing the data it has received. Like any of the other SEND CONTROL options, however, you can code these options on a SEND MAP or SEND TEXT command as well.

- If you're building a logical message, be sure to include ACCUM and PAGING.

- You don't usually need to handle any of the exceptional conditions that can occur as a result of the SEND CONTROL command. They represent errors from which your program can't generally recover.

Coding example

This example shows a SEND CONTROL command that initiates a form feed operation and causes the printer to start printing.

```
EXEC CICS
    SEND CONTROL FORMFEED
                 PRINT
END-EXEC.
```

THE SEND MAP COMMAND

Function

Basic Mapping Support. The SEND MAP command lets you send data to a terminal, mapping it according to the specifications in a BMS map definition.

Syntax

```
EXEC CICS
    SEND MAP (name)
        [ MAPSET(name) ]
        [ FROM(data-area) ]
        [ LENGTH(data-value ]
        [ DATAONLY|MAPONLY ]
        [ ERASEAUP|ERASE ]
        [ ALARM ]
        [ FREEKB ]
        [ FRSET ]
        [ CURSOR [(data-value)] ]
        [ PRINT ]
        [ FORMFEED ]
        [ NLEOM ]                        ┌──────────────┐
        [ ACCUM ]                        │ 1.6 & 1.7 only │
        [ { PAGING          }  ]         └──────────────┘
          { TERMINAL [WAIT] }
        [ LAST ]
          ⎧ L40    ⎫
        [ ⎨ L64    ⎬ ]
          ⎪ L80    ⎪
          ⎩ HONEOM ⎭
        [ REQID(name) ]
END-EXEC.
```

Options

MAP
Specifies the one- to seven-character name of the map to be used to map the output data.

MAPSET
Specifies the one- to eight-character name of the mapset that contains the map. If omitted, the map name is used. This name must be defined in the Processing Program Table (PPT).

FROM
Specifies the data area from which the data to be mapped is obtained.

LENGTH
Specifies a binary halfword (PIC S9(4) COMP) or literal value that indicates the length of the data to be mapped. Required only if less than the entire data area specified in the FROM option is to be used.

DATAONLY

Data from the FROM area is to be mapped, but not constant data included in the BMS map definition.

MAPONLY

Only constant data from the BMS map definition is to be sent; no FROM area is used.

ERASEAUP

Erases all of the unprotected fields on the screen.

ERASE

Erases the entire display screen. When used with the ACCUM option, ERASE causes the display to be erased as each page is displayed, not as each map is written.

ALARM

Sounds the terminal's alarm.

FREEKB

Unlocks the terminal's keyboard.

FRSET

Resets the Modified Data Tag (MDT) bit of each attribute character to zero.

CURSOR

Specifies a binary halfword (PIC S9(4) COMP) or literal value that indicates the position at which the cursor is to be placed. The row and column corresponding to a given cursor position depends on the number of columns in each line; for an 80-column display, column 1 of row 1 is cursor position 0, column 1 of row 2 is cursor position 80, and so on. If you specify CURSOR but omit the data value, the symbolic cursor positioning technique (described in Section 2) is used.

PRINT

When used with a printer, specifies that the data is to be printed; if PRINT is omitted, the data is sent to the printer but not printed.

FORMFEED

(1.6 & 1.7 only) Causes the printer to advance to the top of the next page.

NLEOM

Specifies that BMS is to use new-line (NL) and end-of-message (EOM) orders to build the output; should be used for output intended for a printer.

ACCUM

Specifies that this command is a part of a message building operation.

PAGING

Specifies that output should be held in temporary storage until it can be delivered to its final destination.

TERMINAL

Specifies that output should be sent directly to the terminal.

WAIT

Specifies that the task should be suspended until the output operation has completed.

LAST

For logical units only, specifies the last terminal output operation for the task.

REQID

Specifies a two-character name that's used for message recovery. If omitted, '**' is assumed. All BMS commands for the same logical message must specify the same REQID value.

L40

Specifies that the maximum line length for printed output is 40 characters.

L64

Specifies that the maximum line length for printed output is 64 characters.

L80

Specifies that the maximum line length for printed output is 80 characters.

HONEOM

Specifies that CICS should honor the printer's default end-of-margin setting when determining the maximum print line length.

Exceptional conditions

Note: unless you provide for these conditions with a HANDLE CONDITION command, the task will be terminated if any of them other than or OVER-FLOW occur.

IGREQID

You changed the REQID value for a logical message.

INVMPSZ

The map is too large for the terminal.

INVREQ

The request is invalid; this often means that during the creation of a message, you changed an option—such as PAGING or TERMINAL—that must remain constant for the message.

OVERFLOW

There is not enough room on the screen for the map. When a HANDLE CONDITION command for the OVERFLOW condition is active, control returns to the application program, which can issue additional SEND MAP commands to complete the current page by sending a trailer map and/or a header map for the next page. If no HANDLE CONDITION command for the OVERFLOW condition is issued, OVERFLOW is ignored.

TSIOERR

A temporary storage I/O error has occurred.

Notes and tips

- If you omit the FROM option, BMS adds the letter O to the end of the map name you specify to determine the name of the output data area. So, if the map is named CUSTMAP, the output data area is CUSTMAPO. BMS uses the same convention when it assembles the symbolic map, so if you copy the BMS-generated symbolic mapset into your program, the names will match up. However, you must code FROM if (1) you want to use your own version of the symbolic map or (2) you specify a data name rather than a literal value in the MAP option.

- The DATAONLY and MAPONLY options let you add data to a display. Code DATAONLY when the screen already contains the correct captions, but you want to change the data that's displayed. Code MAPONLY when you want to display just captions with no data. Omit both if you want data from the symbolic map to be combined with captions coded in the BMS map definition. When you code these options, remem-ber that hex zeros (LOW-VALUE) in the symbolic map are *never* sent to the terminal. So, moving LOW-VALUE to the symbolic map and issuing a SEND MAP command without coding MAPONLY or DATAONLY is equivalent to issuing the same command with MAPONLY. Usually, you'll omit both MAPONLY and DATAONLY and move LOW-VALUE to the symbolic map fields that don't need to be sent to the terminal.

- Although the CURSOR option lets you place the cursor at any screen location, you'll usually want to use the symbolic cursor positioning technique instead. Symbolic cursor positioning is described in Section 2.

- If you're building a logical message, be sure to include the ACCUM and PAGING options and test for the OVERFLOW condition. The other exceptional conditions that can occur as a result of the SEND MAP command represent errors from which your program can't generally recover.

Coding example (sending a new map)

This example shows a SEND MAP command used to send a new map to a screen. Here, KEY-MAP is the name of a symbolic map definition created by the programmer; KM-D-OPERATOR-MESSAGE is a field in the map used to display operator messages. You should use a SEND MAP command like this one whenever you're sending a map to a terminal that's currently displaying a different map or no map at all.

```
    1400-SEND-KEY-SCREEN SECTION.
*
        MOVE SPACE TO KEY-MAP.
        MOVE 'PRESS CLEAR TO END SESSION'
            TO KM-D-OPERATOR-MESSAGE.
        EXEC CICS
            SEND MAP('MNTMAP1')
                MAPSET('MNTSET1')
                FROM(KEY-MAP)
                ERASE
        END-EXEC.
```

Coding example (refreshing a display)

This SEND MAP command leaves the current display on the screen, replacing only the fields from the symbolic map.

```
    1300-SEND-ORDER-SCREEN SECTION.
*
        EXEC CICS
            SEND MAP('ORDMAP1')
                MAPSET('ORDSET1')
                FROM(ORDER-ENTRY-MAP)
                DATAONLY
                CURSOR
        END-EXEC.
```

Coding example (message building)

This long example shows how to use SEND MAP commands to build message pages, each consisting of multiple maps. Each page consists of three types of maps: a header map (LSTMAP1), which is displayed at the top of each page; a detail map (LSTMAP2), which is displayed several times on each page; and a trailer map (LSTMAP3), which is displayed at the bottom of each page. The OVER-FLOW condition is tested to determine when header and trailer maps should be sent.

```
   0000-PRODUCE-INVENTORY-LISTING SECTION.
*
   .
   .
   .
       EXEC CICS
           HANDLE CONDITION OVERFLOW(2210-OVERFLOW)
       END-EXEC.
       PERFORM 2230-SEND-HEADER-MAP.
       PERFORM 2000-PRODUCE-INVENTORY-LINE
           UNTIL INVMAST-EOF.
       EXEC CICS
           SEND PAGE OPERPURGE
       END-EXEC.
       EXEC CICS
           RETURN
       END-EXEC.
*
   .
   .
   .

   2000-PRODUCE-INVENTORY-LINE SECTION.
*
       PERFORM 2100-READ-INVENTORY-RECORD.
       IF NOT INVMAST-EOF
           PERFORM 2200-SEND-INVENTORY-LINE.
*
   .
   .
   .

   2200-SEND-INVENTORY-LINE SECTION.
*
     PERFORM 2210-SEND-DETAIL-MAP.
     IF PAGE-OVERFLOW
         PERFORM 2220-SEND-TRAILER-MAP
         PERFORM 2230-SEND-HEADER-MAP
         PERFORM 2210-SEND-DETAIL-MAP
         MOVE 'N' TO PAGE-OVERFLOW-SW.
```

```
*
 2210-SEND-DETAIL-MAP SECTION.
*
     EXEC CICS
         SEND MAP('LSTMAP2')
              MAPSET('LSTSET1')
              FROM(INVENTORY-LISTING-MAP-2)
              ACCUM
              PAGING
              ERASE
     END-EXEC.
     GO TO 2210-EXIT.
*
 2210-OVERFLOW.
*
     MOVE 'Y' TO PAGE-OVERFLOW-SW.
*
 2210-EXIT.
*
     EXIT.
*
 2220-SEND-TRAILER-MAP SECTION.
*
     EXEC CICS
         SEND MAP('LSTMAP3')
              MAPSET('LSTSET1')
              ACCUM
              PAGING
              ERASE
     END-EXEC.
*
 2230-SEND-HEADER-MAP SECTION.
*
     EXEC CICS
         SEND MAP('LSTMAP1')
              MAPSET('LSTSET1')
              FROM(INVENTORY-LISTING-MAP-1)
              ACCUM
              PAGING
              ERASE
     END-EXEC.
```

THE SEND PAGE COMMAND

Function

Basic Mapping Support. The SEND PAGE command writes the last page of a BMS logical message to temporary storage.

Syntax

```
EXEC CICS
      SEND PAGE [ AUTOPAGE|NOAUTOPAGE ]
                [ OPERPURGE ]
END-EXEC.
```

Options

AUTOPAGE
NOAUTOPAGE
Overrides the Terminal Control Table's specification for the terminal's paging status. AUTOPAGE specifies that the pages should be sent to the terminal automatically; NOAUTOPAGE specifies that the pages should be sent to the terminal under operator control.

OPERPURGE
Specifies that the operator must enter a message termination command to delete the message. If you omit OPERPURGE, the message is automatically deleted when the operator enters anything that's not a page-retrieval command.

Exceptional conditions

Note: unless you provide for these conditions with a HANDLE CONDITION command, the task will be terminated if any of them occur.

INVREQ
The request is invalid.

TSIOERR
A temporary storage I/O error has occurred.

Notes and tips

- You should always include a SEND PAGE command in any program that builds a logical message. Usually, you'll omit AUTOPAGE and NOAUTOPAGE so that the terminal's default setting will apply. For display terminals, however, I recommend you always code OPERPURGE. Otherwise, it's all too easy for the operator to accidentally delete the message.

- You don't usually need to handle either of the exceptional conditions that result from the SEND PAGE command. They represent errors from which your program can't generally recover.

Coding example

This example shows a portion of the high-level module of a program that creates a logical message. As you can see, the program issues a SEND PAGE command immediately before it issues a RETURN command. That way, the last page of the logical message will be handled properly.

```
0000-PRODUCE-INVENTORY-LISTING SECTION.
*
        .
        .
        .
    PERFORM 2000-PRODUCE-INVENTORY-LINE
        UNTIL INVMAST-EOF.
    PERFORM 3000-SEND-TOTAL-MAP.
    EXEC CICS
        SEND PAGE
            OPERPURGE
    END-EXEC.
    EXEC CICS
        RETURN
    END-EXEC.
```

THE SEND TEXT COMMAND

Function

Basic Mapping Support. The SEND TEXT command lets you send text to a terminal. A map definition is not used to format the data; instead, BMS automatically formats the data, breaking lines between words where possible.

Syntax

```
    EXEC CICS
        SEND TEXT FROM(data-area) ]
                  LENGTH(data-value ]
                  [ ERASE ]
                  [ ALARM ]
                  [ FREEKB ]
                  [ CURSOR [(data-value)] ]
                  [ PRINT ]
                  [ FORMFEED ]                  1.6 & 1.7 only
                  [ NLEOM ]
                  [ ACCUM ]
                  [ { PAGING              } ]
                    { TERMINAL [WAIT]     }
                  [ LAST ]
                  [ HEADER(data-area) ]
                  [ TRAILER(data-area) ]
                    { JUSTIFY  }
                  [ { JUSFIRST } ]
                    { JUSLAST  }
                    { L40     }
                  [ { L64     } ]
                    { L80     }
                    { HONEOM  }
                  [ REQID(name)

    END-EXEC.
```

Options

FROM
Specifies the data area that contains the data to be sent.

LENGTH
Specifies a binary halfword (PIC S9(4) COMP) or literal value that indicates the length of the data to be sent.

ERASE
Erases the entire display screen. When used with the ACCUM option, ERASE causes the display to be erased as each page is displayed, not as each map is written.

ALARM
Sounds the terminal's alarm.

FREEKB

Unlocks the terminal's keyboard.

CURSOR

Specifies a binary halfword (PIC S9(4) COMP) or literal value that indicates the screen position at which the cursor is to be placed. The row and column corresponding to a given cursor position value depends on the number of columns in each line; for a standard 80-column display, column 1 of row 1 is cursor position 0, column 1 of row 2 is cursor position 80, and so on. If you specify CURSOR but omit the data value, the symbolic cursor positioning technique is used. This technique is described in Section 2.

PRINT

When used with a printer, specifies that the data is to be printed; if PRINT is omitted, the data is sent to the printer but not printed.

FORMFEED

(1.6 & 1.7 only) Causes the printer to advance to the top of the next page.

NLEOM

Specifies that BMS is to use new-line (NL) and end-of-message (EOM) orders to build the output; should be used for output intended for a printer.

ACCUM

Specifies that this command is a part of a message building operation.

PAGING

Specifies that output should be held in temporary storage until it can be delivered to its final destination.

TERMINAL

Specifies that output should be sent directly to the terminal.

WAIT

Specifies that the task should be suspended until the output operation has completed.

LAST

For logical units only, specifies the last terminal output operation for the task.

HEADER

Specifies a data area that contains the data to be used as the header area that's placed at the top of each page. I'll describe the format of the header area data under *Notes and tips*.

TRAILER

Specifies a data area that contains the data to be used as the trailer area that's placed at the bottom of each page. I'll describe the format of the trailer area data under *Notes and tips* .

JUSTIFY

Specifies a binary halfword (PIC S9(4) COMP) or literal value that indicates the number of the line at which the data is to be placed; the first line on the page is line 1. When a data area is specified, the value -1 is the same as specifying JUSFIRST, and -2 is the same as JUSLAST.

JUSFIRST

Specifies that the data is to be placed on the first available line following the header area.

JUSLAST

Specifies that the data is to be placed at the bottom of the page, immediately before the trailer area.

REQID

Specifies a two-character name that's used for message recovery. If omitted, '**' is assumed. All BMS commands for the same logical message must specify the same REQID value.

L40

Specifies that the maximum line length for printed output is 40 characters.

L64

Specifies that the maximum line length for printed output is 64 characters.

L80

Specifies that the maximum line length for printed output is 80 characters.

HONEOM

Specifies that CICS should honor the printer's default end-of-margin setting when determining the maximum print line length.

Exceptional conditions

Note: unless you provide for these conditions with a HANDLE CONDITION command, the task will be terminated if any of them occur.

IGREQID

You changed the REQID value for a logical message.

INVREQ

The request is invalid; this often means that during the creation of a message, you changed an option—such as PAGING or TERMINAL—that must remain constant for the message.

TSIOERR

A temporary storage I/O error has occurred.

Notes and tips

* When you use the SEND TEXT command, BMS formats data by breaking it into lines. Lines are split at spaces, so words aren't split across lines. You can force a line break at any time by including a new-line character (hex 15) in the data.

* When you use message building, be sure to code the ACCUM and PAGING options. The HEADER and TRAILER options let you specify data areas that contain header and trailer information; this data is included in the output if the text data overflows the current page. The header and trailer area must begin with a four-byte prefix that contains control information: the first two bytes make up a binary halfword (PIC S9(4) COMP) that indicates the length of the header area, *not* including the four-byte prefix area; the next byte indicates whether pages should be automatically numbered (I'll explain that in a moment); and the fourth byte is reserved for use by BMS.

* To use automatic page numbering, code a non-blank value in the third byte or a header or trailer prefix area. When an overflow situation occurs, BMS scans the header or trailer data until it finds one or more occurrences of the character you specified in byte 3 of the prefix. Then, it replaces those characters with the current page number. For example, if you specify an asterisk in byte 3 of the header area's prefix, BMS scans the header data until it finds one or more asterisks; then, it places the current page number in the positions occupied by the asterisks.

* The JUSTIFY, JUSTFIRST, and JUSTLAST options let you alter the output data's position. With JUSTIFY, you specify the line number of the line at which you want the output to begin. JUSTFIRST and JUSTLAST let you position data at the top or bottom of the page, allowing for any header or trailer areas. If you omit JUSTIFY, JUSTFIRST, and JUSTLAST, data is positioned starting at the next available line.

* You don't normally need to handle any of the exceptional conditions that result from the SEND TEXT command. They represent errors from which your program can't generally recover.

Coding example (sending a single block of text)

This example shows how to use a SEND TEXT command to send text to a terminal. The example is from an on-line problem reporting system; the data consists of a problem number followed by a free-form textual description of the problem. The fields PROB-NL-1 and PROB-NL-2 contain new-line characters (hex 15) to force line breaks.

```
        .
        .
        .
   01   PROBLEM-DESCRIPTION-AREA.
   *
        05   FILLER              PIC X(16)    VALUE 'PROBLEM NUMBER: '
        05   PROB-NUMBER         PIC X(5).
        05   PROB-NL-1           PIC X        VALUE ' '.
        05   FILLER              PIC X(11)    VALUE 'DESCRIPTION'
        05   PROB-NL-2           PIC X        VALUE ' '.
        05   PROB-DESCRIPTION    PIC X(1000).
   *
        .
        .
        .

        EXEC CICS
            SEND TEXT FROM(PROBLEM-DESCRIPTION-AREA)
                      LENGTH(1034)
                      ERASE
                      FREEKB
        END-EXEC.
```

Coding example (message building)

This long example shows how to use SEND TEXT commands to create a report using message building facilities. Each page of the report has a header area at the top and a trailer area at the bottom. A single SEND TEXT command is used to send each line of the report; whenever BMS detects a page overflow condition, it automatically sends the header and trailer areas. Automatic page numbering is used; the three asterisks in the header area will be replaced by a three-digit page number.

```
        WORKING-STORAGE SECTION.
    *
        .
        .
        .
        .
        01   HEADER-AREA.
    *
            05   HA-PREFIX.
                10   HA-LENGTH      PIC S9(4)      VALUE +153      COMP.
                10   HA-PAGE-CODE   PIC X          VALUE '*'.
                10   FILLER         PIC X          VALUE SPACE.
            05   HEADER-LINE-1.
                10   FILLER         PIC X(20)      VALUE '                    INVE'.
                10   FILLER         PIC X(20)      VALUE 'NTORY LISTING          '.
                10   FILLER         PIC X(10)      VALUE ' PAGE: ***'.
                10   HA1-NL         PIC X          VALUE ' '.
            05   HEADING-LINE-2.
                10   FILLER         PIC X(20)      VALUE 'ITEM      DESCRIPTION '.
                10   FILLER         PIC X(20)      VALUE '                  UNIT'.
                10   FILLER         PIC X(8)       VALUE '    QTY'.
                10   HA2-NL         PIC X          VALUE ' '.
            05   HEADING-LINE-3.
                10   FILLER         PIC X(20)      VALUE ' NO.               '.
                10   FILLER         PIC X(20)      VALUE '                 PRICE'.
                10   FILLER         PIC X(10)      VALUE '   ON HAND'.
                10   HA3-NL         PIC X          VALUE ' '.
    *
        01   INVENTORY-LINE.
    *
            05   IL-ITEM-NUMBER          PIC 9(5).
            05   FILLER                  PIC X(3)       VALUE SPACE.
            05   IL-ITEM-DESCRIPTION     PIC X(20).
            05   FILLER                  PIC X(3)       VALUE SPACE.
            05   IL-UNIT-PRICE           PIC ZZ,ZZ9.99.
            05   FILLER                  PIC X(4)       VALUE SPACE.
            05   IL-ON-HAND-QUANTITY     PIC ZZ,ZZ9.
            05   IL-NL                   PIC X          VALUE ' '.
    *
        01   TRAILER-AREA.
    *
            05   TA-PREFIX.
                10   TA-LENGTH      PIC S9(4)      VALUE +26      COMP.
                10   TA-PAGE-CODE   PIC X          VALUE SPACE.
                10   FILLER         PIC X          VALUE SPACE.
            05   TRAILER-LINE.
                10   TA-NL          PIC X          VALUE ' '.
                10   FILLER         PIC X(20)      VALUE 'CONTINUED ON NEXT PA'.
                10   FILLER         PIC X(5)       VALUE 'GE...'.
```

```
  0000-PRODUCE-INVENTORY-LISTING SECTION.
*
  .
  .
  .
      PERFORM 2000-PRODUCE-INVENTORY-LINE
          UNTIL INVMAST-EOF.
      EXEC CICS
          RETURN
      END-EXEC.
*
  .
  .
  .
  2000-PRODUCE-INVENTORY-LINE SECTION.
*
      PERFORM 2100-READ-INVENTORY-RECORD.
      IF NOT INVMAST-EOF
          PERFORM 2200-SEND-INVENTORY-LINE.
*
  .
  .
  .
  2200-SEND-INVENTORY-LINE SECTION.
*
      MOVE IM-ITEM-NUMBER       TO IL-ITEM-NUMBER.
      MOVE IM-ITEM-DESCRIPTION  TO IL-ITEM-DESCRIPTION.
      MOVE IM-UNIT-PRICE        TO IL-UNIT-PRICE.
      MOVE IM-ON-HAND           TO IL-ON-HAND.
      EXEC CICS
          SEND TEXT FROM(INVENTORY-LINE)
                    LENGTH(51)
                    ACCUM
                    PAGING
                    ERASE
                    HEADER(HEADER-AREA)
                    TRAILER(TRAILER-AREA)
      END-EXEC.
```

THE START COMMAND

Function

Interval control. The START command initiates another task; the task will begin execution when a specified time period has expired. Optionally, the START command can pass data to the task.

Syntax

```
EXEC CICS
    START TRANSID(name)
         [ { INTERVAL(hhmmss) } ]
         [ { TIME(hhmmss)     } ]
         [ TERMID(name) ]
         [ SYSID(name) ]
         [ REQID(name) ]
         [ FROM(data-area) ]
         [ LENGTH(data-value) ]
         [ RTRANSID(name) ]
         [ RTERMID(name) ]
         [ QUEUE(name) ]
         [ NOCHECK ]
         [ PROTECT ]
    END-EXEC.
```

Options

TRANSID

Specifies the one- to four-character transaction identifier that will be used to start the task.

INTERVAL

Specifies a time interval; the task will be started when this interval has elapsed. You can code a literal in the form hhmmss; leading zeros can be omitted. Or, you can code a data name; the data area must be a 7-digit packed decimal field (PIC S9(7) COMP-3); its value must be in the form 0hhmmss. If both INTERVAL and TIME are omitted, INTERVAL(0) is assumed.

TIME

Specifies a time of day; the task will be started at this time. You can code a literal in the form hhmmss; leading zeros can be omitted. Or, you can code a data name; the data area must be a 7-digit packed decimal field (PIC S9(7) COMP-3); its value must be in the form 0hhmmss. If both INTERVAL and TIME are omitted, INTERVAL(0) is assumed.

TERMID

Specifies a one- to four-character terminal identifier that identifies the terminal to which the started task will be attached. If specified, it must be defined in the Terminal Control Table (TCT); if omitted, the task is not attached to any terminal and, as a result, can't do any terminal I/O.

SYSID

Specifies the one- to four-character name of a remote system on which the task is to be started.

REQID

Specifies a one- to eight-character name used to uniquely identify this START command. If specified, a CANCEL command can be issued later to cancel the task before it begins executing. (Once the task has started, however, the CANCEL command has no effect.)

FROM

Specifies a data area that contains data to be passed to the started task. The started task receives this data by issuing a RETRIEVE command with the INTO or SET option.

LENGTH

Specifies a binary halfword (PIC S9(4) COMP) or literal value that indicates the length of the FROM area.

RTERMID

Specifies a one- to four-character name that's passed to the started task; the started task receives the name by issuing a RETRIEVE command with the RTERMID option.

Exceptional conditions

Note: unless you provide for these conditions with a HANDLE CONDITION command, the task will be terminated if any of them occur.

INVREQ

The START command is invalid.

IOERR

An I/O error occurred.

ISCINVREQ

An undeterminable error occurred on the remote system (specified in the SYSID option).

NOTAUTH

(1.7 only) The current transaction's PCT entry specified that resource security checking should be done and the operator is not authorized to access the transaction to be started.

RTRANSID

Specifies a one- to four-character name that's passed to the started task; the started task receives the name by issuing a RETRIEVE command with the RTRANSID option.

QUEUE

Specifies a one- to eight-character name that's passed to the started task; the started task receives the name by issuing a RETRIEVE command with the QUEUE option.

NOCHECK

Specifies that when the started task is to be initiated on another system, the task issuing the START command should *not* wait for confirmation that the START command was successfully processed.

PROTECT

Specifies that the task can not be started until the task issuing the START command issues a syncpoint, either by ending or by issuing a SYNCPOINT command.

SYSIDERR

The system identified by SYSID could not be located or accessed.

TERMIDERR

The terminal identified by the TERMID option isn't defined in the Terminal Control Table (TCT).

TRANSIDERR

The transaction identified by the TRANSID option isn't defined in the Program Control Table (PCT).

Notes and tips

- The START command has two basic uses. The first is when an application function is divided into two or more independent programs that can be executed simultaneously because they don't depend on one another. In this case, use one or more START commands to immediately start one or more tasks. The second is when you need to begin a task at some time in the future. For example, you might use a START command to schedule a task for execution at 6:00 a.m., when the system's usage is low; to do that, issue a START command with the TIME option. Or, you might have a program that needs to restart itself at regular intervals. In that case, the program should issue a START command with the INTERVAL option before it ends.

- Usually, if two or more START commands specify the same expiration time and the same transid, one task will be started for each START command. However, if data is passed to the started task, only one task is started. If this task repeatedly issues RETRIEVE commands to process all of the data sent to it, then no additional tasks are started. But if it does not, the task is started again and again until all of the passed data has been processed.

- You don't usually need to handle any of the exceptional conditions that result from the START command; they represent error conditions from which your program can't generally recover.

Coding example (no data, no terminal)

This example shows how to issue a START command to start the transaction name 'RFK4' at 6:00 a.m. No data is passed to the task and no terminal is associated with the task.

```
EXEC CICS
    START TRANSID('RFK4')
          TIME(060000)
END-EXEC.
```

Coding example (data, terminal)

This example shows how to start a transaction named 'DKM3' in 10 minutes, passing it the 100 bytes of data in the field named DKM3-DATA. The task will be attached to the terminal named L580.

```
EXEC CICS
    START TRANSID('DKM3')
          INTERVAL(1000)
          TERMID('L580')
          FROM(DKM3-DATA)
          LENGTH(100)
END-EXEC.
```

THE STARTBR COMMAND

Function

File control. The STARTBR command initiates a browse operation so records can be retrieved using READNEXT or READPREV commands. The STARTBR command itself does not retrieve a record; it just establishes positioning for subsequent retrieval. The browse operation should always be ended with an ENDBR command.

Syntax

```
EXEC CICS
     STARTBR DATASET(name)
             RIDFLD(data-area)
           [ KEYLENGTH(data-value) ]
           [ GENERIC ]
           [ RBA|RRN ]
           [ GTEQ|EQUAL ]
           [ REQID(data-value) ]
           [ SYSID(name) ]
END-EXEC.
```

Options

DATASET
Specifies the one- to eight-character name of the data set for which a browse operation is to be started.

RIDFLD
Specifies a data area that identifies the record at which the browse operation is to begin. The contents of the RIDFLD field depends on whether RBA or RRN is specified; if neither is specified, the RIDFLD field contains a key for VSAM KSDS or path retrieval. For generic positioning (see the KEYLENGTH and GENERIC options, below), the RIDFLD field must still be as long as the file's defined key length.

To begin a browse operation at the first record in the file, place hexadecimal zeros (LOW-VALUE) in the RIDFLD field. To begin a browse operation at the last record in the file, place hexadecimal FFs (HIGH-VALUE) in the RIDFLD field.

KEYLENGTH
Specifies a binary halfword (PIC S9(4) COMP) or literal value that indicates the length of the key, which must be less than the file's defined key length. Used only for a generic read along with the GENERIC option. Not valid if RBA or RRN is specified.

GENERIC
Specifies that only a part of the key in the RIDFLD field should be used, as indicated by the KEYLENGTH option. Positioning is established at the first record with a key whose leftmost character positions (as specified by KEYLENGTH) match the RIDFLD field.

RBA

Specifies that the RIDFLD field is a Relative Byte Address (RBA) for a VSAM KSDS or ESDS. An RBA is a binary fullword (PIC S9(8) COMP).

RRN

Specifies that the RIDFLD is a Relative Record Number (RRN) for a VSAM RRDS. An RRN is a binary fullword (PIC S9(8) COMP). The RRN of the first record in an RRDS is 1.

GTEQ

Specifies that positioning is to be established at the first record whose key value is greater than or equal to the key specified in the RIDFLD field. This will always establish positioning in the file unless the specified key is greater than the largest key in the file. If you omit GTEQ and EQUAL, GTEQ is assumed.

EQUAL

Specifies that positioning will be established at the record whose key matches the RIDFLD field exactly. If no such record exists, the NOTFND condition is raised and the browse operation is not started.

REQID

Specifies a binary halfword (PIC S9(4) COMP) or literal value that identifies the browse operation; used only when your program controls two or more browse operations at the same time. For each I/O command that's part of the same browse operation, specify the same REQID value.

SYSID

Specifies the one- to four-character name of a remote system that contains the file.

Exceptional conditions

Note: unless you provide for these conditions with a HANDLE CONDITION command, the task will be terminated if any of them occur.

DISABLED

(1.7 only) The data set is disabled, probably as a result of the master terminal operator explicitly dis-abling the file using CEMT SET DISABLE.

DSIDERR

The data set name specified in the DATASET option isn't defined in the File Control Table.

ILLOGIC

A serious VSAM error occurred.

INVREQ

The STARTBR request is prohibited by the file's FCT entry. Can also occur if you specify a REQID value that's already used for another browse operation within the same task.

IOERR

An I/O error occurred.

ISCINVREQ

An undeterminable error occurred on the remote system (specified in the SYSID option).

NOTAUTH

(1.7 only) The transaction's PCT entry specified that resource security checking should be done and the operator is not authorized to access the data set.

NOTFND

The specified record could not be located.

NOTOPEN

The file is not open.

SYSIDERR

The system identified by SYSID could not be located or accessed.

Notes and tips

- You must issue a STARTBR command before you can issue READNEXT or READPREV commands to sequentially retrieve records during a browse operation. Browsing is relatively inefficient because a VSAM string is held for the duration of the browse. (A string is required for each concurrent access to a VSAM file; so if 10 strings are specified for a file, 10 simultaneous accesses are allowed.) Because of this inefficiency, try to avoid browsing whenever possible.

- To browse a file via an alternate index, specify a path name in the DATASET option.

- There are two ways to change positioning during a browse. One is to simply change the value of the RIDFLD field before you issue a READNEXT or READPREV command; the key value you specify establishes a new position for the browse. (This is called skip-sequential processing.) The second is to issue a RESETBR command, whose function is basically the same as the STARTBR command.

- The only exceptional condition you should normally handle for a STARTBR command is NOTFND; the other conditions represent errors from which your program can't generally recover.

Coding example

This example starts a browse operation for a file named ACCOUNT. The browse operation will start at the record indicated by AR-ACCOUNT-NUMBER: if this field contains hex zeros (LOW-VALUE), the browse starts at the beginning of the file; if it contains hex FFs (HIGH-VALUE), the browse starts at the end of the file; otherwise, the browse starts at the indicated record.

```
      1100-START-ACCOUNT-BROWSE SECTION.
*
          EXEC CICS
              HANDLE CONDITION NOTFND(1100-NOTFND)
          END-EXEC.
          EXEC CICS
              STARTBR DATASET('ACCOUNT')
                      RIDFLD(AR-ACCOUNT-NUMBER)
          END-EXEC.
          MOVE 'N' TO END-OF-BROWSE-SW.
          GO TO 1100-EXIT.
*
        1100-NOTFND.
*
          MOVE 'Y' TO END-OF-BROWSE-SW.
*
        1100-EXIT.
*
          EXIT.
```

THE SUSPEND COMMAND

Function

Task control. The SUSPEND command temporarily returns control to CICS. That allows CICS to dispatch other tasks that may have been waiting while your task executes. Control will eventually return to your task. The SUSPEND command is appropriate only for applications that require an unusually large amount of CPU time without an intervening CICS command.

Syntax

```
EXEC CICS
    SUSPEND
END-EXEC.
```

Options

The SUSPEND command has no options.

Exceptional conditions

No exceptional conditions are raised as a result of a SUSPEND command.

Notes and tips

- If your program includes a long processing loop that doesn't involve CICS commands, you should issue a SUSPEND command. If you don't, CICS may cancel your task because it thinks it's a runaway task. You don't have to use SUSPEND if the processing loop issues CICS commands, though. That's because almost all of the CICS commands suspend your task anyway.

Coding example

This example shows how to issue a SUSPEND command once in every 100 invocations of a program routine. In this example, a working storage field named WS-SUSPEND-COUNT is used as a counter to determine when the SUSPEND command should be issued.

```
IF WS-SUSPEND-COUNT = 100
    EXEC CICS
        SUSPEND
    END-EXEC
    MOVE ZERO TO WS-SUSPEND-COUNT.
ADD 1 TO WS-SUSPEND-COUNT.
```

THE SYNCPOINT COMMAND

Function

Recovery. The SYNCPOINT command has two distinct functions. When coded without options, the SYNCPOINT command makes all of the updates applied to protected resources permanent: they aren't reversed if an abend occurs. When coded with the ROLLBACK option, the SYNCPOINT command reverses all updates made since the last SYNCPOINT command was issued (or since the task began).

Syntax

```
EXEC CICS
    SYNCPOINT [ ROLLBACK ]
END-EXEC.
```

Options

ROLLBACK

Specifies that all updates made since the last SYNCPOINT command or the beginning of the task should be reversed. If omitted, the SYNCPOINT command permanently commits all of the updates made so far by the task.

Exceptional conditions

Note: unless you provide for this condition with a HANDLE CONDITION command, the task will be terminated if it occurs.

ROLLEDBACK

(1.7 only) Indicates that a remote system was not able to complete the syncpoint; as a result, a ROLLBACK operation is forced.

Notes and tips

- When a CICS task abends, any updates made to protected resources are normally reversed. Sometimes, however, it's not necessary to reverse all of the updates made by an abending task. In those cases, you can use the SYNCPOINT command to limit the number of updates that are reversed; in short, only those updates made since the last SYNCPOINT command was issued are reversed when a task abends. To illustrate, consider a program that reads a file of invoice records and updates corresponding master records in several files. If the program abends (or if CICS itself abends) after 100 records have been processed, the updates for all 100 records are reversed, even though that's probably not necessary; just the updates for the invoice that was being processed when the abend occurred need to be reversed. So, a SYNCPOINT command should be issued after all of the updates for each invoice record have been made.

- The SYNCPOINT command with the ROLLBACK option invokes the dynamic transaction backout facility as if the task were abended. You might find it useful in error-handling routines when you want to reverse all of the updates made by a task, but you don't want the task to be abended.

- You don't usually need to handle the exceptional condition that results from the SYNCPOINT command (ROLLEDBACK).

Coding example

This example shows how to issue a SYNCPOINT command in a program that updates several files based on records in a transaction file. A SYNCPOINT command is issued after each transaction record has been completely processed.

```
 0000-POST-INVOICE-TRANSACTIONS SECTION.
*
        .
        .
        .
     PERFORM 1000-POST-INVOICE-TRANSACTION
         UNTIL INVOICE-EOF.
        .
        .
        .
*
 1000-POST-INVOICE-TRANSACTION SECTION.
*
     PERFORM 1100-READ-INVOICE-TRANSACTION.
     IF NOT INVOICE-EOF
         PERFORM 1200-UPDATE-MASTER-FILES
         EXEC CICS
             SYNCPOINT
         END-EXEC.
*
        .
        .
        .
```

THE TRACE COMMAND

Function

Trace control. The TRACE command enables or disables the CICS trace facility. When enabled, the trace facility maintains a trace table which can be useful for program debugging.

Syntax

```
EXEC CICS
    TRACE { ON|OFF }
          [ SYSTEM ]
          [ EI ]
          [ USER ]
          [ SINGLE ]
END-EXEC.
```

Options

ON

Specifies that the trace facility is to be enabled.

OFF

Specifies that the trace facility is to be disabled.

SYSTEM

Specifies that this TRACE command applies to all tracing activity in the CICS system.

EI

Specifies that this TRACE command applies only to the tracing activity performed by the EXEC interface program, which processes all CICS commands issued by application programs.

USER

Specifies that this TRACE command applies only to user trace entries created by any task. User trace entries are produced by the ENTER command.

SINGLE

Specifies that this TRACE command applies only to user trace entries created by this task. User trace entries are produced by the ENTER command.

Exceptional conditions

There are no exceptional conditions for the TRACE command.

Notes and tips

- Although the TRACE command might be useful in some situations, it's not really intended for use in application programs. That's because most of its options affect tracing for *all* of the tasks in a CICS system, not just the task that issues the TRACE command. The exception is the SINGLE option: it lets you enable or disable user trace entries (created by the ENTER command) for a single task. If you've coded ENTER commands for debugging purposes, you can use TRACE ON and TRACE OFF to enable or disable those commands.

- A terminal operator with access to the CEMT transaction can also control the trace facility.

Coding example

This example shows a module that enables or disables user trace entries for the task, depending on the setting of a flag.

```
    WORKING-STORAGE SECTION.
*
    01  FLAGS.
*
        05  TRACE-CONTROL-FLAG      PIC 9     VALUE 0.
            88  DISABLE-TRACE                 VALUE 0.
            88  ENABLE-TRACE                  VALUE 1.
      .
      .
      .
*
    PROCEDURE DIVISION.
*
      .
      .
      .
*
    0500-SET-TRACE-FUNCTION SECTION.
*
        IF ENABLE-TRACE
            EXEC CICS
                TRACE ON SINGLE
            END-EXEC
        ELSE IF DISABLE-TRACE
            EXEC CICS
                TRACE OFF SINGLE
            END-EXEC.
```

THE UNLOCK COMMAND

Function

File control. The UNLOCK command releases a record that was held under exclusive control by a READ UPDATE command. If you don't issue an UNLOCK command, the record is released automatically when you issue a SYNCPOINT command or when your task terminates.

Syntax

```
EXEC CICS
    UNLOCK DATASET(name)
         [ SYSID(name) ]
END-EXEC.
```

Options

DATASET
Specifies the one- to eight-character name of the data set containing the record to be released.

SYSID
Specifies the one- to four-character name of a remote system that contains the file.

Exceptional conditions

Note: unless you provide for these conditions with a HANDLE CONDITION command, the task will be terminated if any of them occur.

DISABLED
(1.7 only) The data set is disabled, probably as a result of the master terminal operator explicitly dis-abling the file using CEMT SET DISABLE.

DSIDERR
The data set name specified in the DATASET option isn't defined in the File Control Table.

ILLOGIC
A serious VSAM error occurred.

IOERR
An I/O error occurred.

ISCINVREQ
An undeterminable error occurred on the remote system (specified in the SYSID option).

NOTAUTH
(1.7 only) The transaction's PCT entry specified that resource security checking should be done and the operator is not authorized to access the data set.

NOTOPEN
The file is not open.

SYSIDERR
The system identified by SYSID could not be located or accessed.

Notes and tips

- Whenever you issue a READ UPDATE command, CICS prevents other users from accessing any record in the control interval until your task ends, you issue a SYNCPOINT command, or you issue an UNLOCK command (and you haven't updated or deleted the record). As a result, if your program reads a record with a READ UPDATE command and then decides not to update the record, it should issue an UNLOCK command (unless the program will end immediately after

making the decision not to update the file anyway; don't issue an UNLOCK command if it's the last CICS command issued before the RETURN command).

- You don't usually need to handle any of the exceptional conditions that result from the UNLOCK command; they represent error conditions from which your program can't generally recover.

Coding example

This example shows how to release control of a record in the ACCOUNT file that was previously read with the UPDATE option.

```
    4250-UNLOCK-ACCOUNT-FILE SECTION.
*
        EXEC CICS
            UNLOCK DATASET('ACCOUNT')
        END-EXEC.
```

THE WAIT EVENT COMMAND

Function

Interval control. The WAIT EVENT command delays the task until a previously issued POST command has expired.

Syntax

```
EXEC CICS
     WAIT EVENT ECADDR(pointer-value)
END-EXEC.
```

Options

ECADDR

Specifies a binary fullword (PIC S9(8) COMP) that contains the address of the Timer Event Control Area that must expire before the task can continue. You can obtain this value from the SET option of the POST command that creates the Timer Event Control Area.

Exceptional conditions

Note: unless you provide for this condition with a HANDLE CONDITION command, the task will be terminated if it occurs.

INVREQ

(1.6 & 1.7 only) The Timer Event Control Area address is invalid.

Notes and tips

- One possible, though unlikely, use for the POST and WAIT EVENT commands is to force a minimum response time for terminal transactions. To do that, issue a POST command at the start of the task, specifying the minimum response time (perhaps 3 seconds) in the INTERVAL option. Then, before you issue the final SEND MAP command, issue a WAIT EVENT command. That way, the terminal won't receive output faster than the minimum response time will allow. Of course, this doesn't account for data transmission time, which is often the largest component of total response time.

- You don't usually need to handle the exceptional condition that results from the WAIT EVENT command; it represents an error condition from which your program can't generally recover.

Coding example

This example shows how to issue POST and WAIT EVENT commands to ensure a minimum 3 second response time. Because this type of function affects the high-level coding of the program, I've included all of the program's top level module and parts of several subordinate modules. WS-ECA-POINTER is a working storage field defined as PIC S9(8) COMP.

```
    0000-PROCESS-CUSTOMER-INQUIRY SECTION.
*
        IF EIBCALEN = ZERO
            PERFORM 8000-START-TERMINAL-SESSION
        ELSE
            MOVE DFHCOMMAREA TO COMMUNICATION-AREA
            EXEC CICS
                POST EVENT INTERVAL(3)
                            SET(WS-ECA-POINTER)
            END-EXEC
            PERFORM 1000-PROCESS-INQUIRY-SCREEN.
        IF END-SESSION
            EXEC CICS
                XCTL PROGRAM('MENU1')
            END-EXEC
        ELSE
            EXEC CICS
                RETURN TRANSID('INQ1')
                        COMMAREA(COMMUNICATION-AREA)
                        LENGTH(1)
            END-EXEC.
*
    1000-PROCESS-INQUIRY-SCREEN SECTION.
*
        PERFORM 1100-RECEIVE-INQUIRY-SCREEN.
        IF NOT END-SESSION
            PERFORM 1200-GET-CUSTOMER-DATA
            PERFORM 1300-SEND-INQUIRY-SCREEN.
            .
            .
            .
*
    1300-SEND-INQUIRY-SCREEN SECTION.
*
        EXEC CICS
            WAIT EVENT ECADDR(WS-ECA-POINTER)
        END-EXEC.
        EXEC CICS
            SEND MAP ...
        END-EXEC.
```

THE WAIT JOURNAL COMMAND

Function

Journal control. The WAIT JOURNAL command synchronizes the current task with a previously written journal record by suspending the task until the record has been successfully written to the journal file. The WAIT JOURNAL command is used only for asynchronous journal output; that is, when the JOURNAL command that writes the journal record does *not* specify WAIT.

Syntax

```
EXEC CICS
    WAIT JOURNAL JFILEID(data-value)
                 [ REQID(data-value) ]
                 [ STARTIO ]
END-EXEC.
```

Options

JFILEID
Specifies a binary halfword (PIC S9(4) COMP) that indicates the journal file with which the task is to be synchronized.

REQID
Specifies a binary fullword (PIC S9(8) COMP) that identifies the specific journal record for which the task is to wait. You can obtain this value from the REQID option of the JOURNAL command that creates the record. If you omit REQID, the task is suspended until the record created by the most recently issued JOURNAL command is written.

STARTIO
Specifies that the journal buffer should be written to the journal file immediately.

Exceptional conditions

Note: unless you provide for these conditions with a HANDLE CONDITION command, the task will be terminated if any of them occur.

INVREQ
(1.6 & 1.7 only) The task has not yet issued a JOURNAL command.

IOERR
An I/O error occurred.

JIDERR
The journal identifier you specified in the JFILEID option isn't defined in the Journal Control Table.

NOTAUTH

(1.7 only) The transaction's PCT entry specified that resource security checking should be done and the operator is not authorized to access the journal.

NOTOPEN

The journal data set is not open.

Notes and tips

- The WAIT JOURNAL command can be used to synchronize your task to more than one journal record created asynchronously; whenever you issue a WAIT journal command, your task is suspended until *all* journal records created asynchronously have been written to the journal data set. Thus, your program should issue just one WAIT JOURNAL command even if it's issued more than one asynchronous JOURNAL command.

- If the journal record has already been written to the journal data set, the WAIT JOURNAL command has no effect; control returns immediately to the application program.

- You don't usually need to handle any of the exceptional conditions that result from the WAIT JOURNAL command; they represent error conditions from which your program can't generally recover.

Coding example

This example shows how to delete a data set record after first recording the record in a journal. Asynchronous journal output is used, so the program does not wait for the journal record to be written to disk before it deletes the data set record.

However, a WAIT JOURNAL command is issued so that the program will not continue beyond the DELETE commad before the journal record is written to disk.

```
    3100-DELETE-CUSTOMER-RECORD SECTION.
*
        EXEC CICS
            JOURNAL JFILEID(7)
                    JTYPEID('CD')
                    FROM(CUSTOMER-MASTER-RECORD)
                    LENGTH(97)
                    REQID(WS-REQID)
        END-EXEC.
        EXEC CICS
            DELETE FILE('CUSTMAS')
                   RIDFLD(CM-CUSTOMER-NUMBER)
        END-EXEC.
        EXEC CICS
            WAIT JOURNAL JFILEID(7)
                         REQID(WS-REQID)
        END-EXEC.
```

THE WRITE COMMAND

Function

File control. The WRITE command writes one record to a file. The file can be a VSAM KSDS, ESDS, RRDS, or path. (CICS also supports BDAM, and earlier releases supported ISAM. Those uncommonly used access methods aren't covered here.)

Syntax

```
EXEC CICS
     WRITE DATASET(name)
           FROM(data-area)
         [ LENGTH(data-value) ]
           RIDFLD(data-area)
         [ KEYLENGTH(data-value ]
         [ SYSID(name) ]
         [ RBA|RRN ]
         [ MASSINSERT ]
END-EXEC.
```

Options

DATASET

Specifies the one- to eight-character name of the data set to which a record is to be written.

FROM

Specifies the name of a data area from which the data record is moved.

LENGTH

Specifies a binary halfword (PIC S9(4) COMP) or literal value that indicates the length of the record to be written. Not required if the file has fixed-length records.

RIDFLD

Specifies a data area that identifies the record to be written. The contents of the RIDFLD field depends on whether RBA or RRN is specified; if neither is specified, the RIDFLD field contains a key for a VSAM KSDS or path or an ISAM file.

KEYLENGTH

Specifies a binary halfword (PIC S9(4) COMP) or literal value that indicates the length of the key. Used only when the SYSID option is also specified and RBA or RRN is not specified.

SYSID

Specifies the one- to four-character name of a remote system that contains the file.

RBA

Specifies that the RIDFLD field is a Relative Byte Address (RBA) for a VSAM ESDS. An RBA is a binary fullword (PIC S9(8) COMP). Since ESDS records are always written to the end of the file, the initial value of the RIDFLD field doesn't matter; when control returns, however, the RIDFLD field contains the RBA of the record that was written.

RRN

Specifies that the RIDFLD is a Relative Record Number (RRN) for a VSAM RRDS. An RRN is a binary fullword (PIC S9(8) COMP). The RRN of the first record in an RRDS is 1.

MASSINSERT

Specifies that the WRITE command is a part of a VSAM mass sequential insertion, which improves performance when many records are to be written to the file from a single task.

Exceptional conditions

Note: unless you provide for these conditions with a HANDLE CONDITION command, the task will be terminated if any of them occur.

DISABLED

(1.7 only) The data set is disabled, probably as a result of the master terminal operator explicitly dis abling the file using CEMT SET DISABLE.

DSIDERR

The data set name specified in the DATASET option isn't defined in the File Control Table.

DUPREC

A record with the specified key is already in the file. Can also occur if the record contains an alternate key value that already exists, the alternate index does not allow duplicate keys, and the alternate index is a part of the file's upgrade set or access is via the path.

ILLOGIC

A serious VSAM error occurred.

INVREQ

The WRITE request is prohibited by the file's FCT entry. Can also occur if the key value specified in the RIDFLD field doesn't agree with the key value contained within the record to be written or if the KEYLENGTH value is incorrect.

IOERR

An I/O error occurred.

ISCINVREQ

An undeterminable error occurred on the remote system (specified in the SYSID option).

LENGERR

The length specified in the LENGTH option exceeds the maximum record length allowed for the file.

NOSPACE

There is not enough space allocated to the data set to contain the record.

NOTAUTH

(1.7 only) The transaction's PCT entry specified that resource security checking should be done and the operator is not authorized to access the data set.

NOTOPEN

The file is not open.

SYSIDERR

The system identified by SYSID could not be located or accessed.

Notes and tips

- When you write a record to an ESDS, the record is always added to the end of the file. In that case, the initial value of the RIDFLD is ignored; CICS returns the RBA value of the record that was written in this field.

- If you need to write several records in ascending key sequence, you should use the MASSINSERT operation; MASSINSERT changes the technique VSAM uses to split control intervals and can be more efficient when records are written in sequential order. The

MASSINSERT operation is not considered complete until you issue an UNLOCK command, a SYNCPOINT command, or terminate your task. Usually, that's not significant. But if the same program (that is, the same task) reads records from the file after writing records with the MASSINSERT option, it should first issue an UNLOCK command.

- The only exceptional condition you usually need to handle for a WRITE command is DUPREC; the other conditions result from errors from which your program can't generally recover.

Coding example (fixed-length VSAM KSDS records)

This example writes a fixed-length record to a VSAM KSDS. The record is contained in the field named ACCOUNT-RECORD, and AR-AC-COUNT-NUMBER, which is a part of ACCOUNT-RECORD, contains the record's key value. The DUPREC condition is handled in case the record already exists.

```
   3100-WRITE-ACCOUNT-RECORD SECTION.
*
      EXEC CICS
          HANDLE CONDITION DUPREC(3100-DUPREC)
      END-EXEC.
      EXEC CICS
          WRITE DATASET('ACCOUNT')
                FROM(ACCOUNT-RECORD)
                RIDFLD(AR-ACCOUNT-NUMBER)
      END-EXEC.
      MOVE 'N' TO DUPLICATE-RECORD-SW.
      GO TO 3100-EXIT.
*
   3100-DUPREC.
*
      MOVE 'Y' TO DUPLICATE-RECORD-SW.
*
   3100-EXIT.
*
      EXIT.
```

WRITE

Coding example (variable-length VSAM ESDS records)

This example writes a record to a variable-length VSAM ESDS. The record is contained in AC-COUNT-RECORD, and ACCOUNT-RECORD-LENGTH indicates the record's length (in this case, 250 bytes). After the READ command completes, ACCOUNT-RECORD-RBA will contain the RBA of the account record that was written. No exceptional conditions are handled; any that might occur represent serious errors from which the program can't recover.

```
    3100-WRITE-ACCOUNT-RECORD SECTION.
*
        MOVE 250 TO ACCOUNT-RECORD-LENGTH.
        EXEC CICS
            WRITE DATASET('ACCOUNT')
                  FROM(ACCOUNT-RECORD)
                  LENGTH(ACCOUNT-RECORD-LENGTH)
                  RIDFLD(ACCOUNT-NUMBER-RBA)
                  RBA
        END-EXEC.
```

THE WRITEQ TD COMMAND

Function

Transient data control. The WRITEQ TD command writes a record to a specified transient data queue (also called a destination).

Syntax

```
EXEC CICS
    WRITEQ TD QUEUE(name)
              FROM(data-area)
            [ LENGTH(data-value) ]
            [ SYSID(name) ]
END-EXEC.
```

Options

QUEUE
Specifies the one- to eight-character name of the transient data queue to which data is written.

FROM
Specifies the name of a data area that contains the record to be written.

LENGTH
Specifies a binary halfword (PIC S9(4) COMP) or literal value that indicates the length of the record to be written. Not required for destinations with fixed-length records.

SYSID
Specifies the one- to four-character name of the remote system that contains the destination.

Exceptional conditions

Note: unless you provide for these conditions with a HANDLE CONDITION command, the task will be terminated if any of them occur.

IOERR
An I/O error occurred.

ISCINVREQ
An undeterminable error occurred on the remote system (specified in the SYSID option).

LENGERR
The length specified in the LENGTH option exceeds the maximum record length allowed for the destination.

NOSPACE
There is not enough space allocated to the destination to contain the record.

NOTAUTH

(1.7 only) The transaction's PCT entry specified that resource security checking should be done and the operator is not authorized to access the destination.

NOTOPEN

The destination is not open.

QIDERR

The destination specified in the QUEUE option isn't defined in the Destination Control Table (DCT).

SYSIDERR

The system identified by SYSID could not be located or accessed.

Notes and tips

- There are two types of transient data destinations: intrapartition and extrapartition. All intrapartition destinations are stored in a VSAM file called DFHNTRA; access to these destinations is efficient. Extrapartition destinations, however, are QSAM files managed not by CICS, but by the operating system. Because of the way CICS uses QSAM, extrapartition destinations are relatively inefficient. So avoid using them. (The syntax of the WRITEQ TD command is the same for both types of destinations.)

- An intrapartition destination can be used with automatic transaction initiation (ATI) so that a transaction is started as soon as the number of records in the destination reaches a specified trigger level. Because of this feature, intrapartition destinations are often used for applications in which data from one program needs to be temporarily gathered so it can be processed by another program.

- One common use of ATI is for printer applications: an ATI transaction reads records from a destination, formats the data, and sends it to a printer. This technique removes detailed printer considerations from the application program that creates the data to be printed; all that program has to do is issue WRITEQ TD commands to write records to the proper destination.

- The transient data facility provides no mechanism for holding a destination for exclusive use. If you need to write several uninterrupted records to a destination, use the ENQ and DEQ commands.

- You don't usually need to handle any of the exceptional conditions that result from the WRITEQ TD command; they represent error conditions from which your program can't generally recover.

Coding example

This example shows how to write a record to a destination. The destination's name is stored in a four-character alphanumeric field named DESTINA-TION-ID; the record is in PRINT-AREA, and LINE-LENGTH contains the number of bytes to be written. No exceptional conditions are handled.

```
    2220-WRITE-QUEUE-RECORD SECTION.
*
    EXEC CICS
        WRITE TD QUEUE(DESTINATION-ID)
                 FROM(PRINT-AREA)
                 LENGTH(LINE-LENGTH)
    END-EXEC.
```

THE WRITEQ TS COMMAND

Function

Temporary storage control. The WRITEQ TS command writes a record to a specified temporary storage queue.

Syntax

```
EXEC CICS
    WRITEQ TS QUEUE(name)
              FROM(data-area)
            [ LENGTH(data-value) ]
            [ ITEM(data-area) ]
            [ REWRITE ]
            [ SYSID(name) ]
            [ MAIN|AUXILIARY ]          1.7 only
            [ NOSUSPEND ]
END-EXEC.
```

Options

QUEUE
Specifies the one- to eight-character name of the temporary storage to which data is written.

FROM
Specifies the name of a data area that contains the record to be written.

LENGTH
Specifies a binary halfword (PIC S9(4) COMP) or literal value that indicates the length of the record to be written. Not required for queues with fixed-length records.

ITEM
Specifies a binary halfword data area (PIC S9(4) COMP). If you specify REWRITE, ITEM specifies the item number of the record you want to rewrite. If you don't specify REWRITE, the initial contents of ITEM are ignored; CICS returns the item number of the record in this field.

REWRITE
Specifies that the record should be rewritten.

SYSID
Specifies the one- to four-character name of the remote system that contains the destination.

MAIN
Specifies that the record should be held in main storage.

AUXILIARY
Specifies that the record should be written to the temporary storage data set.

NOSUSPEND
(1.7 only) Specifies that if there is not enough space for the record, the record should not be written; instead, control should be returned immediately to the first statement following the WRITEQ TS command.

Exceptional conditions

Note: unless you provide for these conditions with a HANDLE CONDITION command, the task will be terminated if any of them other than NOSPACE occur.

INVREQ
The LENGTH field specifies zero or the queue is unavailable.

IOERR
An I/O error occurred.

ISCINVREQ
An undeterminable error occurred on the remote system (specified in the SYSID option).

ITEMERR
No record exists for the item number specified by the ITEM option.

NOSPACE
There is not enough temporary storage space to contain the record. Unless a HANDLE CONDITION command is issued for NOSPACE, the task is suspended until space becomes available.

NOTAUTH
(1.7 only) The transaction's PCT entry specified that resource security checking should be done and the operator is not authorized to access the queue.

QIDERR
The specified queue does not exist.

SYSIDERR
The system identified by SYSID could not be located or accessed.

Notes and tips

- Temporary storage queues are automatically created when you write a record to a queue that doesn't yet exist. As a result, no special coding is required to create a queue.

- The MAIN and AUXILIARY options let you specify whether you want the record stored in virtual storage or on disk. If the data is going to exist for more than a few seconds, you should specify AUXILIARY.

- Temporary storage is often used instead of the communication area to save data between executions of a pseudo-conversational program. In general, I recommend you use temporary storage for this purpose unless the amount of data you're saving is small—say, 50 bytes or less. When the amount of data you're saving is that small, you're probably better off using the communication area, because a temporary storage record on disk requires almost that much main storage as overhead.

- In many applications that use temporary storage queues, you'll want the queue names to be unique. To ensure that a queue name is unique, use the terminal-id of the terminal that's attached to your task as a part of the name. The terminal-id is always available in the Execute Interface Block field EIBTERMID.

- You don't usually need to handle any of the exceptional conditions that result from the WRITEQ TS command; they represent error conditions from which your program can't generally recover.

Coding example (write a record)

This example shows how to write a record to a temporary storage queue. The queue's name is stored in an eight-character alphanumeric field named TS-QUEUE-NAME; the record is in TS-CUSTOMER-RECORD, and TS-QUEUE-LENGTH contains the number of bytes to be written. No exceptional conditions are handled.

```
    8100-WRITE-QUEUE-RECORD SECTION.
*
        EXEC CICS
            WRITE TS QUEUE(TS-QUEUE-NAME)
                     FROM(TS-CUSTOMER-RECORD)
                     LENGTH(TS-QUEUE-LENGTH)
        END-EXEC.
```

Coding example (rewrite a record)

This example shows how to rewrite a record in a queue. Here, TS-ITEM-NUMBER is set to 1 so that the first record in the queue is rewritten.

```
    1220-REWRITE-QUEUE-RECORD SECTION.
*
        EXEC CICS
            WRITEQ TS QUEUE(TS-QUEUE-NAME)
                      FROM(CUSTOMER-MASTER-RECORD)
                      LENGTH(TS-RECORD-LENGTH)
                      ITEM(TS-ITEM-NUMBER)
                      REWRITE
        END-EXEC.
```

THE XCTL COMMAND

Function

Program control. The XCTL command terminates the program that's currently executing and invokes the specified program. Data can be passed to the in-voked program. When the invoked program ends, control is not returned to the program that issued the XCTL command.

Syntax

```
EXEC CICS
    XCTL PROGRAM(name)
        [ COMMAREA(data-area) ]
        [ LENGTH(data-value) ]
END-EXEC.
```

Options

PROGRAM

Specifies the one- to eight-character name of the program to be invoked. This name must be defined in the Processing Program Table (PPT).

COMMAREA

Specifies a data area that's passed to the in-voked program as a communication area. The invoked program accesses the com-munication area via its DFHCOMMAREA field, which addresses a separate area of storage in which a copy of the specified data area has been placed. (This works differently than it does for a LINK command; see the description of that command for details.)

LENGTH

Specifies a binary halfword (PIC S9(4) COMP) or literal value that indicates the length of the data area specified in the COM-MAREA option; this option is required if you code COMMAREA.

Exceptional conditions

Note: unless you provide for these conditions with a HANDLE CONDITION command, the task will be terminated if any of them other than NOSPACE occur.

NOTAUTH

(1.7 only) The transaction's PCT entry specified that resource security checking should be done and the operator is not authorized to access the program.

PGMIDERR

The program is not defined in the Processing Program Table (PPT).

Notes and tips

- The XCTL command is commonly used to implement menu applications. The menu program itself uses an XCTL command to transfer control to a program selected by the operator. And application programs return control to the menu program by issuing an XCTL command.

- If you need to return control to the invoking program, you may need to use LINK instead of XCTL. If you invoke a program with LINK, you can return control to the point following the LINK command by issuing a RETURN command. When you use LINK, however, CICS must keep the invoking program in virtual storage while the linked program executes. Since that can be inefficient, use XCTL rather than LINK whenever possible.

- You don't usually need to handle any of the exceptional conditions that result from the XCTL command; they represent error conditions from which your program can't generally recover. In menu applications, you might want to handle the PGMIDERR condition and simply notify the operator that an application is not available if PGMIDERR occurs. And you might want to handle the NOTAUTH condition and notify the operator that he or she isn't authorized to access the application if it occurs.

Coding example

This example shows how the XCTL command might be used in a menu application to transfer control to a program selected by the operator. Since users who are authorized to use the menu may not be authorized to use all of its selections, the NOTAUTH condition is handled. And PGMIDERR is handled in case a program is unavailable. In the XCTL command, OPERATOR-SELECTED-PROGRAM is an 8-byte field defined in the Working-Storage Section; it contains the name of the program to be invoked. A 100-byte communication area is passed to the invoked program.

```
    1000-XFER-TO-APPLICATION SECTION.
*
    EXEC CICS
        HANDLE CONDITION NOTAUTH(1000-NOTAUTH)
                         PGMIDERR(1000-PGMIDERR)
    END-EXEC.
    EXEC CICS
        XCTL PROGRAM(OPERATOR-SELECTED-PROGRAM)
            COMMAREA(COMMUNICATION-AREA)
            LENGTH(100)
    END-EXEC.
*
    1000-NOTAUTH.
*
    MOVE 'Y' TO PROGRAM-ERROR-SW.
    MOVE 'YOU ARE NOT AUTHORIZED TO RUN THAT APPLICATION'
        TO ERROR-MESSAGE.
*
    1000-PGMIDERR.
*
    MOVE 'Y' TO PROGRAM-ERROR-SW.
    MOVE 'THAT APPLICATION IS NOT AVAILABLE'
        TO ERROR-MESSAGE.
*
    1000-EXIT.
*
    EXIT.
```

Section 5

Model CICS programs

This section presents seven complete CICS programs that you can use as models for your own programs. Each of these programs is reproduced from either *Part 1* or *Part 2* of *CICS for the COBOL Programmer*. The seven programs are:

1. The menu program that appeared in Chapter 9 of *Part 1*. This program displays a menu of operator selections on the display, accepts an operator's selection, and branches to an appropriate program.

2. The *order entry program* from Chapter 9 of *Part 1*. This data-entry program accepts data for a customer order, edits it, and writes records to a VSAM file.

3. The *customer maintenance program* from Chapter 4 of *Part 2*. This program lets an operator add, change, or delete records in a customer master file. Temporary storage is used to keep a copy of the customer record across program executions to ensure that another operator doesn't access a record while it's being updated. (A simpler version of this program without the temporary storage function appeared in *Part 1*).

4. The *customer inquiry program* from Chapter 2 of *Part 2*. This program accepts a customer number from the operator and retrieves the corresponding record from the customer master file as well as related records from an invoice file. An alternate index is used to access the invoice file by the alternate key, customer number. The file's primary key is the invoice number.

5. The transient data version of the *inventory listing program* from Chapter 5 of *Part 2*. This program reads records from an inventory file and formats a printed report, which is sent to a printer via a transient data destination. (Another program is responsible for reading records from the queue and writing them on the printer; that program is described in Chapter 8 of *Part 2*.)

6. The SEND TEXT version of the *inventory listing program* from Chapter 6 of *Part 2*. This program uses the SEND TEXT command to create a BMS logical message that can be displayed or printed.

7. The SEND MAP version of the *inventory listing program* from Chapter 6 of *Part 2*. This program is similar to program 6 except that it uses the SEND MAP command and a BMS mapset rather than the SEND TEXT command to format the logical message.

The inventory menu program

```
Program:   INVMENU   Inventory application menu        Page: 1
Designer:  Doug Lowe                                    Date: 08-01-87
----------------------------------------------------------------------
Process specifications
----------------------------------------------------------------------
1.    Accept a single digit representing the operator's program
      selection and branch to the appropriate program using an
      XCTL command.

2.    If the operator presses the clear key, end the session by
      issuing a RETURN command without the TRANSID option.

3.    Use the pseudo-conversational programming technique.  Test the
      communication area length to determine if the operator invoked
      the program directly by entering a trans-id; if the communication
      area length is zero, format the screen and issue a RETURN command
      with the TRANSID option.
```

Specifications for the inventory application menu

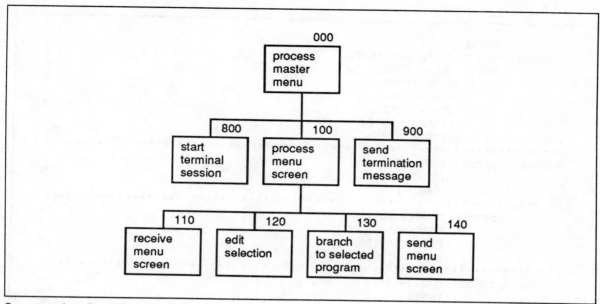

Structure chart for the menu program

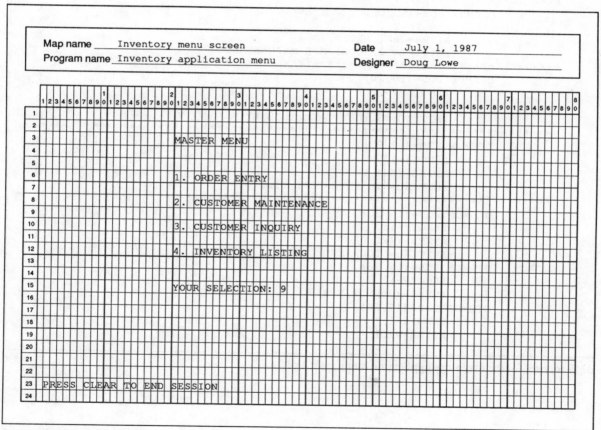

Screen layout for the menu program

```
          PRINT NOGEN
MENUSET   DFHMSD TYPE=&SYSPARM,                                          X
               LANG=COBOL,                                              X
               MODE=INOUT,                                              X
               TERM=3270-2,                                             X
               CTRL=FREEKB,                                             X
               STORAGE=AUTO,                                            X
               TIOAPFX=YES
*******************************************************************
MENUMAP   DFHMDI SIZE=(24,80),                                          X
               LINE=1,                                                  X
               COLUMN=1
*******************************************************************
          DFHMDF POS=(3,20),                                            X
               LENGTH=11,                                               X
               ATTRB=(BRT,PROT),                                        X
               INITIAL='MASTER MENU'
*******************************************************************
          DFHMDF POS=(6,20),                                            X
               LENGTH=14,                                               X
               ATTRB=(BRT,PROT),                                        X
               INITIAL='1. ORDER ENTRY'
*******************************************************************
          DFHMDF POS=(8,20),                                            X
               LENGTH=23,                                               X
               ATTRB=(BRT,PROT),                                        X
               INITIAL='2. CUSTOMER MAINTENANCE'
*******************************************************************
          DFHMDF POS=(10,20),                                           X
               LENGTH=19,                                               X
               ATTRB=(BRT,PROT),                                        X
               INITIAL='3. CUSTOMER INQUIRY'
*******************************************************************
          DFHMDF POS=(12,20),                                           X
               LENGTH=20,                                               X
               ATTRB=(BRT,PROT),                                        X
               INITIAL='4. INVENTORY LISTING'
*******************************************************************
          DFHMDF POS=(15,20),                                           X
               LENGTH=15,                                               X
               ATTRB=(BRT,PROT),                                        X
               INITIAL='YOUR SELECTION:'
SELECT    DFHMDF POS=(15,36),                                           X
               LENGTH=1,                                                X
               ATTRB=(UNPROT,NUM)
          DFHMDF POS=(15,38),                                           X
               LENGTH=1,                                                X
               ATTRB=PROT
```

BMS mapset for the inventory application menu (part 1 of 2)

```
**********************************************************************
          DFHMDF POS=(23,1),                                          X
                LENGTH=26,                                            X
                ATTRB=(BRT,PROT),                                     X
                INITIAL='PRESS CLEAR TO END SESSION'
ERROR     DFHMDF POS=(24,1),                                          X
                LENGTH=77,                                            X
                ATTRB=(BRT,PROT)
DUMMY     DFHMDF POS=(24,79),                                         X
                LENGTH=1,                                             X
                ATTRB=(DRK,PROT,FSET),                                X
                INITIAL=' '
**********************************************************************
          DFHMSD TYPE=FINAL
          END
```

BMS mapset for the inventory application menu (part 2 of 2)

```
 01  MENU-MAP.
*
     05  FILLER                   PIC X(12).
*
     05  MM-L-SELECTION           PIC S9(4)   COMP.
     05  MM-A-SELECTION           PIC X.
     05  MM-D-SELECTION           PIC 9.
*
     05  MM-L-ERROR-MESSAGE       PIC S9(4)   COMP.
     05  MM-A-ERROR-MESSAGE       PIC X.
     05  MM-D-ERROR-MESSAGE       PIC X(77).
*
     05  MM-L-DUMMY               PIC S9(4)   COMP.
     05  MM-A-DUMMY               PIC X.
     05  MM-D-DUMMY               PIC X.
```

Programmer-generated symbolic map for the inventory application menu

```
     IDENTIFICATION DIVISION.
*
     PROGRAM-ID.  INVMENU.
*
     ENVIRONMENT DIVISION.
*
     DATA DIVISION.
*
     WORKING-STORAGE SECTION.
*
     01   SWITCHES.
*
         05   END-SESSION-SW         PIC X     VALUE 'N'.
              88   END-SESSION                 VALUE 'Y'.
         05   VALID-DATA-SW          PIC X     VALUE 'Y'.
              88   VALID-DATA                  VALUE 'Y'.
*
     01   WORK-FIELDS.
*
         05   WS-PROGRAM-NAME        PIC X(8)  VALUE SPACE.
*
     01   END-OF-SESSION-MESSAGE     PIC X(13) VALUE 'SESSION ENDED'.
*
     01   COMMUNICATION-AREA         PIC X.
*
     COPY MENUSET.
*
     LINKAGE SECTION.
*
     01   DFHCOMMAREA                PIC X.
*
     PROCEDURE DIVISION.
*
     000-PROCESS-MASTER-MENU SECTION.
*
         IF EIBCALEN = ZERO
             PERFORM 800-START-TERMINAL-SESSION
         ELSE
             PERFORM 100-PROCESS-MENU-SCREEN.
         IF END-SESSION
             PERFORM 900-SEND-TERMINATION-MESSAGE
             EXEC CICS
                  RETURN
             END-EXEC
         ELSE
             EXEC CICS
                  RETURN TRANSID('MENU')
                         COMMAREA(COMMUNICATION-AREA)
                         LENGTH(1)
             END-EXEC.
*
```

Source listing for the menu program (part 1 of 3)

```
    100-PROCESS-MENU-SCREEN SECTION.
*
        PERFORM 110-RECEIVE-MENU-SCREEN.
        IF NOT END-SESSION
            IF VALID-DATA
                PERFORM 120-EDIT-SELECTION
                IF VALID-DATA
                    PERFORM 130-BRANCH-TO-SELECTED-PROGRAM.
        IF NOT END-SESSION
            PERFORM 140-SEND-MENU-SCREEN.
*
    110-RECEIVE-MENU-SCREEN SECTION.
*
        EXEC CICS
            HANDLE AID CLEAR(110-CLEAR-KEY)
                       ANYKEY(110-ANYKEY)
        END-EXEC.
        EXEC CICS
            RECEIVE MAP('MENUMAP')
                    MAPSET('MENUSET')
                    INTO(MENU-MAP)
        END-EXEC.
        GO TO 110-EXIT.
*
    110-CLEAR-KEY.
*
        MOVE 'Y' TO END-SESSION-SW.
        GO TO 110-EXIT.
*
    110-ANYKEY.
*
        MOVE 'N' TO VALID-DATA-SW.
        MOVE 'INVALID KEY PRESSED' TO MM-D-ERROR-MESSAGE.
*
    110-EXIT.
*
        EXIT.
*
    120-EDIT-SELECTION SECTION.
*
        IF MM-D-SELECTION NOT NUMERIC
            MOVE 'N' TO VALID-DATA-SW
            MOVE 'INVALID SELECTION' TO MM-D-ERROR-MESSAGE
        ELSE IF MM-D-SELECTION = 1
            MOVE 'ORDRENT' TO WS-PROGRAM-NAME
        ELSE IF MM-D-SELECTION = 2
            MOVE 'CUSTMNT' TO WS-PROGRAM-NAME
        ELSE IF MM-D-SELECTION = 3
            MOVE 'CUSTINQ' TO WS-PROGRAM-NAME
        ELSE IF MM-D-SELECTION = 4
            MOVE 'INVLST' TO WS-PROGRAM-NAME
        ELSE
            MOVE 'N' TO VALID-DATA-SW
            MOVE 'INVALID SELECTION' TO MM-D-ERROR-MESSAGE.
```

Source listing for the menu program (part 2 of 3)

```
*
  130-BRANCH-TO-SELECTED-PROGRAM SECTION.
*
      EXEC CICS
          HANDLE CONDITION PGMIDERR(130-PGMIDERR)
      END-EXEC.
      EXEC CICS
          XCTL PROGRAM(WS-PROGRAM-NAME)
      END-EXEC.
      GO TO 130-EXIT.
*
  130-PGMIDERR.
*
      MOVE 'N' TO VALID-DATA-SW.
      MOVE 'THAT PROGRAM CANNOT BE FOUND' TO MM-D-ERROR-MESSAGE.
*
  130-EXIT.
*
      EXIT.
*
  140-SEND-MENU-SCREEN SECTION.
*
      MOVE -1 TO MM-L-SELECTION.
      EXEC CICS
          SEND MAP('MENUMAP')
              MAPSET('MENUSET')
              FROM(MENU-MAP)
              DATAONLY
              CURSOR
      END-EXEC.
*
  800-START-TERMINAL-SESSION SECTION.
*
      MOVE LOW-VALUE TO MENU-MAP.
      MOVE -1 TO MM-L-SELECTION.
      EXEC CICS
          SEND MAP('MENUMAP')
              MAPSET('MENUSET')
              FROM(MENU-MAP)
              ERASE
              CURSOR
      END-EXEC.
*
  900-SEND-TERMINATION-MESSAGE SECTION.
*
      EXEC CICS
          SEND TEXT FROM(END-OF-SESSION-MESSAGE)
                    LENGTH(13)
                    ERASE
                    FREEKB
      END-EXEC.
```

Source listing for the menu program (part 3 of 3)

The order entry program

```
Program:   ORDRENT   Order entry              Page: 1
Designer:  Doug Lowe                           Date: 08-01-87
================================================================
Input/output specifications
----------------------------------------------------------------
File       Description

CUSTMAS    Customer master file
INVMAST    Inventory master file
INVOICE    Invoice file
================================================================
Process specifications
----------------------------------------------------------------
Until the operator indicates the end of the terminal session by using
the CLEAR key in step 1:

1.    Get order data from the entry screen.  If the operator doesn't
      press the CLEAR key, edit the data according to these rules:

            customer number    must be in the customer file
            item number        must be in the inventory file
                               at least one item number must be entered
            quantity           must be numeric and greater than zero
                               must have accompanying item number

2.    If the data edited in step 1 is valid, format and send a
      verification screen to the terminal.  If the data is invalid,
      format an appropriate error message and redisplay the entry
      screen.

3.    If the operator presses the enter key from the verify screen, post
      the order by formatting and writing an invoice record; invoke the
      GETINV subprogram to obtain a valid invoice number.  If the
      operator presses PA1 from the verify screen, redisplay the entry
      screen so the operator can make any required changes.  If the
      operator presses the clear key from the verify screen, erase the
      order data and redisplay the entry screen so the operator can
      start over.

4.    Use the pseudo-conversational programming technique.  Use the
      communication area to keep track of which screen is being
      processed.  When control is transferred to this  program from the
      menu program, no communication area is passed.
```

Specifications for the order entry program

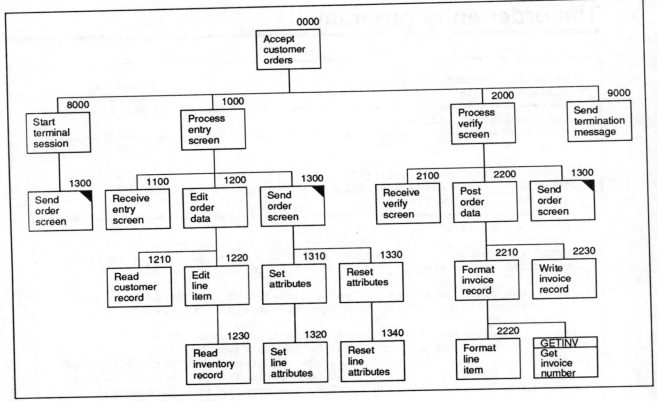

Structure chart for the order entry program

| Map name | Order entry screen | Date | July 1, 1987 |
| Program name | Order entry | Designer | Doug Lowe |

```
          1         2         3         4         5         6         7         8
1234567890123456789012345678901234567890123456789012345678901234567890123456789 0
1  ORDER ENTRY
2
3  CUSTOMER NUMBER: XXXXX        XXXXXXXXXXXXXXXXXXXXXXXXXXXXXX
4  P.O. NUMBER:     XXXXXXXXXX
5
6  ITEM NO   QUANTITY   DESCRIPTION              UNIT PRICE      AMOUNT
7
8   99999     99999    XXXXXXXXXXXXXXXXXXXXXX    ZZ,ZZ9.99    ZZ,ZZ9.99
9   99999     99999    XXXXXXXXXXXXXXXXXXXXXX    ZZ,ZZ9.99    ZZ,ZZ9.99
10  99999     99999    XXXXXXXXXXXXXXXXXXXXXX    ZZ,ZZ9.99    ZZ,ZZ9.99
11  99999     99999    XXXXXXXXXXXXXXXXXXXXXX    ZZ,ZZ9.99    ZZ,ZZ9.99
12  99999     99999    XXXXXXXXXXXXXXXXXXXXXX    ZZ,ZZ9.99    ZZ,ZZ9.99
13  99999     99999    XXXXXXXXXXXXXXXXXXXXXX    ZZ,ZZ9.99    ZZ,ZZ9.99
14  99999     99999    XXXXXXXXXXXXXXXXXXXXXX    ZZ,ZZ9.99    ZZ,ZZ9.99
15  99999     99999    XXXXXXXXXXXXXXXXXXXXXX    ZZ,ZZ9.99    ZZ,ZZ9.99
16  99999     99999    XXXXXXXXXXXXXXXXXXXXXX    ZZ,ZZ9.99    ZZ,ZZ9.99
17  99999     99999    XXXXXXXXXXXXXXXXXXXXXX    ZZ,ZZ9.99    ZZ,ZZ9.99
18
19                                      INVOICE TOTAL:  ZZ,ZZ9.99
20
21
22
23 XXXXXXXXXXXXXXXXXXXXXXXXXXXXXXXXXXXXXXXXXXXXXXXXXXXXXXXXXXXXXXXXXXXXXXXXXXXXXXXX
24 XXXXXXXXXXXXXXXXXXXXXXXXXXXXXXXXXXXXXXXXXXXXXXXXXXXXXXXXXXXXXXXXXXXXXXXXXXXXXXXXX
```

Screen layout for the order entry program

```
            PRINT NOGEN                                                X
ORDSET1     DFHMSD TYPE=&SYSPARM,                                       X
                   LANG=COBOL,                                          X
                   TERM=3270-2,                                         X
                   MODE=INOUT,                                          X
                   CTRL=FREEKB,                                         X
                   STORAGE=AUTO,                                        X
                   TIOAPFX=YES
*************************************************************************
                                                                       X
ORDMAP1     DFHMDI SIZE=(24,80),                                       X
                   LINE=1,
                   COLUMN=1
*************************************************************************
            DFHMDF POS=(1,1),                                          X
                   LENGTH=11,                                          X
                   ATTRB=(BRT,PROT),                                   X
                   INITIAL='ORDER ENTRY'
*************************************************************************
            DFHMDF POS=(3,1),                                          X
                   LENGTH=16,                                          X
                   ATTRB=(BRT,PROT),                                   X
                   INITIAL='CUSTOMER NUMBER:'
CUSTNO      DFHMDF POS=(3,18),                                         X
                   LENGTH=5,                                           X
                   ATTRB=UNPROT
            DFHMDF POS=(3,24),                                         X
                   LENGTH=1,                                           X
                   ATTRB=ASKIP
*************************************************************************
NAME        DFHMDF POS=(3,30),                                         X
                   LENGTH=30,                                          X
                   ATTRB=PROT
*************************************************************************
            DFHMDF POS=(4,1),                                          X
                   LENGTH=12,                                          X
                   ATTRB=(BRT,PROT),                                   X
                   INITIAL='P.O. NUMBER:'
PO          DFHMDF POS=(4,18),                                         X
                   LENGTH=10,                                          X
                   ATTRB=UNPROT
            DFHMDF POS=(4,29),                                         X
                   LENGTH=1,                                           X
                   ATTRB=ASKIP
*************************************************************************
            DFHMDF POS=(6,1),                                          X
                   LENGTH=30,                                          X
                   ATTRB=(BRT,PROT),                                   X
                   INITIAL='ITEM NO  QUANTITY   DESCRIPTION'
            DFHMDF POS=(6,42),                                         X
                   LENGTH=20,                                          X
                   ATTRB=(BRT,PROT),                                   X
                   INITIAL='UNIT PRICE      AMOUNT'
```

BMS mapset for the order entry program (part 1 of 2)

```
*********************************************************************
*          LINE ITEM 1                                              *
*********************************************************************
ITEMNO1  DFHMDF POS=(8,2),                                          X
                LENGTH=5,                                           X
                ATTRB=(UNPROT,NUM),                                 X
                PICIN='9(5)'
         DFHMDF POS=(8,8),                                          X
                LENGTH=1,                                           X
                ATTRB=ASKIP
QTY1     DFHMDF POS=(8,11),                                         X
                LENGTH=5,                                           X
                ATTRB=(UNPROT,NUM),                                 X
                PICIN='9(5)'
         DFHMDF POS=(8,17),                                         X
                LENGTH=1,                                           X
                ATTRB=ASKIP
DESCR1   DFHMDF POS=(8,20),                                         X
                LENGTH=20,                                          X
                ATTRB=PROT
UPRICE1  DFHMDF POS=(8,42),                                         X
                LENGTH=9,                                           X
                ATTRB=PROT,                                         X
                PICOUT='ZZ,ZZ9.99'
AMOUNT1  DFHMDF POS=(8,53),                                         X
                LENGTH=9,                                           X
                ATTRB=PROT,                                         X
                PICOUT='ZZ,ZZ9.99'
         .
         .
         .
```

> The BMS macro instructions that define line items 2 through 10 are similar to those that define line item 1.

```
*********************************************************************
         DFHMDF POS=(19,37),                                        X
                LENGTH=14,                                          X
                ATTRB=(BRT,PROT),                                   X
                INITIAL='INVOICE TOTAL:'
TOTAL    DFHMDF POS=(19,53),                                        X
                LENGTH=9,                                           X
                ATTRB=PROT,                                         X
                PICOUT='ZZ,ZZ9.99'
*********************************************************************
MESSAGE  DFHMDF POS=(23,1),                                         X
                LENGTH=79,                                          X
                ATTRB=(BRT,PROT)
ERROR    DFHMDF POS=(24,1),                                         X
                LENGTH=77,                                          X
                ATTRB=(BRT,PROT)
DUMMY    DFHMDF POS=(24,79),                                        X
                LENGTH=1,                                           X
                ATTRB=(DRK,PROT,FSET),                              X
                INITIAL=' '
*********************************************************************
         DFHMSD TYPE=FINAL
         END
```

BMS mapset for the order entry program (part 2 of 2)

```
    01  ORDER-ENTRY-MAP.
*
        05  FILLER                          PIC X(12).
*
        05  OEM-L-CUSTOMER-NUMBER           PIC S9(4)   COMP.
        05  OEM-A-CUSTOMER-NUMBER           PIC X.
        05  OEM-D-CUSTOMER-NUMBER           PIC X(5).
*
        05  OEM-L-NAME                      PIC S9(4)   COMP.
        05  OEM-A-NAME                      PIC X.
        05  OEM-D-NAME                      PIC X(30).
*
        05  OEM-L-PO-NUMBER                 PIC S9(4)   COMP.
        05  OEM-A-PO-NUMBER                 PIC X.
        05  OEM-D-PO-NUMBER                 PIC X(10).
*
        05  OEM-LINE-ITEM                   OCCURS 10.
*
            10  OEM-L-ITEM-NUMBER           PIC S9(4)   COMP.
            10  OEM-A-ITEM-NUMBER           PIC X.
            10  OEM-D-ITEM-NUMBER           PIC 9(5).
*
            10  OEM-L-QUANTITY              PIC S9(4)   COMP.
            10  OEM-A-QUANTITY              PIC X.
            10  OEM-D-QUANTITY              PIC 9(5).
*
            10  OEM-L-ITEM-DESCRIPTION      PIC S9(4)   COMP.
            10  OEM-A-ITEM-DESCRIPTION      PIC X.
            10  OEM-D-ITEM-DESCRIPTION      PIC X(20).
*
            10  OEM-L-UNIT-PRICE            PIC S9(4)   COMP.
            10  OEM-A-UNIT-PRICE            PIC X.
            10  OEM-D-UNIT-PRICE            PIC ZZ,ZZ9.99
                                            BLANK WHEN ZERO.
*
            10  OEM-L-EXTENSION             PIC S9(4)   COMP.
            10  OEM-A-EXTENSION             PIC X.
            10  OEM-D-EXTENSION             PIC ZZ,ZZ9.99
                                            BLANK WHEN ZERO.
*
        05  OEM-L-INVOICE-TOTAL             PIC S9(4)   COMP.
        05  OEM-A-INVOICE-TOTAL             PIC X.
        05  OEM-D-INVOICE-TOTAL             PIC ZZ,ZZ9.99
                                            BLANK WHEN ZERO.
*
        05  OEM-L-OPERATOR-MESSAGE          PIC S9(4)   COMP.
        05  OEM-A-OPERATOR-MESSAGE          PIC X.
        05  OEM-D-OPERATOR-MESSAGE          PIC X(79).
*
        05  OEM-L-ERROR-MESSAGE             PIC S9(4)   COMP.
        05  OEM-A-ERROR-MESSAGE             PIC X.
        05  OEM-D-ERROR-MESSAGE             PIC X(77).
*
        05  OEM-L-DUMMY                     PIC S9(4)   COMP.
        05  OEM-A-DUMMY                     PIC X.
        05  OEM-D-DUMMY                     PIC X.
```

Programmer-generated symbolic map for the order entry program

```
    01  FIELD-ATTRIBUTE-DEFINITIONS.
*
        05  FAC-UNPROT                     PIC X    VALUE ' '.
        05  FAC-UNPROT-MDT                 PIC X    VALUE 'A'.
        05  FAC-UNPROT-BRT                 PIC X    VALUE 'H'.
        05  FAC-UNPROT-BRT-MDT             PIC X    VALUE 'I'.
        05  FAC-UNPROT-DARK                PIC X    VALUE '<'.
        05  FAC-UNPROT-DARK-MDT            PIC X    VALUE '('.
        05  FAC-UNPROT-NUM                 PIC X    VALUE '&'.
        05  FAC-UNPROT-NUM-MDT             PIC X    VALUE 'J'.
        05  FAC-UNPROT-NUM-BRT             PIC X    VALUE 'Q'.
        05  FAC-UNPROT-NUM-BRT-MDT         PIC X    VALUE 'R'.
        05  FAC-UNPROT-NUM-DARK            PIC X    VALUE '*'.
        05  FAC-UNPROT-NUM-DARK-MDT        PIC X    VALUE ')'.
        05  FAC-PROT                       PIC X    VALUE '-'.
        05  FAC-PROT-MDT                   PIC X    VALUE '/'.
        05  FAC-PROT-BRT                   PIC X    VALUE 'Y'.
        05  FAC-PROT-BRT-MDT               PIC X    VALUE 'Z'.
        05  FAC-PROT-DARK                  PIC X    VALUE '%'.
        05  FAC-PROT-DARK-MDT              PIC X    VALUE ']'.
        05  FAC-PROT-NUM                   PIC X    VALUE '0'.
        05  FAC-PROT-NUM-MDT               PIC X    VALUE '1'.
        05  FAC-PROT-NUM-BRT               PIC X    VALUE '8'.
        05  FAC-PROT-NUM-BRT-MDT           PIC X    VALUE '9'.
        05  FAC-PROT-NUM-DARK              PIC X    VALUE '@'.
        05  FAC-PROT-NUM-DARK-MDT          PIC X    VALUE QUOTE.
```

The FACDEFN COPY member

```
       IDENTIFICATION DIVISION.
*
       PROGRAM-ID.  ORDRENT.
*
       ENVIRONMENT DIVISION.
*
       DATA DIVISION.
*
       WORKING-STORAGE SECTION.
*
       01  SWITCHES.
*
           05  END-SESSION-SW              PIC X   VALUE 'N'.
               88  END-SESSION                     VALUE 'Y'.
           05  VALID-DATA-SW               PIC X   VALUE 'Y'.
               88  VALID-DATA                      VALUE 'Y'.
           05  CUSTOMER-FOUND-SW           PIC X   VALUE 'Y'.
               88  CUSTOMER-FOUND                  VALUE 'Y'.
           05  ITEM-FOUND-SW               PIC X   VALUE 'Y'.
               88  ITEM-FOUND                      VALUE 'Y'.
           05  VALID-QUANTITY-SW           PIC X   VALUE 'Y'.
               88  VALID-QUANTITY                  VALUE 'Y'.
*
       01  FLAGS.
*
           05  ORDER-VERIFICATION-FLAG     PIC X   VALUE '0'.
               88  POST-ORDER                      VALUE '1'.
               88  MODIFY-ORDER                    VALUE '2'.
               88  CANCEL-ORDER                    VALUE '3'.
           05  ATTRIBUTE-CONTROL-FLAG      PIC X   VALUE '0'.
               88  SET-PROTECTED                   VALUE '1'.
               88  SET-UNPROTECTED                 VALUE '2'.
           05  SEND-CONTROL-FLAG           PIC X   VALUE '0'.
               88  SEND-ALL                        VALUE '1'.
               88  SEND-DATAONLY                   VALUE '2'.
*
       01  WORK-FIELDS.
*
           05  LINE-ITEM-SUB               PIC S9(4)     COMP.
           05  LINE-ITEM-COUNT             PIC S9(4)     COMP.
*
       01  TOTAL-LINE.
*
           05  TL-TOTAL-ORDERS    PIC ZZ9.
           05  FILLER             PIC X(15)   VALUE ' ORDERS ENTERED'.
           05  FILLER             PIC X(15)   VALUE '.  PRESS ENTER '.
           05  FILLER             PIC X(15)   VALUE 'TO RETURN TO ME'.
           05  FILLER             PIC X(3)    VALUE 'NU.'.
*
       01  COMMUNICATION-AREA.
*
           05  CA-PROCESS-FLAG            PIC X.
               88  PROCESS-ENTRY-SCREEN   VALUE '1'.
               88  PROCESS-VERIFY-SCREEN  VALUE '2'.
```

Source listing for the order entry program (part 1 of 11)

```
        05   CA-UNIT-PRICE                  OCCURS 10
                                            PIC S9(5)V99   COMP-3.
        05   CA-TOTAL-ORDERS                PIC S9(3)      COMP-3
                                            VALUE ZERO.
    *
      01   INVOICE-RECORD.
    *
        05   INV-INVOICE-NUMBER             PIC 9(5).
        05   INV-INVOICE-DATE               PIC 9(6).
        05   INV-CUSTOMER-NUMBER            PIC X(5).
        05   INV-PO-NUMBER                  PIC X(10).
        05   INV-LINE-ITEM                  OCCURS 10.
             10   INV-ITEM-NUMBER           PIC X(5).
             10   INV-QUANTITY              PIC S9(5)      COMP-3.
             10   INV-UNIT-PRICE            PIC S9(5)V99   COMP-3.
             10   INV-EXTENSION             PIC S9(5)V99   COMP-3.
        05   INV-INVOICE-TOTAL              PIC S9(5)V99   COMP-3.
    *
      01   CUSTOMER-MASTER-RECORD.
    *
        05   CM-CUSTOMER-NUMBER             PIC X(5).
        05   CM-NAME                        PIC X(30).
        05   CM-ADDRESS                     PIC X(30).
        05   CM-CITY                        PIC X(21).
        05   CM-STATE                       PIC XX.
        05   CM-ZIP-CODE                    PIC X(5).
    *
      01   INVENTORY-MASTER-RECORD.
    *
        05   IM-ITEM-NUMBER                 PIC X(5).
        05   IM-ITEM-DESCRIPTION            PIC X(20).
        05   IM-UNIT-PRICE                  PIC S9(5)V99   COMP-3.
        05   IM-ON-HAND-QUANTITY            PIC S9(5)      COMP-3.
    *
    COPY   ORDSET1.
    *
    COPY FACDEFN.
    *
    LINKAGE SECTION.
    *
      01   DFHCOMMAREA                      PIC X(43).
    *
      01   BLL-CELLS.
    *
        05   FILLER                         PIC S9(8)      COMP.
        05   BLL-CWA                        PIC S9(8)      COMP.
    *
      01   COMMON-WORK-AREA.
    *
        05   CWA-DATE                       PIC 9(6).
    *
```

Source listing for the order entry program (part 2 of 11)

```
     PROCEDURE DIVISION.
*
 0000-ACCEPT-CUSTOMER-ORDERS SECTION.
*
     EXEC CICS
         ADDRESS CWA(BLL-CWA)
     END-EXEC.
     IF EIBCALEN = ZERO
         PERFORM 8000-START-TERMINAL-SESSION
     ELSE
         MOVE DFHCOMMAREA TO COMMUNICATION-AREA
         IF PROCESS-ENTRY-SCREEN
             PERFORM 1000-PROCESS-ENTRY-SCREEN
         ELSE IF PROCESS-VERIFY-SCREEN
             PERFORM 2000-PROCESS-VERIFY-SCREEN.
     IF END-SESSION
         PERFORM 9000-SEND-TERMINATION-MESSAGE
         EXEC CICS
             RETURN TRANSID('MENU')
         END-EXEC
     ELSE
         EXEC CICS
             RETURN TRANSID('ORD1')
                    COMMAREA(COMMUNICATION-AREA)
                    LENGTH(43)
         END-EXEC.
*
 1000-PROCESS-ENTRY-SCREEN SECTION.
*
     PERFORM 1100-RECEIVE-ENTRY-SCREEN.
     IF NOT END-SESSION
         IF VALID-DATA
             PERFORM 1200-EDIT-ORDER-DATA.
     IF NOT END-SESSION
         IF VALID-DATA
             MOVE 'PRESS ENTER TO POST ORDER, PA1 TO MODIFY ORDER,
-                  ' OR CLEAR TO CANCEL ORDER'
                 TO OEM-D-OPERATOR-MESSAGE
             MOVE SPACE TO OEM-D-ERROR-MESSAGE
             MOVE '1' TO ATTRIBUTE-CONTROL-FLAG
             MOVE '2' TO SEND-CONTROL-FLAG
             PERFORM 1300-SEND-ORDER-SCREEN
             MOVE '2' TO CA-PROCESS-FLAG
         ELSE
             MOVE 'ERRORS DETECTED--MAKE CORRECTIONS OR PRESS CLEA
-                  'R TO END SESSION' TO OEM-D-OPERATOR-MESSAGE
             MOVE '0' TO ATTRIBUTE-CONTROL-FLAG
             MOVE '2' TO SEND-CONTROL-FLAG
             PERFORM 1300-SEND-ORDER-SCREEN
             MOVE '1' TO CA-PROCESS-FLAG.
*
```

Source listing for the order entry program (part 3 of 11)

```
    1100-RECEIVE-ENTRY-SCREEN SECTION.
*
        EXEC CICS
            HANDLE AID CLEAR(1100-CLEAR-KEY)
                       ANYKEY(1100-ANYKEY)
        END-EXEC.
        EXEC CICS
            RECEIVE MAP('ORDMAP1')
                    MAPSET('ORDSET1')
                    INTO(ORDER-ENTRY-MAP)
        END-EXEC.
        GO TO 1100-EXIT.
*
    1100-CLEAR-KEY.
*
        MOVE 'Y' TO END-SESSION-SW.
        GO TO 1100-EXIT.
*
    1100-ANYKEY.
*
        MOVE LOW-VALUE TO ORDER-ENTRY-MAP.
        MOVE -1 TO OEM-L-CUSTOMER-NUMBER.
        MOVE 'N' TO VALID-DATA-SW.
        MOVE 'INVALID KEY PRESSED' TO OEM-D-ERROR-MESSAGE.
*
    1100-EXIT.
*
        EXIT.
*
    1200-EDIT-ORDER-DATA SECTION.
*
        MOVE FAC-UNPROT-NUM-MDT TO OEM-A-CUSTOMER-NUMBER.
*
        MOVE ZERO TO LINE-ITEM-COUNT
                     INV-INVOICE-TOTAL.
        PERFORM 1220-EDIT-LINE-ITEM
            VARYING LINE-ITEM-SUB FROM 10 BY -1
            UNTIL LINE-ITEM-SUB < 1.
        MOVE INV-INVOICE-TOTAL TO OEM-D-INVOICE-TOTAL.
        IF LINE-ITEM-COUNT = ZERO
            MOVE FAC-UNPROT-NUM-BRT-MDT TO OEM-A-ITEM-NUMBER(1)
            MOVE -1 TO OEM-L-ITEM-NUMBER(1)
            MOVE 'YOU MUST ENTER AT LEAST ONE LINE ITEM'
                TO OEM-D-ERROR-MESSAGE.
*
        IF OEM-L-CUSTOMER-NUMBER = ZERO
            MOVE FAC-UNPROT-NUM-BRT-MDT TO OEM-A-CUSTOMER-NUMBER
            MOVE -1 TO OEM-L-CUSTOMER-NUMBER
            MOVE 'YOU MUST ENTER A CUSTOMER NUMBER'
                TO OEM-D-ERROR-MESSAGE
            MOVE SPACE TO OEM-D-NAME
```

Source listing for the order entry program (part 4 of 11)

```
            ELSE
                PERFORM 1210-READ-CUSTOMER-RECORD
                IF CUSTOMER-FOUND
                    MOVE CM-NAME TO OEM-D-NAME
                ELSE
                    MOVE FAC-UNPROT-NUM-BRT-MDT TO OEM-A-CUSTOMER-NUMBER
                    MOVE -1 TO OEM-L-CUSTOMER-NUMBER
                    MOVE 'CUSTOMER NOT IN FILE' TO OEM-D-ERROR-MESSAGE
                    MOVE SPACE TO OEM-D-NAME.
*
            IF OEM-D-ERROR-MESSAGE NOT = LOW-VALUE
                MOVE 'N' TO VALID-DATA-SW.
*
        1210-READ-CUSTOMER-RECORD SECTION.
*
            EXEC CICS
                HANDLE CONDITION NOTFND(1210-NOTFND)
            END-EXEC.
            EXEC CICS
                READ DATASET('CUSTMAST')
                     INTO(CUSTOMER-MASTER-RECORD)
                     RIDFLD(OEM-D-CUSTOMER-NUMBER)
            END-EXEC.
            GO TO 1210-EXIT.
*
        1210-NOTFND.
*
            MOVE SPACE TO CM-NAME.
            MOVE 'N' TO CUSTOMER-FOUND-SW.
*
        1210-EXIT.
*
            EXIT.
*
        1220-EDIT-LINE-ITEM SECTION.
*
            MOVE 'N' TO ITEM-FOUND-SW.
            MOVE 'Y' TO VALID-QUANTITY-SW.
            MOVE FAC-UNPROT-NUM-MDT TO OEM-A-ITEM-NUMBER(LINE-ITEM-SUB)
                                       OEM-A-QUANTITY(LINE-ITEM-SUB).
*
            IF OEM-L-ITEM-NUMBER(LINE-ITEM-SUB) = ZERO
                IF OEM-L-QUANTITY(LINE-ITEM-SUB) NOT = ZERO
                    MOVE FAC-UNPROT-NUM-BRT-MDT
                        TO OEM-A-QUANTITY(LINE-ITEM-SUB)
                    MOVE -1 TO OEM-L-QUANTITY(LINE-ITEM-SUB)
                    MOVE 'QUANTITY INVALID WITHOUT ITEM NUMBER'
                        TO OEM-D-ERROR-MESSAGE.
```

Source listing for the order entry program (part 5 of 11)

```
*
        IF OEM-L-ITEM-NUMBER(LINE-ITEM-SUB) NOT = ZERO
            IF OEM-L-QUANTITY(LINE-ITEM-SUB) = ZERO
                MOVE 'N' TO VALID-QUANTITY-SW
                MOVE FAC-UNPROT-NUM-BRT-MDT
                    TO OEM-A-QUANTITY(LINE-ITEM-SUB)
                MOVE -1 TO OEM-L-QUANTITY(LINE-ITEM-SUB)
                MOVE 'YOU MUST ENTER A QUANTITY'
                    TO OEM-D-ERROR-MESSAGE
            ELSE IF OEM-D-QUANTITY(LINE-ITEM-SUB) NOT NUMERIC
                MOVE 'N' TO VALID-QUANTITY-SW
                MOVE FAC-UNPROT-NUM-BRT-MDT
                    TO OEM-A-QUANTITY(LINE-ITEM-SUB)
                MOVE -1 TO OEM-L-QUANTITY(LINE-ITEM-SUB)
                MOVE 'QUANTITY MUST BE NUMERIC'
                    TO OEM-D-ERROR-MESSAGE
            ELSE IF OEM-D-QUANTITY(LINE-ITEM-SUB) NOT  ZERO
                MOVE 'N' TO VALID-QUANTITY-SW
                MOVE FAC-UNPROT-NUM-BRT-MDT
                    TO OEM-A-QUANTITY(LINE-ITEM-SUB)
                MOVE -1 TO OEM-L-QUANTITY(LINE-ITEM-SUB)
                MOVE 'QUANTITY MUST BE GREATER THAN ZERO'
                    TO OEM-D-ERROR-MESSAGE.
        IF OEM-L-ITEM-NUMBER(LINE-ITEM-SUB) = ZERO
            MOVE SPACE TO OEM-D-ITEM-DESCRIPTION(LINE-ITEM-SUB)
            MOVE ZERO  TO OEM-D-UNIT-PRICE(LINE-ITEM-SUB)
                          OEM-D-EXTENSION(LINE-ITEM-SUB)
        ELSE
            ADD 1 TO LINE-ITEM-COUNT
            PERFORM 1230-READ-INVENTORY-RECORD
            IF ITEM-FOUND
                MOVE IM-ITEM-DESCRIPTION
                    TO OEM-D-ITEM-DESCRIPTION.(LINE-ITEM-SUB)
                MOVE IM-UNIT-PRICE
                    TO OEM-D-UNIT-PRICE(LINE-ITEM-SUB)
                       CA-UNIT-PRICE(LINE-ITEM-SUB)
            ELSE
                MOVE SPACE TO OEM-D-ITEM-DESCRIPTION(LINE-ITEM-SUB)
                MOVE ZERO  TO OEM-D-UNIT-PRICE(LINE-ITEM-SUB)
                              OEM-D-EXTENSION(LINE-ITEM-SUB)
                MOVE FAC-UNPROT-NUM-BRT-MDT
                    TO OEM-A-ITEM-NUMBER(LINE-ITEM-SUB)
                MOVE -1 TO OEM-L-ITEM-NUMBER(LINE-ITEM-SUB)
                MOVE 'ITEM NOT IN INVENTORY FILE'
                    TO OEM-D-ERROR-MESSAGE.
```

Source listing for the order entry program (part 6 of 11)

```
*
     IF        ITEM-FOUND
        AND VALID-QUANTITY
        MULTIPLY OEM-D-QUANTITY(LINE-ITEM-SUB)
             BY IM-UNIT-PRICE
             GIVING OEM-D-EXTENSION(LINE-ITEM-SUB)
                    INV-EXTENSION(LINE-ITEM-SUB)
             ON SIZE ERROR
                 MOVE 'N' TO VALID-QUANTITY-SW
                 MOVE ZERO TO OEM-D-EXTENSION(LINE-ITEM-SUB)
                 MOVE FAC-UNPROT-NUM-BRT-MDT
                     TO OEM-A-QUANTITY(LINE-ITEM-SUB)
                 MOVE -1 TO OEM-L-QUANTITY(LINE-ITEM-SUB)
                 MOVE 'QUANTITY TOO LARGE'
                     TO OEM-D-ERROR-MESSAGE.
*
     IF        ITEM-FOUND
        AND VALID-QUANTITY
        ADD INV-EXTENSION(LINE-ITEM-SUB)
             TO INV-INVOICE-TOTAL
             ON SIZE ERROR
                 MOVE 99999.99 TO INV-INVOICE-TOTAL
                 MOVE -1 TO OEM-L-ITEM-NUMBER(1)
                 MOVE 'INVOICE TOTAL TOO LARGE'
                     TO OEM-D-ERROR-MESSAGE.
*
 1230-READ-INVENTORY-RECORD SECTION.
*
     EXEC CICS
         HANDLE CONDITION NOTFND(1230-NOTFND)
     END-EXEC.
     MOVE 'Y' TO ITEM-FOUND-SW.
     MOVE OEM-D-ITEM-NUMBER(LINE-ITEM-SUB) TO IM-ITEM-NUMBER.
     EXEC CICS
         READ DATASET('INVMAST')
              INTO(INVENTORY-MASTER-RECORD)
              RIDFLD(IM-ITEM-NUMBER)
     END-EXEC.
     GO TO 1230-EXIT.
*
 1230-NOTFND.
*
     MOVE SPACE TO IM-ITEM-DESCRIPTION.
     MOVE ZERO  TO IM-UNIT-PRICE.
     MOVE 'N' TO ITEM-FOUND-SW.
*
 1230-EXIT.
*
     EXIT.
```

Source listing for the order entry program (part 7 of 11)

```
*
 1300-SEND-ORDER-SCREEN SECTION.
*
     IF SET-PROTECTED
         PERFORM 1310-SET-ATTRIBUTES
     ELSE IF SET-UNPROTECTED
         PERFORM 1330-RESET-ATTRIBUTES.
     IF SEND-ALL
         EXEC CICS
             SEND MAP ('ORDMAP1')
                  MAPSET ('ORDSET1')
                  FROM (ORDER-ENTRY-MAP)
                  ERASE
                  CURSOR
         END-EXEC
     ELSE IF SEND-DATAONLY
         EXEC CICS
             SEND MAP ('ORDMAP1')
                  MAPSET ('ORDSET1')
                  FROM (ORDER-ENTRY-MAP)
                  DATAONLY
                  CURSOR
         END-EXEC.
*
 1310-SET-ATTRIBUTES SECTION.
*
     MOVE FAC-PROT-MDT TO OEM-A-CUSTOMER-NUMBER
                          OEM-A-PO-NUMBER.
     PERFORM 1320-SET-LINE-ATTRIBUTES
         VARYING LINE-ITEM-SUB FROM 1 BY 1
         UNTIL LINE-ITEM-SUB > 10.
*
 1320-SET-LINE-ATTRIBUTES SECTION.
*
     MOVE FAC-PROT-MDT TO OEM-A-ITEM-NUMBER(LINE-ITEM-SUB)
                          OEM-A-QUANTITY(LINE-ITEM-SUB).
*
 1330-RESET-ATTRIBUTES SECTION.
*
     MOVE FAC-UNPROT-NUM-MDT TO OEM-A-CUSTOMER-NUMBER.
     MOVE FAC-UNPROT-MDT     TO OEM-A-PO-NUMBER.
     PERFORM 1340-RESET-LINE-ATTRIBUTES
         VARYING LINE-ITEM-SUB FROM 1 BY 1
         UNTIL LINE-ITEM-SUB > 10.
*
 1340-RESET-LINE-ATTRIBUTES SECTION.
*
     MOVE FAC-UNPROT-NUM-MDT TO OEM-A-ITEM-NUMBER(LINE-ITEM-SUB)
                                OEM-A-QUANTITY(LINE-ITEM-SUB).
```

Source listing for the order entry program (part 8 of 11)

```
*
 2000-PROCESS-VERIFY-SCREEN SECTION.
*
     PERFORM 2100-RECEIVE-VERIFY-SCREEN.
     IF POST-ORDER
         PERFORM 2200-POST-ORDER-DATA
         MOVE LOW-VALUE TO ORDER-ENTRY-MAP
         MOVE -1 TO OEM-L-CUSTOMER-NUMBER
         MOVE 'ORDER POSTED--ENTER NEXT ORDER OR PRESS CLEAR TO EN
-            'D SESSION' TO OEM-D-OPERATOR-MESSAGE
         MOVE '0' TO ATTRIBUTE-CONTROL-FLAG
         MOVE '1' TO SEND-CONTROL-FLAG
         PERFORM 1300-SEND-ORDER-SCREEN
         MOVE '1' TO CA-PROCESS-FLAG
     ELSE IF MODIFY-ORDER
         MOVE LOW-VALUE TO ORDER-ENTRY-MAP
         MOVE -1 TO OEM-L-CUSTOMER-NUMBER
         MOVE 'ENTER MODIFICATIONS OR PRESS CLEAR TO END SESSION'
             TO OEM-D-OPERATOR-MESSAGE
         MOVE '2' TO ATTRIBUTE-CONTROL-FLAG
         MOVE '2' TO SEND-CONTROL-FLAG
         PERFORM 1300-SEND-ORDER-SCREEN
         MOVE '1' TO CA-PROCESS-FLAG
     ELSE IF CANCEL-ORDER
         MOVE LOW-VALUE TO ORDER-ENTRY-MAP
         MOVE -1 TO OEM-L-CUSTOMER-NUMBER
         MOVE 'ORDER CANCELLED--ENTER NEXT ORDER OR PRESS CLEAR TO
-            ' END SESSION' TO OEM-D-OPERATOR-MESSAGE
         MOVE '0' TO ATTRIBUTE-CONTROL-FLAG
         MOVE '1' TO SEND-CONTROL-FLAG
         PERFORM 1300-SEND-ORDER-SCREEN
         MOVE '1' TO CA-PROCESS-FLAG
     ELSE
         MOVE LOW-VALUE TO ORDER-ENTRY-MAP
         MOVE 'PRESS ENTER TO POST ORDER, PA1 TO MODIFY ORDER, OR
-            'CLEAR TO CANCEL ORDER' TO OEM-D-OPERATOR-MESSAGE
         MOVE '0' TO ATTRIBUTE-CONTROL-FLAG
         MOVE '2' TO SEND-CONTROL-FLAG
         PERFORM 1300-SEND-ORDER-SCREEN
         MOVE '2' TO CA-PROCESS-FLAG.
*
 2100-RECEIVE-VERIFY-SCREEN SECTION.
*
     EXEC CICS
         HANDLE AID PA1(2100-PA1-KEY)
                    CLEAR(2100-CLEAR-KEY)
                    ANYKEY(2100-ANYKEY)
     END-EXEC.
     MOVE '1' TO ORDER-VERIFICATION-FLAG.
     EXEC CICS
         RECEIVE MAP('ORDMAP1')
                 MAPSET('ORDSET1')
                 INTO(ORDER-ENTRY-MAP)
     END-EXEC.
     GO TO 2100-EXIT.
```

Source listing for the order entry program (part 9 of 11)

```
*
 2100-PA1-KEY.
*
     MOVE '2' TO ORDER-VERIFICATION-FLAG.
     GO TO 2100-EXIT.
*
 2100-CLEAR-KEY.
*
     MOVE '3' TO ORDER-VERIFICATION-FLAG.
     GO TO 2100-EXIT.
*
 2100-ANYKEY.
*
     MOVE '0' TO ORDER-VERIFICATION-FLAG.
     MOVE 'INVALID KEY PRESSED' TO OEM-D-ERROR-MESSAGE.
*
 2100-EXIT.
*
     EXIT.
*
 2200-POST-ORDER-DATA SECTION.
*
     PERFORM 2210-FORMAT-INVOICE-RECORD.
     PERFORM 2230-WRITE-INVOICE-RECORD.
     ADD 1 TO CA-TOTAL-ORDERS.
*
 2210-FORMAT-INVOICE-RECORD SECTION.
*
     EXEC CICS
         LINK PROGRAM('GETINV')
             COMMAREA(INV-INVOICE-NUMBER)
             LENGTH(5)
     END-EXEC.
     MOVE OEM-D-CUSTOMER-NUMBER TO INV-CUSTOMER-NUMBER.
     MOVE OEM-D-PO-NUMBER        TO INV-PO-NUMBER.
     MOVE CWA-DATE               TO INV-INVOICE-DATE.
     MOVE ZERO                   TO INV-INVOICE-TOTAL.
     PERFORM 2220-FORMAT-LINE-ITEM
         VARYING LINE-ITEM-SUB FROM 1 BY 1
         UNTIL LINE-ITEM-SUB > 10.
*
 2220-FORMAT-LINE-ITEM SECTION.
*
     IF OEM-L-ITEM-NUMBER(LINE-ITEM-SUB) = ZERO
         MOVE ZERO TO INV-ITEM-NUMBER(LINE-ITEM-SUB)
                      INV-QUANTITY(LINE-ITEM-SUB)
                      INV-UNIT-PRICE(LINE-ITEM-SUB)
                      INV-EXTENSION(LINE-ITEM-SUB)
     ELSE
         MOVE OEM-D-ITEM-NUMBER(LINE-ITEM-SUB)
             TO INV-ITEM-NUMBER(LINE-ITEM-SUB)
         MOVE OEM-D-QUANTITY(LINE-ITEM-SUB)
             TO INV-QUANTITY(LINE-ITEM-SUB)
```

Source listing for the order entry program (part 10 of 11)

```
            MOVE CA-UNIT-PRICE(LINE-ITEM-SUB)
                TO INV-UNIT-PRICE(LINE-ITEM-SUB)
            COMPUTE INV-EXTENSION(LINE-ITEM-SUB)=
                    INV-QUANTITY(LINE-ITEM-SUB) *
                    INV-UNIT-PRICE(LINE-ITEM-SUB)
            ADD INV-EXTENSION(LINE-ITEM-SUB) TO INV-INVOICE-TOTAL.
*
 2230-WRITE-INVOICE-RECORD SECTION.
*
     EXEC CICS
         WRITE DATASET('INVOICE')
               FROM(INVOICE-RECORD)
               RIDFLD(INV-INVOICE-NUMBER)
     END-EXEC.
*
 8000-START-TERMINAL-SESSION SECTION.
*
     MOVE LOW-VALUE TO ORDER-ENTRY-MAP.
     MOVE -1 TO OEM-L-CUSTOMER-NUMBER.
     MOVE 'PRESS CLEAR TO END SESSION' TO OEM-D-OPERATOR-MESSAGE.
     MOVE '0' TO ATTRIBUTE-CONTROL-FLAG.
     MOVE '1' TO SEND-CONTROL-FLAG.
     PERFORM 1300-SEND-ORDER-SCREEN.
     MOVE '1' TO CA-PROCESS-FLAG.
*
 9000-SEND-TERMINATION-MESSAGE SECTION.
*
     MOVE CA-TOTAL-ORDERS TO TL-TOTAL-ORDERS.
     EXEC CICS
         SEND TEXT FROM(TOTAL-LINE)
                   LENGTH(51)
                   ERASE
                   FREEKB
     END-EXEC.
```

Source listing for the order entry program (part 11 of 11)

```
       IDENTIFICATION DIVISION.
*
       PROGRAM-ID. GETINV.
*
       ENVIRONMENT DIVISION.
*
       DATA DIVISION.
*
       WORKING-STORAGE SECTION.
*
       01  INVCTL-RECORD.
*
           05  IR-RECORD-KEY            PIC X    VALUE '0'.
           05  IR-NEXT-INVOICE-NUMBER   PIC 9(5).
*
       LINKAGE SECTION.
*
       01  DFHCOMMAREA                  PIC 9(5).
*
       PROCEDURE DIVISION.
*
       000-GET-INVOICE-NUMBER SECTION.
*
           EXEC CICS
               READ DATASET('INVCTL')
                    INTO(INVCTL-RECORD)
                    RIDFLD(IR-RECORD-KEY)
                    UPDATE
           END-EXEC.
           MOVE IR-NEXT-INVOICE-NUMBER TO DFHCOMMAREA.
           ADD 1 TO IR-NEXT-INVOICE-NUMBER.
           EXEC CICS
               REWRITE DATASET('INVCTL')
                       FROM(INVCTL-RECORD)
           END-EXEC.
           EXEC CICS
               RETURN
           END-EXEC.
```

The GETINV program

The customer maintenance program

```
Program:   CUSTMNT   Customer maintenance        Page: 1
Designer:  Doug Lowe                             Date: 08-01-87
=================================================================
Input/output specifications
-----------------------------------------------------------------
File       Description

CUSTMAS    Customer master file
=================================================================
Process specifications
-----------------------------------------------------------------
Until the operator indicates the end of the terminal session by using
the CLEAR key in step 1:

1.    Get a customer key from the key screen and attempt to read the
      corresponding record in the customer file.  If the record exists,
      format the data screen with the record's data and allow the
      operator to make changes or to delete the record by pressing PF1.
      If the record doesn't exist, display the entry screen with no data
      and let the operator enter data for a new record.

2.    For an addition or a change, all data fields must be entered;
      however, no other field edits are required.

3.    For a change or deletion, maintain an image of the record in
      temporary storage across program executions.  If the data in the
      record changes in any way between program executions, inform the
      operator and abort the change or delete operation.

4.    Use the pseudo-conversational programming technique.  Use the
      communication area to keep track of which screen is being
      processed.  When control is transferred to this program from the
      menu program, no communication area is passed.
```

Specifications for the customer maintenance program

Map name	Key screen	Date	July 1, 1987
Program name	Customer maintenance	Designer	Doug Lowe

```
1  CUSTOMER MAINTENANCE
4  CUSTOMER NUMBER: XXXXX
23 XXXXXXXXXXXXXXXXXXXXXXXXXXXXXXXXXXXXXXXXXXXXXXXXXXXXXXXXXXXXXXXXXXXXXXXXXXXXXXX
24 XXXXXXXXXXXXXXXXXXXXXXXXXXXXXXXXXXXXXXXXXXXXXXXXXXXXXXXXXXXXXXXXXXXXXXXXXXXX  X
```

Map name	Customer data screen	Date	July 1, 1987
Program name	Customer maintenance	Designer	Doug Lowe

```
1  CUSTOMER MAINTENANCE
4  CUSTOMER NUMBER: XXXXX
6  NAME:            XXXXXXXXXXXXXXXXXXXXXXXXXXXXXX
7  ADDRESS:         XXXXXXXXXXXXXXXXXXXXXXXXXXXXXX
8  CITY/STATE/ZIP:  XXXXXXXXXXXXXXXXXXXX XX  XXXXX
23 XXXXXXXXXXXXXXXXXXXXXXXXXXXXXXXXXXXXXXXXXXXXXXXXXXXXXXXXXXXXXXXXXXXXXXXXXXXXXXX
24 XXXXXXXXXXXXXXXXXXXXXXXXXXXXXXXXXXXXXXXXXXXXXXXXXXXXXXXXXXXXXXXXXXXXXXXXXXXX  X
```

Screen layouts for the customer maintenance program

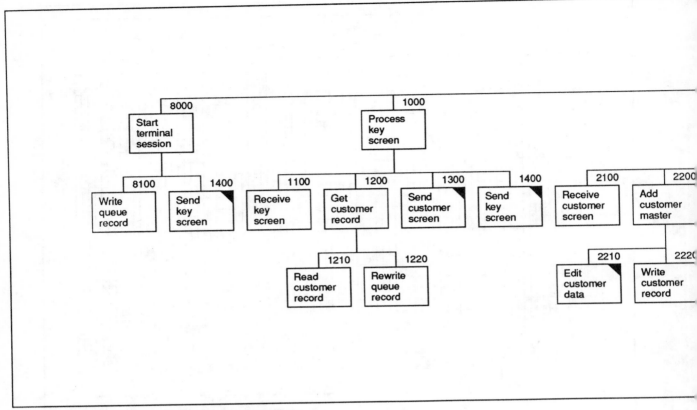

Structure chart for the customer maintenance program

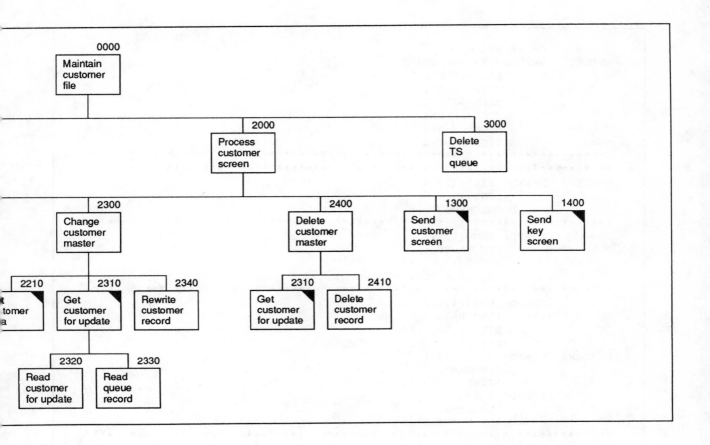

```
           PRINT NOGEN
MNTSET1  DFHMSD TYPE=&SYSPARM,                                             X
                LANG=COBOL,                                               X
                MODE=INOUT,                                               X
                TERM=3270-2,                                              X
                CTRL=FREEKB,                                              X
                STORAGE=AUTO,                                             X
                TIOAPFX=YES
*****************************************************************************
*****************************************************************************
MNTMAP1  DFHMDI SIZE=(24,80),                                             X
                LINE=1,                                                   X
                COLUMN=1
*****************************************************************************
         DFHMDF POS=(1,1),                                                X
                LENGTH=20,                                                X
                ATTRB=(BRT,PROT),                                         X
                INITIAL='CUSTOMER MAINTENANCE'
*****************************************************************************
         DFHMDF POS=(4,1),                                                X
                LENGTH=16,                                                X
                ATTRB=(BRT,PROT),                                         X
                INITIAL='CUSTOMER NUMBER:'
NUMBER1  DFHMDF POS=(4,18),                                               X
                LENGTH=5,                                                 X
                ATTRB=(UNPROT,IC)
         DFHMDF POS=(4,24),                                               X
                LENGTH=1,                                                 X
                ATTRB=ASKIP
*****************************************************************************
MESSAG1  DFHMDF POS=(23,1),                                               X
                LENGTH=79,                                                X
                ATTRB=(BRT,PROT)
ERROR1   DFHMDF POS=(24,1),                                               X
                LENGTH=77,                                                X
                ATTRB=(BRT,PROT)
DUMMY1   DFHMDF POS=(24,79),                                              X
                LENGTH=1,                                                 X
                ATTRB=(DRK,PROT,FSET),                                    X
                INITIAL=' '
*****************************************************************************
*****************************************************************************
MNTMAP2  DFHMDI SIZE=(24,80),                                             X
                LINE=1,                                                   X
                COLUMN=1
*****************************************************************************
         DFHMDF POS=(1,1),                                                X
                LENGTH=20,                                                X
                ATTRB=(BRT,PROT),                                         X
                INITIAL='CUSTOMER MAINTENANCE'
*****************************************************************************
```

BMS mapset for the customer maintenance program (part 1 of 3)

```
          DFHMDF POS=(4,1),                                            X
                 LENGTH=16,                                            X
                 ATTRB=(BRT,PROT),                                     X
                 INITIAL='CUSTOMER NUMBER:'
NUMBER2   DFHMDF POS=(4,18),                                           X
                 LENGTH=5,                                             X
                 ATTRB=(PROT,FSET)
          DFHMDF POS=(4,24),                                           X
                 LENGTH=1,                                             X
                 ATTRB=ASKIP
*********************************************************************
          DFHMDF POS=(6,1),                                            X
                 LENGTH=5,                                             X
                 ATTRB=(BRT,PROT),                                     X
                 INITIAL='NAME:'
NAME      DFHMDF POS=(6,18),                                           X
                 LENGTH=30,                                            X
                 ATTRB=(UNPROT,FSET)
          DFHMDF POS=(6,49),                                           X
                 LENGTH=1,                                             X
                 ATTRB=ASKIP
*********************************************************************
          DFHMDF POS=(7,1),                                            X
                 LENGTH=8,                                             X
                 ATTRB=(BRT,PROT),                                     X
                 INITIAL='ADDRESS:'
ADDRESS   DFHMDF POS=(7,18),                                           X
                 LENGTH=30,                                            X
                 ATTRB=(UNPROT,FSET)
          DFHMDF POS=(7,49),                                           X
                 LENGTH=1,                                             X
                 ATTRB=ASKIP
*********************************************************************
          DFHMDF POS=(8,1),                                            X
                 LENGTH=15,                                            X
                 ATTRB=(BRT,PROT),                                     X
                 INITIAL='CITY/STATE/ZIP:'
CITY      DFHMDF POS=(8,18),                                           X
                 LENGTH=21,                                            X
                 ATTRB=(UNPROT,FSET)
STATE     DFHMDF POS=(8,40),                                           X
                 LENGTH=2,                                             X
                 ATTRB=(UNPROT,FSET)
ZIP       DFHMDF POS=(8,43),                                           X
                 LENGTH=5,                                             X
                 ATTRB=(UNPROT,FSET)
          DFHMDF POS=(8,49),                                           X
                 LENGTH=1,                                             X
                 ATTRB=ASKIP
```

BMS mapset for the customer maintenance program (part 2 of 3)

```
**************************************************************** X
MESSAG2   DFHMDF  POS=(23,1),                                   X
                  LENGTH=79,
                  ATTRB=(BRT,PROT)
                                                                X
ERROR2    DFHMDF  POS=(24,1),                                   X
                  LENGTH=77,
                  ATTRB=(BRT,PROT)
                                                                X
DUMMY2    DFHMDF  POS=(24,79),                                  X
                  LENGTH=1,                                     X
                  ATTRB=(DRK,PROT,FSET),
                  INITIAL=' '
****************************************************************
          DFHMSD  TYPE=FINAL
          END
```

BMS mapset for the customer maintenance program (part 3 of 3)

```
    01   KEY-MAP.
*
    05   FILLER                      PIC X(12).
*
    05   KM-L-TITLE                  PIC S9(4)    COMP.
    05   KM-A-TITLE                  PIC X.
    05   KM-D-TITLE                  PIC X(79).
*
    05   KM-L-CUSTOMER-NUMBER        PIC S9(4)    COMP.
    05   KM-A-CUSTOMER-NUMBER        PIC X.
    05   KM-D-CUSTOMER-NUMBER        PIC X(5).
*
    05   KM-L-OPERATOR-MESSAGE       PIC S9(4)    COMP.
    05   KM-A-OPERATOR-MESSAGE       PIC X.
    05   KM-D-OPERATOR-MESSAGE       PIC X(79).
*
    05   KM-L-ERROR-MESSAGE          PIC S9(4)    COMP.
    05   KM-A-ERROR-MESSAGE          PIC X.
    05   KM-D-ERROR-MESSAGE          PIC X(77).
*
    05   KM-L-DUMMY                  PIC S9(4)    COMP.
    05   KM-A-DUMMY                  PIC X.
    05   KM-D-DUMMY                  PIC X.
*
    01   CUSTOMER-DATA-MAP.
*
    05   FILLER                      PIC X(12).
*
    05   CDM-L-TITLE                 PIC S9(4)    COMP.
    05   CDM-A-TITLE                 PIC X.
    05   CDM-D-TITLE                 PIC X(79).
*
    05   CDM-L-CUSTOMER-NUMBER       PIC S9(4)    COMP.
    05   CDM-A-CUSTOMER-NUMBER       PIC X.
    05   CDM-D-CUSTOMER-NUMBER       PIC X(5).
*
    05   CDM-L-NAME                  PIC S9(4)    COMP.
    05   CDM-A-NAME                  PIC X.
    05   CDM-D-NAME                  PIC X(30).
*
    05   CDM-L-ADDRESS               PIC S9(4)    COMP.
    05   CDM-A-ADDRESS               PIC X.
    05   CDM-D-ADDRESS               PIC X(30).
*
    05   CDM-L-CITY                  PIC S9(4)    COMP.
    05   CDM-A-CITY                  PIC X.
    05   CDM-D-CITY                  PIC X(21).
*
    05   CDM-L-STATE                 PIC S9(4)    COMP.
    05   CDM-A-STATE                 PIC X.
    05   CDM-D-STATE                 PIC XX.
*
    05   CDM-L-ZIP-CODE              PIC S9(4)    COMP.
    05   CDM-A-ZIP-CODE              PIC X.
    05   CDM-D-ZIP-CODE              PIC X(5).
```

Programmer-generated symbolic mapset for the customer maintenance program (part 1 of 2)

```
 *
       05   CDM-L-OPERATOR-MESSAGE    PIC S9(4)    COMP.
       05   CDM-A-OPERATOR-MESSAGE    PIC X.
       05   CDM-D-OPERATOR-MESSAGE    PIC X(79).
 *
       05   CDM-L-ERROR-MESSAGE       PIC S9(4)    COMP.
       05   CDM-A-ERROR-MESSAGE       PIC X.
       05   CDM-D-ERROR-MESSAGE       PIC X(77).
 *
       05   CDM-L-DUMMY               PIC S9(4)    COMP.
       05   CDM-A-DUMMY               PIC X.
       05   CDM-D-DUMMY               PIC X.
 *
```

Programmer-generated symbolic mapset for the customer maintenance program (part 2 of 2)

```
      IDENTIFICATION DIVISION.
*
      PROGRAM-ID.   CUSTMNT2.
*
      ENVIRONMENT DIVISION.
*
      DATA DIVISION.
*
      WORKING-STORAGE SECTION.
*
      01   SWITCHES.
*
           05   END-SESSION-SW              PIC X         VALUE 'N'.
                88   END-SESSION                          VALUE 'Y'.
           05   CANCEL-ENTRY-SW             PIC X         VALUE 'N'.
                88   CANCEL-ENTRY                         VALUE 'Y'.
           05   VALID-DATA-SW               PIC X         VALUE 'Y'.
                88   VALID-DATA                           VALUE 'Y'.
           05   PF-KEY-1-SW                 PIC X         VALUE 'N'.
                88   PF-KEY-1                             VALUE 'Y'.
*
      01   COMMUNICATION-AREA.
*
           05   CA-PROCESS-FLAG             PIC X.
                88   PROCESS-KEY-SCREEN                   VALUE '1'.
                88   PROCESS-CUSTOMER-SCREEN              VALUE '2'.
           05   CA-CUSTOMER-FOUND-SW        PIC X         VALUE 'Y'.
                88   CA-CUSTOMER-FOUND                    VALUE 'Y'.
*
      COPY MNTSET1.
*
      01   CUSTOMER-MASTER-RECORD.
*
           05   CM-CUSTOMER-NUMBER          PIC X(5).
           05   CM-NAME                     PIC X(30).
           05   CM-ADDRESS                  PIC X(30).
           05   CM-CITY                     PIC X(21).
           05   CM-STATE                    PIC XX.
           05   CM-ZIP-CODE                 PIC X(5).
*
      01   TEMPORARY-STORAGE-FIELDS.
*
           05   TS-QUEUE-NAME.
                10   TS-TERMINAL-ID         PIC X(4).
                10   FILLER                 PIC X(4)      VALUE 'MNT2'.
           05   TS-ITEM-NUMBER              PIC S9(4)  COMP   VALUE +1.
           05   TS-CUSTOMER-RECORD          PIC X(93).
           05   TS-RECORD-LENGTH            PIC S9(4)  COMP   VALUE +93.
*
      LINKAGE SECTION.
*
      01   DFHCOMMAREA                      PIC X(2).
*
```

Source listing for the customer maintenance program (part 1 of 9)

```
PROCEDURE DIVISION.
*
0000-MAINTAIN-CUSTOMER-FILE SECTION.
*
    MOVE EIBTRMID TO TS-TERMINAL-ID.
    MOVE LOW-VALUE TO KEY-MAP
                      CUSTOMER-DATA-MAP.
    IF EIBCALEN = ZERO
        PERFORM 8000-START-TERMINAL-SESSION
    ELSE
        MOVE DFHCOMMAREA TO COMMUNICATION-AREA
        IF PROCESS-KEY-SCREEN
            PERFORM 1000-PROCESS-KEY-SCREEN
        ELSE
            PERFORM 2000-PROCESS-CUSTOMER-SCREEN.
    IF END-SESSION
        PERFORM 3000-DELETE-TS-QUEUE
        EXEC CICS
            XCTL PROGRAM('INVMENU')
        END-EXEC
    ELSE
        EXEC CICS
            RETURN TRANSID('MNT2')
                   COMMAREA(COMMUNICATION-AREA)
                   LENGTH(2)
        END-EXEC.
*
1000-PROCESS-KEY-SCREEN SECTION.
*
    PERFORM 1100-RECEIVE-KEY-SCREEN.
    IF NOT END-SESSION
        IF NOT VALID-DATA
            PERFORM 1400-SEND-KEY-SCREEN
        ELSE
            IF      KM-D-CUSTOMER-NUMBER = SPACE
                 OR KM-L-CUSTOMER-NUMBER = ZERO
                MOVE 'YOU MUST ENTER A CUSTOMER NUMBER'
                    TO KM-D-ERROR-MESSAGE
                PERFORM 1400-SEND-KEY-SCREEN
            ELSE
                PERFORM 1200-GET-CUSTOMER-RECORD
                MOVE KM-D-CUSTOMER-NUMBER TO CDM-D-CUSTOMER-NUMBER
                MOVE CM-NAME              TO CDM-D-NAME
                MOVE CM-ADDRESS           TO CDM-D-ADDRESS
                MOVE CM-CITY              TO CDM-D-CITY
                MOVE CM-STATE             TO CDM-D-STATE
                MOVE CM-ZIP-CODE          TO CDM-D-ZIP-CODE
                MOVE -1 TO CDM-L-NAME
                MOVE '2' TO CA-PROCESS-FLAG
                PERFORM 1300-SEND-CUSTOMER-SCREEN.
*
```

Source listing for the customer maintenance program (part 2 of 9)

```
    1100-RECEIVE-KEY-SCREEN SECTION.
*
        EXEC CICS
            HANDLE AID CLEAR(1100-CLEAR-KEY)
                       ANYKEY(1100-ANYKEY)
        END-EXEC.
        EXEC CICS
            RECEIVE MAP('MNTMAP1')
                    MAPSET('MNTSET1')
                    INTO(KEY-MAP)
        END-EXEC.
        GO TO 1100-EXIT.
*
    1100-CLEAR-KEY.
*
        MOVE 'Y' TO END-SESSION-SW.
        GO TO 1100-EXIT.
*
    1100-ANYKEY.
*
        MOVE 'N' TO VALID-DATA-SW.
        MOVE 'INVALID KEY PRESSED' TO KM-D-ERROR-MESSAGE.
*
    1100-EXIT.
*
        EXIT.
*
    1200-GET-CUSTOMER-RECORD SECTION.
*
        PERFORM 1210-READ-CUSTOMER-RECORD.
        IF CA-CUSTOMER-FOUND
            PERFORM 1220-REWRITE-QUEUE-RECORD.
*
    1210-READ-CUSTOMER-RECORD SECTION.
*
        MOVE 'Y' TO CA-CUSTOMER-FOUND-SW.
        EXEC CICS
            HANDLE CONDITION NOTFND(1210-NOTFND)
        END-EXEC.
        EXEC CICS
            READ DATASET('CUSTMAS')
                 INTO(CUSTOMER-MASTER-RECORD)
                 RIDFLD(KM-D-CUSTOMER-NUMBER)
        END-EXEC.
        MOVE 'ENTER CHANGES OR PRESS PF1 TO DELETE CUSTOMER OR CLEAR
    -        'TO START OVER' TO CDM-D-OPERATOR-MESSAGE.
        MOVE SPACE TO CDM-D-ERROR-MESSAGE.
        GO TO 1210-EXIT.
*
```

Source listing for the customer maintenance program (part 3 of 9)

```
     1210-NOTFND.
*
         MOVE SPACE TO CUSTOMER-MASTER-RECORD.
         MOVE 'N' TO CA-CUSTOMER-FOUND-SW.
         MOVE 'ENTER DATA FOR NEW CUSTOMER OR PRESS CLEAR TO START OVE
    -        'R' TO CDM-D-OPERATOR-MESSAGE.
         MOVE SPACE TO CDM-D-ERROR-MESSAGE.
*
     1210-EXIT.
*
         EXIT.
*
     1220-REWRITE-QUEUE-RECORD SECTION.
*
         EXEC CICS
             WRITEQ TS QUEUE(TS-QUEUE-NAME)
                       FROM(CUSTOMER-MASTER-RECORD)
                       LENGTH(TS-RECORD-LENGTH)
                       ITEM(TS-ITEM-NUMBER)
                       REWRITE
         END-EXEC.
*
     1300-SEND-CUSTOMER-SCREEN SECTION.
*
         EXEC CICS
             SEND MAP('MNTMAP2')
                  MAPSET('MNTSET1')
                  FROM(CUSTOMER-DATA-MAP)
                  CURSOR
         END-EXEC.
*
     1400-SEND-KEY-SCREEN SECTION.
*
         MOVE 'PRESS CLEAR TO END SESSION' TO KM-D-OPERATOR-MESSAGE.
         EXEC CICS
             SEND MAP('MNTMAP1')
                  MAPSET('MNTSET1')
                  FROM(KEY-MAP)
                  ERASE
         END-EXEC.
*
     2000-PROCESS-CUSTOMER-SCREEN SECTION.
*
         PERFORM 2100-RECEIVE-CUSTOMER-SCREEN.
         IF VALID-DATA
             IF NOT CANCEL-ENTRY
                 IF CA-CUSTOMER-FOUND
                     IF PF-KEY-1
                         PERFORM 2400-DELETE-CUSTOMER-MASTER
                     ELSE
                         PERFORM 2300-CHANGE-CUSTOMER-MASTER
                 ELSE
                     PERFORM 2200-ADD-CUSTOMER-MASTER
             ELSE
                 MOVE 'NO ACTION TAKEN' TO KM-D-ERROR-MESSAGE.
```

Source listing for the customer maintenance program (part 4 of 9)

```
        IF VALID-DATA
            PERFORM 1400-SEND-KEY-SCREEN
            MOVE '1' TO CA-PROCESS-FLAG
        ELSE
            PERFORM 1300-SEND-CUSTOMER-SCREEN
            MOVE '2' TO CA-PROCESS-FLAG.
*
    2100-RECEIVE-CUSTOMER-SCREEN SECTION.
*
        EXEC CICS
            HANDLE AID CLEAR(2100-CLEAR-KEY)
                       PF1(2100-PF1-KEY)
                       ANYKEY(2100-ANYKEY)
        END-EXEC.
        EXEC CICS
            RECEIVE MAP('MNTMAP2')
                    MAPSET('MNTSET1')
                    INTO(CUSTOMER-DATA-MAP)
        END-EXEC.
        GO TO 2100-EXIT.
*
    2100-CLEAR-KEY.
*
        MOVE 'Y' TO CANCEL-ENTRY-SW.
        GO TO 2100-EXIT.
*
    2100-PF1-KEY.
*
        IF CA-CUSTOMER-FOUND
            MOVE 'Y' TO PF-KEY-1-SW
        ELSE
            MOVE 'N' TO VALID-DATA-SW
            MOVE 'INVALID KEY PRESSED' TO CDM-D-ERROR-MESSAGE.
        GO TO 2100-EXIT.
*
    2100-ANYKEY.
*
        MOVE 'N' TO VALID-DATA-SW.
        MOVE 'INVALID KEY PRESSED' TO CDM-D-ERROR-MESSAGE.
*
    2100-EXIT.
*
        EXIT.
*
```

Source listing for the customer maintenance program (part 5 of 9)

```
    2200-ADD-CUSTOMER-MASTER SECTION.
*
        PERFORM 2210-EDIT-CUSTOMER-DATA.
        IF VALID-DATA
            MOVE CDM-D-CUSTOMER-NUMBER TO CM-CUSTOMER-NUMBER
            MOVE CDM-D-NAME             TO CM-NAME
            MOVE CDM-D-ADDRESS          TO CM-ADDRESS
            MOVE CDM-D-CITY             TO CM-CITY
            MOVE CDM-D-STATE            TO CM-STATE
            MOVE CDM-D-ZIP-CODE         TO CM-ZIP-CODE
            MOVE 'RECORD ADDED' TO KM-D-ERROR-MESSAGE
            PERFORM 2220-WRITE-CUSTOMER-RECORD.
*
     2210-EDIT-CUSTOMER-DATA SECTION.
*
        IF       CDM-D-ZIP-CODE = SPACE
            OR CDM-L-ZIP-CODE = ZERO
            MOVE -1 TO CDM-L-ZIP-CODE
            MOVE 'YOU MUST ENTER A ZIP CODE'
                TO CDM-D-ERROR-MESSAGE.
*
        IF       CDM-D-STATE = SPACE
            OR CDM-L-STATE = ZERO
            MOVE -1 TO CDM-L-STATE
            MOVE 'YOU MUST ENTER A STATE'
                TO CDM-D-ERROR-MESSAGE.
*
        IF       CDM-D-CITY = SPACE
            OR CDM-L-CITY = ZERO
            MOVE -1 TO CDM-L-CITY
            MOVE 'YOU MUST ENTER A CITY'
                TO CDM-D-ERROR-MESSAGE.
*
        IF       CDM-D-ADDRESS = SPACE
            OR CDM-L-ADDRESS = ZERO
            MOVE -1 TO CDM-L-ADDRESS
            MOVE 'YOU MUST ENTER AN ADDRESS'
                TO CDM-D-ERROR-MESSAGE.
*
        IF       CDM-D-NAME = SPACE
            OR CDM-L-NAME = ZERO
            MOVE -1 TO CDM-L-NAME
            MOVE 'YOU MUST ENTER A NAME'
                TO CDM-D-ERROR-MESSAGE.
*
        IF CDM-D-ERROR-MESSAGE NOT =  LOW-VALUE
            MOVE 'N' TO VALID-DATA-SW.
*
```

Source listing for the customer maintenance program (part 6 of 9)

```
    2220-WRITE-CUSTOMER-RECORD SECTION.
*
        EXEC CICS
            HANDLE CONDITION DUPREC(2220-DUPREC)
        END-EXEC.
        EXEC CICS
            WRITE DATASET('CUSTMAS')
                  FROM(CUSTOMER-MASTER-RECORD)
                  RIDFLD(CM-CUSTOMER-NUMBER)
        END-EXEC.
        GO TO 2220-EXIT.
*
    2220-DUPREC.
*
        MOVE 'ERROR--CUSTOMER RECORD ALREADY EXISTS'
            TO KM-D-ERROR-MESSAGE.
*
    2220-EXIT.
*
        EXIT.
*
    2300-CHANGE-CUSTOMER-MASTER SECTION.
*
        PERFORM 2210-EDIT-CUSTOMER-DATA.
        IF VALID-DATA
            PERFORM 2310-GET-CUSTOMER-FOR-UPDATE
            IF CA-CUSTOMER-FOUND
                MOVE CDM-D-NAME          TO CM-NAME
                MOVE CDM-D-ADDRESS       TO CM-ADDRESS
                MOVE CDM-D-CITY          TO CM-CITY
                MOVE CDM-D-STATE         TO CM-STATE
                MOVE CDM-D-ZIP-CODE      TO CM-ZIP-CODE
                PERFORM 2340-REWRITE-CUSTOMER-RECORD
                MOVE 'RECORD UPDATED' TO KM-D-ERROR-MESSAGE.
*
    2310-GET-CUSTOMER-FOR-UPDATE SECTION.
*
        PERFORM 2320-READ-CUSTOMER-FOR-UPDATE.
        IF CA-CUSTOMER-FOUND
            PERFORM 2330-READ-QUEUE-RECORD.
*
    2320-READ-CUSTOMER-FOR-UPDATE SECTION.
*
        EXEC CICS
            HANDLE CONDITION NOTFND(2320-NOTFND)
        END-EXEC.
        EXEC CICS
            READ DATASET('CUSTMAS')
                 INTO(CUSTOMER-MASTER-RECORD)
                 RIDFLD(CDM-D-CUSTOMER-NUMBER)
                 UPDATE
        END-EXEC.
        MOVE 'Y' TO CA-CUSTOMER-FOUND-SW.
        GO TO 2320-EXIT.
*
```

Source listing for the customer maintenance program (part 7 of 9)

```
     2320-NOTFND.
*
         MOVE 'ERROR--CUSTOMER RECORD DOES NOT EXIST'
             TO KM-D-ERROR-MESSAGE.
         MOVE 'N' TO CA-CUSTOMER-FOUND-SW.
*
     2320-EXIT.
*
         EXIT.
*
     2330-READ-QUEUE-RECORD SECTION.
*
         EXEC CICS
             READQ TS QUEUE(TS-QUEUE-NAME)
                      INTO(TS-CUSTOMER-RECORD)
                      LENGTH(TS-RECORD-LENGTH)
                      ITEM(TS-ITEM-NUMBER)
         END-EXEC.
         IF TS-CUSTOMER-RECORD NOT = CUSTOMER-MASTER-RECORD
             MOVE 'ERROR--ANOTHER OPERATOR HAS UPDATED THAT CUSTOMER'
                 TO KM-D-ERROR-MESSAGE
             MOVE 'N' TO CA-CUSTOMER-FOUND-SW.
*
     2340-REWRITE-CUSTOMER-RECORD SECTION.
*
         EXEC CICS
             REWRITE DATASET('CUSTMAS')
                     FROM(CUSTOMER-MASTER-RECORD)
         END-EXEC.
*
     2400-DELETE-CUSTOMER-MASTER SECTION.
*
         PERFORM 2310-GET-CUSTOMER-FOR-UPDATE.
         IF CA-CUSTOMER-FOUND
             PERFORM 2410-DELETE-CUSTOMER-RECORD
             MOVE 'RECORD DELETED' TO KM-D-ERROR-MESSAGE.
*
     2410-DELETE-CUSTOMER-RECORD SECTION.
*
         EXEC CICS
             DELETE DATASET('CUSTMAS')
         END-EXEC.
*
     3000-DELETE-TS-QUEUE SECTION.
*
         EXEC CICS
             DELETEQ TS QUEUE(TS-QUEUE-NAME)
         END-EXEC.
*
```

Source listing for the customer maintenance program (part 8 of 9)

```
 8000-START-TERMINAL-SESSION SECTION.
*
     PERFORM 8100-WRITE-QUEUE-RECORD.
     PERFORM 1400-SEND-KEY-SCREEN.
     MOVE '1' TO CA-PROCESS-FLAG.
*
 8100-WRITE-QUEUE-RECORD SECTION.
*
     MOVE LOW-VALUE TO TS-CUSTOMER-RECORD.
     EXEC CICS
         WRITEQ TS QUEUE(TS-QUEUE-NAME)
                   FROM(TS-CUSTOMER-RECORD)
                   LENGTH(TS-RECORD-LENGTH)
     END-EXEC.
```

Source listing for the customer maintenance program (part 9 of 9)

The customer inquiry program

```
Program:   CUSTINQ   Customer inquiry              Page: 1
Designer:  Doug Lowe                                Date: 08-01-87
================================================================
Input/output specifications
----------------------------------------------------------------

File       Description

CUSTMAS    Customer master file
INVPATH    Invoice file (customer number path)
================================================================
Process specifications
----------------------------------------------------------------
Until the operator indicates the end of the terminal session by using
the CLEAR key in step 1:

1.   Let the operator select the customer to display by using one
     of these AID keys:

          ENTER  Use the customer key entered by the operator.
          PF1    Display the first record in the file.
          PF2    Display the last record in the file.
          PF3    Display the next record in the file.
          PF4    Display the previous record in the file.

2.   For each inquiry, display the information from the customer
     record as well as information from the first 10 related
     invoice records.  Access the invoice file via the INVPATH
     path to read invoice records in customer-number sequence.

3.   Use the pseudo-conversational programming technique.  Use the
     communication area to keep track of which screen is being
     processed.  When control is transferred to this program from the
     menu program, no communication area is passed.
```

Specifications for the customer inquiry program

Map name _____ Customer inquiry screen _____ Date _____ July 1, 1987 _____

Program name _Customer inquiry_ _____ Designer _Doug Lowe_ _____

```
    1234567890123456789012345678901234567890123456789012345678901234567890123456789 0
 1  CUSTOMER INQUIRY
 2
 3
 4  CUSTOMER NUMBER: XXXXX
 5
 6  NAME:           XXXXXXXXXXXXXXXXXXXXXXXXXXXXXX
 7  ADDRESS:        XXXXXXXXXXXXXXXXXXXXXXXXXXXXXX
 8  CITY/STATE/ZIP: XXXXXXXXXXXXXXXXXXXX XX  XXXXX
 9
10  INVOICE   PO NUMBER      DATE        TOTAL
11
12    99999   XXXXXXXXXX   Z9/Z9/99   ZZ,ZZ9.99
13    99999   XXXXXXXXXX   Z9/Z9/99   ZZ,ZZ9.99
14    99999   XXXXXXXXXX   Z9/Z9/99   ZZ,ZZ9.99
15    99999   XXXXXXXXXX   Z9/Z9/99   ZZ,ZZ9.99
16    99999   XXXXXXXXXX   Z9/Z9/99   ZZ,ZZ9.99
17    99999   XXXXXXXXXX   Z9/Z9/99   ZZ,ZZ9.99
18    99999   XXXXXXXXXX   Z9/Z9/99   ZZ,ZZ9.99
19    99999   XXXXXXXXXX   Z9/Z9/99   ZZ,ZZ9.99
20    99999   XXXXXXXXXX   Z9/Z9/99   ZZ,ZZ9.99
21    99999   XXXXXXXXXX   Z9/Z9/99   ZZ,ZZ9.99
22
23
24  ENTER = CUST; PF1 = FIRST; PF2 = LAST; PF9 = PREV; PF5 = NEXT; CLEAR = MENU
```

Screen layout for the customer inquiry program

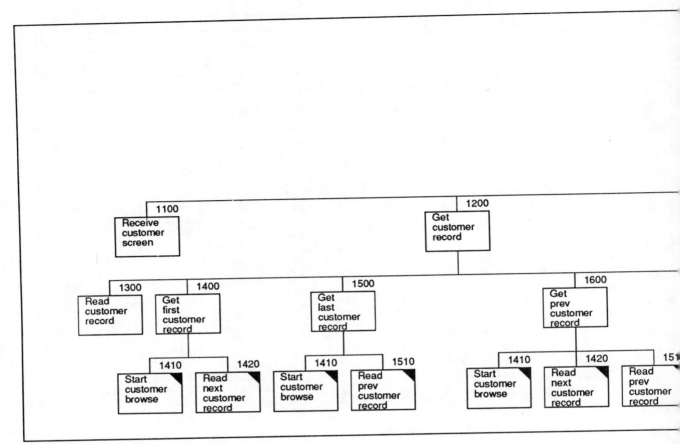

Structure chart for the customer inquiry program

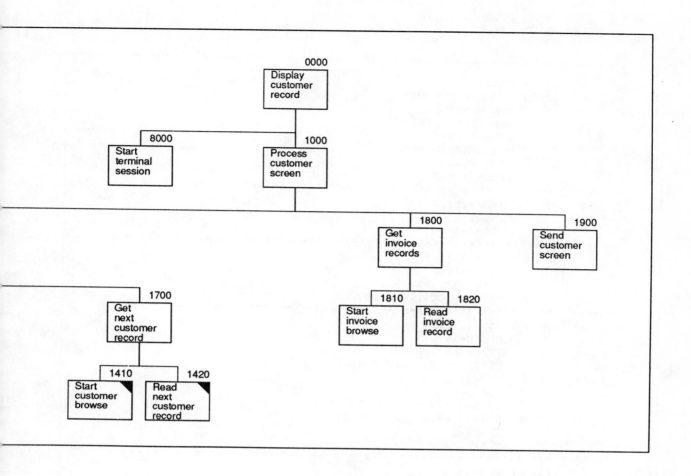

```
        PRINT NOGEN
INQSET2 DFHMSD TYPE=&SYSPARM,                                              X
            LANG=COBOL,                                                    X
            MODE=INOUT,                                                    X
            TERM=3270-2,                                                   X
            CTRL=FREEKB,                                                   X
            STORAGE=AUTO,                                                  X
            TIOAPFX=YES
***************************************************************************
INQMAP1 DFHMDI SIZE=(24,80),                                              X
            LINE=1,                                                        X
            COLUMN=1
***************************************************************************
        DFHMDF POS=(1,1),                                                 X
            LENGTH=16,                                                     X
            ATTRB=(BRT,PROT),                                              X
            INITIAL='CUSTOMER INQUIRY'
***************************************************************************
        DFHMDF POS=(4,1),                                                 X
            LENGTH=16,                                                     X
            ATTRB=(BRT,PROT),                                              X
            INITIAL='CUSTOMER NUMBER:'
NUMBER  DFHMDF POS=(4,18),                                                X
            LENGTH=5,                                                      X
            ATTRB=(IC,UNPROT,FSET)
        DFHMDF POS=(4,24),                                                X
            LENGTH=1,                                                      X
            ATTRB=ASKIP
***************************************************************************
        DFHMDF POS=(6,1),                                                 X
            LENGTH=16,                                                     X
            ATTRB=(BRT,PROT),                                              X
            INITIAL='CUSTOMER NAME:'
NAME    DFHMDF POS=(6,18),                                                X
            LENGTH=30,                                                     X
            ATTRB=PROT
***************************************************************************
        DFHMDF POS=(7,1),                                                 X
            LENGTH=8,                                                      X
            ATTRB=(BRT,PROT),                                              X
            INITIAL='ADDRESS:'
ADDRESS DFHMDF POS=(7,18),                                                X
            LENGTH=30,                                                     X
            ATTRB=PROT
***************************************************************************
        DFHMDF POS=(8,1),                                                 X
            LENGTH=15,                                                     X
            ATTRB=(BRT,PROT),                                              X
            INITIAL='CITY/STATE/ZIP:'
CITY    DFHMDF POS=(8,18),                                                X
            LENGTH=21,                                                     X
            ATTRB=PROT
```

BMS mapset for the customer inquiry program (part 1 of 2)

```
     STATE      DFHMDF POS=(8,40),                                        X
                       LENGTH=2,                                          X
                       ATTRB=PROT
     ZIP        DFHMDF POS=(8,43),                                        X
                       LENGTH=5,                                          X
                       ATTRB=PROT
     *******************************************************************
                DFHMDF POS=(10,1),                                        X
                       LENGTH=40,                                         X
                       ATTRB=(BRT,PROT),                                  X
                       INITIAL='INVOICE  PO NUMBER     DATE        TOTAL'
     *******************************************************************
     *          LINE 1
     *******************************************************************
     INVNO1     DFHMDF POS=(12,2),                                        X
                       LENGTH=5,                                          X
                       ATTRB=PROT
     PO1        DFHMDF POS=(12,10),                                       X
                       LENGTH=10,                                         X
                       ATTRB=PROT
     DATE1      DFHMDF POS=(12,22),                                       X
                       LENGTH=8,                                          X
                       ATTRB=PROT,                                        X
                       PICOUT='Z9/99/99'
     TOT1       DFHMDF POS=(12,32),                                       X
                       LENGTH=9,                                          X
                       ATTRB=PROT,                                        X
                       PICOUT='ZZ,ZZ9.99'
                   .
                   .
                   .
                   .
                   .
                   .
                   .
```

> The BMS macro
> instructions for lines 2
> through 10 are similar
> to those for line 1.

```
     *******************************************************************
                DFHMDF POS=(23,1),                                        X
                       LENGTH=75,                                         X
                       ATTRB=(BRT,PROT),                                  X
                       INITIAL='ENTER = CUST; PF1 = FIRST; PF2 = LAST; PF4 = PRX
                       EV; PF5 = NEXT; CLEAR = MENU'
     ERROR      DFHMDF POS=(24,1),                                        X
                       LENGTH=77,                                         X
                       ATTRB=(BRT,PROT)
     DUMMY      DFHMDF POS=(24,79),                                       X
                       LENGTH=1,                                          X
                       ATTRB=(DRK,PROT,FSET),                             X
                       INITIAL=' '
     *******************************************************************
                DFHMSD TYPE=FINAL
                END
```

BMS mapset for the customer inquiry program (part 2 of 2)

```
01    INQUIRY-MAP.
*
      05    FILLER                    PIC X(12).
*
      05    IM-L-CUSTOMER-NUMBER      PIC S9(4)      COMP.
      05    IM-A-CUSTOMER-NUMBER      PIC X.
      05    IM-D-CUSTOMER-NUMBER      PIC X(5).
*
      05    IM-L-NAME                 PIC S9(4)      COMP.
      05    IM-A-NAME                 PIC X.
      05    IM-D-NAME                 PIC X(30).
*
      05    IM-L-ADDRESS              PIC S9(4)      COMP.
      05    IM-A-ADDRESS              PIC X.
      05    IM-D-ADDRESS              PIC X(30).
*
      05    IM-L-CITY                 PIC S9(4)      COMP.
      05    IM-A-CITY                 PIC X.
      05    IM-D-CITY                 PIC X(21).
*
      05    IM-L-STATE                PIC S9(4)      COMP.
      05    IM-A-STATE                PIC X.
      05    IM-D-STATE                PIC XX.
*
      05    IM-L-ZIP-CODE             PIC S9(4)      COMP.
      05    IM-A-ZIP-CODE             PIC X.
      05    IM-D-ZIP-CODE             PIC X(5).
*
      05    IM-INVOICE-GROUP          OCCURS 10.
*
            10    IM-L-INVOICE-NUMBER PIC S9(4)      COMP.
            10    IM-A-INVOICE-NUMBER PIC X.
            10    IM-D-INVOICE-NUMBER PIC 9(5).
*
            10    IM-L-PO-NUMBER      PIC S9(4)      COMP.
            10    IM-A-PO-NUMBER      PIC X.
            10    IM-D-PO-NUMBER      PIC X(10).
*
            10    IM-L-INVOICE-DATE   PIC S9(4)      COMP.
            10    IM-A-INVOICE-DATE   PIC X.
            10    IM-D-INVOICE-DATE   PIC Z9/99/99.
*
            10    IM-L-INVOICE-TOTAL  PIC S9(4)      COMP.
            10    IM-A-INVOICE-TOTAL  PIC X.
            10    IM-D-INVOICE-TOTAL  PIC ZZ,ZZ9.99.
*
      05    IM-L-ERROR-MESSAGE        PIC S9(4)      COMP.
      05    IM-A-ERROR-MESSAGE        PIC X.
      05    IM-D-ERROR-MESSAGE        PIC X(77).
*
      05    IM-L-DUMMY                PIC S9(4)      COMP.
      05    IM-A-DUMMY                PIC X.
      05    IM-D-DUMMY                PIC X.
```

Programmer-generated symbolic mapset for the customer inquiry program

```
     IDENTIFICATION DIVISION.
*
     PROGRAM-ID. CUSTINQ2.
*
     ENVIRONMENT DIVISION.
*
     DATA DIVISION.
*
     WORKING-STORAGE SECTION.
*
 01   SWITCHES.
*
     05   END-SESSION-SW          PIC X            VALUE 'N'.
          88   END-SESSION                         VALUE 'Y'.
     05   CUSTOMER-FOUND-SW       PIC X            VALUE 'Y'.
          88   CUSTOMER-FOUND                      VALUE 'Y'.
     05   MORE-INVOICES-SW        PIC X            VALUE 'Y'.
          88   MORE-INVOICES                       VALUE 'Y'.
*
 01   FLAGS.
*
     05   PF-KEY-FLAG             PIC X            VALUE '0'.
          88   ENTER-KEY                           VALUE '0'.
          88   PF-KEY-1                            VALUE '1'.
          88   PF-KEY-2                            VALUE '2'.
          88   PF-KEY-4                            VALUE '4'.
          88   PF-KEY-5                            VALUE '5'.
          88   INVALID-KEY                         VALUE SPACE.
*
 01   COMMUNICATION-AREA          PIC X            VALUE SPACE.
*
 01   CUSTOMER-MASTER-RECORD.
*
     05   CM-CUSTOMER-NUMBER      PIC X(5).
     05   CM-NAME                 PIC X(30).
     05   CM-ADDRESS              PIC X(30).
     05   CM-CITY                 PIC X(21).
     05   CM-STATE                PIC XX.
     05   CM-ZIP-CODE             PIC X(5).
*
 01   INVOICE-RECORD.
*
     05   INV-INVOICE-NUMBER      PIC 9(5).
     05   INV-INVOICE-DATE        PIC 9(6).
     05   INV-CUSTOMER-NUMBER     PIC X(5).
     05   INV-PO-NUMBER           PIC X(10).
     05   INV-LINE-ITEM           OCCURS 10.
          10   INV-ITEM-NUMBER    PIC 9(5).
          10   INV-QUANTITY       PIC S9(5)        COMP-3.
          10   INV-UNIT-PRICE     PIC S9(5)V99     COMP-3.
          10   INV-EXTENSION      PIC S9(5)V99     COMP-3.
     05   INV-INVOICE-TOTAL       PIC S9(5)V99     COMP-3.
*
 01   INVOICE-SUB                 PIC S9(4)        COMP.
*
```

Source listing for the customer inquiry program (part 1 of 7)

```
       COPY INQSET2.
     *
       LINKAGE SECTION.
     *
       01   DFHCOMMAREA                  PIC X.
     *
       PROCEDURE DIVISION.
     *
       0000-DISPLAY-CUSTOMER-RECORD SECTION.
     *
           IF EIBCALEN = ZERO
               PERFORM 8000-START-TERMINAL-SESSION
           ELSE
               PERFORM 1000-PROCESS-CUSTOMER-SCREEN.
           IF END-SESSION
               EXEC CICS
                   XCTL PROGRAM('INVMENU')
               END-EXEC
           ELSE
               EXEC CICS
                   RETURN TRANSID('INQ2')
                       COMMAREA(COMMUNICATION-AREA)
                       LENGTH(1)
               END-EXEC.
     *
       1000-PROCESS-CUSTOMER-SCREEN SECTION.
     *
           PERFORM 1100-RECEIVE-CUSTOMER-SCREEN.
           IF NOT END-SESSION
               PERFORM 1200-GET-CUSTOMER-RECORD
               PERFORM 1800-GET-INVOICE-RECORDS
               MOVE CM-CUSTOMER-NUMBER TO IM-D-CUSTOMER-NUMBER
               MOVE CM-NAME            TO IM-D-NAME
               MOVE CM-ADDRESS         TO IM-D-ADDRESS
               MOVE CM-CITY            TO IM-D-CITY
               MOVE CM-STATE           TO IM-D-STATE
               MOVE CM-ZIP-CODE        TO IM-D-ZIP-CODE
               PERFORM 1900-SEND-CUSTOMER-SCREEN.
     *
       1100-RECEIVE-CUSTOMER-SCREEN SECTION.
     *
           EXEC CICS
               HANDLE AID CLEAR(1100-CLEAR-KEY)
                          PF1(1100-PF1-KEY)
                          PF2(1100-PF2-KEY)
                          PF4(1100-PF4-KEY)
                          PF5(1100-PF5-KEY)
                          ANYKEY(1100-ANYKEY)
           END-EXEC.
           EXEC CICS
               RECEIVE MAP('INQMAP1')
                       MAPSET('INQSET2')
                       INTO(INQUIRY-MAP)
           END-EXEC.
           GO TO 1100-EXIT.
```

Source listing for the customer inquiry program (part 2 of 7)

```
*
 1100-CLEAR-KEY.
*
     MOVE 'Y' TO END-SESSION-SW.
     GO TO 1100-EXIT.
*
 1100-PF1-KEY.
*
     MOVE '1' TO PF-KEY-FLAG.
     GO TO 1100-EXIT.
*
 1100-PF2-KEY.
*
     MOVE '2' TO PF-KEY-FLAG.
     GO TO 1100-EXIT.
*
 1100-PF4-KEY.
*
     MOVE '4' TO PF-KEY-FLAG.
     GO TO 1100-EXIT.
*
 1100-PF5-KEY.
*
     MOVE '5' TO PF-KEY-FLAG.
     GO TO 1100-EXIT.
*
 1100-ANYKEY.
*
     MOVE SPACE TO PF-KEY-FLAG.
     MOVE LOW-VALUE TO INQUIRY-MAP.
     MOVE 'INVALID KEY PRESSED' TO IM-D-ERROR-MESSAGE.
*
 1100-EXIT.
*
     EXIT.
*
 1200-GET-CUSTOMER-RECORD SECTION.
*
     MOVE SPACE TO CM-NAME
                   CM-ADDRESS
                   CM-CITY
                   CM-STATE
                   CM-ZIP-CODE.
     IF ENTER-KEY
         MOVE IM-D-CUSTOMER-NUMBER TO CM-CUSTOMER-NUMBER
         PERFORM 1300-READ-CUSTOMER-RECORD
     ELSE IF PF-KEY-1
         PERFORM 1400-GET-FIRST-CUSTOMER-RECORD
     ELSE IF PF-KEY-2
         PERFORM 1500-GET-LAST-CUSTOMER-RECORD
     ELSE IF PF-KEY-4
         PERFORM 1600-GET-PREV-CUSTOMER-RECORD
     ELSE IF PF-KEY-5
         PERFORM 1700-GET-NEXT-CUSTOMER-RECORD.
```

Source listing for the customer inquiry program (part 3 of 7)

```
*
 1300-READ-CUSTOMER-RECORD SECTION.
*
     EXEC CICS
         HANDLE CONDITION NOTFND(1300-NOTFND)
     END-EXEC.
     EXEC CICS
         READ DATASET('CUSTMAS')
             INTO(CUSTOMER-MASTER-RECORD)
             RIDFLD(CM-CUSTOMER-NUMBER)
     END-EXEC.
     GO TO 1300-EXIT.
*
 1300-NOTFND.
*
     MOVE 'CUSTOMER RECORD NOT FOUND' TO IM-D-ERROR-MESSAGE.
*
 1300-EXIT.
*
     EXIT.
*
 1400-GET-FIRST-CUSTOMER-RECORD SECTION.
*
     MOVE LOW-VALUE TO CM-CUSTOMER-NUMBER.
     PERFORM 1410-START-CUSTOMER-BROWSE.
     IF CUSTOMER-FOUND
         PERFORM 1420-READ-NEXT-CUSTOMER-RECORD.
*
 1410-START-CUSTOMER-BROWSE SECTION.
*
     EXEC CICS
         HANDLE CONDITION NOTFND(1410-NOTFND)
     END-EXEC.
     EXEC CICS
         STARTBR DATASET('CUSTMAS')
                 RIDFLD(CM-CUSTOMER-NUMBER)
     END-EXEC.
     GO TO 1410-EXIT.
*
 1410-NOTFND.
*
     MOVE 'N' TO CUSTOMER-FOUND-SW.
     MOVE 'CUSTOMER RECORD NOT FOUND' TO IM-D-ERROR-MESSAGE.
*
 1410-EXIT.
*
     EXIT.
*
```

Source listing for the customer inquiry program (part 4 of 7)

```
    1420-READ-NEXT-CUSTOMER-RECORD SECTION.
*
        EXEC CICS
            HANDLE CONDITION ENDFILE(1420-ENDFILE)
        END-EXEC.
        EXEC CICS
            READNEXT DATASET('CUSTMAS')
                     INTO(CUSTOMER-MASTER-RECORD)
                     RIDFLD(CM-CUSTOMER-NUMBER)
        END-EXEC.
        GO TO 1420-EXIT.
*
    1420-ENDFILE.
*
        MOVE 'THERE ARE NO MORE RECORDS IN THE FILE'
            TO IM-D-ERROR-MESSAGE.
*
    1420-EXIT.
*
        EXIT.
*
    1500-GET-LAST-CUSTOMER-RECORD SECTION.
*
        MOVE HIGH-VALUE TO CM-CUSTOMER-NUMBER.
        PERFORM 1410-START-CUSTOMER-BROWSE.
        IF CUSTOMER-FOUND
            PERFORM 1510-READ-PREV-CUSTOMER-RECORD.
*
    1510-READ-PREV-CUSTOMER-RECORD SECTION.
*
        EXEC CICS
            HANDLE CONDITION ENDFILE(1510-ENDFILE)
        END-EXEC.
        EXEC CICS
            READPREV DATASET('CUSTMAS')
                     INTO(CUSTOMER-MASTER-RECORD)
                     RIDFLD(CM-CUSTOMER-NUMBER)
        END-EXEC.
        GO TO 1510-EXIT.
*
    1510-ENDFILE.
*
        MOVE 'THERE ARE NO MORE RECORDS IN THE FILE'
            TO IM-D-ERROR-MESSAGE.
*
    1510-EXIT.
*
        EXIT.
*
```

Source listing for the customer inquiry program (part 5 of 7)

```
 1600-GET-PREV-CUSTOMER-RECORD SECTION.
*
     MOVE IM-D-CUSTOMER-NUMBER TO CM-CUSTOMER-NUMBER.
     PERFORM 1410-START-CUSTOMER-BROWSE.
     IF CUSTOMER-FOUND
         PERFORM 1420-READ-NEXT-CUSTOMER-RECORD
         PERFORM 1510-READ-PREV-CUSTOMER-RECORD
         PERFORM 1510-READ-PREV-CUSTOMER-RECORD.
*
 1700-GET-NEXT-CUSTOMER-RECORD SECTION.
*
     MOVE IM-D-CUSTOMER-NUMBER TO CM-CUSTOMER-NUMBER.
     PERFORM 1410-START-CUSTOMER-BROWSE.
     IF CUSTOMER-FOUND
         PERFORM 1420-READ-NEXT-CUSTOMER-RECORD
         IF IM-D-CUSTOMER-NUMBER = CM-CUSTOMER-NUMBER
             PERFORM 1420-READ-NEXT-CUSTOMER-RECORD.
*
 1800-GET-INVOICE-RECORDS SECTION.
*
     PERFORM 1810-START-INVOICE-BROWSE.
     EXEC CICS
         HANDLE CONDITION DUPKEY(1820-DUPKEY)
     END-EXEC.
     PERFORM 1820-READ-INVOICE-RECORD
         VARYING INVOICE-SUB FROM 1 BY 1
         UNTIL   INVOICE-SUB > 10
             OR NOT MORE-INVOICES.
*
 1810-START-INVOICE-BROWSE SECTION.
*
     EXEC CICS
         HANDLE CONDITION NOTFND(1810-NOTFND)
     END-EXEC.
     EXEC CICS
         STARTBR DATASET('INVPATH')
                 RIDFLD(CM-CUSTOMER-NUMBER)
                 EQUAL
     END-EXEC.
     GO TO 1810-EXIT.
*
 1810-NOTFND.
*
     MOVE 'N' TO MORE-INVOICES-SW.
*
 1810-EXIT.
*
     EXIT.
*
```

Source listing for the customer inquiry program (part 6 of 7)

```
 1820-READ-INVOICE-RECORD SECTION.
*
     EXEC CICS
         READNEXT DATASET('INVPATH')
                  INTO(INVOICE-RECORD)
                  RIDFLD(CM-CUSTOMER-NUMBER)
     END-EXEC.
     MOVE 'N' TO MORE-INVOICES-SW.
*
 1820-DUPKEY.
*
     MOVE INV-INVOICE-NUMBER TO IM-D-INVOICE-NUMBER(INVOICE-SUB).
     MOVE INV-PO-NUMBER      TO IM-D-PO-NUMBER(INVOICE-SUB).
     MOVE INV-INVOICE-DATE   TO IM-D-INVOICE-DATE(INVOICE-SUB).
     MOVE INV-INVOICE-TOTAL  TO IM-D-INVOICE-TOTAL(INVOICE-SUB).
*
 1820-EXIT.
*
     EXIT.
*
 1900-SEND-CUSTOMER-SCREEN SECTION.
*
     EXEC CICS
         SEND MAP('INQMAP1')
              MAPSET('INQSET2')
              FROM(INQUIRY-MAP)
              ERASE
     END-EXEC.
*
 8000-START-TERMINAL-SESSION SECTION.
*
     MOVE LOW-VALUE TO INQUIRY-MAP.
     EXEC CICS
         SEND MAP('INQMAP1')
              MAPSET('INQSET2')
              FROM(INQUIRY-MAP)
              ERASE
     END-EXEC.
```

Source listing for the customer inquiry program (part 7 of 7)

The inventory listing program (transient data)

```
Program:   INVLST1   Inventory listing (transient data)   Page: 1
Designer:  Doug Lowe                                       Date: 08-01-87
------------------------------------------------------------------------
Process specifications
------------------------------------------------------------------------
1.  For each record in the inventory file, list the item number,
    item description, unit price, and quantity on hand.  At the
    end of the listing, list the number of records in the file.

2.  Use a transient data destination to route the output data to
    a printer.  An installation-developed utility program will be
    responsible for reading data from the destination and writing
    it to the printer.
3.  Use ASA control characters in the first byte of each record to
    control printer spacing.  The control characters are:

    blank     skip one line before printing
    0         skip two lines before printing
    -         skip three lines before printing
    1         skip to the top of the next page before printing
```

Specifications for the inventory listing program (transient data version)

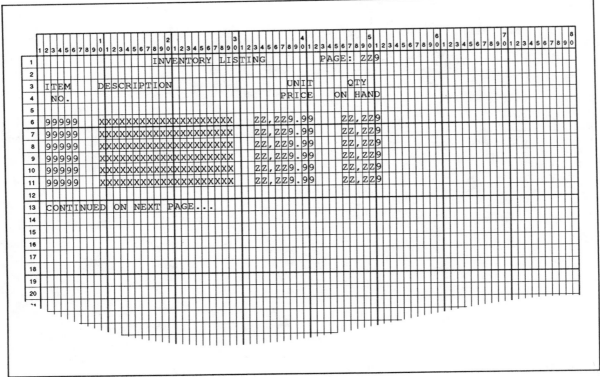

Print chart for the inventory listing program (transient data version)

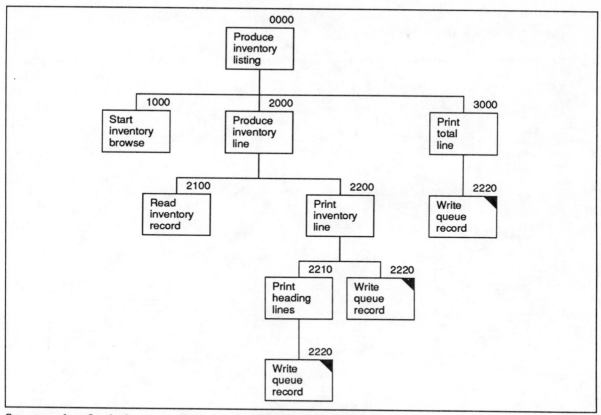

Structure chart for the inventory listing program (transient data version)

```
      IDENTIFICATION DIVISION.
 *
      PROGRAM-ID.  INVLST1.
 *
      ENVIRONMENT DIVISION.
 *
      DATA DIVISION.
 *
      WORKING-STORAGE SECTION.
 *
      01    SWITCHES.
 *
            05    INVMAST-EOF-SW    PIC X          VALUE 'N'.
                  88  INVMAST-EOF                  VALUE 'Y'.
 *
      01    WORK-FIELDS.
 *
            05    RECORD-COUNT      PIC S9(5)  VALUE ZERO   COMP-3.
 *
      01    PRINT-FIELDS.
 *
            05    LINE-COUNT        PIC S99    VALUE +50    COMP-3.
            05    LINES-ON-PAGE     PIC S99    VALUE +50    COMP-3.
            05    PAGE-NO           PIC S999   VALUE +1     COMP-3.
            05    PRINT-AREA        PIC X(133).
            05    LINE-LENGTH       PIC S9(4)               COMP.
 *
      01    HDG-LINE-1.
 *
            05    HDG1-CC           PIC X      VALUE '1'.
            05    FILLER            PIC X(20)  VALUE '               INVE'.
            05    FILLER            PIC X(20)  VALUE 'NTORY LISTING       '.
            05    FILLER            PIC X(7)   VALUE ' PAGE: '.
            05    HDG1-PAGE-NO      PIC ZZ9.
 *
      01    HDG-LINE-2.
 *
            05    HDG2-CC           PIC X      VALUE '0'.
            05    FILLER            PIC X(20)  VALUE 'ITEM    DESCRIPTION '.
            05    FILLER            PIC X(20)  VALUE '               UNIT'.
            05    FILLER            PIC X(8)   VALUE '     QTY'.
 *
      01    HDG-LINE-3.
 *
            05    HDG3-CC           PIC X      VALUE ' '.
            05    FILLER            PIC X(20)  VALUE ' NO.               '.
            05    FILLER            PIC X(20)  VALUE '            PRICE'.
            05    FILLER            PIC X(10)  VALUE '   ON HAND'.
 *
```

Source listing for the inventory listing program (transient data version) (part 1 of 4)

```
    01   INVENTORY-LINE.
*
         05   IL-CC                 PIC X              VALUE SPACE.
         05   IL-ITEM-NUMBER        PIC 9(5).
         05   FILLER                PIC X(3)           VALUE SPACE.
         05   IL-ITEM-DESCRIPTION   PIC X(20).
         05   FILLER                PIC X(3)           VALUE SPACE.
         05   IL-UNIT-PRICE         PIC ZZ,ZZ9.99.
         05   FILLER                PIC X(4)           VALUE SPACE.
         05   IL-ON-HAND-QUANTITY   PIC ZZ,ZZ9.
*
    01   TOTAL-LINE.
*
         05   TL-CC              PIC X        VALUE '-'.
         05   TL-RECORD-COUNT    PIC ZZ,ZZ9.
         05   FILLER             PIC X(20)    VALUE ' RECORDS IN THE INVE'.
         05   FILLER             PIC X(10)    VALUE 'NTORY FILE'.
*
    01   EOJ-MESSAGE.
*
         05   FILLER             PIC X(20)    VALUE 'INVENTORY LISTING PR'.
         05   FILLER             PIC X(6)     VALUE 'INTED.'.
*
    01   INVENTORY-MASTER-RECORD.
*
         05   IM-ITEM-NUMBER       PIC X(5).
         05   IM-ITEM-DESCRIPTION  PIC X(20).
         05   IM-UNIT-PRICE        PIC S9(5)V99    COMP-3.
         05   IM-ON-HAND-QUANTITY  PIC S9(5)       COMP-3.
*
    01   DESTINATION-ID           PIC X(4)          VALUE 'L86P'.
*
    PROCEDURE DIVISION.
*
    0000-PRODUCE-INVENTORY-LISTING SECTION.
*
         PERFORM 1000-START-INVENTORY-BROWSE.
         EXEC CICS
             HANDLE CONDITION ENDFILE(2100-ENDFILE)
         END-EXEC.
         EXEC CICS
             ENQ RESOURCE(DESTINATION-ID)
                 LENGTH(4)
         END-EXEC.
         PERFORM 2000-PRODUCE-INVENTORY-LINE
             UNTIL INVMAST-EOF.
         PERFORM 3000-PRINT-TOTAL-LINE.
         EXEC CICS
             DEQ RESOURCE(DESTINATION-ID)
                 LENGTH(4)
         END-EXEC.
```

Source listing for the inventory listing program (transient data version) (part 2 of 4)

```
            EXEC CICS
                SEND TEXT FROM(EOJ-MESSAGE)
                          LENGTH(26)
                          ERASE
                          FREEKB
            END-EXEC.
            EXEC CICS
                RETURN
            END-EXEC.
        *
         1000-START-INVENTORY-BROWSE SECTION.
        *
            EXEC CICS
                HANDLE CONDITION NOTFND(1000-NOTFND)
            END-EXEC.
            MOVE ZERO TO IM-ITEM-NUMBER.
            EXEC CICS
                STARTBR DATASET('INVMAST')
                        RIDFLD(IM-ITEM-NUMBER)
            END-EXEC.
            GO TO 1000-EXIT.
        *
         1000-NOTFND.
        *
            MOVE 'Y' TO INVMAST-EOF-SW.
        *
         1000-EXIT.
        *
            EXIT.
        *
         2000-PRODUCE-INVENTORY-LINE SECTION.
        *
            PERFORM 2100-READ-INVENTORY-RECORD.
            IF NOT INVMAST-EOF
                PERFORM 2200-PRINT-INVENTORY-LINE.
        *
         2100-READ-INVENTORY-RECORD SECTION.
        *
            EXEC CICS
                READNEXT DATASET('INVMAST')
                         INTO(INVENTORY-MASTER-RECORD)
                         RIDFLD(IM-ITEM-NUMBER)
            END-EXEC.
            ADD 1 TO RECORD-COUNT.
            GO TO 2100-EXIT.
        *
         2100-ENDFILE.
        *
            MOVE 'Y' TO INVMAST-EOF-SW.
        *
         2100-EXIT.
        *
            EXIT.
        *
```

Source listing for the inventory listing program (transient data version) (part 3 of 4)

```
    2200-PRINT-INVENTORY-LINE SECTION.
*
        IF LINE-COUNT = LINES-ON-PAGE
            PERFORM 2210-PRINT-HEADING-LINES.
        MOVE IM-ITEM-NUMBER       TO IL-ITEM-NUMBER.
        MOVE IM-ITEM-DESCRIPTION TO IL-ITEM-DESCRIPTION.
        MOVE IM-UNIT-PRICE        TO IL-UNIT-PRICE.
        MOVE IM-ON-HAND-QUANTITY TO IL-ON-HAND-QUANTITY.
        MOVE INVENTORY-LINE TO PRINT-AREA.
        MOVE 51 TO LINE-LENGTH.
        PERFORM 2220-WRITE-QUEUE-RECORD.
        ADD 1 TO LINE-COUNT.
        MOVE SPACE TO IL-CC.
*
    2210-PRINT-HEADING-LINES SECTION.
*
        MOVE PAGE-NO TO HDG1-PAGE-NO.
        MOVE HDG-LINE-1 TO PRINT-AREA.
        MOVE 51 TO LINE-LENGTH.
        PERFORM 2220-WRITE-QUEUE-RECORD.
        ADD 1 TO PAGE-NO.
        MOVE HDG-LINE-2 TO PRINT-AREA.
        MOVE 49 TO LINE-LENGTH.
        PERFORM 2220-WRITE-QUEUE-RECORD.
        MOVE HDG-LINE-3 TO PRINT-AREA.
        MOVE 51 TO LINE-LENGTH.
        PERFORM 2220-WRITE-QUEUE-RECORD.
        MOVE '0' TO IL-CC.
        MOVE ZERO TO LINE-COUNT.
*
    2220-WRITE-QUEUE-RECORD SECTION.
*
        EXEC CICS
            WRITEQ TD QUEUE(DESTINATION-ID)
                      FROM(PRINT-AREA)
                      LENGTH(LINE-LENGTH)
        END-EXEC.
*
    3000-PRINT-TOTAL-LINE SECTION.
*
        MOVE RECORD-COUNT TO TL-RECORD-COUNT.
        MOVE TOTAL-LINE TO PRINT-AREA.
        MOVE 37 TO LINE-LENGTH.
        PERFORM 2220-WRITE-QUEUE-RECORD.
```

Source listing for the inventory listing program (transient data version) (part 4 of 4)

The inventory listing program (SEND TEXT)

```
Program:   INVLST2   Inventory listing (SEND TEXT)       Page: 1
Designer:  Doug Lowe                                      Date: 08-01-87
-------------------------------------------------------------------------
Process specifications
-------------------------------------------------------------------------
1.  For each record in the inventory file, list the item number,
    item description, unit price, and quantity on hand.  At the
    end of the listing, list the number of records in the file.

2.  Use basic mapping support's message building facilities and
    the SEND TEXT command to create the listing.
```

Specifications for the inventory listing program (SEND TEXT version)

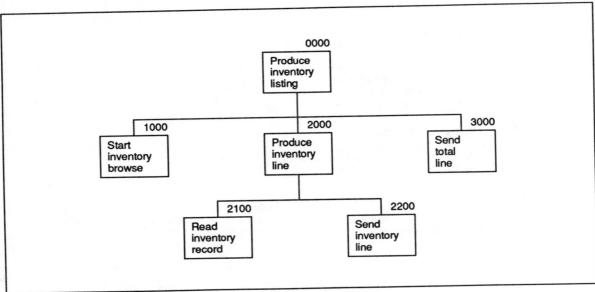

Structure chart for the inventory listing program (SEND TEXT version)

Output on all pages of the message except the last

```
          1         2         3         4         5         6         7         8
 12345678901234567890123456789012345678901234567890123456789012345678901234567890
1                     INVENTORY LISTING            PAGE: ZZ9
2
3  ITEM     DESCRIPTION                     UNIT        QTY
4  NO.                                      PRICE       ON HAND
5
6  99999    XXXXXXXXXXXXXXXXXXXX            ZZ,ZZ9.99     ZZ,ZZ9
7  99999    XXXXXXXXXXXXXXXXXXXX            ZZ,ZZ9.99     ZZ,ZZ9
8  99999    XXXXXXXXXXXXXXXXXXXX            ZZ,ZZ9.99     ZZ,ZZ9
9  99999    XXXXXXXXXXXXXXXXXXXX            ZZ,ZZ9.99     ZZ,ZZ9
10 99999    XXXXXXXXXXXXXXXXXXXX            ZZ,ZZ9.99     ZZ,ZZ9
11 99999    XXXXXXXXXXXXXXXXXXXX            ZZ,ZZ9.99     ZZ,ZZ9
12 99999    XXXXXXXXXXXXXXXXXXXX            ZZ,ZZ9.99     ZZ,ZZ9
13 99999    XXXXXXXXXXXXXXXXXXXX            ZZ,ZZ9.99     ZZ,ZZ9
14 99999    XXXXXXXXXXXXXXXXXXXX            ZZ,ZZ9.99     ZZ,ZZ9
15 99999    XXXXXXXXXXXXXXXXXXXX            ZZ,ZZ9.99     ZZ,ZZ9
16 99999    XXXXXXXXXXXXXXXXXXXX            ZZ,ZZ9.99     ZZ,ZZ9
17 99999    XXXXXXXXXXXXXXXXXXXX            ZZ,ZZ9.99     ZZ,ZZ9
18 99999    XXXXXXXXXXXXXXXXXXXX            ZZ,ZZ9.99     ZZ,ZZ9
19 99999    XXXXXXXXXXXXXXXXXXXX            ZZ,ZZ9.99     ZZ,ZZ9
20 99999    XXXXXXXXXXXXXXXXXXXX            ZZ,ZZ9.99     ZZ,ZZ9
21 99999    XXXXXXXXXXXXXXXXXXXX            ZZ,ZZ9.99     ZZ,ZZ9
22 99999    XXXXXXXXXXXXXXXXXXXX            ZZ,ZZ9.99     ZZ,ZZ9
23
24 CONTINUED ON NEXT PAGE...
```

- Header — lines 1–4
- Inventory line — lines 6–22
- Trailer — lines 23–24

Output on the last page of the message

```
10 99999    XXXXXXXXXXXXXXXXXXXX            ZZ,ZZ9.99     ZZ,ZZ9
11 99999    XXXXXXXXXXXXXXXXXXXX            ZZ,ZZ9.99     ZZ,ZZ9
12
13 ZZ,ZZ9 RECORDS IN THE INVENTORY FILE
14
15
```

- Total line — line 13

Screen layout for the inventory listing program (SEND TEXT version)

```
        IDENTIFICATION DIVISION.
    *
        PROGRAM-ID.   INVLST2.
    *
        ENVIRONMENT DIVISION.
    *
        DATA DIVISION.
    *
        WORKING-STORAGE SECTION.
    *
        01    SWITCHES.
    *
            05    INVMAST-EOF-SW    PIC X           VALUE 'N'.
                  88    INVMAST-EOF                 VALUE 'Y'.
    *
        01    WORK-FIELDS.
    *
            05    RECORD-COUNT      PIC S9(5)  VALUE ZERO     COMP-3.
    *
        01    HEADER-AREA.
    *
            05    HA-PREFIX.
                  10    HA-LENGTH     PIC S9(4)  VALUE +153      COMP.
                  10    HA-PAGE-CODE  PIC X      VALUE '*'.
                  10    FILLER        PIC X      VALUE SPACE.
            05    HEADER-LINE-1.
                  10    FILLER        PIC X(20)  VALUE '                    INVE'.
                  10    FILLER        PIC X(20)  VALUE 'NTORY LISTING        '.
                  10    FILLER        PIC X(10)  VALUE ' PAGE: ***'.
                  10    HA1-NL        PIC XX     VALUE '  '.
            05    HEADER-LINE-2.
                  10    FILLER        PIC X(20)  VALUE 'ITEM    DESCRIPTION '.
                  10    FILLER        PIC X(20)  VALUE '                UNIT'.
                  10    FILLER        PIC X(8)   VALUE '     QTY'.
                  10    HA2-NL        PIC X      VALUE ' '.
            05    HEADER-LINE-3.
                  10    FILLER        PIC X(20)  VALUE ' NO.                '.
                  10    FILLER        PIC X(20)  VALUE '              PRICE'.
                  10    FILLER        PIC X(10)  VALUE '   ON HAND'
                  10    HA3-NL        PIC XX     VALUE '  '.
    *
        01    INVENTORY-LINE.
    *
            05    IL-ITEM-NUMBER        PIC 9(5).
            05    FILLER                PIC X(3)        VALUE SPACE.
            05    IL-ITEM-DESCRIPTION   PIC X(20).
            05    FILLER                PIC X(3)        VALUE SPACE.
            05    IL-UNIT-PRICE         PIC ZZ,ZZ9.99.
            05    FILLER                PIC X(4)        VALUE SPACE.
            05    IL-ON-HAND-QUANTITY   PIC ZZ,ZZ9.
            05    IL-NL                 PIC X           VALUE ''.
    *
```

Source listing for the inventory listing program (SEND TEXT version) (part 1 of 4)

```
     01   TOTAL-LINE.
     *
          05   TL-NL              PIC X        VALUE ' '.
          05   TL-RECORD-COUNT    PIC ZZ,ZZ9.
          05   FILLER             PIC X(20)    VALUE ' RECORDS IN THE INVE'.
          05   FILLER             PIC X(10)    VALUE 'NTORY FILE'.
     *
     01   TRAILER-AREA.
     *
          05   TA-PREFIX.
               10   TA-LENGTH     PIC S9(4)    VALUE +26      COMP.
               10   FILLER        PIC XX       VALUE SPACE.
          05   TRAILER-LINE.
               10   TA-NL         PIC X        VALUE ' '.
               10   FILLER        PIC X(20)    VALUE 'CONTINUED ON NEXT PA'.
               10   FILLER        PIC X(5)     VALUE 'GE...'.
     *
     01   INVENTORY-MASTER-RECORD.
     *
          05   IM-ITEM-NUMBER       PIC X(5).
          05   IM-ITEM-DESCRIPTION  PIC X(20).
          05   IM-UNIT-PRICE        PIC S9(5)V99    COMP-3.
          05   IM-ON-HAND-QUANTITY  PIC S9(5)       COMP-3.
     *
      PROCEDURE DIVISION.
     *
      0000-PRODUCE-INVENTORY-LISTING SECTION.
     *
          PERFORM 1000-START-INVENTORY-BROWSE.
          EXEC CICS
              HANDLE CONDITION ENDFILE(2100-ENDFILE)
          END-EXEC.
          PERFORM 2000-PRODUCE-INVENTORY-LINE
              UNTIL INVMAST-EOF.
          PERFORM 3000-SEND-TOTAL-LINE.
          EXEC CICS
              SEND PAGE
                      OPERPURGE
          END-EXEC.
          EXEC CICS
              RETURN
          END-EXEC.
     *
      1000-START-INVENTORY-BROWSE SECTION.
     *
          EXEC CICS
              HANDLE CONDITION NOTFND(1000-NOTFND)
          END-EXEC.
          MOVE ZERO TO IM-ITEM-NUMBER.
          EXEC CICS
              STARTBR DATASET('INVMAST')
                      RIDFLD(IM-ITEM-NUMBER)
          END-EXEC.
          GO TO 1000-EXIT.
```

Source listing for the inventory listing program (SEND TEXT version) (part 2 of 4)

```
       *
        1000-NOTFND.
       *
            MOVE 'Y' TO INVMAST-EOF-SW.
       *
        1000-EXIT.
       *
            EXIT.
       *
        2000-PRODUCE-INVENTORY-LINE SECTION.
       *
            PERFORM 2100-READ-INVENTORY-RECORD.
            IF NOT INVMAST-EOF
                PERFORM 2200-SEND-INVENTORY-LINE.
       *
        2100-READ-INVENTORY-RECORD SECTION.
       *
            EXEC CICS
                READNEXT DATASET('INVMAST')
                         INTO(INVENTORY-MASTER-RECORD)
                         RIDFLD(IM-ITEM-NUMBER)
            END-EXEC.
            ADD 1 TO RECORD-COUNT.
            GO TO 2100-EXIT.
       *
        2100-ENDFILE.
       *
            MOVE 'Y' TO INVMAST-EOF-SW.
       *
        2100-EXIT.
       *
            EXIT.
       *
        2200-SEND-INVENTORY-LINE SECTION.
       *
            MOVE IM-ITEM-NUMBER      TO IL-ITEM-NUMBER.
            MOVE IM-ITEM-DESCRIPTION TO IL-ITEM-DESCRIPTION.
            MOVE IM-UNIT-PRICE       TO IL-UNIT-PRICE.
            MOVE IM-ON-HAND-QUANTITY TO IL-ON-HAND-QUANTITY.
            EXEC CICS
                SEND TEXT FROM(INVENTORY-LINE)
                          LENGTH(51)
                          ACCUM
                          PAGING
                          ERASE
                          HEADER(HEADER-AREA)
                          TRAILER(TRAILER-AREA)
            END-EXEC.
```

Source listing for the inventory listing program (SEND TEXT version) (part 3 of 4)

```
*
 3000-SEND-TOTAL-LINE SECTION.
*
     MOVE RECORD-COUNT TO TL-RECORD-COUNT.
     EXEC CICS
         SEND TEXT FROM(TOTAL-LINE)
                   LENGTH(37)
                   ACCUM
                   PAGING
                   ERASE
     END-EXEC.
```

Source listing for the inventory listing program (SEND TEXT version) (part 4 of 4)

The inventory listing program (SEND MAP)

```
Program:   INVLST3   Inventory listing (SEND MAP)        Page: 1
Designer:  Doug Lowe                                      Date: 08-01-87
-----------------------------------------------------------------------
Process specifications
-----------------------------------------------------------------------
1.   For each record in the inventory file, list the item number,
     item description, unit price, and quantity on hand.  At the
     end of the listing, list the number of records in the file.

2.   Use basic mapping support's message building facilities and
     the SEND MAP command to create the listing.
```

Specifications for the inventory listing program (SEND MAP version)

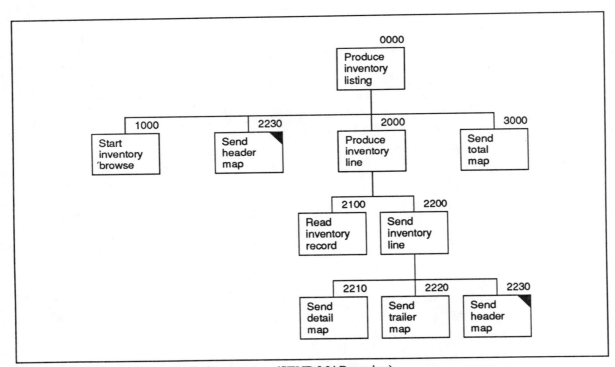

Structure chart for the inventory listing program (SEND MAP version)

Output on all pages of the message except the last

Output on the last page of the message

Screen layout for the inventory listing program (SEND MAP version)

```
        PRINT NOGEN                                                       X
LSTSET1 DFHMSD TYPE=&SYSPARM,                                             X
               LANG=COBOL,                                               X
               MODE=INOUT,                                               X
               TERM=3270-2,                                              X
               CTRL=FREEKB,                                              X
               STORAGE=AUTO,                                             X
               TIOAPFX=YES
*********************************************************************************
*********************************************************************************
LSTMAP1  DFHMDI SIZE=(5,80),                                             X
                JUSTIFY=FIRST,                                           X
                HEADER=YES
*********************************************************************************
         DFHMDF POS=(1,17),                                              X
                LENGTH=17,                                               X
                ATTRB=PROT,                                              X
                INITIAL='INVENTORY LISTING'
         DFHMDF POS=(1,42),                                              X
                LENGTH=5,                                                X
                ATTRB=PROT,                                              X
                INITIAL='PAGE:'
PAGENO   DFHMDF POS=(1,48),                                              X
                LENGTH=3,                                                X
                ATTRB=PROT,                                              X
                PICOUT='ZZ9'
         DFHMDF POS=(3,1),                                               X
                LENGTH=19,                                               X
                ATTRB=PROT,                                              X
                INITIAL='ITEM      DESCRIPTION'
         DFHMDF POS=(3,37),                                              X
                LENGTH=12,                                               X
                ATTRB=PROT,                                              X
                INITIAL='UNIT      QTY'
         DFHMDF POS=(4,2),                                               X
                LENGTH=3,                                                X
                ATTRB=PROT,                                              X
                INITIAL='NO.'
         DFHMDF POS=(4,36),                                              X
                LENGTH=15,                                               X
                ATTRB=PROT,                                              X
                INITIAL='PRICE     ON HAND'
*********************************************************************************
```

BMS mapset for the inventory listing program (SEND MAP version) (part 1 of 2)

```
****************************************************************
LSTMAP2   DFHMDI SIZE=(1,80),                                 X
                 LINE=NEXT,                                   X
                 COLUMN=1
****************************************************************
ITEMNO    DFHMDF POS=(1,1),                                   X
                 LENGTH=5,                                    X
                 ATTRB=PROT
DESCR     DFHMDF POS=(1,9),                                   X
                 LENGTH=20,                                   X
                 ATTRB=PROT
UPRICE    DFHMDF POS=(1,32),                                  X
                 LENGTH=9,                                    X
                 ATTRB=PROT,                                  X
                 PICOUT='ZZ,ZZ9.99'
ONHAND    DFHMDF POS=(1,45),                                  X
                 LENGTH=6,                                    X
                 ATTRB=PROT,                                  X
                 PICOUT='ZZ,ZZ9'
****************************************************************
****************************************************************
LSTMAP3   DFHMDI SIZE=(2,80),                                 X
                 JUSTIFY=LAST,                                X
                 TRAILER=YES
****************************************************************
          DFHMDF POS=(2,1),                                   X
                 LENGTH=25,                                   X
                 ATTRB=PROT,                                  X
                 INITIAL='CONTINUED ON NEXT PAGE...'
****************************************************************
****************************************************************
LSTMAP4   DFHMDI SIZE=(2,80),                                 X
                 LINE=NEXT,                                   X
                 COLUMN=1,                                    X
                 TRAILER=YES
****************************************************************
COUNT     DFHMDF POS=(2,1),                                   X
                 LENGTH=6,                                    X
                 ATTRB=PROT,                                  X
                 PICOUT='ZZ,ZZ9'
          DFHMDF POS=(2,8),                                   X
                 LENGTH=29,                                   X
                 ATTRB=PROT,                                  X
                 INITIAL='RECORDS IN THE INVENTORY FILE'
****************************************************************
          DFHMSD TYPE=FINAL
          END
```

BMS mapset for the inventory listing program (SEND MAP version) (part 2 of 2)

```
 01   INVENTORY-LISTING-MAP-1.
*
      05   FILLER                         PIC X(12).
*
      05   ILM1-L-PAGE-NO                 PIC S9(4)      COMP.
      05   ILM1-A-PAGE-NO                 PIC X.
      05   ILM1-D-PAGE-NO                 PIC ZZ9.
*
 01   INVENTORY-LISTING-MAP-2.
*
      05   FILLER                         PIC X(12).
*
      05   ILM2-L-ITEM-NUMBER             PIC S9(4)   COMP.
      05   ILM2-A-ITEM-NUMBER             PIC X.
      05   ILM2-D-ITEM-NUMBER             PIC 99999.
*
      05   ILM2-L-ITEM-DESCRIPTION PIC S9(4)   COMP.
      05   ILM2-A-ITEM-DESCRIPTION PIC X.
      05   ILM2-D-ITEM-DESCRIPTION PIC X(20).
*
      05   ILM2-L-UNIT-PRICE              PIC S9(4)   COMP.
      05   ILM2-A-UNIT-PRICE              PIC X.
      05   ILM2-D-UNIT-PRICE              PIC ZZ,ZZ9.99.
*
      05   ILM2-L-ON-HAND-QUANTITY PIC S9(4)   COMP.
      05   ILM2-A-ON-HAND-QUANTITY PIC X.
      05   ILM2-D-ON-HAND-QUANTITY PIC ZZ,ZZ9.
*
 01   INVENTORY-LISTING-MAP-4.
*
      05   FILLER                         PIC X(12).
*
      05   ILM4-L-RECORD-COUNT            PIC S9(4)   COMP.
      05   ILM4-A-RECORD-COUNT            PIC X.
      05   ILM4-D-RECORD-COUNT            PIC ZZ,ZZ9.
```

Programmer-generated symbolic mapset for the inventory listing program (SEND MAP version)

```
      IDENTIFICATION DIVISION.
*
      PROGRAM-ID.  INVLST3.
*
      ENVIRONMENT DIVISION.
*
      DATA DIVISION.
*
      WORKING-STORAGE SECTION.
*
      01  SWITCHES.
*
          05  INVMAST-EOF-SW        PIC X        VALUE 'N'.
              88  INVMAST-EOF                     VALUE 'Y'.
          05  PAGE-OVERFLOW-SW      PIC X        VALUE 'N'.
              88  PAGE-OVERFLOW                   VALUE 'Y'.
*
      01  WORK-FIELDS.
*
          05  RECORD-COUNT          PIC S9(5)    VALUE ZERO   COMP-3.
          05  PAGE-NO               PIC S9(3)    VALUE +1     COMP-3.
*
      COPY LSTSET1.
*
      01  INVENTORY-MASTER-RECORD.
*
          05  IM-ITEM-NUMBER        PIC X(5).
          05  IM-ITEM-DESCRIPTION   PIC X(20).
          05  IM-UNIT-PRICE         PIC S9(5)V99             COMP-3.
          05  IM-ON-HAND-QUANTITY   PIC S9(5)                COMP-3.
*
      PROCEDURE DIVISION.
*
      0000-PRODUCE-INVENTORY-LISTING SECTION.
*
          MOVE LOW-VALUE TO INVENTORY-LISTING-MAP-1
                            INVENTORY-LISTING-MAP-2
                            INVENTORY-LISTING-MAP-4.
          PERFORM 1000-START-INVENTORY-BROWSE.
          EXEC CICS
              HANDLE CONDITION ENDFILE(2100-ENDFILE)
                               OVERFLOW(2210-OVERFLOW)
          END-EXEC.
          PERFORM 2230-SEND-HEADER-MAP.
          PERFORM 2000-PRODUCE-INVENTORY-LINE
              UNTIL INVMAST-EOF.
          PERFORM 3000-SEND-TOTAL-MAP.
          EXEC CICS
              SEND PAGE
                   OPERPURGE
          END-EXEC.
          EXEC CICS
              RETURN
          END-EXEC.
```

Source listing for the inventory listing program (SEND MAP version) (part 1 of 4)

```
*
 1000-START-INVENTORY-BROWSE SECTION.
*
     EXEC CICS
         HANDLE CONDITION NOTFND(1000-NOTFND)
     END-EXEC.
     MOVE ZERO TO IM-ITEM-NUMBER.
     EXEC CICS
         STARTBR DATASET('INVMAST')
                 RIDFLD(IM-ITEM-NUMBER)
     END-EXEC.
     GO TO 1000-EXIT.
*
 1000-NOTFND.
*
     MOVE 'Y' TO INVMAST-EOF-SW.
*
 1000-EXIT.
*
     EXIT.
*
 2000-PRODUCE-INVENTORY-LINE SECTION.
*
     PERFORM 2100-READ-INVENTORY-RECORD.
     IF NOT INVMAST-EOF
         PERFORM 2200-SEND-INVENTORY-LINE.
*
 2100-READ-INVENTORY-RECORD SECTION.
*
     EXEC CICS
         READNEXT DATASET('INVMAST')
                  INTO(INVENTORY-MASTER-RECORD)
                  RIDFLD(IM-ITEM-NUMBER)
     END-EXEC.
     ADD 1 TO RECORD-COUNT.
     GO TO 2100-EXIT.
*
 2100-ENDFILE.
*
     MOVE 'Y' TO INVMAST-EOF-SW.
*
 2100-EXIT.
*
     EXIT.
*
 2200-SEND-INVENTORY-LINE SECTION.
*
     MOVE IM-ITEM-NUMBER        TO ILM2-D-ITEM-NUMBER.
     MOVE IM-ITEM-DESCRIPTION TO ILM2-D-ITEM-DESCRIPTION.
     MOVE IM-UNIT-PRICE         TO ILM2-D-UNIT-PRICE.
     MOVE IM-ON-HAND-QUANTITY TO ILM2-D-ON-HAND-QUANTITY.
```

Source listing for the inventory listing program (SEND MAP version) (part 2 of 4)

```
            PERFORM 2210-SEND-DETAIL-MAP.
            IF PAGE-OVERFLOW
                PERFORM 2220-SEND-TRAILER-MAP
                PERFORM 2230-SEND-HEADER-MAP
                PERFORM 2210-SEND-DETAIL-MAP
                MOVE 'N' TO PAGE-OVERFLOW-SW.
       *
        2210-SEND-DETAIL-MAP SECTION.
       *
            EXEC CICS
                SEND MAP('LSTMAP2')
                     MAPSET('LSTSET1')
                     FROM(INVENTORY-LISTING-MAP-2)
                     ACCUM
                     PAGING
                     ERASE
            END-EXEC.
            GO TO 2210-EXIT.
       *
        2210-OVERFLOW.
       *
            MOVE 'Y' TO PAGE-OVERFLOW-SW.
       *
        2210-EXIT.
       *
            EXIT.
       *
        2220-SEND-TRAILER-MAP SECTION.
       *
            EXEC CICS
                SEND MAP('LSTMAP3')
                     MAPSET('LSTSET1')
                     MAPONLY
                     ACCUM
                     PAGING
                     ERASE
            END-EXEC.
       *
        2230-SEND-HEADER-MAP SECTION.
       *
            MOVE PAGE-NO TO ILM1-D-PAGE-NO.
            EXEC CICS
                SEND MAP('LSTMAP1')
                     MAPSET('LSTSET1')
                     FROM(INVENTORY-LISTING-MAP-1)
                     ACCUM
                     PAGING
                     ERASE
            END-EXEC.
            ADD 1 TO PAGE-NO.
       *
```

Source listing for the inventory listing program (SEND MAP version) (part 3 of 4)

```
    3000-SEND-TOTAL-MAP SECTION.
*
        MOVE RECORD-COUNT TO ILM4-D-RECORD-COUNT.
        EXEC CICS
            SEND MAP('LSTMAP4')
                    MAPSET('LSTSET1')
                    FROM(INVENTORY-LISTING-MAP-4)
                    ACCUM
                    PAGING
                    ERASE
        END-EXEC.
```

Source listing for the inventory listing program (SEND MAP version) (part 4 of 4)

Section 6

JCL procedures for CICS program development

This section shows you the JCL you need to code to prepare BMS mapsets and command-level COBOL programs for execution under two operating system environments: MVS and DOS/VSE. Under MVS, standard cataloged procedures make CICS program development a straightforward process. Under DOS/VSE, however, CICS program development is awkward at best. That's because DOS/VSE doesn't really have a good procedure facility. To simplify the DOS/VSE examples presented in this section, I assume you're using ICCF.

After I describe the CICS program development process and the JCL requirements for DOS/VSE and MVS users, I'll give you some tips for using interactive systems like ISPF, ICCF, and VM/CMS for CICS program development. Naturally, you'll have to adapt the procedures I present here so they'll work at your installation.

At the end of this chapter, I briefly describe the translator and compiler options you're likely to use for CICS program development.

CICS program development

Figure 6-1 illustrates the basic CICS program development process; this process applies to both MVS and DOS/VSE. The left side of the figure shows how BMS mapsets are prepared. Here, a source program containing BMS macro instructions is processed by the assembler to produce an object module (the physical map) and a symbolic map. The physical map is then processed by the linkage editor to produce a load module, used by CICS at execution time.

The right side of figure 6-1 shows how a command-level COBOL program is prepared. Here, a source program containing a mixture of standard COBOL statements and CICS commands is processed by the command-level translator, which translates the CICS commands to equivalent COBOL statements. (Each command results in a series of MOVE statements followed by a CALL statement.) Then, the translated program, also in source form, is processed by the COBOL compiler to produce an object module, which is then processed by the linkage editor to produce a load

module. Notice that the COBOL compiler also processes the symbolic map produced by the assembler.

Since the translator and compiler execute as separate job steps, you get two sets of source listings and diagnostics. The translator output contains a listing of the source program as you wrote it plus any diagnostic messages related to CICS commands. The compiler output contains a listing of the translated program plus any diagnostics related to standard COBOL statements. As a result, you have to examine both listings to determine if your program was processed without errors.

Which source listing should you use when testing and debugging your program? You really need to use both. You need the compiler listing since it contains the expansions of all COPY members included in your program. However, it also contains expansions of all CICS commands, which makes the compiler's listing of the Procedure Division almost unreadable.

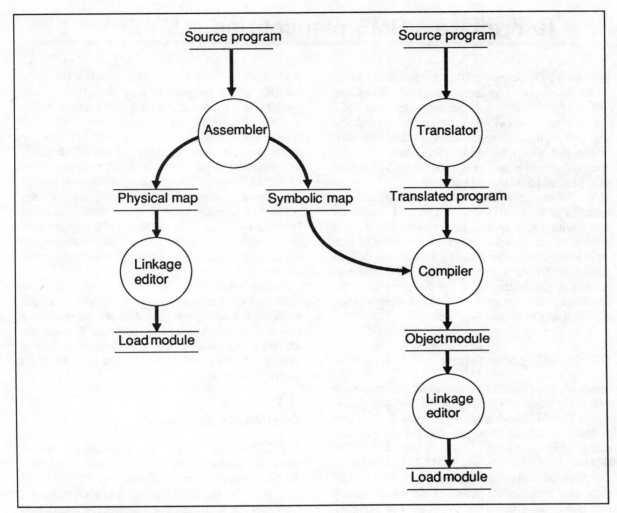

Figure 6-1 CICS program development

How to prepare a BMS mapset under MVS

The best way to prepare a BMS mapset under MVS is to use the standard cataloged procedure *DFHMAPS*. This procedure processes the BMS mapset source file twice to produce both a symbolic map and a physical map. Many installations have customized the DFHMAPS procedure or have created different procedures altogether. So find out what procedures to use at your shop.

To invoke the DFHMAPS procedure, you specify PROC=DFHMAPS on an EXEC statement along with any required parameters. Then, you supply one or more DD statements to identify data sets required by the procedure. To code the JCL to invoke DFHMAPS properly, you need to know about the parameters used by the procedure, the processing done by each of the procedure's steps, and the data sets required by each job.

DFHMAPS parameters

There are three symbolic parameters you may need to specify when you invoke the DFHMAPS procedure. The MAPLIB parameter specifies the name of the load library that will contain the physical map. For example, you code MAPLIB='MMA2.LOADLIB' to use MMA2.LOADLIB for the physical map load library. The DSECTLIB parameter specifies the name of the source library that will contain the symbolic map. For example, you code MAPLIB='MMA2.COPYLIB' to use MMA2.COPYLIB for the symbolic map source library. The MAPNAME parameter specifies the member name to use for the map in both the physical map load library and the symbolic map source library. At most shops, the MAPLIB and DSECTLIB parameters have appropriate default values. So you need to code only the MAPNAME parameter on the EXEC statement when you invoke DFHMAPS.

DFHMAPS job steps

The DFHMAPS procedure consists of four job steps named COPY, ASMMAP, LINKMAP, and ASMDSECT. The COPY step invokes the IEBGENER utility program to copy the BMS source program to a temporary data set that's used as input to the assembler in the ASMMAP and ASMDSECT job steps. The ASMMAP step invokes the assembler, specifying SYSPARM(MAP) to create a physical map (an object module). The LINKMAP step invokes the linkage-editor to process the object module produced in the ASMMAP step; the result is a load module that can be used by CICS. The ASMDSECT step invokes the assembler again, this time specifying SYSPARM(DSECT). As a result, a symbolic map is created.

Notice that both the ASMMAP and the ASMDSECT job steps set the SYSPARM variable to indicate whether the assembler should produce a physical map or a symbolic map. As a result, the DFHMAPS procedure won't work properly unless you specify TYPE=&SYSPARM in the DFHMSD macro instruction.

DFHMAPS data sets

For DFHMAPS to work, you must supply one or more DD statements to allocate required data sets. At the minimum, you must supply a SYSUT1 DD statement for the COPY step; this DD statement identifies the source program (usually, a member of a partitioned data set or an in-stream data set). If you want the load module to be stored in a library other than the procedure's default, you can supply a SYSLMOD DD statement for the LINKMAP step. And if you want to redirect the symbolic map output, you can specify a SYSPUNCH DD statement for the ASMDSECT step. Alternatively, you can use the MAPLIB and DSECTLIB procedure parameters to specify a library for the physical or symbolic maps. For the symbolic map, I often code SYSOUT=A on the SYSPUNCH DD statement. Then, I use the resulting printed copy of the symbolic map to verify the symbolic map I create.

A DFHMAPS example

The following example shows how to invoke the DFHMAPS procedure to process a mapset named ORDSET1. The source module is in a library named MMA2.CICS.ASM; the physical map will be placed in MMA2.CICS.LOADLIB, and the symbolic map will be printed.

```
//MMA2MAP   JOB  (job accounting information)
//          EXEC PROC=DFHMAPS,MAPNAME=ORDSET1,
//              MAPLIB='MMA2.CICS.LOADLIB'
//COPY.SYSUT1       DD DSNAME=MMA2.CICS.ASM(ORDSET1),DISP=SHR
//ASMDSECT.SYSPUNCH DD SYSOUT=A
//
```

How to prepare a command-level COBOL program under MVS

To prepare a command-level COBOL program under MVS, you use the standard cataloged procedure *DFHEITCL*. This procedure translates, compiles, and link-edits a command-level program. Like DFHMAPS, many shops have customized the DFHEITCL procedure or developed their own. So find out what procedures to use at your installation. To use DFHEITCL properly, you must know about the parameters, job steps, and data sets the procedure uses.

DFHEITCL parameters

None of the DFHEITCL symbolic parameters are of general interest to application programmers. However, you can use the PARM parameter on the EXEC statement to specify options for the translator or the compiler. To specify translator options, specify TRN.PARM on the EXEC statement; to specify compiler options, specify COB.PARM. Later in this section, I'll describe translator and compiler options.

If you specify COB.PARM, check the procedure to find out what compiler options you're overriding and be sure to include them along with the options you want to specify. Usually, you'll need to specify NOTRUNC, NODYNAM, and LIB. You may also need to specify BUF and SIZE.

DFHEITCL job steps

DFHEITCL has three job steps. The TRN step translates the source program, producing a translated version of the source program in a temporary data set. The COB step compiles the translated program produced by the TRN step. And the LKED step link-edits the object module produced by the COB step.

DFHEITCL data sets

For DFHEITCL to work, you must supply several DD statements to allocate required data sets. First, you must supply a SYSIN DD statement for the TRN step to identify the source program, usually a partitioned data set member or an in-stream data set. For the COB step, you may or may not need to supply a SYSLIB DD statement, depending on whether or not your system's version of the DFHEITCL procedure allocates the source statement libraries your program needs.

For the LKED step, you must identify the member name for the load module. You can do that in one of two ways. If you want the member to be stored in the procedure's default load library, you can specify a LKED.SYSLIN DD statement that includes a NAME statement as in-stream data. If you want to use a library other than the procedure's default, however, you can include a LKED.SYSLMOD DD statement that provides a complete data set and member name.

A DFHEITCL example (default load library)

The following example shows how to invoke the DFHEITCL procedure to compile a source program named ORDRENT stored in a source library named MMA2.CICS.COBOL. A COPY library named MMA2.COPYLIB is concatenated to the procedure's COB.SYSLIB DD statement. The load module will be stored in the procedure's default load library with ORDRENT as the member name.

```
//MMA2TRAN JOB   (job accounting information)
//          EXEC PROG=DFHEITCL
//TRN.SYSIN  DD DSNAME=MMA2.CICS.COBOL(ORDRENT),DISP=SHR
//COB.SYSLIB DD
//           DD DSNAME=MMA2.COPYLIB,DISP=SHR
//LKED.SYSLIN DD *
 NAME ORDRENT (R)
/*
//
```

DFHEITCL example (private load library)

The following example shows how to invoke the DFHEITCL procedure to compile a source program named ORDRENT stored in a source library named MMA2.CICS.COBOL. A COPY library named MMA2.COPYLIB is concatenated to the procedure's COB.SYSLIB DD statement. And the load module (LKED.SYSLMOD) is written to a member of MMA2.CICS.LOADLIB.

```
//MMA2TRAN JOB   (job accounting information)
//          EXEC PROG=DFHEITCL
//TRN.SYSIN  DD DSNAME=MMA2.CICS.COBOL(ORDRENT),DISP=SHR
//COB.SYSLIB DD
//           DD DSNAME=MMA2.COPYLIB,DISP=SHR
//LKED.SYSLMOD DD DSNAME=MMA2.CICS.LOADLIB(ORDRENT),DISP=SHR
//
```

How to prepare a BMS mapset under DOS/VSE

The following job processes an ICCF source member named MNTSET1 twice to produce both a physical map and a symbolic map. In the first job step, the assembler is invoked to produce the physical map (SYSPARM='MAP'); the physical map is link-edited into a core-image library in the second job step. The third job step invokes the assembler again, this time specifying SYSPARM='DSECT' in the OPTION statement so that a symbolic map is produced. SYSPCH output from the assembler is routed to a temporary disk file, which is then processed as input to the MAINT program in the fourth job step; the linkage editor catalogs the symbolic map in a source statement library. The fifth job step invokes the SSERV program to print the symbolic map. The two /INCLUDE statements copy the specified ICCF library member into the job stream when you submit the job for background processing.

For this job to work on your system, you'll have to change (1) the name of the ICCF library member that contains the BMS mapset, (2) the phase name on the PHASE statement, (3) the DLBL and EXTENT statements that describe the temporary disk file, and (4) the LIBDEF statements that identify the libraries that will contain the physical and symbolic maps. You may also need to add POWER JECL statements.

```
// JOB MAPSET
// OPTION CATAL,NODECK,ALIGN,SYSPARM='MAP'
   PHASE MNTSET1,*
// EXEC ASSEMBLY
/INCLUDE MNTSET1
/*
// LIBDEF CL,TO=USRCL2
// EXEC LNKEDT
// DLBL IJSYSPH,'CICS.MAPSET.PUNCH',0,SD
// EXTENT SYSPCH,SYSWK1,1,0,111770,1000
   ASSGN SYSPCH,DISK,VOL=SYSWK1,SHR
// OPTION DECK,SYSPARM='DSECT'
// EXEC ASSEMBLY
   PUNCH ' CATALS C.MNTSET1'
/INCLUDE MNTSET1
/*
   CLOSE SYSPCH,PUNCH
// DLBL IJSYSIN,'CICS.MAPSET.PUNCH',0,SD
// EXTENT SYSIPT
   ASSGN SYSIPT,DISK,VOL=SYSWK1,SHR
// LIBDEF SL,TO=USRSL2
// EXEC MAINT
// EXEC SSERV
   DSPLY A.MNTSET1
/*
   CLOSE SYSIPT,SYSRDR
/&
```

How to prepare a command-level COBOL program under DOS/VSE

The following job stream contains three job steps. The first invokes the CICS command level translator (DFHECP1$) to process the source program, which is included in the job via an ICCF /INCLUDE statement. The output from the translator is directed via SYSPCH to a temporary disk file. The second job step invokes the COBOL compiler to process the translated source program; to do that, the compiler's input (SYSIPT) is assigned to the disk file created in the first job step. The third job step link-edits the compiled program to produce an executable load module.

For this job to work properly on your system, you should change (1) the member name specified in the /INCLUDE statement, (2) the phase name on the PHASE statement, (3) the DLBL and EXTENT statements that define the temporary disk file, (4) the CBL card, which provides translator and compiler options, and (5) the LIBDEF statements that identify the compiler's source statement library search sequence and the linkage-editor output library. You may also need to add POWER JECL statements.

If you're not using ICCF, you'll have to replace the /INCLUDE statement with the actual source text for the command-level program. Unlike the mapset assembly job, however, that doesn't present any additional complications because the source text is required only once by the CICSTRAN job.

```
// JOB CICSTRAN
// LIBDEF SL,SEARCH=(USRSL2,USRSL1,PRDSLA,PRDSLB)
// DLBL IJSYSPH,'CICS.TRANSL.PUNCH',0,SD
// EXTENT SYSPCH,SYSWK1,1,0,111770,1000
   ASSGN SYSPCH,DISK,VOL=SYSWK1,SHR
// EXEC DFHECP1$
 CBL LIB,APOST,LANGLVL(1),NOTRUNC
/INCLUDE ORDRENT
/*
   CLOSE SYSPCH,02D
// DLBL IJSYSIN,'CICS.TRANSL.PUNCH',0,SD
// EXTENT SYSIPT
   ASSGN SYSIPT,DISK=VOL=SYSWK1,SHR
// OPTION SYM,ERRS,NODECK,CATAL
   PHASE ORDRENT
   INCLUDE DFHECI
// EXEC FCOBOL
   CLOSE SYSIPT,SYSRDR
// LIBDEF CL,TO=USRCL2
// EXEC LNKEDT
/&
```

Tips for interactive users

When you use an interactive system such as TSO/ISPF, ICCF, or VM/CMS to develop CICS programs and mapsets, you must develop techniques for submitting CICS program development jobs for processing either as a background job or, under VM/CMS, as a job in a guest operating system. In general, there are three approaches to doing that. The first is to code the JCL and source file together as a single library member (or file under VM/CMS) and submit the entire member for processing when necessary. When you use this technique, the source file can be treated as in-stream data. Although this is the easiest technique, it has two drawbacks. First, it forces you to duplicate the required JCL statements for each map or program you develop. To simplify things, you can keep model JCL statements in a separate library member and copy it into each new source member you create. But that doesn't eliminate the second drawback of this approach: keeping two different types of records (JCL and COBOL or assembler statements) in the same library member may short circuit some of your text editor's features for editing specific record types.

The second approach is to create model jobs in separate library members. The JCL refers to the source program not as in-stream data, but as a member of the appropriate library (under MVS with TSO) or via an /INCLUDE statement (under DOS/VSE with ICCF). When you're ready to process a source member, you edit the model JCL to provide the correct member name. Then, you submit the JCL member for processing. The obvious drawback of this approach is that you have to frequently edit the JCL to provide the correct member name. However, in actual practice, you don't have to do that often. Most programmers work on just one or two programs at a time. (Under CMS,

this technique doesn't work very well. That's because CMS doesn't provide a good facility for including text from another file when a file is punched to another machine.)

The third approach is to eliminate the need to manually edit the JCL by using a procedure (under TSO, a CLIST or a customized ISPF dialog; under ICCF or VM/CMS, a procedure). Basically, this procedure creates the appropriate JCL statements (or edits an existing model) and submits it for processing. Here's a simple CLIST (TSO) that does that:

```
PROC 1 MEM
EDIT MMA2.CICS.CNTL(TRAN)
CHANGE 1 99999 'MEMBER' '&MEM' A
LL
SUBMIT
END NOSAVE
WRITE JOB SUBMITTED
```

The JCL in the TRAN member contains the word MEMBER whenever a member name is specified; the CLIST changes each occurrence of that word with the value of the MEM symbolic parameter. Thus, to invoke this CLIST (which is named TRAN) to translate the member named ORDRENT, you would code this:

```
TRAN ORDRENT
```

Of course, this procedure could be expanded to include other symbolic parameters to let you change the default libraries or compiler options. You can use this example as a starting point for developing your own program development CLISTs. And you can develop similar procedures that will work under ICCF or VM/CMS.

Translator and compiler options

You can influence how the translator and compiler work by passing options to them. Figure 6-2 shows the more important translator and compiler options, divided into three groups. The first group of options affects the printed output produced by the translator and compiler. The second group affects the debugging facilities available for the program. And the third group affects miscellaneous translator and compiler features.

To pass options to the translator or compiler, you can either code the options on the appropriate EXEC (MVS) or OPTION (DOS/VSE) statement or include them in a CBL statement that's placed in the source program before the IDENTIFICATION DIVISION header. If you use a CBL statement, you code translator options within the XOPTS option, like this:

```
CBL XOPTS(COBOL2,APOST),FDUMP
```

Here, the translator uses the COBOL2 and APOST options because they're coded within the XOPTS option; the FDUMP option is passed on to the compiler because it's coded after and outside of the XOPTS option.

Category	Translator	VS COBOL	VS COBOL II	Function
Options that affect printed output	SOURCE	SOURCE	SOURCE	Print a listing of the source program.
		CLIST	OFFSET	Print a condensed listing that shows the offset of each Procedure Division statement.
		PMAP	LIST	Print an assembler language listing of the object module.
		DMAP	MAP	Print a map showing the offset of each data field.
		XREF		Print a data cross reference.
		SXREF	XREF	Print a sorted data cross reference.
	VBREF			Print a CICS command cross reference.
Options for debugging	DEBUG			Enables EDF for the program.
			FDUMP	Print a formatted dump if the program abends.
Miscellaneous options	QUOTE	QUOTE	QUOTE	Use the ANSI standard quote (") to delimit literals.
	APOST	APOST	APOST	Use the apostrophe (') to delimit literals.
	COBOL2			The VS COBOL II compiler will be used to compile the program.

Section 7

Resource definition

For a CICS application to operate, CICS must know about the transactions, programs, maps, files, and other resources required by the application. This information is stored in a variety of control tables, such as the Program Control Table (PPT) for transactions, the Processing Program Table (PPT) for programs, and the File Control Table (FCT) for files. Normally, these tables are maintained by system programmers according to tightly defined procedures. However, there may be occasions when you are able to create those table entries yourself. As a result, this section presents information about the PPT, PCT, and FCT, since they're the most commonly required tables.

There are two ways to maintain CICS control tables: you can code special macro instructions that are processed by the assembler or you can use an on-line facility called Resource Definition On-line (RDO). I'll first describe how to code the macro instructions to define a PPT, PCT, and FCT entry. Then, I'll describe how you use RDO to accomplish the same thing.

Since most installations have well-established procedures and standards for CICS table maintenance, I'll present only a small subset of the options you can code for each macro instruction. I won't include options that provide for performance improvements, security facilities, inter-system communication, or non-3270 devices. In short, I'll present just the minimum CICS table entry requirements. Using the options that are included here, you can define resources well enough to make your applications operational for testing purposes. However, those resource definitions will have to be refined to make the applications perform well in a production environment.

Defining programs and maps in the PPT

To define a program or mapset in the Processing Program Table, you code a DFHPPT macro that specifies TYPE=ENTRY. (Other forms of the DFHPPT macro identify the start and end of the table or define groups of programs; you don't need to worry about those forms.)

Syntax

```
name        DFHPPT TYPE=ENTRY
                  ,PROGRAM=program-name
                  ,PGMLANG=langauge
              [ ,USAGE=MAP ]
              [ ,RES=YES ]
```

Parameters

TYPE

TYPE=ENTRY specifies that this DFHPPT macro instruction defines an individual program.

PROGRAM

Specifies the one- to seven-character name of the program. This name must correspond to the program's member name in the on-line CICS load library.

PGMLANG

Specifies the language in which the program is written; for COBOL programs, specify PGMLANG=COBOL; for assembler-language programs and mapsets, specify PGMLANG=ASM or omit the PGMLANG parameter altogether.

USAGE

Specifies that the program is to be loaded into an area of storage called the MAP area. Specifying USAGE=MAP has nothing to do with whether or not the PPT entry is defining a mapset; any assembler language program can be placed in the MAP area. USAGE=MAP should be specified only for the most infrequently used mapsets.

RES

Specifies that the program (or mapset) is to be made permanently resident; resident programs are loaded into storage when CICS is initialized and remain there permanently. RES=YES should be coded for all but the most infrequently used programs and mapsets.

Coding example

The following example shows two DFHPPT macros: the first defines a COBOL program named ORDRENT; the second defines a mapset named ORDSET1. Because the order entry application is frequently used, both table entries specify RES=YES.

```
ORDRENT   DFHPPT TYPE=ENTRY,
                 PROGRAM=ORDRENT,
                 PGMLANG=COBOL,
                 RES=YES

ORDSET1   DFHPPT TYPE=ENTRY,
                 PROGRAM=ORDSET1,
                 RES=YES
```

Defining transactions in the PCT

To define a transaction in the Program Control Table, you code a DFHPCT macro that specifies TYPE=ENTRY. (Other forms of the DFHPCT macro identify the start or end of the table or define groups of transactions.)

Syntax

```
name       DFHPCT TYPE=ENTRY
                  ,TRANSID=transaction-identifier
                  ,PROGRAM=program-name
               [ ,DTB=YES ]
               [ ,DUMP=YES ]
```

Parameters

TYPE
TYPE=ENTRY specifies that this DFHPCT macro defines an individual transaction.

TRANSID
Specifies the one- to four-character transaction identifier that's used to initiate the transaction.

PROGRAM
Specifies the name of the program to be invoked when the transaction is started. There must be a corresponding entry in the PPT.

DTB
DTB=YES specifies that dynamic transaction backout is in effect for the transaction; if the transaction abends, any updates made to protected data sets will be reversed.

DUMP
DUMP=YES specifies that a transaction dump should be produced if the transaction abends.

Coding example

This example shows how to define a transaction whose trans-id is ORD1. When this transaction is started, the program ORDRENT will be invoked.

DTB is in effect for the transaction and a dump will be produced if the transaction abends.

```
ORD1       DFHPCT TYPE=ENTRY,
                  TRANSID=ORD1,
                  PROGRAM=ORDRENT,
                  DTB=YES,
                  DUMP=YES
```

Defining files in the FCT

To define a file in the File Control Table, you code a DFHFCT macro, specifying TYPE=DATASET. (Other forms of the DFHFCT macro let you iden-tify the start or end of the table, define files on remote systems, or specify the characteristics of buffer pools.)

Syntax

```
name        DFHFCT TYPE=DATASET
              ,DATASET=file-name
              ,ACCMETH=(VSAM [,type])
            [ ,BASE=base-cluster ]
            [ ,RECFORM=FIXED ]
            [ ,LOG=YES ]
            [ ,SERVREQ=(option,option,...) ]
            [ ,STRNO=strings ]
```

Parameters

TYPE

TYPE=DATASET specifies that this DFHFCT macro defines an individual data set.

DATASET

Specifies the one- to eight-character data set name (under DOS/VSE, the limit is seven characters). This name is used both in the DATASET option of file control commands that process the data set and in the JCL state-ments that allocate the data set. (Under MVS, the name must match the DD statement's ddname; under DOS/VSE, the name must match the DLBL statement's filename.) For an alternate index, the DATASET parameter names the path, not the base cluster.

ACCMETH

ACCMETH=VSAM specifies that the file is a VSAM file. You can also specify KSDS, RRDS, or ESDS for type; if you omit the type, KSDS is assumed (and you can omit the parentheses).

BASE

(MVS only) Specifies the data set name of the base cluster associated with the path you're defining. The file you specify must have its own FCT entry.

RECFORM

RECFORM=FIXED specifies that the VSAM file has fixed length records, so the LENGTH option can be omitted from file control com-mands. If you omit RECFORM=FIXED, you must code LENGTH on all file control com-mands that access data in the file.

LOG

LOG=YES specifies that the data set is protected; any updates made to the data set are recorded in a log so they can be reversed in case the task abends or the entire system crashes.

SERVREQ

Specifies one or more service requests which are valid for the file. You can code any or all of the following:

BROWSE	Browse commands are allowed for the file.
DELETE	DELETE commands are allowed for the file.
GET	READ commands are allowed for the file.
NEWREC	Records can be added to the file.
UPDATE	REWRITE commands are allowed for the file.

If you omit SERVREQ, CICS assumes SERVREQ=READ. So you'll be able to retrieve records randomly, but you won't be able to add, delete, or update the file. Nor will you be able to sequentially browse the file.

STRNO

Specifies the number of concurrent accesses CICS allows for the file. The default, STRNO=1, means that only one task at a time may access the file. In most cases, this is unacceptable; certainly for testing you should specify STRNO=2 or STRNO=3 so you can properly test the effect of simultaneous file updates. (For VSAM files that use Local Shared Resources, STRNO is ignored.)

Coding example (base cluster)

This example shows how to define a file named IN-VOICE. The file has fixed-length records, is protected, allows all file control operations, and permits four concurrent accesses.

```
INVOICE   DFHFCT TYPE=DATASET,
                 DATASET=INVOICE,
                 ACCMETH=(VSAM,KSDS),
                 RECFORM=FIXED,
                 LOG=YES,
                 SERVREQ=(BROWSE,DELETE,GET,NEWREC,UPDATE),
                 STRNO=4
```

Coding example (path)

This example shows how to define a path used to access the INVOICE file via an alternate index. The path is named INVPATH, and the SERVREQ parameter specifies that it can be used only for retrieval; invoice records can't be added, deleted, or updated via this path.

```
INVPATH   DFHFCT TYPE=DATASET,
                 DATASET=INVPATH,
                 BASE=INVOICE,
                 ACCMETH=(VSAM,KSDS),
                 SERVREQ=(BROWSE,GET),
                 STRNO=4
```

Resource Definition Online (RDO)

With CICS Release 1.6, IBM announced a new facility called *Resource Definition Online* (or *RDO*). RDO lets you define certain CICS resources interactively while CICS is running; there's no need to code and assemble macro instructions and restart CICS to make the new definitions active. Specifically, RDO lets you define terminals, programs, and transactions interactively. You still have to code macro instructions for other resources, including VSAM files.

RDO maintains the resource specifications you give it in a VSAM file called the *CICS System Definition file*, or just *CSD*. When CICS is started, information from the CSD is used to create the internal tables that manage resources, such as the PPT and PCT. CICS provides three service transactions (CEDA, CEDB, and CEDC) that let you maintain the CSD. The CEDA transaction performs three basic functions: it lets you display data from the CSD, change data in the CSD, and install changed resource definitions so they become effective. The CEDB and CEDC transactions are subsets of CEDA; CEDB lets you display or change CSD resource definitions, but not install them and CEDC lets you display resource definitions, but not look at them.

Within RDO, resources are defined in *groups*, which are normally used to classify resources by ap-plication. For example, a group named ORDPROC might contain all of the resource definitions required by the order processing application. If necessary, several groups can be combined to make a *list*, which is simply a listing of group names. RDO provides many commands that let you operate on individual resources, groups of resources, or lists of groups. If you use RDO, you need to know your shop's guidelines for creating and using groups and lists.

The RDO transactions (CEDA, CEDB, and CEDC) work much like the extended master terminal transaction (CEMT). It's command driven, but most commands yield a panel that lets you key in specific data. The initial display lists the commands you can enter. To define a program named ORDRENT, you enter a command like this:

```
DEFINE PROGRAM(ORDRENT)
```

CEDA responds by displaying a panel in which you can enter additional data to complete the resource definition.

Because of the menu-driven orientation of CEDA, it's relatively easy to use. So I won't provide additional reference material for it here.

Section 8

Master terminal and other operator transactions

To use CICS effectively for program development, you need to know how to use the various *service transactions* that are supplied with CICS. This section provides reference information for service transactions designed for CICS terminal operators; these transactions let you sign on and sign off of a CICS system (CSSN, CESN, and CSSF), perform master terminal operations (CEMT and CEST), route messages (CMSG), and retrieve message pages (CSPG). Other important CICS service transactions are covered in other sections: the transactions for Resource Definition Online (CEDA, CEDB, and CEDC) are covered in Section 7 and three transactions that are useful for testing (CEDF, CECI, and CEBR) are covered in Section 9.

The sign-on transaction for CICS 1.6 (CSSN)

The CSSN transaction lets you sign on to a CICS release 1.6 system. (For release 1.7, you use the CESN transaction.) If you're going to run an application that uses CICS security checking facilities or RACF security, you'll have to sign on using CSSN. If you're not accessing resources protected by CICS or RACF security, sign-on is unnecessary.

Syntax

```
CSSN [ NAME=name ] [, PS=password ] [, NEWPS=password ]
```

Options

If you enter the trans-id CSSN without additional data, CSSN displays a data-entry screen that lets you enter the required information.

NAME
Your one- to twenty-character CICS operator name.

PS
Your one- to eight-character CICS password.

NEWPS
A one- to eight-character password that will replace your current password.

Example

This example shows how to sign on using DLOWE as the operator name and B39ZSN5C as the password.

```
CSSN NAME=DLOWE,PS=B39ZSN5C
```

The sign-on transaction for CICS 1.7 (CESN)

The CESN transaction lets you sign on to a CICS release 1.7 system. (For release 1.6, you use the CSSN transaction.) If you're going to run an application that uses CICS security checking facilities or RACF security, you'll have to sign on using CESN. If you're not accessing resources protected by CICS or RACF security, sign-on is unnecessary. The difference between CESN and CSSN is that CSSN uses a 20-character operator name for user validation and CESN uses an eight-character RACF user-id. As a result, CESN is more compatible with RACF than CSSN.

Syntax

```
CESN [ USER=user-id ] [, PS=password ] [, NEWPS=password ]
```

Options

If you enter the trans-id CESN without additional data, CESN displays a data-entry screen that lets you enter the required information.

USER

Your one- to eight-character RACF user-id.

PS

Your one- to eight-character CICS password.

NEWPS

A one- to eight-character password that will replace your current password.

Example

This example shows how to sign on using DLOWE as the user-id and B39ZSN5C as the password.

```
CESN USER=DLOWE,PS=B39ZSN5C
```

The sign-off transaction (CSSF)

The sign-off transaction detaches you as a user from the CICS system and optionally detaches your terminal from the CICS system.

Syntax

```
CSSF [ { LOGOFF    } ]
     { GOODNIGHT }
```

Options

If you code CSSF alone, you are signed off of the CICS system, but your terminal remains attached to it. In other words, you can continue to communicate with CICS by entering another trans-id, including CSSN or CESN. However, when you are signed off, you can't access any resources that are protected by CICS or RACF security.

LOGOFF

CSSF LOGOFF breaks the connection between your terminal and CICS (unless the terminal is a non-switched BTAM terminal, in which case the connection cannot be broken). CSSF LOGOFF leaves your terminal in TRANSCIEVE status, which means that when you reestablish your terminal's connection to CICS, you can enter a trans-id (such as CSSN/CESN) to continue processing.

GOODNIGHT

CSSF GOODNIGHT is similar to CSSF LOGOFF, but your terminal is placed in RECEIVE status. That means that even if you reconnect your terminal to CICS, you cannot initiate any processing because CICS won't recognize any input from your terminal. To continue processing on a terminal in RECEIVE status, either change the terminal's status by using the CEOT or CEMT transactions from another terminal or wait until CICS is restarted, when terminals return to their default status. (The GOODNIGHT option is designed to shut your terminal down for the night; in the morning, when CICS is restarted, the terminal returns to its normal status.)

The terminal status transaction (CEOT)

CEOT is designed to let terminal users who aren't authorized to use CEMT inquire into and change the status of a terminal. Using CEOT, you can dis-play the status of any terminal, but you can change the status of only your own.

Syntax

```
CEOT  [PAGEABLE|AUTOPAGEABLE]  [ATI|NOATI]  [TTI|NOTTI]
```

Options

If you enter CEOT without options, CEOT displays the current status of your terminal and prompts you for more information.

PAGEABLE|AUTOPAGEABLE

If you specify PAGEABLE, pages of a multiple-page message are displayed only when you request them using the CSPG transaction. If you specify AUTOPAGEABLE, pages are automatically sent to the terminal.

ATI|NOATI

If you specify ATI, the terminal can be used for transactions that are invoked via Automatic Transaction Initiation (ATI)

facilities. NOATI means that the terminal can *not* be used for those transactions.

TTI|NOTTI

If you specify TTI, the terminal can be used for transactions initiated from the terminal; in other words, CICS accepts and processes input from the terminal. NOTTI means that the terminal is output only; no input data is accepted from the terminal.

The Master Terminal Transaction (CEMT)

CEMT lets you display and change the status of resources (including programs, transactions, data sets, queues, and terminals). In addition, you use CEMT to shut down a CICS system. To invoke CEMT, you enter the trans-id CEMT with or without a command. Once you've started CEMT, you can enter commands in the command line (at the top of the display) or you can overtype data directly on the data display.

If you don't enter complete information for a CEMT command, CEMT prompts you for the additional information, showing all of the valid choices.

You can abbreviate any CICS command option with as few characters as are required to make the abbreviation unique within the context. For the keyword PERFORM, for example, you can enter P, PE, PER, PERF, and so on. However, if another keyword *at the same level* begins with the letter P, you would have to use at least two letters in the abbreviation.

The three basic CEMT commands you're likely to use are INQUIRE (usually abbreviated INQ), SET, and PERFORM.

INQUIRE command syntax

```
                        ⎧ DATASET [(name)]       ⎫
                        ⎪ PROGRAM [(name)]       ⎪
  CEMT INQUIRE          ⎨ QUEUE [(name)]         ⎬
                        ⎪ TASK [(number)]        ⎪
                        ⎪ TERMINAL [(term-id)]   ⎪
                        ⎩ TRANSACTION [(trans-id)]⎭
```

Commonly used SET command syntax

```
  CEMT SET DATASET(name) {ENABLED|DISABLED} {OPEN|CLOSED}

  CEMT SET PROGRAM (name) {ENABLED|DISABLED} [NEWCOPY]

  CEMT SET QUEUE (name) {ENABLED|DISABLED} {OPEN|CLOSED}
       [TRIGGER(number)]

  CEMT SET TASK (number) {PURGE|FORCEPURGE}

  CEMT SET TERMINAL (term-id) {INSERVICE|OUTSERVICE}
       {PURGE|FORCEPURGE} {PAGE|AUTOPAGE} {ATI|NOATI}

  CEMT SET TRANSACTION (trans-id) {ENABLED|DISABLED}
```

PERFORM SHUTDOWN command syntax

```
  CEMT PERFORM SHUTDOWN   [IMMEDIATE]
```

Options

DATASET
Inquires or sets data set information. If you omit the file-name, CEMT displays a list of all data sets.

PROGRAM
Inquires or sets program information. If you omit the program name, CEMT displays a list of all programs.

QUEUE
Inquires or sets transient data information. If you omit the destination name, CEMT displays a list of all transient data queues.

TASK
Inquires or sets task information. If you omit the task identifier, CEMT displays a list of all active tasks.

TERMINAL
Inquires or sets terminal information. If you omit the terminal-id, CEMT displays a list of all terminals.

TRANSACTION
Inquires or sets transaction information. If you omit the trans-id, CEMT displays a list of all transactions.

ENABLED | DISABLED
Changes the status of the facility to ENABLED or DISABLED. Disabling a facility is often a good way to get out of a processing loop. For example, if your terminal is tied up by a pseudo-conversational transaction that keeps restarting itself, simply disable the transaction from another terminal.

OPEN | CLOSED
Changes the status of a data set or queue to OPEN or CLOSED.

NEWCOPY
Establishes a new copy of a program or map-set. You should issue CEMT SET PROGRAM(name) NEWCOPY each time you recompile or reassemble a program or mapset.

TRIGGER
Changes the trigger level for an ATI task associated with a transient data queue.

PURGE | FORCEPURGE
Cancels a running task: for SET TASK, cancels the task indicated by the task identifier; for SET TERMINAL, cancels the task associated with the terminal. PURGE cancels the task only if CICS can insure system integrity; FORCEPURGE cancels a task without regard to integrity. Always try PURGE first.

INSERVICE/OUTSERVICE
Specifies whether or not the terminal is available for use.

PAGE | AUTOPAGE
Specifies how a terminal handles multiple page messages. If PAGE is specified, the operator must retrieve message pages with the CSPG transaction; if AUTOPAGE is specified, message pages are delivered one after another. PAGE is usually specified for display devices, and AUTOPAGE is usually specified for printer devices.

ATI | NOATI
Specifies whether or not the terminal is eligible for ATI transactions.

SHUTDOWN
Terminates the CICS system.

IMMEDIATE
Specifies that CICS should be terminated immediately, even if there are tasks still running. If you omit IMMEDIATE, CICS waits until any active tasks complete.

The message switching transaction (CMSG)

The CMSG transaction lets you send a message to other CICS users. You can specify that the message is to be sent to a specific terminal or operator or to all operators of a particular class. And you can specify that the message should be delivered immediately or in the future.

CMSG is "command driven": to use it, enter the trans-id CMSG followed by one or more operands.

CMSG is somewhat interactive, in that if you don't enter all the required operands, you'll be prompted to enter more data. But it doesn't use a full-screen fill-in-the-blanks approach like CEMT or CECI. (CECI will be presented in the next section.) If you wish, you can abbreviate all of the CMSG operands (except CANCEL) as a single letter.

Syntax

```
CMSG [MSG=]'message' [,ROUTE=route-list]
    [,OPCLASS=operator-class] [,TIME=time]
    [,DATE=date] [,ID=(message-title)]
    [,HEADING={YES|NO}] ,{SEND|CANCEL}
```

Parameters

MSG

Specifies the message text, which must be enclosed in apostrophes. The word MSG= is optional. To include an apostrophe in the message, code two apostrophes in a row. If you omit the closing apostrophe, CMSG asks you to continue the message.

ROUTE

Specifies the terminals and/or operators to which the message should be delivered. The ROUTE parameter has a complicated format, but it's usually coded in one of these simple forms:

ROUTE=ALL
    Send the message to all terminals.

ROUTE=(term-id [,term-id...])
    Send the message to the specified terminals.

ROUTE=(/operator [,/operator...])
    Send the message to the specified operators; note that each operator-id must be preceded by a slash.

ROUTE=(.term-list [,.term-list...])
    Send the message to all terminals in the specified terminal lists; note that each term-list identifier must be preceded by a period. Terminal lists are defined in a system table called the Terminal List Table (TLT) and are used to group related terminals.

OPCLASS

Specifies one or more operator classes; the message will be delivered only to operators of the specified class.

TIME

Specifies when the message should be delivered. You can specify a time of day as hhmm, or you can specify a relative time as +hhmm, +mm, or +m.

DATE

Specifies the date when the message should be delivered. You can specify the date in the form yy.ddd, mm/dd, mm/dd/yy, or +d.

ID

Specifies a title of up to 62 characters (enclosed in parentheses); this title is associated with the message and is displayed when the terminal operator requests a list of pending messages.

HEADING

HEADING=YES adds a heading to the message; the heading includes the current time and date and the terminal-id of the terminal from which the message originated.

SEND | CANCEL

SEND tells CICS to send the message; CANCEL tells CICS to cancel the message request. If you don't code SEND or CANCEL, CMSG prompts you to enter additional parameters.

Abbreviations

You can abbreviate all CMSG parameters to a single letter, as follows:

D	DATE
H	HEADING
I	ID
M	MSG
O	OPCLASS
R	ROUTE
T	TIME

Examples

This example sends a message to terminal L401; the message is delivered immediately.

```
CMSG 'THE FCT TABLE ASSEMBLY IS COMPLETED',R=L401
```

This example sends a message to all terminal users; the message is delivered at 5:30 pm (1730).

```
CMSG 'CICS WILL BE SHUT DOWN IN 30 MINUTES',R=ALL,T=1730
```

This example sends a message to all terminals specified in the terminal list table entry named ADMIN1A. Because the message is long, two terminal interactions are used; after the operator enters the first line, CMSG responds 'CONTINUE INPUT', after which the operator enters the second line. Notice that the closing apostrophe is omitted on the first line so that the message can be continued on the second line.

```
CMSG 'DON''T FORGET--TOMORROW IS THE LAST DAY TO SUBMIT FORM 1023-A

CMSG '  PLEASE HAVE YOUR SUBMISSIONS IN BY NOON',R=(.ADMIN1A)
```

The page retrieval transaction (CSPG)

CICS page retrieval functions let a terminal operator manage the display of multi-page messages by entering page retrieval commands. Although you don't normally invoke page retrieval functions using a trans-id like you invoke other service transactions, the page retrieval functions are implemented as a single transaction named CSPG. CICS itself interprets page retrieval commands the operator enters and invokes the CSPG transaction when necessary.

A facility called *Single Keystroke Retrieval*, or *SKR*, lets an installation specify PF key assignments for certain page retrieval commands. For ex-

ample, your shop might specify that PF1 retrieves the next page in sequence, while PF3 ends the page retrieval session. Since those PF key assignments are installation dependent, you'll have to find out how your shop uses them.

There are two basic page retrieval commands you're likely to use: getpage and msgterm. Both commands can be associated with a prefix determined by the installation; usually, the prefix for the getpage command is P/ and the prefix for the msgterm command is T/. If your shop uses a different prefix, use it wherever you see P/ or T/ in this section.

The getpage command

P / n   Retrieve page n.

P / +n   Retrieve the page that's n pages past the current page.

P / -n   Retrieve the page that's n pages before the current page.

P / L   Retrieve the last page.

P / N   Retrieve the next page.

P / P   Retrieve the previous page.

P / C   Redisplay the current page.

P / x, message-id
Retrieve a page from the specified message; x can be any of the above options (n, +n, -n, L, N, P, or C) and message-id is the message identifier for the message you want to display. (You can determine the message identifier of an undelivered message by issuing the P/Q command.)

P / Q
Display a list of pending messages for this terminal.

The msgterm command

T / B
Terminate the page retrieval session and purge the message being displayed.

Section 9

Testing and debugging

This section contains reference material that you'll use as you test and debug your command-level programs. Here, you'll find a list of things to watch for as you test a command-level program, instructions for using three IBM-supplied transactions that are helpful during testing (CECI, CEBR, and CEDF), basic techniques for using a transaction dump, and a list of commonly encountered transaction abend codes.

A checklist for program testing

When you test a CICS program, it's often difficult to keep track of all that happens during the test run. As a result, you should use a checklist like this one to make sure you've detected all errors.

What to check for as you examine the appearance of the screen:

Are all headings and captions placed correctly?
Are the operator instructions displayed properly?
Is there any garbage on the screen?
Are there any misspellings?
Do all the fields have the correct attributes?
Is the cursor in the correct initial location?
Does the cursor move correctly from field to field?

What to check for as you enter valid data:

Are all program screens displayed in the correct sequence?
Do all AID keys work correctly?
Are the operator messages always correct?
Are the functions of all AID keys indicated?
Does the program properly acknowledge receipt of valid data?
Are work fields properly cleared after each valid transaction?
Are control totals accumulated properly?
Are files updated properly?

What to check for as you enter individual errors:

Does each case of invalid data for each field yield an appropriate error message?
Do lookup routines work properly?
Is the field in error highlighted?
Is the cursor positioned at the field in error?
When you correct the error, does the error message go away?
Does the program post transactions even though errors are detected?

What to check for as you enter compound errors:

Are all errors detected or does the program detect just the first error on the screen?
Is the cursor positioned under the first field in error and is the corresponding error message displayed?
Are all errors highlighted?

The command-level interpreter (CECI)

The command-level interpreter (CECI) is an IBM-supplied transaction that interactively executes CICS commands. With it, you can perform almost any CICS operation interactively, without developing a separate program. So you'll use it often to display maps, read or write VSAM file records, and so on.

Syntax

```
CECI [ command ]
```

Operation

CECI lets you interactively enter and execute CICS commands; although you can code a complete CICS command along with the CECI trans-id, you usually don't. Instead, you enter the CECI trans-id alone and the work on the full-screen entry panel CECI provides. On the top line of that panel, you enter all or part of a CICS command; CECI responds by displaying that command's complete syntax, with the options you've chosen highlighted. You can then code additional options on the top line, or type directly over the command syntax in the display portion of the screen.

When you have entered a command correctly, CECI displays the message "ABOUT TO EXECUTE COMMAND." If you press the enter key, CECI executes the command and updates the display with the message "COMMAND EXECUTION COMPLETE." Any input data that was received by the command is displayed with its related option (usually INTO). If the received data can't be displayed on a single line, you can move the cursor to the start of the data and press the enter key; CECI will then display all of the data.

Abbreviations

CECI lets you abbreviate CICS commands to as few as one character, as long as the keyword you're abbreviating is unique within the command. For example, you can use I instead of INTO in a READ command; however, you can't specify R because several READ command options begin with R (RBA, RRN, and RIDFLD). You can also omit the words EXEC CICS and END-EXEC, apostrophes around literal values, and input options like INTO, which are assumed by default.

Variables

CECI lets you use variables to pass data from one command to another within a CECI session. And, with a few tricks, you can pass variables forward to subsequent CECI sessions. Variables are especially useful for updating VSAM file records. First, issue a READ command with the UPDATE option, specifying a variable in the INTO option. Then, after making appropriate changes to the variable data, issue a REWRITE command specifying the same variable in the FROM option.

There are several ways to define a variable. The simplest is to name it in an option that receives input data, like INTO. To use a variable in a CECI command, specify the variable name preceded with an ampersand, like this: INTO(&RECORD). Here, the RECORD variable will be used to store the input data that's associated with the INTO option.

If you execute a command without specifying a variable in an INTO option, you can position the cursor at the data and press the enter key; the resulting display lets you enter the name of a variable which will be used to store the data.

A more direct way to create a variable is to press PF5, which takes you to a display of all the current CECI variables. Using this display, you can define a new variable, specifying the variable's name and length. And you can change the value of a variable by overtyping the variable's data area. (If a variable's data doesn't fit on one line, position the cursor to the data and press enter; the resulting display shows the entire variable.)

One more way to create a variable is to enter a new variable name in the FROM field of the CECI syntax display. When you do that, a variable is created and the CICS command currently displayed is stored in it. You can later recall this command by typing the variable name (preceded by an ampersand) on the top line of the CECI display.

A useful trick for passing a variable forward to subsequent executions of CECI is to use temporary storage. To do that, issue a WRITEQ TS command to write the variable to a temporary storage queue. Then, when you invoke CECI later, you can issue a READQ TS command to retrieve the variable. To make this easier, CECI has two default variables: &DFHW contains a WRITEQ TS command and &DFHR contains a READQ TS command. So if you enter &DFHW on the top line of the screen, CECI will respond by displaying a skeleton WRITEQ TS command; you can modify this command to specify the variable you want written and then execute it. &DFHR can be used in a similar way to read a previously saved variable.

The temporary storage browse transaction (CEBR)

CEBR lets you browse the contents of a specified temporary storage queue; that's something you may need to do if you're testing a program that uses temporary storage. In addition to browsing a temporary storage queue, CEBR lets you delete the queue. And you can write the contents of the queue to a transient data destination or read the contents of a destination into the queue.

Syntax

```
CEBR [ queue-name ]
```

Operation

If you omit *queue-name* from the CEBR transaction, CEBR uses a default queue name that consists of the letters CEBR followed by your terminal's term-id. So if you're using terminal L1T4, the default queue name is CEBRL1T4.

CEBR's data display shows each record in the queue and lets you use PF keys to scroll forward or backward through the queue; the meaning of each PF key is displayed at the bottom of the screen. At the top of the screen is a command line in which you can enter any of the commands listed below.

CEBR commands

QUEUE xxxxxxxx
Changes the display to the temporary storage queue you specify.

TERMINAL xxxx
Changes the last four characters of the queue's name to the characters you specify.

PURGE
Deletes the queue.

TOP
Scrolls to the first record in the queue.

BOTTOM
Scrolls to the last record in the queue.

FIND /string/
Searches for the string enclosed within the delimiter. You can use any character for the delimiter as long as that character isn't in the search string. If the search string doesn't contain spaces, you can omit the second delimiter character.

LINE nnn
Scrolls to the specified line.

COLUMN nnn
Scrolls to the specified column.

GET xxxx
Reads the specified transient data destination into the current temporary storage queue. Remember that when you do this, the records in the destination are effectively deleted.

PUT xxxx
Writes the contents of the current temporary storage queue to the specified transient data destination.

The execution diagnostics facility (CEDF)

CEDF is the tool most commonly used to debug CICS programs. Basically, it lets you monitor a command-level program by intercepting all CICS commands the program issues. Although it's not the most powerful on-line debugging tool available, it has two advantages: (1) programs require no special preparation to work with EDF and (2) EDF is a standard component of CICS, so all shops have it.

Syntax

```
CEDF [ term-id ]
```

Operation

You can use CEDF in one of two basic modes: single-terminal mode or two-terminal mode. You invoke CEDF in single-terminal mode by entering the CEDF trans-id without options; CEDF attaches itself to your terminal and monitors the next transaction you initiate. You initiate two-terminal mode by entering CEDF with a terminal-id; CEDF attaches itself to your terminal but monitors the transaction running at the terminal you specify. Usually, you'll use single-terminal mode. Two-terminal mode is useful in two circumstances: (1) when you want to monitor a transaction which has already started and (2) when you want to monitor a transaction that's attached to a printer terminal, which can't directly support CEDF.

As a task executes, CICS interrupts it at several key points: before a new program begins to execute, before any CICS command is executed, after any CICS command is executed, before a program ends, before a task ends, whenever an abend occurs, and before a task ends abnormally. At any of these points, you can examine or change the contents of working storage or the Execute Interface Block. EDF remembers most of these displays and you can move forward or backward through the remembered displays using PF10 and PF11.

You can temporarily suspend EDF displays by pressing PF4; then, EDF won't interrupt your program until one of several conditions occur. By default, these conditions are a CICS error condition, an abend, or a normal end of task. However, you can use PF9 to tell CEDF to resume its displays whenever your program issues a particular type of CICS command (like SEND MAP or ENDBR) or whenever a particular exceptional condition occurs.

In single-terminal mode, EDF displays alternately with your programs displays. For example, suppose EDF displays a screen telling you your program is about to issue a SEND MAP command. When you press the enter key, your program issues the command; the next display you see is the output from the SEND MAP command. Press the enter key again and another EDF display appears, this time telling you that the SEND MAP command is complete. You can display the current program screen at any time by pressing PF6.

To view or change working storage, press PF5; that takes you to a display that's similar to a storage dump. To locate a particular working storage field, you'll have to use the DMAP output from the compiler to determine the field's offset. To change data, simply overtype the data on the screen.

In a pseudo-conversational program, you need to enter YES in the REPLY field of the task termination screen. If you don't, the CEDF session will be terminated when the current task ends and it won't resume when the pseudo-conversational program restarts.

Transaction dump debugging

CEDF and other on-line debugging tools are useful during program testing, but if a production program abends, you'll probably have to use a transaction dump to find out what caused the abend. Here, I'll summarize three essential transaction dump debugging techniques: (1) how to determine the abend code; (2) how to determine the instruction that caused the abend; and (3) how to locate a working-storage field. Figure 9-1 shows a portion of a CICS storage dump; it should help you understand these three simple techniques. (This storage dump was produced under CICS 1.6; other releases may produce dumps in slightly different formats.)

How to determine the abend code

- The abend code is always printed at the start of a transaction dump; it's item 1 in part 1 of figure 9-1.

- If the abend code is ASRA (program check), you'll have to look in the PSW to determine the type of check. Item 2 in part 1 of figure 9-1 shows where to look; here, the code B means the abend was a decimal divide exception. The PSW program check codes are summarized later in this section.

How to determine the instruction that caused the abend

- Determine the interrupt address (item 3 in part 1 of figure 9-1) and the program load point (item 4).

- Subtract the load point from the interrupt address. In figure 9-1, the load point (4A7ED0) minus the interrupt address (4A7050) is E80. That's the displacement at which the interrupt occurred.

- Use the CLIST output from the compiler to determine which COBOL statement that caused the abend.

How to locate a field in working storage

- Use the DMAP and REGISTER ASSIGNMENT portion of the compiler output to determine which register is assigned to the field's base locator.

- Determine the contents of the base register (item 5 in part 1 of figure 9-1 shows the contents of register 6, the base register used in this example).

- Use the DMAP to determine the field's displacement; add the displacement to the base register value. For example, if the DMAP displacement for the field is 3F and the base register value is 18904C (as in figure 9-1), the field's address is 18908B.

- Locate the portion of the transaction dump that shows user transaction storage in a range that contains the address you're looking for.

- Scan the address column (the rightmost column) to find the line that contains the field you're looking for; then, count across that line to find the field. In part 2 of figure 9-1, item 1 indicates the line that contains the field and items 2 and 3 indicate the field's hex and character data.

```
CUSTOMER INFORMATION CONTROL SYSTEM STORAGE DUMP   CODE=ASRA   TASK=MOR1      DATE=10/14/83   TIME=17:14:10   PAGE    1
                                                          (1)
SYMPTOMS= AB/UASRA PIDS/5740XX100 FLDS/F000KC RIDS/MORCAL1

CICS/VS LEVEL = 0160
                                  (3)         (2)                                                        (4)
PSW               47800000    004A7ED0    0006000B    00000000

REGS 14-4         5052A522    604A88F8    00000168    004A7E4A          004A7B42    00000168    0018451C

REGS 5-11         80188FC8    0018904C    001894B3    001894B4          004A812E    004A7050    004A7050
                                  (5)
TASK CONTROL AREA (USER AREA)        ADDRESS 00184140 TO 00184EEF    LENGTH 000DB0

00000000   00184000 004D5E8C 01531278 0055BE70  00184680 00000000 14006500 043100A0   *.. ..(;.........................*   00184140
00000020   0554C8F8 00000000 00000000 00000000  00000000 00000000 00000000 00000000   *..H8............................*   00184160
00000040   00000000 00000000 00000000 00000000  00000000 00000000 5052A522 00189590   *..........................V...N.*   00184180
00000060   4052A3B4 C1E2D9C1 00000168 00006000  0052ABE8 00000006 004D5BF0 0052A154   * .T.ASRA......-....Y.....($0....*   001841A0
00000080   FE000000 00000000 C5E3F140 C1E2D9C1  478D0000 004A7ED0 0006000B 00000000   *.........ET1 ASRA......=........*   001841C0
000000A0   5052A522 604A88F8 00000168 004A7E4A  004A7B42 00000168 0018451C 80188FC8   *..V.-.H8.......=...............H*   001841E0
000000C0   0018904C 001894B3 001894B4 004A812E  004A7050 004A7050 18020000 0000077E   *......M...M...A................=*   00184200
000000E0   00189590 8C0000A8 24F40000 00000000  00000000 00000000 00000000 00000000   *..N....Y.4......................*   00184220
00000100   00000000 00000000 00000000 00000000  00000000 00000000 00000000 00000000   *................................*   00184240
00000120   LINES TO 000002E0 SAME AS ABOVE                                                                                   00184260
00000300   8C000028 00184440 00000000 00528BE4  00000000 00000000 00000000 00000000   *....... .......U................*   00184440
00000320   00000000 00000000 00000028 00184440  00000190 00184470 001845D0 00000000   *............... ................*   00184460
00000340   00000000 00000000 00000000 40404040  00531278 00000000 00000000 00000000   *...........     ................*   00184480
00000360   00000000 00000000 00000000 00000000  00000000 00000000 00000000 00000000   *................................*   001844A0
00000380   00000000 00000000 00000000 00000000  00000000 00184F80 00000000 00000000   *................................*   001844C0
000003A0   00000000 00000000 00000000 00000000  00000000 00008200 00140000 00000000   *......................B.........*   001844E0
000003C0   00000000 00184EF0 00000000 00000004  00000000 00010000 00000000 001845D0   *......+0........................*   00184500
000003E0   80188FC8 001892AC 0018904C 00000000  004D5BF8 001892AC 5055952A 004A7050   *...H..K...........($8..K...N....*   00184520
00000400   004D5BF8 0018451C 004A7090 00189010  004A7098 0052B760 00184000 004A7050   *.($8................Q...-.. ....*   00184540
00000420   005592E4 004A795E 00528A98 80184470  00184140 00000000 00000000 00000000   *..KU...;...Q....... ............*   00184560
00000440   00000000 00000000 0018451C 80184520  00000000 00000000 00000000 00000000   *................................*   00184580
00000460   00000000 00000000 00000000 00000000  001845D0 00189558 00000000 00000000   *......................N.........*   001845A0
00000480   00000000 00000000 40C4C6C8 C5C9C240  0171410C 0083287F D4D6D9F1 0000244C   *........ DFHEIB .....C..MOR1....*   001845C0
000004A0   C8F4F0F0 00000103 00017D18 02000000  00000000 00000000 00000000 00000000   *H400......'.....................*   001845E0
000004C0   00000040 40404040 40404000 00000000  00000000 00000000 00000000 00000000   *...         ....................*   00184600
000004E0   000001B0 00184470 00000000 0017D790  00000001 0017C82C 00000001 0017C92C   *..............P.......H.......I.*   00184620
00000500   00000001 00000000 00000000 00000000  00000000 00000000 00000000 00000000   *................................*   00184640
00000520   00000000 00000000 00000000 00000000  00000000 00000000 D3C9C6D6 E2E3D6D9   *........................LIFOSTOR*   00184660
00000540   42000068 00000000 FF1846E8 5051FA9C  9051FBAE 00000005 00189558 0018928C   *..........Y...............N...K.*   00184680
00000560   00189274 0018906C 00189284 00182000  00000002 00559C2C 0051F9B0 00531278   *..K.......KD...............9.....*   001846A0
00000580   00184470 00184140 0055B870 FE1846E8  F000D2C3 005578E0 00000000 00000000   *....... .......YO.KC............*   001846C0
000005A0   00000000 00000000 48000060 00184680  FF184748 4051D538 5051D428 00000054   *...........-......... .N...M.....*   001846E0
000005C0   00184000 0051D674 00189274 00184680  00189284 00184000 48000060 00559C2C   *.. ...O...K........KD.. ....-....*   00184700
000005E0   00000000 00531278 01531278 00184140  0055B870 FE184748 FA00D4C3 0051D674   *............... ..........MC..O.*   00184720
00000600   01000000 00000000 480001D8 001846E8  FF184920 4052B09C 00503F74 C0000200   *..........G...Y.... ............*   00184740
00000620   00184130 0052ABE8 8052AF94 004D5BF0  0052A154 00184000 480001D8 00000002   *........Y...M.($0...... ....Q....*   00184760
00000640   000003A8 0052AC90 8052B058 00184140  0055B870 FE184920 FA00D4C3 005211A0   *...Y........... ..........MC....*   00184780
00000660   01020000 00000000 0002C505 00000020  C1D3F140 00531278 D4D6D9D4 C1D7F140   *.................AL1 ....MORMAP1 *   001847A0
00000680   D4D6D9E2 C5E3F140 005592E4 FFFFFFFE  00000000 00184810 00000000 00000000   *MORSET1 ..KU.....................*   001847C0
000006A0   00000000 001809E0 00531284 00000000  00000000 07800000 00000000 00000000   *...........D....................*   001847E0
000006C0   00000000 00000000 001809E0 00184814  00000000 00000000 00000000 00000000   *................................*   00184800
000006E0   00110000 00000000 00000000 00000000  00000000 00000000 00000000 00000000   *................................*   00184820
```

Figure 9-1 Part of a CICS transaction dump (part 1 of 2)

Figure 9-1   Part of a CICS transaction dump (part 2 of 2)

Abend codes

When a task abends, a four-character abend code is issued to indicate the cause of the abend. In many cases, this code alone gives you enough information to correct the problem that caused the abend. If not, the abend code gives you an idea of what to look for when you examine a transaction dump or use EDF to figure out what caused the abend.

The IBM manual *CICS Messages and Codes* documents all of the abend codes; here, I'll just describe the ones most commonly encountered.

ABMB

> *Basic Mapping Support.* You used the absolute cursor positioning technique and supplied a cursor position that's beyond the limit of the output device.

ABM0

> *Basic Mapping Support.* The specified map isn't in the mapset. The map name is misspelled either in the program or in the mapset or the program specifies the wrong mapset.

AEIx and AEYx

> *Execute Interface Program.* These codes occur when an exceptional condition is raised and the program has not handled the condition, either by issuing a HANDLE CONDITION command, an IGNORE CONDITION command, or by specifying the NOHANDLE option. The abend code indicates which exceptional condition occurred, as figure 9-2 shows.

AEIA	ERROR	AEI9	MAPFAIL
AEID	EOF	AEYA	INVERRTERM
AEIE	EODS	AEYB	INVMPSZ
AEIG	INBFMH	AEYC	IGREQID
AEIH	ENDINPT	AEYE	INVLDC
AEII	NONVAL	AEYG	JIDERR
AEIJ	NOSTART	AEYH	QIDERR
AEIK	TERMIDERR	AEYJ	DSSTAT
AEIL	DSIDERR	AEYK	SELNERR
AEIM	NOTFND	AEYL	FUNCERR
AEIN	DUPREC	AEYM	UNEXPIN
AEIO	DUPKEY	AEYN	NOPASSBKRD
AEIP	INVREQ	AEYO	NOPASSBKWR
AEIQ	IOERR	AWYP	SEGIDERR
AEIR	NOSPACE	AEYQ	SYSIDERR
AEIS	NOTOPEN	AEYR	ISINVREQ
AEIT	ENDFILE	AEYT	ENVDEFERR
AEIU	ILLOGIC	AEYU	IGREQCD
AEIV	LENGERR	AEYV	SESSERR
AEIW	QZERO	AEYY	NOTALLOC
AEIZ	ITEMERR	AEYZ	CBIDERR
AEI0	PGMIDERR	AEY0	INVEXITREQ
AEI1	TRANSIDERR	AEY1	INVPARTNSET
AEI2	ENDDATA	AEY2	INVPARTN
AEI3	INVTSREQ	AEY3	PARTNFAIL
AEI8	TSIOERR	AEY7	NOTAUTH

Figure 9-2 AEIx and AEYx abend codes

AFCA

File Control. The data set has been disabled.

AICA

Task Control. The task exceeded the execution time limit for runaway tasks; in other words, the task was looping. If the program needs to run so long legitimately, you can avoid this problem by issuing SUSPEND commands.

AKCP

Task Control. The task was cancelled because CICS was in a stall situation.

AKCS

Task Control. The task was cancelled because it was suspended for a period longer than the transaction's defined deadlock timeout period. This is sometimes caused by programming practices that lead to deadlock situations, but it can also be caused by problems internal to CICS.

AKCT

Task Control. The task was cancelled because it was waiting for terminal input for a period longer than the transaction's defined terminal read-time-out period. This happens when an operator starts a conversational program and then leaves the terminal unattended for a long period of time.

APCT

Program Control. The program could not be found or is disabled. This occurs when an operator enters a valid trans-id, but the program associated with the trans-id is missing or disabled. When a CICS command encounters the same situation, the PGMIDERR condition is raised; if that condition isn't handled, the program abends with return code AEI0.

ASCF

Storage Control. A FREEMAIN command specified an invalid address.

ASCR

Storage Control. A GETMAIN command specified too much storage (or zero storage).

ASRA

System Recovery Program. A program check occurred. The Program Status Word contains a one-byte code identifying the type of program check:

1	Operation exception
2	Privileged operation
3	Execute exception
4	Protection exception
5	Addressing exception
6	Specification exception
7	Data exception
8	Fixed-point overflow
9	Fixed-point divide exception
A	Decimal overflow
B	Decimal divide exception
C	Exponent overflow
D	Exponent underflow
E	Significance exception
F	Floating-point divide exception

ASRB

System Recovery Program. An operating system abend has occurred; CICS was able to abend the transaction.

ATCH

Terminal Control. The master terminal operator purged the task.

ATCI

Terminal Control. The master terminal operator purged the task, specifying FORCEPURGE to cancel the task immediately.

ATDD

Transient Data Control. The destination is disabled.

Section 10

AMS commands to define and manipulate VSAM files

To use CICS effectively, you need to know how to define and maintain the VSAM files your CICS application processes. And that means you must know how to use Access Method Services (AMS or IDCAMS) and its commands. This section begins by describing the rules you must follow when you code an AMS command. Then, it shows you how to issue AMS commands from five system environments: MVS using JCL, MVS using TSO, DOS/VSE using JCL, DOS/VSE using ICCF, and VM using CMS. Finally, it describes nine basic AMS control statements: DEFINE CLUSTER, DEFINE ALTERNATEINDEX, DEFINE PATH, BLDINDEX, ALTER, DELETE, LISTCAT, REPRO, and PRINT. For each command, you'll find the command's syntax, an explanation of each of its parameters, and one or more coding examples.

How to code AMS commands

Quite frankly, AMS commands have relatively complicated formatting requirements. To begin with, you can code AMS commands anywhere in columns 2 through 72. It's easy to code your commands in column 1, so be sure to avoid that common mistake.

Each AMS command follows this general format:

```
verb    parameters ...
```

Verb is the name of a command (like DEFINE CLUSTER or LISTCAT) and the *parameters* supply additional information that tells AMS what you want it to do.

Parameters and continuation lines

Most AMS commands require more than one parameter and many of them require more parameters than you can code on a single line. To continue an AMS command from one line to the next, the last character on the line to be continued must be a hyphen; if you omit the hyphen, AMS will reject your command. There's no limit to the number of continuation lines you can code; it's common for an AMS command to require ten or more lines. In fact, I recommend that you use lots of continuation lines, coding only one parameter on each line. That makes your AMS listings much easier to read.

Most AMS parameters have one or more abbreviated forms. For example, you can abbreviate RECORDS as REC. And you can code CISZ or CNVSZ instead of CONTROLINTERVALSIZE. Most of the abbreviations are more trouble to remember than they're worth. So I only use abbreviations for long parameters like CONTROLINTERVALSIZE or ALTERNATEINDEX.

Parameter values and subparameter lists

Most parameters require values in parentheses, such as RECORDS(500). If a parameter requires more than one value, you code a *subparameter list*, separating each value with a space or comma, as in KEYS(5 0).

Some parameters allow multiple sets of subparameter lists, like this:

```
KEYRANGES((0001 4000) (4001 7000)
```

Here, the KEYRANGES parameter consists of two subparameter lists, each of which consists of two values.

Parameter groups and parentheses

Often, entire groups of parameters must be grouped together by parentheses. For example, consider this command:

```
DEFINE CLUSTER ( NAME(AR.TRANS)           -
                 INDEXED                   -
                 RECORDSIZE(150 200)       -
                 KEYS(12 0) )              -
        DATA    ( NAME(AR.TRANS.DATA)      -
                  VOLUMES(261 262)         -
                  CYLINDERS(50 50) )       -
        INDEX   ( NAME(AR.TRANS.INDEX)     -
                  VOLUMES(271) )
```

Here, the first four parameters—NAME, IN-DEXED, RECORDSIZE, and KEYS—are grouped together within parentheses. That's a requirement of the DEFINE CLUSTER command; if you omit these parentheses, AMS will reject the command. Following the first group of parameters, you can code two other groups on a DEFINE CLUSTER command, labelled DATA and INDEX. Each group is enclosed in its own set of parentheses. Notice that two parameters—NAME and VOLUMES—are coded more than once. AMS interprets the meaning of each depending on the group in which the parameter is coded.

Comments

You can include comments anywhere in an AMS command stream by beginning the comment with /* and ending it with */, like this:

```
/* THIS IS A COMMENT */
```

You can place the comment on its own line, or you can place it within a command.

How to invoke AMS under MVS using JCL

To invoke AMS under MVS using JCL, you code an EXEC statement specifying IDCAMS in the PGM parameter. Then, you provide two DD statements: SYSPRINT and SYSIN. SYSPRINT directs AMS printed output, and SYSIN identifies the file that contains the AMS control statements. Usually, you'll code the control statements in the job stream as in-stream data and you'll specify the SYSPRINT DD statement as a SYSOUT data set. If the control statements you code require that AMS process a VSAM data set, you may have to provide a DD statement for it too.

The DD statement for VSAM files

When you code a DD statement for a VSAM file, you need to specify just two parameters: DSNAME to identify the file's name, and DISP=SHR to specify that the file can be shared. The first qualifier of the data set name identifies the catalog that owns the file.

```
//CUSTMAST   DD   DSNAME=MMA2.CUSTMAST,DISP=SHR
```

Coding example

The following example shows how to invoke AMS using MVS JCL.

```
//LISTCAT    JOB   (job accounting information)
//           EXEC PGM=IDCAMS
//SYSPRINT   DD   SYSOUT=A
//SYSIN      DD   *
  LISTCAT ENTRIES(AR.OPEN.ITEMS)              -
          VOLUME
/*
//
```

How to invoke AMS under MVS using TSO

You can issue AMS commands directly under MVS/TSO; TSO recognizes AMS commands and automatically invokes AMS to process them. AMS output is automatically routed back to your terminal. If your AMS commands require access to a data set, you'll have to issue an ALLOCATE command for it before you issue the IDCAMS command.

The ALLOCATE command for VSAM files

When you code an ALLOCATE command for a VSAM file, you specify just three parameters: DSNAME identifies the file's data set name, DDNAME identifies the ddname associated with the data set, and SHR specifies that the data set can be shared. The first qualifier of the data set name identifies the catalog that owns the file.

```
ALLOCATE DSNAME(MMA2.CUSTMAST) DDNAME(CUSTMAST) SHR
```

Coding example

In this example, the lower-case text represents data entered by the terminal operator and the upper-case text is a TSO message.

```
READY
listcat entries(ar.open.items) volume
   .
   .
   .
```

How to invoke AMS from DOS/VSE using JCL

To invoke AMS under DOS/VSE using JCL, you specify IDCAMS in an EXEC statement. (You must also specify SIZE=AUTO on the EXEC statement.) After the EXEC statement, code your AMS commands. And after the AMS commands, you code an end-of-data statement (/*). If the AMS commands you code actually process a data set, you'll also have to provide a DLBL statement for the VSAM file.

The DLBL statement for VSAM files

When you code a DLBL statement for a VSAM file, you need to code just four parameters: the file-name used by the program to refer to the file, the file-id used by VSAM to identify the file, VSAM to indicate that the file is a VSAM file, and CAT to identify the catalog that owns the file. If the file is owned by the job catalog or the master catalog, you can omit CAT. You don't code an EXTENT statement for a VSAM file. (Be sure to code two commas before the word VSAM.)

```
// DLBL CUSTMAS,'CUSTOMER.MASTER.FILE',,VSAM,CAT=UCAT08
```

Coding example

The following example shows how to invoke AMS using DOS/VSE JCL.

```
// JOB      LISTCAT
// EXEC     IDCAMS,SIZE=AUTO
   LISTCAT  ENTRIES(AR.OPEN.ITEMS)      -
            CATALOG(AR.USER.CATALOG)    -
            VOLUME
/*
/&
```

How to invoke AMS under DOS/VSE using ICCF

To invoke AMS under DOS/VSE using ICCF, you must code a procedure that issues a /LOAD statement to invoke IDCAMS. After the /LOAD statement, code an /OPTION statement that specifies GETVIS=AUTO. Then, code the AMS statements. Any VSAM files processed by the AMS control statements must be allocated (with DLBL statements) to the partition in which ICCF is running.

Coding example

The following example shows how to invoke AMS using an ICCF procedure.

```
/LOAD IDCAMS
/OPTION GETVIS=AUTO
 LISTCAT ENTRIES(AR.OPEN.ITEMS)            -
         CATALOG(AR.USER.CATALOG)          -
         VOLUME
```

How to invoke AMS under VM/CMS

You invoke AMS under VM/CMS by issuing the AMSERV command. On the AMSERV command, you specify the name of a CMS file that contains the AMS control statements you want to process. If you want the AMS output directed to a printer, you should specify (PRINT on the AMSERV command too.

Coding example

In this example, the lower-case text represents data entered by the terminal operator and the upper-case text represents CMS messages.

```
CP:
edit listcat amserv
NEW FILE:
EDIT:
input
  listcat entries(ar.open.items)         -
          catalog(ar.user.catalog)       -
          volume
file
CP:
amserv listcat (print
 .
 .
 .
```

The DEFINE CLUSTER command

The DEFINE CLUSTER command defines a VSAM data set, specifying the file's name, organization, space requirements, and other characteristics.

Syntax

```
DEFINE CLUSTER    (    NAME(entry-name)
                      [ OWNER(owner-id) ]
                      [ FOR(days) | TO(date) ]
                      [ INDEXED | NONINDEXED | NUMBERED ]
                      [ RECORDSIZE(avg max) ]
                      [ SPANNED | NONSPANNED ]
                      [ KEYS(length offset) ]
                      [ FREESPACE(ci-space ca-space) ]
                      [ IMBED | NOIMBED ]
                      [ REPLICATE | NOREPLICATE ]
                      [ VOLUMES(vol-ser...) ]

                         ⎧ CYLINDERS ⎫
                      [  ⎨ TRACKS    ⎬  (primary [secondary]) ]
                         ⎪ BLOCKS    ⎪
                         ⎩ RECORDS   ⎭

                      [ UNIQUE | SUBALLOCATION ]
                      [ FILE (ddname) ]
                      [ SHAREOPTIONS(a b) ]
                      [ MODEL(entry-name[/password]) ]

          [ DATA     ( [ NAME(entry-name) ]
                      [ VOLUMES(vol-ser...) ]
                      [ CISZ(size) ]

                         ⎧ CYLINDERS ⎫
                      [  ⎨ TRACKS    ⎬  (primary [secondary]) ] ) ]
                         ⎪ BLOCKS    ⎪
                         ⎩ RECORDS   ⎭

          [ INDEX    ( [ NAME(entry-name) ]
                      [ VOLUMES(vol-ser...) ]

                         ⎧ CYLINDERS ⎫
                      [  ⎨ TRACKS    ⎬  (primary [secondary]) ] ) ]
                         ⎪ BLOCKS    ⎪
                         ⎩ RECORDS   ⎭

          [ CATALOG(name[/password]) ]
```

Options

NAME

Specifies the name of the cluster or component.

OWNER

Specifies a one- to eight-character owner-id.

FOR
TO

Specifies a retention period for the file.

INDEXED
NONINDEXED
NUMBERED

Specifies whether you're defining a KSDS (INDEXED), ESDS (NONINDEXED) or RRDS (NUMBERED) file. If omitted, INDEXED is assumed.

RECORDSIZE

Specifies the average and maximum length of the file's records. If omitted, (4089 4089) is assumed for nonspanned records; (4089 32600) is assumed for spanned records.

SPANNED
NONSPANNED

Specifies whether logical records can span control intervals. NONSPANNED is the default.

KEYS

Specifies, for a KSDS, the length and offset of the primary key.

FREESPACE

Specifies the percentage of free space that should be reserved for record insertions. *ci-space* specifies what percentage of each control interval should be left free; *ca-space* specifies what percentage of the control intervals in each control area should be left free. (KSDS only)

IMBED
NOIMBED

IMBED specifies that the lowest level of the data set's index component should be stored together with the data component. Because this almost always improves performance, you should code IMBED for all key-sequenced data sets. NOIMBED is the default. (KSDS only)

REPLICATE
NOREPLICATE

Specifies whether or not index records should be repeated as many times as possible on each track. You should usually specify REPLICATE. NOREPLICATE is the default.

VOLUMES

Specifies one or more volumes that will contain the cluster or component.

primary

Specifies how much space to initially allocate to the cluster or component, expressed in cylinders, tracks, records, or blocks.

secondary

Specifies the secondary space allocation for the cluster. Ignored for unique files under DOS.

UNIQUE
SUBALLOCATION

Specifies whether the file is unique (occupies its own data space) or suballocated (shares space with other files). SUBALLOCATION is the default.

FILE

For OS, required only if the volume is not permanently mounted. For DOS, required if UNIQUE is specified.

SHAREOPTIONS

Specifies how the file may be shared among regions (a) and among systems (b). See next page for the values you can code for a and b.

MODEL

Specifies the name of an already defined cluster on which this cluster is to be modeled.

CISZ

Specifies the size of the data component's control intervals. For most files, you'll specify 2048, 4096, or 6144.

CATALOG

Specifies the name and password of the catalog that will own the cluster. If omitted, the stepcat, jobcat, master catalog, or (MVS only) high-level qualifier of the cluster name identifies the catalog.

Calculating space requirements

You can use the following table to calculate the number of cylinders required to hold a VSAM file.

CI size	CIs per cylinder with IMBED/NOIMBED				
	3330	3340	3350	3375	3380
512	360/380	132/144	783/810	440/480	644/690
1024	198/209	77/84	435/450	275/300	434/456
2048	108/114	33/36	232/240	154/168	252/270
4096	54/57	33/36	116/120	88/96	140/150
6144	36/38	11/12	77/80	51/56	84/90
8192	26/28	16/18	58/60	44/48	70/75

Share options

Cross-region share option (a)

1 The file can be processed simultaneously by multiple jobs as long as all jobs open the file for input only. If a job opens the file for output, no other job can open the file.

2 The file can be processed simultaneously by multiple jobs as long as only one job opens the file for output; all other jobs must open the file for input only.

3 Any number of jobs can process the file simultaneously for input or output; VSAM does nothing to ensure the integrity of the file.

4 Any number of jobs can process the file simultaneously for input or output; VSAM imposes these restrictions:

- direct retrieval always reads data from disk even if the desired index or data records are already in a VSAM buffer

- data may not be added to the end of the file

- a control area split is not allowed

Cross-system share options (b)

3 Any number of jobs on any system can process the file simultaneously for input or output; VSAM does nothing to ensure the integrity of the file.

4 Any number of jobs on any system can process the file simultaneously for input or output; VSAM imposes the same restrictions as for cross-region share option 4.

Coding example (KSDS)

This example shows how to define a key-sequenced
data set named MMA2.CUSTOMER.MASTER.

```
    DEFINE CLUSTER ( NAME(MMA2.CUSTOMER.MASTER)        -
                     OWNER(DLOWE2)                     -
                     INDEXED                           -
                     RECORDSIZE(200 200)               -
                     KEYS(6 0)                         -
                     UNIQUE                            -
                     VOLUMES(MPS800)                   -
                     TO(88365)                         -
                     SHAREOPTIONS(2 3)                 -
                     IMBED                             -
                     REPLICATE )                       -
         DATA      ( NAME(MMA2.CUSTOMER.MASTER.DATA)   -
                     CYLINDERS(6 0)                    -
                     CISZ(4096) )                      -
         INDEX     ( NAME(MMA2.CUSTOMER.MASTER.INDEX) )
```

Coding example (ESDS)

This example shows how to define an entry-se-
quenced data set name MMA2.AR.TRAN.

```
    DEFINE CLUSTER ( NAME(MMA2.AR.TRAN)                -
                     OWNER(DLOWE2)                     -
                     NONINDEXED                        -
                     RECORDSIZE(190 280)               -
                     UNIQUE                            -
                     VOLUMES(MPS800)                   -
                     FOR(365)                          -
         DATA      ( NAME(MMA2.AR.TRAN.DATA)           -
                     CYLINDERS(10 1) )
```

Coding example (RRDS)

This example shows how to define a relative-record
data set named MMA2.GL.ACCOUNT.MASTER.

```
DEFINE CLUSTER ( NAME(MMA2.GL.ACCOUNT.MASTER          -
                 OWNER(ACCT1)                          -
                 NUMBERED                              -
                 RECORDSIZE(502 502)                   -
                 UNIQUE                                -
                 VOLUMES(MPS800)                       -
                 FOR(365)                              -
                 SHAREOPTIONS(1 3) )                   -
        DATA    ( NAME(MMA2.GL.ACCOUNT.MASTER.DATA)    -
                  CYLINDERS(10 1) )
```

The DEFINE ALTERNATEINDEX command

The DEFINE ALTERNATEINDEX command defines an alternate index. The alternate index is related to a base cluster via the RELATE option. However, to process the base cluster via the alternate index, you must create a path using the DEFINE PATH command. Although you can spell it out if you wish, the keyword ALTERNATEINDEX is almost always abbreviated AIX.

Syntax

```
DEFINE AIX  (    NAME(entry-name)
                 RELATE(entry-name/password)
            [ OWNER(owner-id) ]
            [ FOR(days) | TO(date) ]
            [ KEYS(length offset) ]
            [ UNIQUEKEY | NONUNIQUEKEY ]
            [ UPGRADE | NOUPGRADE ]
            [ VOLUMES(vol-ser...) ]

                ⎧ CYLINDERS ⎫
            [   ⎨ TRACKS    ⎬   (primary [secondary]) ]
                ⎪ BLOCKS    ⎪
                ⎩ RECORDS   ⎭

            [ UNIQUE | SUBALLOCATION ]
            [ FILE(ddname) ]
            [ SHAREOPTIONS(a b) ]
            [ MODEL(entry-name[/password]) ]

     [ DATA  ( [ NAME(entry-name) ]
               [ VOLUMES(vol-ser...) ]

                  ⎧ CYLINDERS ⎫
              [   ⎨ TRACKS    ⎬   (primary [secondary])  ]    ) ]
                  ⎪ BLOCKS    ⎪
                  ⎩ RECORDS   ⎭

     [ INDEX ( [ NAME(entry-name) ]
               [ VOLUMES(vol-ser...) ]

                  ⎧ CYLINDERS ⎫
              [   ⎨ TRACKS    ⎬   (primary [secondary])  ]    ) ]
                  ⎪ BLOCKS    ⎪
                  ⎩ RECORDS   ⎭

     [ CATALOG(name[/password]) ]
```

Options

NAME

Specifies the name of the alternate index or component.

RELATE

Specifies the name and, if required, password of the base cluster to which this alternate index is related.

OWNER

Specifies a one- to eight-character owner- id for the alternate index.

FOR
TO

Specifies a retention period for the alternate index.

KEYS

Specifies, for a KSDS, the length and offset of the alternate key.

UNIQUEKEY
NONUNIQUEKEY

Specifies whether duplicate key values are allowed. NONUNIQUEKEY is the default.

UPGRADE
NOUPGRADE

Specifies whether the alternate index is a part of the base cluster's upgrade set. UPGRADE is the default.

VOLUMES

Specifies one or more volumes that will contain the alternate index or component.

primary

Specifies how much space to initially allocate to the alternate index or component, expressed in cylinders, tracks, records, or blocks.

secondary

Specifies the secondary space allocation for the alternate index. Ignored for unique files under DOS.

UNIQUE
UBALLOCATION

Specifies whether the alternate index is unique (occupies its own data space) or suballocated (shares space with other files). If omitted, SUBALLOCATION is assumed.

FILE

For OS, required only if the volume is not permanently mounted. For DOS, required if UNIQUE is specified.

SHAREOPTIONS

Specifies how the alternate index may be shared among regions (a) and among systems (b). See the description of the SHAREOPTIONS values under the DEFINE CLUSTER command for details. Abbreviation: SHR.

MODEL

Specifies the name of an already defined alternate index on which this alternate index is to be modeled.

CATALOG

Specifies the name and password of the catalog that will own the alternate index. If omitted, the stepcat, jobcat, master catalog, or (MVS only) high-level qualifier of the cluster name identifies the catalog.

Coding example

This example shows how to define an alternate index named MMA2.EMPMAST.SSN.AIX for a base cluster named MMA2.EMPLOYEE.-MASTER. The alternate keys are nine bytes long, starting in the thirteenth byte (displacement 12) of each record. (The alternate key values are employee social security numbers.) Duplicates are not allowed (UNIQUEKEY) and the alternate index is *not* a part of the base cluster's upgrade set (NOUPGRADE).

```
DEFINE AIX    ( NAME(MMA2.EMPMAST.SSN.AIX)        -
                RELATE(MMA2.EMPLOYEE.MASTER)      -
                OWNER(DLOWE2)                     -
                TO(87365)                         -
                KEYS(9 12)                        -
                UNIQUEKEY                         -
                NOUPGRADE                         -
                VOLUMES(MPS800)                   -
                UNIQUE )                          -
       DATA   ( NAME(MMA2.EMPMAST.SSN.AIX.DATA)   -
                CYLINDERS(1 1) )                  -
       INDEX  ( NAME(MMA2.EMPMAST.SSN.AIX.INDEX) )
```

The DEFINE PATH command

The DEFINE PATH command defines the processing link between an alternate index and its base
cluster.

Syntax

```
DEFINE PATH (    NAME(entry-name)
                 PATHENTRY(entry-name[/password])
             [ UPDATE | NOUPDATE ]
             [ FOR(days) | TO(date) ]
             [ MODEL(entry-name[/password]) ] )
        [ CATALOG(name[/password]) ]
```

Options

NAME
Specifies the name of the path.

PATHENTRY
Specifies the name of the alternate index to
which the path is related.

UPDATE
NOUPDATE
Specifies whether the upgrade set should be
updated when this path is processed. UP-
DATE is the default.

FOR
TO
Specifies a retention period (in the format
dddd) or an expiration date (in the format
yyddd) for the path.

MODEL
Specifies the name of an existing path to use
as a model.

CATALOG
Specifies the name of the catalog that contains the alternate index. If omitted, the stepcat, jobcat, master catalog, or high-level
qualifier (MVS only) of the alternate index
name identifies the catalog.

Coding example

This example shows how to define a path that links an alternate index named MMA2.EMPMAST.-SSN.AIX to its base cluster.

```
DEFINE PATH ( NAME(MMA2.EMPMAST.SSN.PATH)      -
              PATHENTRY(MMA2.EMPMAST.SSN.AIX)   -
              UPDATE   )
```

The BLDINDEX command

The BLDINDEX command creates the key entries necessary to access a base cluster via a path. You use it initially to load key entries into an alternate index. And you use it periodically to rebuild alternate indexes so they can be processed efficiently.

Syntax

```
BLDINDEX      { INFILE(ddname[/password])    }
              { INDATASET(ddname[/password]) }

              { OUTFILE(ddname[/password])    }
              { OUTDATASET(ddname[/password]) }

              [ EXTERNALSORT | INTERNALSORT ]

              { WORKFILES(ddname ddname) }
              { WORKVOLUMES(vol-ser...)  }

              [ CATALOG(name[/password]) ]
```

Options

INFILE
Specifies the name of a DD or DLBL statement that identifies the base cluster.

INDATASET
Specifies the name of the base cluster.

OUTFILE
Specifies the name of a DD or DLBL statement that identifies the alternate index.

OUTDATASET
Specifies the name of the alternate index.

EXTERNALSORT
INTERNALSORT
Specifies whether VSAM is to sort the alternate index records in virtual storage (INTERNALSORT) or using disk storage (EXTERNALSORT). If you specify INTERNALSORT and enough virtual storage isn't available to sort the records, an external sort is performed. INTERNALSORT is the default.

WORKFILES
WORKVOLUMES
WORKFILES (MVS only) supplies the ddnames for the work files used by an external sort. DD statements for these files must be provided. If omitted, IDCUT1 and IDCUT2 are used. WORKVOLUMES (DOS only) specifies the volumes (up to 10) that will contain the two work files. No DLBL statements are required.

CATALOG
Specifies the name and password of the catalog that will own the sort work files. If omitted, the stepcat or jobcat is used if available; otherwise, the master catalog is used. On MVS systems, if the data set names are supplied on the DD statements for the work files, the high-level qualifiers of those names identify the catalog.

Coding example (MVS)

This example shows how to build the alternate index that was defined in the coding example for the DEFINE ALTERNATEINDEX command on an MVS system.

```
//           EXEC PGM=IDCAMS
//SYSPRINT DD   SYSOUT=A
//IDCUT1    DD   UNIT=SYSDA,VOL=SER=MPS800,DISP=SHR
//IDCUT2    DD   UNIT=SYSDA,VOL=SER=MPS800,DISP=SHR
//SYSIN     DD   *
  BLDINDEX INDATASET(MMA2.EMPLOYEE.MASTER)    -
           OUTDATASET(MMA2.EMPMAST.SSN.AIX)   -
           CATALOG(MMA2)
  /*
```

Coding example (DOS/VSE)

This example shows how to build the alternate index that was defined in the coding example for the DEFINE ALTERNATEINDEX command on a DOS/VSE system.

```
// DLBL IJSYSUC,'MMA.USER.CATALOG',,VSAM,CAT=IJSYSCT
// EXEC IDCAMS,SIZE=AUTO
  BLDINDEX INDATASET(MMA2.EMPLOYEE.MASTER)    -
           OUTDATASET(MMA2.EMPMAST.SSN.AIX)   -
           WORKVOLUMES(SYSWK2)                 -
           CATALOG(MMA.USER.CATALOG)
  /*
```

The LISTCAT command

The LISTCAT command lists information about
data sets and other VSAM objects that are defined
in VSAM catalogs.

Syntax

```
LISTCAT [ CATALOG(name[/password]) ]
        { ENTRIES(entry-name[/password]...)}
        { LEVEL(level)                     }
        [ entry-type ]
            / NAME       \
            | HISTORY    |
        [ < VOLUME     > ]
            | ALLOCATION |
            \ ALL        /
        [ NOTUSABLE ]
        [ CREATION(days) ]
        [ EXPIRATION(days) ]
        [ OUTFILE(ddname) ]
```

Options

CATALOG
Specifies the name and, if required, password
of the catalog from which entries are to be
listed.

ENTRIES
Specifies the names of the entries you want to
list. If omitted, all entries in the catalog are
listed. Under MVS, you can specify a
generic entry name by replacing one or more
of the file name levels with an asterisk.

LEVEL
Specifies one or more levels of qualification.
Any data sets whose names match those
levels are listed. (MVS only)

entry-type
Specifies the type of entries you want listed.
For all versions of VSAM, you can code any
of the following entry types:

ALIAS (*MVS only*)
ALTERNATEINDEX
CLUSTER
DATA
GENERATIONDATAGROUP (*MVS only*)
INDEX
NONVSAM
PAGESPACE (*MVS only*)
PATH
SPACE
USERCATALOG

You can abbreviate GENERATION-
DATAGROUP as GDG.

NAME

Specifies that only the names and types of the specified entries are to be listed. NAME is the default.

HISTORY

Specifies that the information listed by NAME, plus the history information (such as creation and expiration dates), is to be listed. (MVS only)

VOLUME

Specifies that the information listed by HISTORY, plus the volume locations of the specified entries, is to be listed.

ALLOCATION

Specifies that the information listed by VOLUME, plus detailed extent information, is to be listed.

ALL

Specifies that all available catalog information for the specified entries is to be listed.

NOTUSABLE

Specifies that only damaged catalog entries are to be listed.

CREATION

Specifies that only entries which were created on or before the specified number of days before the current date should be listed. (MVS only)

EXPIRATION

Specifies that only entries which will expire on or before the specified number of days after the current date should be listed. (MVS only)

OUTFILE

Specifies the name of a DD statement that should receive the output from the LISTCAT command. If omitted, output is sent to SYSPRINT. (MVS only)

Device codes that appear in LISTCAT output

If you specify VOLUMES, ALLOCATION, or ALL in a LISTCAT command, VSAM indicates the device type for each volume that contains the file. Unfortunately, the device type is given in a coded format. You can use the following table to look up the device code given in the LISTCAT output.

Device code in LISTCAT output	Device type
30008001	9 track tape
3040200A	3340 (35 or 70 MB)
30502006	2305-1
30502007	2305-2
30502009	3330-1 or 3330-2
3050200B	3350
3050200D	3330-11
30582009	3330 MSS virtual volume
30808001	7 track tape
30C02008	2314 or 2319
3010200C	3375
3010200E	3380

Coding example

The following example shows how to list the names
of all data sets that begin with MMA2.

```
LISTCAT LEVEL(MMA2) -
        NAMES
```

Coding example

The following example shows how to list all available information for a data set named MMA2.CUS-
TOMER.MASTER.

```
LISTCAT ENTRIES(MMA2.CUSTOMER.MASTER) -
        ALL
```

The ALTER command

The ALTER command lets you change a VSAM file's name, volume allocation, and other characteristics assigned to the file when you defined it.

And you can inhibit the file so that it can be read but not updated.

Syntax

```
ALTER       name[/password]
            [ CATALOG(name[/password]) ]
            [ NEWNAME(name) ]
            [ ADDVOLUMES(volser...) ]
            [ REMOVEVOLUMES(volser...) ]
            [ INHIBIT | UNINHIBIT ]
```

Options

Note: Although not indicated in the ALTER command's syntax, you can specify many of the DEFINE CLUSTER options on an ALTER command.

name
>   Specifies the name and, if required, password of the object whose catalog entry is to be altered.

CATALOG
>   Identifies the catalog that contains the object to be altered. Required only if catalog can't be located by standard search sequence.

NEWNAME
>   Specifies a new name for the entry.

ADDVOLUMES
>   Adds the specified volumes to the list of volumes on which space may be allocated to the object.

REMOVEVOLUMES
>   Removes the specified volumes from the list of volumes on which space may be allocated to the object. Ignored if space has already been allocated on the specified volumes.

INHIBIT
UNINHIBIT
>   INHIBIT sets the data set to read-only; UNINHIBIT returns the data set to normal status.

Coding example

The following example changes the name and free space specification for a file. The old name is MMA2.CUSTOMER.MASTER and the new name is MMA2.CUSTMAST.

```
ALTER MMA2.CUSTOMER.MASTER        -
      NEWNAME(MMA2.CUSTMAST)      -
      FREESPACE(10 10)
```

The DELETE command

The DELETE command deletes a VSAM file or other object.

Syntax

```
DELETE ( entry-name[/password]... )
       [ CATALOG(name[/password]) ]
       [ entry-type ]
       [ FORCE | NOFORCE ]
       [ PURGE | NOPURGE ]
       [ ERASE | NOERASE ]
```

Options

entry-name
Specifies the name and password of the entry or entries to be deleted. If you specify just one entry name, you can omit the list in parentheses. To delete a space, specify a vol-ser as the entry name.

CATALOG
Specifies the name and password of the catalog that owns the entries to be deleted. Required only if the correct catalog can't be found using the standard search order.

entry-type
Specifies that only entries of the listed types should be deleted. The valid entry types are the same as for the LISTCAT command.

FORCE
NOFORCE
When SPACE is specified along with FORCE, data spaces are deleted even if they contain data sets. If you specify NOFORCE, only empty spaces are deleted. NOFORCE is the default.

PURGE
NOPURGE
PURGE means that an object should be deleted even if its retention period has not expired. NOPURGE means to delete entries only if their retention periods have expired. NOPURGE is the default.

ERASE
NOERASE
ERASE means that the data component of a cluster or alternate index should be erased (overwritten with binary zeros). NOERASE means that the data component should not be erased. NOERASE is the default.

Coding example

This example shows two DELETE commands. The first deletes three entries; the PURGE option specifies that they should be deleted regardless of their expiration dates. The second deletes all alternate indexes whose names follow the form MMA2.CUSTMAST.*.AIX.

```
DELETE  (MMA2.CUSTOMER.MASTER            -
         MMA2.CUSTMAST.DISTRICT.AIX      -
         MMA2.CUSTMAST.DISTRICT.PATH)    -
         PURGE
DELETE  MMA2.CUSTMAST.*.AIX             -
         ALTERNATEINDEX
```

The PRINT command

The PRINT command prints all or a specified portion of a VSAM file in character, hex, or dump format.

Syntax

```
PRINT   { INDATASET(entry-name[/password]) }
        { INFILE(ddname[/password])        }

        [ { CHARACTER }  ]
          { HEX       }
          { DUMP      }

        [ { SKIP(count)           }  ]
          { FROMKEY(key)          }
          { FROMNUMBER(number)    }
          { FROMADDRESS(address)  }

        [ { COUNT(count)        }  ]
          { TOKEY(key)          }
          { TONUMBER(number)    }
          { TOADDRESS(address)  }
```

Options

INDATASET
Specifies the file name of the VSAM file to be printed. A DD or DLBL statement is not required if you code INDATASET rather than INFILE.

INFILE
Specifies the ddname or DLBL file name of the file to be printed.

CHARACTER
HEX
DUMP
Specifies the format of the output; CHARACTER and HEX print the data in character or hex format; DUMP prints data in both character and hex format. DUMP is the default.

SKIP
For count, specify a numeric value to indicate the number of records to be skipped before the print operation begins. Valid for all file types.

FROMKEY
For key, specify the value of the key at which the print operation should begin. Valid only when printing a KSDS.

FROMNUMBER
For number, specify the relative record number at which the print operation should begin. Valid only when printing an RRDS.

FROMADDRESS
For address, specify the RBA of the first record to be printed. Valid only when printing a KSDS or ESDS.

COUNT

For count, specify a numeric value to indicate the number of records to be printed. Valid for all file types.

TOKEY

For key, specify the value of the key at which the print operation should end. Valid only when printing a KSDS.

TONUMBER

For number, specify the relative record number at which the print operation should end. Valid only when printing an RRDS.

TOADDRESS

For address, specify an RBA that lies within the last record to be printed. Valid only when printing a KSDS or ESDS.

Coding example

This example shows how to print the contents of a VSAM file in character format.

```
    PRINT INDATASET(MMA2.CUSTOMER.MASTER)
```

Coding example

This example shows how to print 3 records starting at the 29th record of a file. The data is printed in dump format.

```
    PRINT INDATASET(MMA2.CUSTOMER.MASTER)   -
           SKIP(28)                         -
           COUNT(3)                         -
           DUMP
```

The REPRO command

The REPRO command copies the contents of a data set into another data set. Usually, you use it to copy one VSAM file to another or to copy a non-VSAM file to a VSAM file. If the output file is a VSAM file, it must first be defined with a DEFINE CLUSTER command.

Syntax

```
REPRO     {INDATASET(entry-name[/password])}
          {INFILE(ddname[/password])       }

          {OUTDATASET(entry-name[/password])}
          {OUTFILE(ddname[/password])       }

       [  {SKIP(count)            }  ]
          {FROMKEY(key)           }
          {FROMNUMBER(number)     }
          {FROMADDRESS(address)   }

       [  {COUNT(count)           }  ]
          {TOKEY(key)             }
          {TONUMBER(number)       }
          {TOADDRESS(address)     }

          [ REPLACE | NOREPLACE ]
```

Options

INDATASET
Specifies the name of the file to be copied.

INFILE
Specifies the name of a DD or DLBL statement that identifies the file to be copied.

OUTDATASET
Specifies the name of the data set to which the input file is to be copied.

OUTFILE
Specifies the name of a DD or DLBL statement that identifies the file to which the input file is to be copied.

SKIP
For count, specify a numeric value to indicate the number of records to be skipped before the copy operation begins. Valid for all file types.

FROMKEY
For key, specify the value of the key at which the copy operation should begin. Valid only when copying a KSDS or ISAM file.

FROMNUMBER
For number, specify the relative record number at which the copy operation should begin. Valid only when copying an RRDS.

FROMADDRESS
For address, specify the RBA of the first record to be copied. Valid only when copying a KSDS or ESDS.

COUNT
For count, specify a numeric value to indicate the number of records to be copied. Valid for all file types.

TOKEY

For key, specify the value of the key at which the copy operation should end. Valid only when copying a KSDS or ISAM file.

TONUMBER

For number, specify the relative record number at which the copy operation should end. Valid only when copying an RRDS.

TOADDRESS

For address, specify an RBA that lies within the last record to be copied. Valid only when copying a KSDS or ESDS.

REPLACE
NOREPLACE

Specifies how duplicate records should be handled. If you specify REPLACE, duplicate records are replaced; if you specify NOREPLACE, duplicate records are treated as errors. NOREPLACE is the default.

Coding example

This example shows how to copy a data set named MMA2.EMPLOYEE.MASTER to MMA2.EMP-LOYEE.COPY. Note that MMA2.EMPLOYEE.- COPY must first be defined with a DEFINE CLUSTER command.

```
REPRO INDATASET(MMA2.EMPLOYEE.MASTER) -
      OUTDATASET(MMA2.EMPLOYEE.COPY)
```

Section 11

ISPF, ICCF, and CMS

To be an effective CICS programmer, you need to master the interactive system you use for program development. Under MVS, that interactive system is probably ISPF; under DOS/VSE, it's probably ICCF. However, if your shop uses VM, you'll probably use CMS for program development. In this section, you'll find extensive reference information for each of these interactive program development environments.

ISPF

Although ISPF is becoming available for other operating system environments, it's still most commonly used under MVS. As a result, the reference information presented here assumes you're using an MVS system. The variations for other systems are minor.

ISPF menu selections

Although you can work your way through ISPF menus one level at a time, you'll often want to go directly from one menu to another, without passing through any intermediate menus. You can do that from the primary option menu by entering the complete menu selection in the form x.y, where x represents the first-level menu selection and y represents the sub-menu you want to select. From any other ISPF panel, you must prefix your selection with an equals sign (=x.y).

0	ISPF parms
0.1	Specify terminal characteristics
0.2	Specify log and list defaults
0.3	Specify program function keys
0.4	Specify screen display characteristics
0.5	Specify list data set characteristics
1	Browse
2	Edit
3	Utilities
3.1	Library utility
3.2	Data set utility
3.3	Move/copy utility
3.4	Data set list utility
3.5	Reset statistics utility
3.6	Hardcopy utility
3.7	List VTOC utility
3.8	Outlist utility
3.9	Command table utility
3.10	Convert menus/messages
4	Foreground
4.1	System assembler
4.2	OS/VS COBOL compiler
4.3	VS FORTRAN compiler
4.4	PL/I checkout compiler
4.5	PL/I optimizing compiler
4.6	PASCAL/VS compiler
4.7	Linkage editor
4.9	SCRIPT/VS
4.10	COBOL interactive debug
4.11	FORTRAN interactive debug
4.12	Member parts list

5	Batch
5.1	System assembler
5.2	OS/VS COBOL compiler
5.3	VS FORTRAN compiler
5.4	PL/I checkout compiler
5.5	PL/I optimizing compiler
5.6	PASCAL/VS compiler
5.7	Linkage editor
5.12	Member parts list
6	TSO command
7	Dialog test
7.1	Functions
7.2	Panels
7.3	Variables
7.4	Tables
7.5	Log
7.6	Dialog services
7.7	Traces
7.8	Breakpoints
8	Library management
8.1	Controls
8.2	User set
8.3	Distribution
8.4	Activate
8.5	Review
T	Tutorial
X	Exit

PA and PF key default assignments

Here are the default function assignments for PA and PF keys. You can change these assignments using option 0.3.

PA1	ATTENTION	Interrupt a TSO command.
PA2	RESHOW	Redisplay the current screen.
PF1/13	HELP	Tutorial.
PF2/14	SPLIT	Enter split screen mode.
PF3/15	END	End the current operation.
PF4/16	RETURN	End the current operation and return to the primary option menu.
PF5/17	RFIND	Repeat the previous FIND command.
PF6/18	RCHANGE	Repeat the previous CHANGE command.
PF7/19	UP	Move the window up by the current scroll amount.
PF8/20	DOWN	Move the window down by the current scroll amount.
PF9/21	SWAP	Alternate between spit screens.
PF10/22	LEFT	Move the window left by the current scroll amount.
PF11/23	RIGHT	Move the window right by the current scroll amount.
PF12/24	CURSOR	Move the cursor to the command area.

Scroll amounts

You can specify any of these values in the SCROLL field to control scrolling.

HALF	Move the screen window half a page (usually 11 lines or 40 columns).
PAGE	Move the screen window one page (usually 22 lines or 80 columns).
n	Move the screen window n lines or columns.
MAX	Move the screen window to the top, bottom, left, or right margin.
CSR	Move the screen window so the data at the cursor position ends up at the top, bottom, left, or right of the screen.

Member list commands

Whenever ISPF displays a member list, you can use the following commands to affect one or more of the displayed members. You enter the primary commands in the command area; line commands are entered next to the member name.

Primary commands

L member-name   Scrolls the display to the specified member.

S member-name   Selects the specified member.

Line commands

S Select the member (any option other than 3.1).
P Print the member (option 3.1 only).
R Rename the member (option 3.1 only).
D Delete the member (option 3.1 only).
B Browse the member (option 3.1 only)

Browse commands

When you're in browse mode, you can enter any of the following primary commands in the command area:

The LOCATE command

Scrolls the text to a particular line, identified by a line number or by a label associated with the line.

```
LOCATE   {line-number|label}
```

To establish a label, enter the following command:

```
.label
```

The FIND command

Searches the file to find an occurrence of a specified text string.

```
FIND string   [scope] [condition] [line-range] [col-range]
```

The *string* component of the FIND command is described later in this section. The word FIND can be abbreviated F. You can code the options in any order. *Scope* can be NEXT, PREV, FIRST, LAST, or ALL. *Condition* can be CHARS, PREFIX, SUF-FIX, or WORD. *Line-range* can be one or two line labels; *col-range* can be one or two column numbers.

The HEX command

Controls the display of hexadecimal data.

```
HEX   [ON|OFF]   [DATA|VERT]
```

Edit profiles

An *edit profile* controls various options of the editor during a particular editing session. Normally, the edit profile is determined by the library type (the library's third data set name qualifier). However, you can specify a different profile when you invoke the editor, if you wish.

The edit profile consists of: (1) mode settings, which control things like whether data is automatically numbered, whether nulls (hex zeros) are displayed, and so on; (2) boundary settings, which specify the left and right column margins; (3) edit masks used as default data when lines are inserted, and (4) tab settings.

Edit modes

You can activate or deactivate any of the following modes by entering the mode name followed by the word ON or OFF.

AUTOSAVE

Controls whether data should be automatically saved when you leave the editor. You can also specify AUTOSAVE OFF PROMPT or AUTOSAVE OFF NOPROMPT to control whether or not ISPF should prompt you before it terminates the editor without saving any text changes you made.

AUTONUM

Controls whether line numbers should be maintained automatically.

AUTOLIST

Controls whether the member should be listed automatically when you leave the editor. If AUTOLIST is on, the member is listed only if it's changed.

CAPS

Controls automatic conversion of lowercase data to uppercase.

HEX

Controls hexadecimal display. You can also specify HEX ON VERTICAL or HEX ON DATA to control the format of the hexadecimal display.

NULLS

Controls how trailing blanks are handled on the 3270 screen: NULLS OFF causes all blanks to be sent to the screen; NULLS ON causes null characters (hex zeros) to be sent in place of trailing blanks. If you specify NULLS ON ALL, *all* trailing blanks are converted to nulls; if you omit ALL, ISPF retains one trailing blank on each line.

NUMBER

Controls how line numbers are maintained. Besides ON or OFF, you can specify three options: STD, COBOL, and DISPLAY. STD places line numbers in the standard line number field (the last eight characters for fixed-length records, the first eight characters for variable-length records). COBOL places line numbers in the COBOL line number field (the first six characters of each record). DISPLAY causes the line numbers to be displayed in the text window; if you omit DISPLAY, which you normally will, ISPF automatically scrolls the display left or right.

PACK

Specifies whether data should be stored in compressed format to save disk space.

RECOVERY

Controls the automatic journal kept for recovery purposes.

STATS

Controls automatic maintenance of library statistics.

Edit boundaries

You can specify the left and right margin using one of two commands: the BNDS line command or the BOUNDS primary command. To use the BNDS line command, enter BNDS in the line command area of any line; ISPF displays a boundary line, into

TABS

Controls logical and hardware tabbing. Besides ON or OFF, you can specify a character that's used for the logical tab character, like this: TABS ON &. Here, the ampersand (&) is used as the tab character. If you omit the tab character, hardware tabbing is assumed.

which you can key a less-than symbol (<) to indicate the left margin and a greater-than symbol (>) to indicate the right margin.

The BOUNDS primary command has this format:

```
BOUNDS [left right]
```

If you omit *left* and *right*, the default boundaries are established. You can abbreviate BOUNDS BNDS or BND.

Edit masks

If you enter MASK in the line command area, ISPF displays the edit mask, which you can modify by overtyping. The contents of the mask are used as default data for each line of text inserted by the I line command.

Tabs

ISPF supports two types of tabs: logical and hardware. When you use logical tabs, you enter a special character whenever you want to align data on a tab stop; ISPF inserts spaces to that position to properly align your data. When you use hardware tabs, attribute bytes are placed on the screen so that you can use the 3270 terminal's tab key for tabbing. The drawback of hardware tabbing is that the position occupied by the attribute byte isn't available for other data. You can use both logical and hardware tabs at the same time.

Tabs are controlled by two commands. The TABS primary command controls whether or not tabs are active, and what character is used for the logical tab character. (If you omit the tab character, hardware tabbing is assumed.) The TABS line command causes ISPF to display the tabs line, which you can modify by overtyping to indicate the tab stops you want to define. To define a tab stop, you enter an asterisk immediately to the left of the desired tab position. These tab positions are used by both hardware and logical tabbing.

Edit primary commands

You can enter any of the following edit primary commands in the command area. Although ISPF supports several other edit commands, these are the ones most commonly used.

The CANCEL command

Ends the editing session without saving the edited file.

```
CANCEL
```

The CHANGE command

Changes one or more occurrences of a text string.

```
CHANGE string-1 string-2 [scope] [condition]
       [line-range] [col-range]
```

The *string* components of the CHANGE command are described later in this section. The word CHANGE can be abbreviated CHG or just C. You can code the options in any order, except that string-2 must follow immediately after string-1. *Scope* can be NEXT, PREV, FIRST, LAST, or ALL. *Condition* can be CHARS, PREFIX, SUFFIX, or WORD. *Line-range* can be one or two line labels; *col-range* can be one or two column numbers.

The COPY command

Copies data from another member into the current member.

```
COPY [member-name]    { BEFORE label }
                      { AFTER  label }
```

The CREATE command

Stores data from the current member in a new member.

```
CREATE   [member-name] [line-1|label-1] [line-2|label-2]
```

The FIND command

Searches the current member for an occurrence of the specified text string.

```
FIND   string-1 [scope] [condition] [line-range] [col-range]
```

The *string* component of the FIND command is described later in this section. The word FIND can be abbreviated F. You can code the options in any order. *Scope* can be NEXT, PREV, FIRST, LAST, or ALL. *Condition* can be CHARS, PREFIX, SUFFIX, or WORD. *Line-range* can be one or two line labels; *col-range* can be one or two column numbers.

The LOCATE command

The LOCATE command has two basic formats. The first is used to scroll to a specified label or line number.

```
LOCATE   {line-number|label}
```

The second is used to scroll to a particular type of line.

```
LOCATE  [{ NEXT
           PREV
           FIRST
           LAST }] [type] [label-1 [label-2] ]
```

In the second format, *type* can be LABEL, COMMAND, ERROR, CHANGE, SPECIAL, or EXCLUDED.

The MOVE command

Copies data from the specified member into the current member; the specified member is deleted after the copy operation is completed.

```
     MOVE [member-name]    { BEFORE label }
                           { AFTER label  }
```

The REPLACE command

Replaces the specified member with data from the current member.

```
     REPLACE   [member-name] [line-1|label-1]
               [line-2|label-2]
```

The word REPLACE can be abbreviated REPL or REP.

The RESET command

Resets various editor settings to their default values.

```
     RESET   [LABEL] [COMMAND] [ERROR] [CHANGE]
             [SPECIAL] [EXCLUDED] [label-1 label-2]
```

If no options are entered, all entry types except labels are reset.

The SAVE command

Saves the current member.

```
SAVE
```

The SUBMIT command

Submits the current member for background
processing.

```
SUBMIT   [label-1 label-2]
```

FIND and CHANGE command strings

The strings you use in the FIND and CHANGE commands can be coded in any of these formats:

String	Meaning
string	A string containing no blanks or commas. Case doesn't matter; any combination of upper- or lower-case text can be used to match the string.
'string'	A delimited string enclosed in apostrophes or quotes; the string can't contain the character used as a delimiter. Case doesn't matter; any combination of upper- or lower-case text can be used to match the string.
C'string'	A character string. Case does matter; to match the string, text must have exactly the same combination of upper- and lower-case characters as the string.
X'hex-digits'	A hexadecimal string.
P'picture'	A picture string.
*	Use string from previous FIND or CHANGE.

The following characters are valid in picture strings:

Character	Meaning
=	Any character
¬	Any non-blank character
.	Any undisplayable character
#	Any numeric character
-	Any non-numeric character (including a blank)
@	Any alphabetic character
<	Any lowercase alphabetic character
>	Any uppercase alphabetic character
$	Any special character

Editor line commands

Copying and moving lines

C	Copy this line.
C*n*	Copy *n* lines starting with this line.
CC	Copy a block of lines.
M	Move this line.
M*n*	Move *n* lines starting with this line.
MM	Move a block of lines.
A	Place the copied or moved lines after this line.
A*n*	Repeat the copied or moved lines *n* times after this line.
B	Place the copied or moved lines before this line.
B*n*	Repeat the copied or moved lines *n* times before this line.

Deleting lines

D	Delete this line.
D*n*	Delete *n* lines.
DD	Delete a block of lines.

Inserting lines

I	Insert a single line following this line.
I*n*	Insert *n* lines following this line.

Repeating lines

R	Repeat this line.
R*n*	Repeat this line *n* times.
RR	Repeat a block of lines.
R*n*	Repeat a block of lines *n* times.

Shifting data

Data shift command	Column shift command	Meaning
<	(	Shift this line left two positions.
<*n*	(*n*	Shift this line left *n* positions.
<<	((	Shift a block of lines left two positions.
<<*n*	((*n*	Shift a block of lines left *n* positions.
>	)	Shift this line right two positions.
> *n*	)*n*	Shift this line right *n* positions.
>>	))	Shift a block of lines right two positions.
>>*n*	))*n*	Shift a block of lines right *n* positions.

ICCF

ICCF is one of two interactive program development environments commonly used on DOS systems; the other is VM/CMS. ICCF is a command-driven system, which makes it rather difficult to use. There are three classes of ICCF commands: *system commands*, which let you control your terminal environment and manipulate ICCF library members; *editor commands*, which can be used only within the editor, and *procedures and macros*, which are supplied with ICCF and perform commonly needed functions. The distinction between system commands and procedures and macros is mostly unimportant, so I'll describe them together first. Then, I'll describe the editor commands.

System commands, procedures, and macros

The ASSEMBLE procedure

Assembles a source member.

```
ASSEMBLE source-member [OBJ object-member] [options]
```

The /ASYNC command

Places your terminal in asynchronous mode so that you can do other work while an interactive job is running. Issue the /SYNC command to return to synchronous mode.

```
/ASYNC
```

The /CANCEL command

Terminates the current operation.

```
/CANCEL
```

The COBOL procedure

Compiles a COBOL source program.

```
COBOL source-member [OBJ object-member] [CBL] [options]
```

The /CONNECT command

Connects a specified library to your primary
library, enabling you to retrieve members from the
connected library.

```
/CONNECT   {library-number|OFF}
```

The /CONTINU command

Places your terminal in continuous output mode or
disables continuous output mode if you specify

OFF. The number indicates how many seconds
ICCF should pause between each display page.

```
/CONTINU   [OFF|nn]
```

The COPYFILE procedure

Copies a member from the primary library or a connected library to the primary library.

```
COPYFILE in-name out-name [in-password]
```

The COPYMEM procedure

For ICCF 2.1 only; copies a member from a
specified library to another library.

```
COPYMEM in-name [in-password] in-lib
        out-name [out-password] out-lib [PURGE]
```

The CPYLIB procedure

Copies a member from one library to another.

```
CPYLIB in-name [in-password] in-lib out-lib
```

The /DISPC command

Displays a file in continuous mode.

```
/DISPC [start [end]] [member-name [password]]
```

The /DISPLAY command

Displays a file at the terminal.

```
/DISPLAY [start [end]] [member-name [password]]
```

The /ECHO command

Displays the specified text on the screen; usually
used in macros.

```
/ECHO text
```

The @ED macro

Invokes the full-screen editor.

```
@ED [member-name [password]]
```

The /EDIT command

Invokes the context editor.

```
/EDIT [member-name [password]]
```

The /END command

Terminates input mode.

```
/END
```

The /ERASEP command

Removes a job from a POWER queue.

```
/ERASEP queue job-name [job-number] [PWD=password]
```

The /EXEC command

Invokes a procedure.

```
/EXEC member-name [password] [CLIST [parameters]]
```

The @FSEDPF macro

Establishes the PF key settings for use with the editor.

```
@FSEDPF
```

The GETL procedure

Retrieves a file from the POWER list queue.

```
GETL job-name [job-number] [class] [PRINT|NOPRINT]
            [KEEP|DELETE] [MEM=member-name] [PWD=password]
```

The GETP procedure

Retrieves a file from the POWER punch queue.

```
GETP job-name [job-number] [class] [PRINT|NOPRINT]
               [KEEP|DELETE ] [MEM=member-name] [PWD=password]
```

The GETR procedure

Retrieves a file from the POWER punch queue.

```
GETR job-name [job-number] [class] [PRINT|NOPRINT]
               [KEEP|DELETE] [MEM=member-name] [PWD=password]
```

The /GROUP command

Manages generation member groups.

```
          ⎧ CREATE name [password] [PRIV|PUBL] [member-count] ⎫
/GROUP    ⎨ UNGROUP name [password]                           ⎬
          ⎩ REGROUP name [password]                           ⎭
```

The /HARDCOPY command

Manages hardcopy mode by activating or deactivating it, directing it to a printer or destination, and starting a printer task to print data directed to a destination.

```
            ⎧ [ON|OFF]               ⎫
            ⎪ printer-id             ⎪
/HARDCPY    ⎨ dest-id                ⎬
            ⎩ START printer-id dest-id ⎭
```

The @HC macro

Executes a single command in hardcopy mode. Issue a /HARDCPY command first to set the printer or destination.

```
@HC command operands
```

The /INPUT command

Places your terminal in input mode; any data you enter is placed in the input area.

```
/ INPUT
```

The /INSERT command

Inserts the specified member into the input area.

```
/INSERT member-name [password]
```

The /LIBC command

Displays information about the current ICCF libraries. This command is the same as the /LIBRARY command.

```
/LIBC [CON|COM] [FULL[ALL]|*abcdefg]
```

The /LIBRARY command

Displays information about the current ICCF libraries. This command is the same as the /LIBC command.

```
/LIBRARY [CON|COM] [FULL[ALL]|*abcdefg]
```

The LIBRC procedure

Stores an ICCF library member in a DOS/VSE
library. Valid only for ICCF 2.1.

```
    LIBRC   VSE-library-spec [ICCF-member|$$PUNCH] [password]
                             [REPLACE] [DATA=YES] [EOD=nn]
```

The LIBRL procedure

Prints a member from a DOS/VSE library. Valid
only for ICCF 2.1.

```
    LIBRL   VSE-library-spec [ICCF-member|$$PUNCH] [password]
                             [REPLACE] [DATA=YES] [EOD=nn]
```

The LIBRP procedure

Punches a member from a DOS/VSE library. Valid
only for ICCF 2.1.

```
    LIBRP   VSE-library-spec [ICCF-member|$$PUNCH] [password]
                             [REPLACE] [DATA=YES] [EOD=nn]
```

The /LIST command

Lists all or part of the specified member.

```
    /LIST [start [end]] [member-name [password]]
```

The /LISTC command

Lists all or part of the specified member in continuous display mode.

```
    /LISTC [start [end]] [member-name [password]]
```

The /LISTP command

Lists output from the POWER list queue. If more than one job in the POWER list queue has the same name, specify the job's number as well. The default class is Q, so if the job has a different class, you must specify the class parameter.

```
/LISTP job-name [job-number] [class] [PWD=password]
```

The /LISTX command

Lists all or part of the specified member in hexadecimal notation.

```
/LISTX [start [end]] [member-name [password]]
```

The LOAD procedure

Link-edits, loads, and executes a program that's been processed by a compiler or assembler. The JES option specifies a member that contains job entry statements for the program. The DATA option specifies a member that contains card input data that's processed by the program. The options parameter lets you specify a variety of processing options including GETVIS=AUTO (for programs that process VSAM files) and various language translator options (like XREF and DECK).

```
LOAD [object=member] [JES JES-member] [DATA data-member]
     [options]
```

The /LOCP statement

Locates a text string in a POWER queue file; you must first issue a /LISTP command to display the file.

```
/LOCP /string/
```

The /LOGOFF command

Terminates your ICCF session.

```
/LOGOFF
```

The /LOGON command

Establishes an ICCF session

```
/LOGON user-id
```

The /MAIL command

Displays messages which aren't displayed automatically during logon.

```
/MAIL
```

The MSG command

Displays messages sent to you from other users.

```
/MSG
```

The MVLIB procedure

Moves a member from one library to another.

```
MVLIB in-name [in-password] in-lib out-lib
```

The @PRINT macro

Prints the specified member in hardcopy mode. Issue a /HARDCPY command first to set the printer or destination.

```
@PRINT [member-name [password]]
```

The /PROTECT command

Establishes security options for a member. Specify new-password to add or change a password; NOPASS removes password protection. PRIV makes the member private; a private member can be accessed only by its owner. PUBL makes the member public so anyone can access it. DATE updates the member's last modification date. And USER changes the member's owner.

```
                                      ⎛ new-password    ⎞
                                      ⎜ NOPASS          ⎟
                                      ⎜ PRIV            ⎟
/PROTECT name [old-password]  ⎨ PUBL            ⎬
                                      ⎜ DATE            ⎟
                                      ⎝ USER new-user-id ⎠
```

The PSERV procedure

Retrieves data from a VSE procedure library.

```
          ⎛ DSPLY VSE-member-name                          ⎞
PSERV ⎨ PUNCH VSE-member-name [INTO ICCF-member-name] ⎬
          ⎝ DSPCH VSE-member-name [INTO ICCF-member-name] ⎠
```

The /PURGE command

Erases a member.

```
/PURGE member-name [password]
```

The /PURGEP command

Deletes a file from a POWER queue.

```
/PURGEP queue job-name [job-number] [PWD=password]
```

The @RELIST macro

Prints a member on the central system printer.

```
@RELIST [member-name [password]]
```

The /RENAME command

Changes the name of an ICCF library member.

```
/RENAME old-member-name new-member-name [password]
```

The /REPLACE command

Stores text in the input area in an existing library
member and exits input mode.

```
/REPLACE member-name [password]
```

The /ROUTEP command

Routes a POWER queue file to a printer or punch.

```
/ROUTEP queue jobname [job-number] [CLASS=class] [PWD=password]
```

The /RUN command

Runs a program that has been loaded.

```
/RUN
```

The /SAVE command

Saves all or part of the data in the input area in the
specified member and exits input mode.

```
/SAVE member-name [password] [start-line [end-line]]
               [PRIV|PUBL]
```

The SDSERV procedure

Displays sorted directory information for the
primary or a connected ICCF library.

```
              ⎧*abcdefg⎫   ⎧NAME⎫
SDSERV        ⎨CONN    ⎬   ⎨USER⎬
              ⎩COM     ⎭   ⎩DATE⎭
```

The /SEND command

Sends a message to a specified user or to all users.

```
/SEND   ┌ user-id ┐
        │ COPER   │   text
        └ ALL     ┘
```

The /SET commands

These commands set various system attributes.

```
/SET BUFFER nnnn
```

```
/SET CLASS n
```

```
/SET COMLIB {ON|OFF}
```

```
/SET DELAY   ┌ nnn    ┐
             │ TIME   │
             │ BYPASS │
             └ RESET  ┘
```

```
/SET IMPEX {ON|OFF}
```

```
/SET LOG {ON|OFF}   ┌ INPUT  ┐
                    │ OUTPUT │
                    └ INOUT  ┘
```

```
/SET MSGAUTO {ON|OFF}
```

```
/SET PFnn data
```

The SETTIME command

Sets system time limits.

```
/SETTIME  { execution-units [total-processing-time] }
          { TIMEOUT nnnn                             }
```

The /SHOW commands

Display various system information

```
/SHOW BUFFER
```

```
/SHOW CLASS
```

```
/SHOW DATE
```

```
/SHOW DELAY
```

```
/SHOW EXEC
```

```
/SHOW LIBRARIES
```

```
/SHOW LOG
```

```
/SHOW MSG
```

```
/SHOW PF
```

```
/SHOW PGED
```

```
/SHOW TERM
```

```
/SHOW TIME
```

```
/SHOW USER
```

The /SKIP command

Skips forward or backward during display of a print
member.

```
/SKIP  { [n|-n]              }
       { [S+n|S-n]           }
       { [P+n|P-n]           }
       { [TOP|BOTTOM|END]    }
```

The SORT procedure

Sorts the records in a member. The sort sequence is
in the form abbcc... where *a* is A or D to indicate
the sort direction, *bb* indicates the beginning
columns number, and *cc* indicates the field length
position. You can specify up to four fields, so
A1005A2005 indicates two 5-byte ascending sort
fields, starting in columns 10 and 20.

```
SORT in-name [in-password] [SEQ sequence-spec] [PUNCH out-name]
```

The /SQUEEZE command

Compresses a member to save disk space.

```
/SQUEEZE member-name [password]
```

The /SSERV procedure

Retrieves data from a VSE source library.

```
         ┌DSPLY VSE-member-name                                ┐
SSERV   { PUNCH VSE-member-name [INTO ICCF-member-name]        }
         └DSPCH VSE-member-name [INTO ICCF-member-name]        ┘
```

The /STATUSP command

Displays the status of a POWER job.

```
/STATUSP job-name [job-number]
```

The /SUMRY command

Displays the JCL statements in an ICCF member,
omitting any records that don't contain JCL.

```
/SUMRY member-name [password]
```

The /SWITCH command

Changes the primary library to a specified library,
to the connected library, or to the default established by your user profile.

```
           ┌ library ┐
           │ LIBS    │
SWITCH    {  RESET    }
           └ OFF     ┘
```

The /SYNC command

Returns your terminal to synchronous execution
mode.

```
/SYNCH
```

The /TIME command

Displays the current time and date and the number
of execution units for the most recently completed
background job.

```
/TIME
```

The /USERS command

Displays the number of active terminal users,
defaults in your user profile, statistics about your
system usage, or a list of your current libraries.

```
/USERS [PROF|STATS|LIB]
```

The full-screen editor

ICCF provides two text editors: the older and less often used context editor and the newer and more commonly used full-screen editor. The full-screen editor processes three types of commands. *Type I commands* are entered at the top of the screen and are unique to the full-screen editor. *Type II commands* are also entered at the top of the screen; they are common to both the full-screen editor and the context editor. *Type III commands* are unique to the full-screen editor; they're entered in the right-hand margin of each line. (You can change this to the left-hand margin, if you wish.) I'll describe the type I and type II commands together, since the distinction isn't important when you're using the full-screen editor. Then, I'll describe the type III commands.

You invoke the full-screen by entering the @ED macro, specifying the name of the member you wish to edit.

Editor type I and type II commands

The ALIGN command

Aligns data on the right and left margin by left-justifying the text and then adding extra spaces between words. INDENT means to align on the right margin only, without first left-justifying the text.

```
ALIGN [INDENT]
```

The ALTER command

Changes a particular character to another character within a range of lines. *Lines* specifies how many lines beyond the current line to search (the default is 1); * means to search the entire file from the current line. G means to change all occurrences of the character.

```
ALTER  old-char new-char   [n|*]  [G]
```

The BACKWARD command

Scrolls backwards towards the beginning of the file.

```
BACKWARD n
```

The BOTTOM command

Scrolls to the end of the file.

```
BOTTOM
```

The CANCEL command

Leaves the full-screen editor.

```
CANCEL
```

The CASE command

Controls upper/lower case entry. M allows upper
or lower case, U allows only upper case.

```
CASE {M|U}
```

The CENTER command

Centers the data on the line by adding extra spaces
before the leftmost characters or after the rightmost
characters.

```
CENTER
```

The CHANGE command

Changes a character string to another character
string. *Lines* specifies how many lines beyond the
current line to search (the default is 1); * means to
search the entire file from the current line. G
means to change all occurrences of the character
string.

```
CHANGE /old-string/new-string/ [n|*] [G]
```

The CURSOR command

Moves the cursor to a particular screen position. Various forms of the CURSOR command are usually associated with PF keys to simplify their use.

```
CURSOR     ⎧ CURRENT       ⎫
           ⎪ INPUT         ⎪
           ⎨ LINE [n]      ⎬
           ⎪ TABBACK [n]   ⎪
           ⎩ TABFORWARD [n] ⎭
```

The DELETE command

Deletes one or more lines from the file. If you specify a string, lines are deleted from the current line to the first line that contains the string. (The line that contains the string isn't deleted.)

```
DELETE     ⎧ n        ⎫
           ⎨ *        ⎬
           ⎩ /string/ ⎭
```

The DELIM command

Changes the delimiter character used for strings. The default is the slash (/).

```
DELIM character
```

The DOWN command

Scrolls down (towards the end of the file) a specified number of lines. A DOWN command is often associated with a PF key to simplify scrolling.

```
DOWN n
```

The DUP command

Duplicates the current line the specified number of times. The default is one.

```
DUP [n]
```

The END command

Same as the QUIT command. Leaves the editor. Changes made to the input area should first be saved; if you're editing a library member, however, you don't have to save changes; they're saved as you go.

```
END
```

The ENTER command

Lets you edit another file, either in the same screen window or another screen window. By using the SCREEN command to establish screen windows and the ENTER command, you can edit several library members at the same time.

```
ENTER [member-name [password]]
```

The FILE command

Save the input area in a library member and terminate the editor. Issuing FILE is equivalent to issuing SAVE and QUIT.

```
FILE member-name [password] [PRIV|PUBL]
```

The FIND command

Locates the line that contains the specified text string. Only non-blank characters in the text string are matched.

```
FIND text
```

The FORMAT command

Establishes the format of the current screen window; each format area can display a separate part of the file currently being edited in the window. For each format area, code 1, 2, or 3 to indicate the number of display lines to use for each source record, followed by a number to indicate how many source records to display. Use the asterisk to suppress the type III command area for the format area.

```
FORMAT [ [*] {1|2|3}-n ] ...
```

The FORWARD command

Scrolls the display forward a specified number of lines. The FORWARD command is often associated with a PF key to simplify scrolling.

```
FORWARD n
```

The GETFILE command

Copies all or part of a library member into the input area so it can be edited.

```
GETFILE member-name [password] [start [count]]
```

The INPUT command

Lets you insert new lines below the current line.

```
INPUT
```

The INSERT command

Inserts a new line into the file after the current line.

```
INSERT string
```

The JUSTIFY command

Adds space at the beginning or ending of each line
to justify it against the right or left margin.

```
JUSTIFY [LEFT|RIGHT]
```

The LADD command

Adds blank lines to the file, beginning after the current line.

```
LADD n
```

The LEFT command

Scrolls the display the specified number of columns
to the left.

```
LEFT nn
```

The LOCATE command

Searches from the current record to the bottom of
the file until the specified text is found.

```
LOCATE text
```

The LOCUP command

Searches from the current record to the top of the
file until the specified text is found.

```
LOCUP text
```

The LOCNOT command

Searches from the current record to the bottom of
the file until the first line that does not contain the
specified text is found.

```
LOCATE text
```

The NEXT command

Scrolls the display forward the specified number of
lines. Same as FORWARD or DOWN.

```
NEXT n
```

The QUIT command

Same as the END command.

```
QUIT
```

The RENUM command

Renumbers records in the source member.

```
RENUM [increment [starting-col [length [starting-number]]]]
```

The REPEAT command

Specifies that the next ALIGN, BLANK, CENTER, JUSTIFY, or SHIFT command should be repeated the specified number of times (* means to repeat the command once for each line remaining in the file).

```
REPEAT [n|*]
```

The REPLACE command

Stores the input area in the specified file.

```
REPLACE member-name [password] [PRIV|PUBL]
```

The RIGHT command

Scrolls the display the specified number of columns to the right.

```
RIGHT n
```

The SAVE command

Saves the input area in a library member.

```
SAVE member-name [password] [PRIV|PUBL]
```

The SCREEN command

Partitions the screen into multiple windows, specifying the size of each.

```
SCREEN [nn] [nn] ...
```

The SEARCH command

Searches each line in the file for the specified text.

```
SEARCH text
```

The SET commands

Set various editor options.

```
SET CASE {INPUT|OUTPUT} {UPPER|MIXED}
```

```
SET NULLS {ON|OFF}
```

```
SET NUMBERS {ON|OFF}
```

```
SET PFnn data
```

```
SET TAB=x
```

The SHIFT command

Shifts data left or right the specified number of characters.

```
SHIFT {LEFT|RIGHT} nn
```

The SHOW commands

Display the status of various editor settings.

```
SHOW
```

```
SHOW CASE
```

```
SHOW CHAR
```

```
SHOW NAMES
```

```
SHOW PF
```

```
SHOW TABCHAR
```

```
SHOW TABS
```

The SPLIT command

Splits the current line into two lines; the line is split
following the specified text string or at the specified
column.

```
SPLIT {text|column}
```

The TABSET command

Sets tabs for commonly-used environments. *Option* can be ASSEMBLER, BASIC, COBOL, FORTRAN, PL1, PLI, RPG, or TENS.

```
TABSET    { nn ...
            OFF
            CLEAR
            option  }
```

The TOP command

Scrolls the display to the first line in the file. The TOP command is often associated with a PF key to make scrolling easier.

```
TOP
```

The UP command

Scrolls the display up the specified number of lines; same as the BACKWARD command.

```
UP  n
```

The VERIFY command

Activates the full-screen editor. The first number specifies the line (within the line display area) on which the current line is to be displayed; the second number specifies how many lines to use for the type I/II command area.

```
VERIFY FULL [n] [n]
```

The VIEW command

Controls what portion of the file's records are displayed on the screen. H indicates hexadecimal display.

```
VIEW [[H]first-col last-col] [, [H]first-col last-col] ...
```

The ZONE command

Specifies the range of column positions within which editing operations apply.

```
ZONE left-col right-col
```

Editor Type III commands

Scrolling

/   Establishes the line as the current line.

Copying and moving lines

C[nn]   Copy the specified number of lines to the stack.
M[nn]   Move the specified number of lines to the stack.
K[nn]   Append the specified number of lines to the stack.
I   Insert copied or moved lines following this line.

Adding and deleting lines

A[nn]   Add the specified number of lines following this line.
D[nn]   Delete the specified number of lines.

Repeating lines

"[nn]   Duplicate the specified number of lines.

Shifting data

[cc[,nnn]   Shift the data cc columns to the right; the shift operation is to be repeated for nnn lines.
[cc[,nnn]   Shift the data cc columns to the left; the shift operation is to be repeated for nnn lines.

Text manipulation

TA[nn]   Align text in nn lines (see the ALIGN command).
TC[nn]   Center text in nn lines (see the CENTER command).
TL[nn]   Left justify text in nn lines (see the LEFT command).
TR[nn]   Right justify text in nn lines (see the RIGHT command).
TS nn   Split the line at column nn .

VM/CMS

In many of the following VM/CMS commands, I've used the word *file* (as in *file-1* or *output-file*) to indicate that you need to code a complete file specification (name, type, and mode). Also, I've followed the IBM VM/CMS manuals' convention of indicating command abbreviations with capital letters. Thus, for CHange, you can use the complete command name (CHANGE) or the abbreviation (CH). Finally, notice that some of the commands have options that are set off from the rest of the command with a left parenthesis. For those commands, you can omit the parenthesis if you don't code any options.

CMS and CP commands

The AMSERV CMS command

Invokes the Access Method Services program to manipulate VSAM files.

```
AMserv file-1 [file-2] ([PRINT] [TAPIN tape-unit]
    [TAPOUT tape-unit]
```

File-1 contains the AMS control statements; *file-2* is used for the AMS output listing. *Tape-unit* is 18n or TAPn, where n is 1-4.

The #CP CP command

Executes a CP command from within CMS. Depending on how CMS is set up, commands that CMS doesn't recognize may or may not be passed to CP. So you may not have to code #CP before a CP command.

```
#CP command
```

The CHANGE CP command

Changes the characteristics of a file spooled in a virtual reader, punch, or printer.

```
CHange {READER|PUNCH|PRINTER} spool-id [HOLD|NOHOLD] [CLASS x]
```

The CLOSE CP command

Closes a virtual reader, punch, or printer. PURGE
is valid only for printer or punch devices.

```
Close   { READER  }   [HOLD|NOHOLD]  [PURGE]
        { PUNCH   }
        { PRINTER }
        { vaddr   }
```

The COMMANDS CP command

Lists the CP commands you're allowed to use.

```
COMMands
```

The COMPARE CMS command

Compares CMS files and displays records that dif-
fer.

```
COMpare file-1 file-2 [(start-pos end-pos)]
```

The COPYFILE CMS command

Copies CMS files. To make an exact copy of a file,
you don't need to specify any options; just the input
and output file names.

```
COPYfile file-1 [file-2...] [output-file] ([TYPE|NOTYPE]
    [NEWDATE|OLDDATE] [NEWFILE|REPLACE] [PROMPT|NOPROMPT]
    [FROM record-no|FRLABEL xxxxxxxx]
    [FOR count|TOLABEL xxxxxxxx]
    [SPECS|NOSPECS] [OVLY|APPEND] [RECFM {F|V}] [LRECL nnnnn]
    [TRUNC|NOTRUNC] [PACK|UNPACK] [FILL {c|hh}] [EBCDIC]
    [UPCASE|LOWCASE] [TRANS]
```

If you code SPECS, you'll be prompted to enter specifications that let you rearrange data in the input records. For each output record field, you code two operands: the first specifies a range of column positions from which data is derived from the input records, a string constant enclosed between slashes, or a hex constant preceded with the letter h; the second specifies the output column position. For example, h00 1 /ABC/ 2 1-50 4 indicates that the hex constant 00 should be placed in the first byte of the output record, the letters ABC should be placed starting in the second byte of the output record, and the first 50 bytes of the input record should be placed in the output record starting in colum 4.

The DETACH CP command

Detaches a virtual device. You can detach a range of devices by specifying two virtual addresses separated by a hyphen.

```
DETach vaddr [vaddr...]
```

The DIAL CP command

Connects your terminal to an active virtual machine. This is the normal way to gain access to a CICS system running under a guest DOS/VSE or MVS operating system.

```
DIAL user-id [vaddr]
```

The DISCONN CP command

Disconnects your terminal from a virtual machine, but leaves that machine running. You regain access to the virtual machine by issuing another LOGON command.

```
DISConn [HOLD]
```

The ERASE CMS command

Deletes a CMS file.

```
ERASE name type [mode] ([TYPE|NOTYPE]
```

If you specify an asterisk instead of a file name, type, or mode, all CMS file names, types, and modes are deleted. For example, ERASE * CNTL A deletes all CNTL-type files on the A disk; ERASE * * A deletes all files of any type on the A disk.

The EXEC CMS command

Executes a CMS EXEC file. The arguments you can specify depend on the EXEC file you execute.

The word EXEC can be omitted if IMPEX mode is on.

```
    [EXec] name [arguments...]
```

The FILEDEF CMS command

Allocates a file or virtual device. Used to specify the files processed by the MOVEFILE command.

To allocate a CMS file

```
    FIledef ddname DISK name type mode ([PERM] [CHANGE|NOCHANGE]
```

To allocate an OS data set

```
    FIledef ddname [DISK name type mode] DSN {?|data-set-name}
        ([PERM] [CHANGE|NOCHANGE] [RECFM a] [LRECL nnnnn]
        [BLKSIZE nnnnn|BLOCKSIZE nnnnn] [XTENT nnnnn] [DISP MOD]
        [MEMBER member-name] [CONCAT] [DSORG {PS|PO|DA}]
```

To allocate a tape data set

```
    FIledef ddname TAPn [    ⎧ LABOFF                        ⎫ ]
                            ⎪ BLP [n]                        ⎪
                            ⎪ SL [n]    [VOLID vol-ser]      ⎬
                            ⎨ SUL [n]   [VOLID vol-ser]      ⎪
                            ⎪ NL [n]                         ⎪
                            ⎩ NSL filename                   ⎭

        [PERM] [CHANGE|NOCHANGE] [RECFM a] [LRECL nnnnn]
        [BLKSIZE nnnnn|BLOCKSIZE nnnnn] [DISP MOD] [LEAVE|NOEOV]
```

To allocate a spool device

```
FIledef ddname  { PRINTER }   ([PERM]  [CHANGE|NOCHANGE]
                { PUNCH   }
                { READER  }

        [RECFM a]  [LRECL nnnnn]  [BLKSIZE nnnnn|BLOCKSIZE nnnnn]
```

To clear a previously allocated file or device

```
FIledef {ddname|*} CLEAR
```

The FILELIST CMS command

Lists CMS files and lets you operate on them by
typing a CMS command directly on the list or using
a set of predefined PF keys.

```
FILEList [name [type [mode]]]
         ([APPEND] [FILELIST|NOFILELIST] [PROFILE name]
```

In the name, type, and mode operands, you can use
an asterisk (*) or a percent sign (%) as wild cards;
an asterisk represents any number of wild-card characters and a percent sign represents a single
wild-card character.

The HELP CMS command

Displays helpful information about command syntax and error messages.

To display information about how to use the HELP facility

```
Help HELP
```

To display an extended description of an error message

```
            ┌ message-id         ┐
    Help    │ MESSAGE message-id │
            └ MSG message-id     ┘
```

To display information about a particular CMS or CP command

```
    Help command
```

The HT CMS immediate command

Halts terminal output.   HT is especially useful
during output from the TYPE command.

```
    HT
```

The IDENTIFY CMS command

Displays your user-id and the current time and date.

```
    IDentify
```

The INDICATE CP command

Displays information about the current system
usage, either for the whole system (LOAD) or for
your virtual machine (USER).

```
    INDicate [LOAD|USER]
```

The IPL CP command

Initiates an IPL operation within your virtual machine; this loads an operating system such as CMS. IPL occurs from cylinder zero of the specified virtual volume or from the specified system name.

```
Ipl [vaddr|systemname]
```

The LINK CP command

Connects a device owned by another user to your virtual machine. Access to that device depends on how it is defined to the user who owns it.

```
LINK [TO] user-id vaddr-1 [AS] vaddr-2 [mode]
     [[PASS=] password]
```

The LISTFILE CMS command

Lists information about CMS files.

```
Listfile [name [type [mode]]] ([HEADER|NOHEADER]
     [FNAME] [FTYPE] [FMODE] [FORMAT] [ALLOC] [DATE] [LABEL]
```

To specify all file names, types, or modes, code an asterisk instead of a *name*, *type*, or *mode*. BLOCKS says to show the total number of blocks used by the files listed. Each option after FNAME implies the presence of the preceding options (except HEADER); so if you code FMODE, FTYPE and FNAME are assumed as well.

The LOGOFF CP command

Terminates your virtual machine session; the virtual machine is removed from the system.

```
LOGoff [HOLD]
```

The LOGON CP command

Connects you to the VM system and creates a virtual machine on your behalf or reconnects you to a previously disconnected virtual machine.

```
Logon user-id [password]
```

The MOVEFILE CMS command

Copies data from one file to another.

```
MOVEfile [inddname] [outddname] [(PDS)]
```

The files must be allocated with FILEDEF commands. The defaults for *inddname* and *outddname* are INMOVE and OUTMOVE. PDS copies each member of a partitioned data set to a separate CMS file.

The MSG CP command

Sends a message to the system operator or another user. MSG can be spelled out MESSAGE.

```
Msg {user-id|OP} message-text
```

The NOTREADY CP command

Changes a virtual device to not-ready status; this prevents data from being written to or read from it.

```
NOTReady vaddr
```

The PEEK CMS command

Displays the contents of a file in a virtual reader.

```
PEEK [spoolid] ([FROM record-no] [FOR count] [PROFILE name]
```

The PRINT CMS command

Prints the contents of a file on a virtual printer.

```
PRint name type [mode] ([CC|CC HEADER|NOCC] [UPCASE]
      [TRC|NOTRC] [LINECOUN nnn] [MEMBER {name|*}] [HEX]
```

The PUNCH CMS command

Punches the contents of a file on a virtual punch.

```
PUnch name type [mode] ([HEADER|NOHEADER] [MEMBER {name|*}]
```

The QUERY CMS command

Displays information about various CMS facilities.

To display the current disk search order

```
Query SEARCH
```

To display the status of a disk

```
Query DISK mode
```

To display the status of all read/write disks

```
Query DISK R/W
```

To display the disk that has the most available space

```
Query DISK MAX
```

To display system, user, or all synonyms

```
Query SYNONYM    ⎧SYSTEM⎫
                 ⎨USER  ⎬
                 ⎩ALL   ⎭
```

To display current file allocations

```
Query FILEDEF
```

To display the current CMS release

```
Query CMSLEVEL
```

The QUERY CP command

Displays various CP information.

To display the current time

```
Query TIME
```

To display the status of virtual devices

```
Query VIRTUAL    ⎛DASD          ⎞
                 ⎜TAPE          ⎟
                 ⎜UR            ⎟
                 ⎜ALL           ⎟
                 ⎝vaddr[-vaddr] ⎠
```

To display all users linked to the specified virtual device

```
Query LINKS vaddr
```

To display the names of all currently logged on users

```
Query NAMES
```

To display information about your virtual reader, printer, or punch.

```
Query {  READER
         PRINTER    [HOLD|NOHOLD] [ALL]
         PUNCH  }
```

To display the current settings for a PF key

```
Query PF[nn]
```

To display your userid

```
Query USERID
```

To display the number of logged-on users

```
Query USERS
```

The RDR CMS command

Displays information about the next file in your virtual reader.

```
RDR [class]
```

The RDRLIST CMS command

Lists files in your virtual reader and lets you operate on them by typing a CMS command directly on the list or using a set of predefined PF keys.

```
{RDRList|RList} ([PROFILE name] [APPEND]
```

The READY CP command

Places the specified virtual device in ready status.

```
READY vaddr
```

The RECEIVE CMS command

Copies a file from your virtual reader to a CMS disk.

```
RECEIVE [spool-id] [name [type [mode]]] ([PURGE] [REPLACE]
```

The RENAME CMS command

Changes the name of a CMS file.

```
Rename  old-name old-type old-mode new-name new-type new-mode
```

You can rename more than one file by coding an asterisk (*) for the old name, type, and/or mode specification. To keep the same name, type, or mode, code an equals sign (=) for the new name, type, and/or mode specification.

The RESET CP command

Simulates a reset operation for the specified virtual device, which clears any pending I/O activity.

```
RESET vaddr
```

The REWIND CP command

Rewinds the specified virtual tape drive.

```
REWind vaddr
```

The SENDFILE CMS command

Sends a file to another user, either on your VM system or on another system attached to your network.

```
{SENDFile|SFile} name type [mode] [TO] user...
    ([ACK|NOACK] [FILELIST|NOFILELIST]
```

To specify a user on your system, code just the user-id for *user*. To specify a user on another system, code user-id AT node. The FILELIST option indicates that the specified file is a list of files created by the LISTFILE command; rather than send this file, CMS sends each of the files listed in it.

The SET CP command

Sets various CP features; the only one covered here
is PF key definition.

```
SET PFnn [data]
```

To include more than one command in the PF key
definition, separate the commands with pound signs
(#). If you do that, prefix the SET command with
#CP. If you omit the data for a PF key, the
specified key is unassigned.

The SLEEP CP command

Temporarily suspends CP activity for the specified
time period. (However, messages continue to display.)

```
SLeep nn [SEC|MIN|HRS]
```

The SORT CMS command

Sorts the contents of a CMS file.

```
SORT in-name in-type in-mode out-name out-type out-mode
```

You'll be prompted to enter the sort fields; enter
one or more fields in the form xx yy, where xx is the
starting position and yy is the ending position.
Separate the starting and ending positions from one
another with a space and separate xx yy pairs from
one another with a space.

The SPOOL CP command

Sets the characteristics of your virtual reader,
printer, or punch.

To set the characteristics of a virtual reader

```
SPool {READER|vaddr} [CLASS [x|*]] [CONT|NOCONT] [EOF|NOEOF]
```

To set the characteristics of a virtual printer or punch

```
        ⎧ PRINTER ⎫
SPool   ⎨ PUNCH   ⎬  [TO {user-id|*}] [HOLD|NOHOLD] [CONT|NOCONT]
        ⎩ vaddr   ⎭
```

The TAPE CMS command

Dumps and loads CMS files to tape. Files created
with TAPE have a special format and can only be
read with the TAPE command.

To dump, load, scan, or skip a CMS tape file

```
          ⎧ DUMP ⎫
          ⎪ LOAD ⎪
TAPE      ⎨ SCAN ⎬  name type [mode]  ([WTM|NOWTM] [BLKSIZE {800|4096}]
          ⎩ SKIP ⎭

     ⎧ NOPRINT ⎫        ⎧ EOT   ⎫
  [  ⎨ PRINT   ⎬  ]  [  ⎨ EOF n ⎬ ]  [TAPn]
     ⎪ TERM    ⎪        ⎩       ⎭
     ⎩ DISK    ⎭
```

To display or write a VOL1 label

```
        ⎧ DVOL1               ⎫
TAPE    ⎨ WVOL1 vol-ser [owner] ⎬   ([TAPn] [REWIND|LEAVE]
        ⎩                      ⎭
```

To issue a tape command one or more times

Command can be:

BSF	Backspace *n* files	FSR	Space forward *n* files.
BSR	Backspace *n* records.	REW	Rewind tape.
ERG	Erase defective portion of tape.	RUN	Rewind and unload tape.
FSF	Space forward *n* files.	WTM	Write tape mark.

```
TAPE command  ([TAPn]
```

The TRANSFER CP command

Transfers one or more spool files to or from another
user's queue.

To transfer a spool file to another users queue

```
                 ┌ PRINTER ┐   ┌ spool-id ┐
TRANsfer [ { PUNCH  } ] { CLASS x  }
                 └ READER  ┘   └ ALL      ┘

                              ┌ PRINTER ┐
        TO {user-id|*} [ { PUNCH  } ]
                              └ READER  ┘
```

To transfer a spool file from another users queue

```
                 ┌ PRINTER ┐   ┌ spool-id ┐
TRANsfer [ { PUNCH  } ] { CLASS x  }
                 └ READER  ┘   └ ALL      ┘

                                  ┌ PRINTER ┐
        FROM {user-id|ALL} [ { PUNCH  } ]
                                  └ READER  ┘
```

The TYPE CMS command

Displays a CMS file at your terminal. You can interrupt the output operation at any time by entering
an HT command.

```
Type name type [mode]  [starting-record [ending-record]]
    ([COL xxxxx-yyyyy] [HEX]
```

The XEDIT CMS command

Invokes the editor. You can omit the left parenthesis if you don't code any options; you can always omit the right parenthesis.

```
Xedit [name [type [mode]]] ([PROFILE name] [NOPROFILE]
```

XEDIT subcommands and macros

You can enter any of the following commands and
macros in the XEDIT command area. Some of
these commands have functions that are duplicated
by prefix commands. When that's the case, I suggest you use the prefix command instead.

Many of the XEDIT commands let you specify a
target to limit the scope of the command's operation. The format of a target can be (1) a line number preceded by a colon, such as :100; (2) a displacement which may be preceded with a plus or
minus sign, such as +50, -100, or 75; (3) a top-of-
file indicator (-*) or a bottom of file indicator (* or
+*); (4) a line label preceded by a period, such as
.PROC; or (5) a string enclosed within slashes, such
as /PROCEDURE DIVISION/.

The Add subcommand

Adds one or more blank lines following the current
line.

```
ADD [n]
```

The BACKWARD subcommand

Scrolls backwards (towards the beginning of the
file) the specified number of pages. (The size of
each page is the number of lines that can be displayed on the screen at one time.)

```
BAckward [n]
```

The BOTTOM subcommand

Scrolls to the last record in the file.

```
Bottom
```

The CANCEL macro

Cancels the editing session for all files and returns
to CMS.

```
CANCEL
```

The CHANGE subcommand

Changes one or more occurrences of a specified
string to another string.

```
Change /string-1/string2/ [target] [count|*] [occurrence]
```

Code an asterisk for *target* to search from the current line to the end of the file. *Count* is an integer
that specifies how many occurrences of *string-1* in
each line should be changed; if you specify an
asterisk, all occurrences of the string are changed.
Occurrence is an integer that specifies which occurrence of the string on each line should be changed;
if omitted, 1 is assumed.

The CMS subcommand

Passes a command directly to CMS.

```
CMS command
```

The COMPRESS subcommand

Compresses a file by replacing all occurrences of
multiple spaces that immediately precede tab settings with tab characters. You can then change the
tab settings and issue an EXPAND command.

```
COMPress [target]
```

If you omit *target*, only the current line is compressed.

The COPY subcommand

Copies a range of lines.

```
COpy target-1 target-2
```

The copy begins with the current line and extends through *target-1*. The lines are inserted following *target-2*.

The COUNT subcommand

Displays the number of occurrences of the specified string.

```
COUnt /string [/target]
```

The search begins with the current line and extends to the target line, unless *target* is omitted, in which case only the current line is searched.

The DELETE subcommand

Deletes lines from the current line to the target.

```
DELete target
```

The DOWN subcommand

Scrolls the display down, toward the end of the file.

```
Down [n|*]
```

An asterisk scrolls the screen to the last line in the file.

The DUPLICAT subcommand

Duplicates lines starting from the current line through the target line.

```
DUPlicat [count] [target]
```

The lines are duplicated a specified number of times, and the duplicated lines are inserted immediately after the target line. If *target* is omitted, only the current line is duplicated.

The EXPAND subcommand

Replaces all tab characters with one or more spaces to align text at the current tab stops.

```
EXPand [target]
```

The FILE subcommand

Saves the current file on disk.

```
FILE [name [type [mode]]]
```

If you omit all options, the current file is replaced. Otherwise, a new file is created. Code an equals sign for any option to keep the current file's name, type, or mode specification.

The FIND subcommand

Locates the first line following the current line that contains the specified text. If you first issue SET WRAP ON, the entire file will be searched; if WRAP is off, the search stops at the end of the file.

```
Find text
```

The FINDUP subcommand

Locates the first line before the current line that contains the specified text. If you first issue SET WRAP ON, the entire file is searched; if WRAP is off, the search stops at the beginning of the file.

```
{FINDUp|FUp} text
```

The FORWARD subcommand

Scrolls the display forward the specified number of screen pages.

```
FOrward [n|*]
```

Code an asterisk (*) to display the last file record.

The GET subcommand

Loads records from a CMS file and inserts them following the current line.

```
GET [name [type [mode [start-rec [count|*]]]]]
```

If you don't code a name, type, and mode specification, the records saved by the last PUT command (with no options) are retrieved. Code an equals sign (=) for name, type, or mode to use the corresponding value of the current file. If you omit *start-rec* and *count*, the entire file is loaded.

The HELP subcommand

Displays information about using XEDIT.

```
Help  ⎧ MENU       ⎫
      ⎪ TASK       ⎪
      ⎨ PREFIX     ⎬
      ⎪ HELP       ⎪
      ⎩ subcommand ⎭
```

MENU displays a list of XEDIT subcommands and macros; TASK displays task-related help information; PREFIX displays a list of prefix commands; HELP displays information about using the HELP facility. If you specify a subcommand, information about that subcommand is displayed.

ISPF, ICCF, and CMS

The HEXTYPE macro

Displays one or more records in hexadecimal and EBCDIC notation.

```
HEXType [target]
```

The INPUT subcommand

Opens an input area below the current line and places XEDIT in input mode.

```
Input
```

The LEFT subcommand

Scrolls the display left, moving text on the screen to the right.

```
LEft [n]
```

If you omit *n*, the display is scrolled one character position.

The LOCATE subcommand

Searches forward through the file to locate the specified target.

```
Locate target [subcommand]
```

If a subcommand is specified, that subcommand is executed when the target is located.

The LOWERCAS subcommand

Changes all upper case letters from the current line through the target line to upper case. If no target is specified, only the current line is changed.

```
LOWercas [target]
```

The MOVE subcommand

Moves a range of lines.

```
MOve target-1 target-2
```

The move begins with the current line and extends through *target-1*. The lines are deleted from their current position and inserted immediately following *target-2*.

The NEXT subcommand

Scrolls the display down the specified number of lines. Same as the DOWN command.

```
Next [n|*]
```

The NFIND subcommand

Locates the first line following the current line that does *not* contain the specified text. If you first issue SET WRAP ON, the entire file will be searched; if WRAP is off, the search stops at the end of the file.

```
NFind text
```

The NFINDUP subcommand

Locates the first line before the current line that does *not* contain the specified text. If you first issue SET WRAP ON, the entire file will be searched; if WRAP is off, the search stops at the beginning of the file.

```
{NFINDUp|NFUp} text
```

The PRESERVE subcommand

Saves various XEDIT mode settings; these settings can be restored by issuing a RESTORE command.

```
PREServe
```

The PUT subcommand

Saves a range of lines.

```
PUT [target] [name [type [mode]]]
```

The save begins with the current line and extends up to (but not including) the target line in a new CMS file or the end of an existing CMS file. If you don't code a file specification, data is saved in a temporary file, which can be retrieved by issuing a GET subcommand with no operands. If you omit *target*, only the current line is saved. You can code an equals sign (=) for *name*, *type*, or *mode* to use the corresponding value from the current file.

The PUTD subcommand

Saves a range of lines.

```
PUTD [target] [name [type [mode]]]
```

The save begins with the current line and extends up to (but not including) the target line in a new CMS file or the end of an existing CMS file; the lines in the current file are deleted. If you don't code a file specification, data is saved in a temporary file, which can be retrieved by issuing a GET subcommand with no operands. If you omit *target*, only the current line is saved. You can code an equals sign (=) for *name*, *type*, or *mode* to use the corresponding value for the current file.

The QUERY subcommand

Displays the current value of various XEDIT options. For details, see the SET commands later in this section; each option set with the SET command can be queried simply by coding QUERY instead of SET.

```
Query option
```

The QUIT subcommand

Terminates XEDIT without saving the current file. If the file has been changed, you'll be prompted to make sure this is what you want to do.

```
QUIT
```

The RECOVER subcommand

Inserts one or more lines that were previously deleted by a DELETE or PUTD subcommand or a D prefix command.

```
RECover [n|*]
```

The REPEAT subcommand

Advances the current line pointer and reexecutes the most recently entered subcommand. This continues until the target line is reached. If no target is specified, the previous subcommand is executed once.

```
REPEat [target]
```

The RESTORE subcommand

Restores XEDIT option settings that were saved by a PRESERVE command.

```
RESTore
```

The RGTLEFT macro

Scrolls the display right or left, depending on the current position of the displayed data.

```
RGTLEFT [n]
```

In normal usage, issuing RGTLEFT once scrolls the display right; issuing it again returns the display to the left margin. If you specify *n*, the display is scrolled the specified number of column positions; if you omit *n*, XEDIT determines the scroll amount. RGTLEFT is initially assigned to PF10.

The RIGHT subcommand

Scrolls the display right, moving text on the screen to the left.

```
RIght [n]
```

If you omit *n*, the display is scrolled one character position.

The SAVE subcommand

Saves the current file without terminating the editor.

```
SAVE [name [type [mode]]]
```

If you omit the file specification, the current file is replaced. You can code an equals sign (=) for *name, type,* or *mode* to retain the current file's name, type, or mode.

The SCHANGE subcommand

SCHANGE must be assigned to a PF key to work; it lets you enter a CHANGE subcommand in the command area, then selectively change occurrences of the text specified in the CHANGE command by pressing one of two PF keys: one to confirm the change, the other to skip the change and locate the next occurrence of the string. Initially, PF5 is assigned to the SCHANGE command, and PF6 is assigned as the PF key to confirm the change operation.

```
SCHANGE PF-key
```

The SET AUTOSAVE subcommand

Controls whether or not XEDIT is to periodically save your file.

```
SET AUtosave {n|OFF} [mode]
```

If you specify *n*, XEDIT saves the file every time *n* changes are made.

The SET CASE subcommand

Specifies whether or not lowercase text is converted to uppercase and whether the distinction is important during target searches.

```
SET CASE {Uppercase|Mixed} [Respect|Ignore]
```

The SET CMDLINE subcommand

Controls the position of the command line.

```
SET CMDline {On|OFf|Top|Bottom}
```

The SET CURLINE subcommand

Defines the screen location of the current line.

```
SET CURLine ON [M]  [+n|-n]
```

M means the middle of the screen; if omitted, the current line is positioned relative to the top of the screen. You must code M, +n, or -n.

The SET FULLREAD subcommand

Specifies whether nulls within lines are to be retained and converted to spaces.

```
SET FULLread {ON|OFF}
```

The SET HEX subcommand

Specifies whether hexadecimal constants are allowed in targets. If allowed, they are coded like this: /X'C140C2'/.

```
SET HEX {ON|OFF}
```

The SET LINEND subcommand

Specifies the character used to indicate the logical end of a line. The default is the pound sign (#).

```
SET LINENd {ON|OFF} [char]
```

The SET MASK subcommand

Lets you change the current mask, which is used whenever lines are inserted.

```
SET MASK  ⎧Define        ⎫
          ⎨Modify        ⎬
          ⎩Immed [text]  ⎭
```

DEFINE displays a scale line in the command area, which you can overtype; M displays the current mask in the command area, which you can over-type; I specifies the text of the mask directly.

The SET MSGLINE subcommand

Defines the position and size of the message area.

```
SET MSGLine {ON|OFF} [M] [+n|-n]
```

M represents the middle of the screen; if you omit M, the message line is positioned relative to the top of the screen.

The SET MSGMODE subcommand

Specifies whether or not messages should be displayed and whether or not displayed messages should be presented in long or short form.

```
SET MSGMode {ON|OFF} [Short|Long]
```

The SET NULLS subcommand

Specifies how trailing blanks are handled.

```
SET NULls {ON|OFF}
```

ON converts trailing blanks to null characters (hex 00); OFF leaves them as spaces.

The SET NUMBER subcommand

Specifies whether or not line numbers are displayed
in the prefix area.

```
SET NUMber {ON|OFF}
```

The SET PA subcommand

Associates a command string with a PA key. If no
string is specified, the PA key is unassigned.

```
SET PAn [string]
```

The SET PACK subcommand

Specifies whether the editor should store the file in
packed format.

```
SET PACK {ON|OFF}
```

The SET PF subcommand

Associates a command string with a PF key. If no
string is specified, the PF key is unassigned.

```
SET PFn [string]
```

The SET SCALE subcommand

Specifies whether or not a scale line should be displayed.

```
SET SCALe {ON|OFF} [M] [+n|-n]
```

If you specify ON but provide no position, the scale
line is displayed under the current line. M refers to
the middle of the screen; if you omit M, the scale
line is positioned relative to the top of the screen.

The SET SCREEN subcommand

Divides the screen into one or more logical screens, each of which can edit a different file or a different portion of the same file.

```
SET SCReen n    {SIZE size-1 [size-2...] }
                {WIDTH width-1 [width-2...]}
```

The screen can be split horizontally (SIZE) or vertically (WIDTH); a horizonally split screen can be no smaller than five lines, and a vertically split screen can be no smaller than 20 characters.

The SET TABLINE subcommand

Specifies whether or not a tab line should be displayed. Usually, you'll want to place it on the same line as the scale line.

```
SET TABLine {ON|OFF} [M] [+n|-n]
```

M refers to the middle of the screen; if you omit M, the tab line is positioned relative to the top of the screen.

The SET TABS subcommand

Establishes tab positions.

```
SET TABS tab-1 [tab-2...]
```

The SET WRAP subcommand

Specifies whether, during a search, the editor should stop at the top or bottom of the file (WRAP OFF) or continue from the bottom to the top (or from the top to the bottom, depending on the search direction).

```
SET WRap {ON|OFF}
```

The SHIFT subcommand

Shifts a range of lines starting with the current line
and continuing through the target line one or more
characters to the right or left.

```
SHift {Left|Right} [columns] [target]
```

The SORT macro

Sorts a range of lines starting with the current line
and continuing through the target line based on one
or more sort fields.

```
SORT target [A|D]   col-1 col-2   [col-1 col-2]...
```

A or D specifies whether the lines are to be sorted
in ascending or descending sequence.

The TOP subcommand

Scrolls the display to the first record in the file.

```
TOP
```

The UP subcommand

Scrolls the display the specified number of lines
toward the beginning of the file.

```
Up [n|*]
```

The UPPERCAS subcommand

Translates all lowercase letters within the target range to uppercase. If you omit target, only the current line is changed.

```
UPPercas [target]
```

The & subcommand

Code an ampersand (&) in column one of the command area to cause the subcommand you want to execute to be redisplayed. Then, you can press the enter key to execute the subcommand again, or you can make changes to it before you reexecute it.

```
& [subcommand]
```

The = subcommand

Reexecutes the last XEDIT subcommand or macro. If you code a subcommand on the = subcommand, that subcommand is executed first; then, the previous subcommand is reexecuted.

```
= [subcommand]
```

The ? subcommand

Redisplays the previous subcommand. You can modify it if you wish, then press the enter key to execute it.

```
?
```

The XEDIT Prefix subcommands and macros

Adding and deleting lines

A	Add one line.
An or nA	Add *n* lines.
I	Insert one line.
In or nl	Insert *n* lines.
D	Delete one line.
Dn or nD	Delete *n* lines.

Copying and moving lines

C	Copy one line.
Cn or nC	Copy *n* lines.
CC	Move a range of lines.
M	Move one line.
Mn or nM	Move *n* lines.
MM	Move a range of lines.
F	Insert copied/moved lines following this line.
P	Insert copied/moved lines preceding this line.

Duplicating lines

"	Duplicate one line.
"n or n"	Duplicate *n* lines.
""	Duplicate a range of lines.
""n or n""	Duplicate a range of lines *n* times.

Shifting data

<	Shift one line left one column.
<n or n<	Shift one line left *n* columns.
<<	Shift a block of lines left one column.
<<n or n<<	Shift a block of lines left *n* columns.
>	Shift one line right one column.
>n or n>	Shift one line right *n* columns.
>>	Shift a block of lines right one column.
>>n or n>>	Shift a block of lines right *n* columns.

Other prefix subcommands and macros

SCALE	Display a scale line.
TABL	Display a tab line.
.xxxx	Set a symbolic name.
/	Set the current line.

XEDIT default PA and PF key settings

Key	Assignment
PF1	HELP MENU
PF2	Add a blank line after the cursor line.
PF3	QUIT
PF4	Advance to the next tab position.
PF5	Invoke SCHANGE operation.
PF6	Redisplay previous subcommand.
PF7	Scroll backward one page.
PF8	Scroll forward one page.
PF9	Reexecute previous subcommand
PF10	Scroll display right or left.
PF11	Split or join lines.
PF12	Move cursor to home position.

Section 12

Reference tables

Hex/binary equivalents

Hex digit	Bit pattern		Hex digit	Bit pattern
0	0000		8	1000
1	0001		9	1001
2	0010		A	1010
3	0011		B	1011
4	0100		C	1100
5	0101		D	1101
6	0110		E	1110
7	0111		F	1111

EBCDIC code table

Dec	Hex	EBCDIC	Dec	Hex	EBCDIC
0	00	NUL	48	30	
1	01	SOH	49	31	
2	02	STX	50	32	SYN
3	03	ETX	51	33	IR
4	04	SEL	52	34	PP
5	05	HT	53	35	TRN
6	06	RNL	54	36	NBS
7	07	DEL	55	37	EOT
8	08	GE	56	38	SBS
9	09	SPS	57	39	IT
10	0A	RPT	58	3A	RFF
11	0B	VT	59	3B	CU3
12	0C	FF	60	3C	DC4
13	0D	CR	61	3D	NAK
14	0E	SO	62	3E	
15	0F	SI	63	3F	SUB
16	10	DLE	64	40	space
17	11	DC1	65	41	RSP
18	12	DC2	66	42	
19	13	DC3	67	43	
20	14	RES/ENP	68	44	
21	15	NL	69	45	
22	16	BS	70	46	
23	17	POC	71	47	
24	18	CAN	72	48	
25	19	EM	73	49	
26	1A	UBS	74	4A	¢
27	1B	CU1	75	4B	.
28	1C	IFS	76	4C	<
29	1D	IGS	77	4D	(
30	1E	IRS	78	4E	+
31	1F	ITB/IUS	79	4F	|
32	20	DS	80	50	&
33	21	SOS	81	51	
34	22	FS	82	52	
35	23	WUS	83	53	
36	24	BYP/INP	84	54	
37	25	LF	85	55	
38	26	ETB	86	56	
39	27	ESC	87	57	
40	28	SA	88	58	
41	29	SFE	89	59	
42	2A	SM/SW	90	5A	!
43	2B	CSP	91	5B	$
44	2C	MFA	92	5C	*
45	2D	ENQ	93	5D	)
46	2E	ACK	94	5E	;
47	2F	BEL	95	5F	¬

Dec	Hex	EBCDIC		Dec	Hex	EBCDIC
96	60	-		144	90	
97	61	/		145	91	j
98	62			146	92	k
99	63			147	93	l
100	64			148	94	m
101	65			149	95	n
102	66			150	96	o
103	67			151	97	p
104	68			152	98	q
105	69			153	99	r
106	6A	|		154	9A	
107	6B	,		155	9B	
108	6C	%		156	9C	
109	6D	_		157	9D	
110	6E	>		158	9E	
111	6F	?		159	9F	
112	70			160	A0	
113	71			161	A1	~
114	72			162	A2	s
115	73			163	A3	t
116	74			164	A4	u
117	75			165	A5	v
118	76			166	A6	w
119	77			167	A7	x
120	78			168	A8	y
121	79	`		169	A9	z
122	7A	:		170	AA	
123	7B	#		171	AB	
124	7C	@		172	AC	
125	7D	'		173	AD	
126	7E	=		174	AE	
127	7F	"		175	AF	
128	80			176	B0	
129	81	a		177	B1	
130	82	b		178	B2	
131	83	c		179	B3	
132	84	d		180	B4	
133	85	e		181	B5	
134	86	f		182	B6	
135	87	g		183	B7	
136	88	h		184	B8	
137	89	i		185	B9	
138	8A			186	BA	
139	8B			187	BB	
140	8C			188	BC	
141	8D			189	BD	
142	8E			190	BE	
143	8F			191	BF	

Dec	Hex	EBCDIC	Dec	Hex	EBCDIC
192	C0	{	224	E0	\
193	C1	A	225	E1	NSP
194	C2	B	226	E2	S
195	C3	C	227	E3	T
196	C4	D	228	E4	U
197	C5	E	229	E5	V
198	C6	F	230	E6	W
199	C7	G	231	E7	X
200	C8	H	232	E8	Y
201	C9	I	233	E9	Z
202	CA	SHY	234	EA	
203	CB		235	EB	
204	CC		236	EC	
205	CD		237	ED	
206	CE		238	EE	
207	CF		239	EF	
208	D0	}	240	F0	0
209	D1	J	241	F1	1
210	D2	K	242	F2	2
211	D3	L	243	F3	3
212	D4	M	244	F4	4
213	D5	N	245	F5	5
214	D6	O	246	F6	6
215	D7	P	247	F7	7
216	D8	Q	248	F8	8
217	D9	R	249	F9	9
218	DA		250	FA	
219	DB		251	FB	
220	DC		252	FC	
221	DD		253	FD	
222	DE		254	FE	
223	DF		255	FF	EO

Attribute bytes

Protection	Shift	Intensity	MDT	Hex	Char.
unprot				40	SPACE
unprot			MDT	C1	A
unprot		bright		C8	H
unprot		bright	MDT	C9	I
unprot		dark		4C	<
unprot		dark	MDT	4D	(
unprot	num			50	&
unprot	num		MDT	D1	J
unprot	num	bright		D8	Q
unprot	num	bright	MDT	D9	R
unprot	num	dark		5C	*
unprot	num	dark	MDT	5D	)
prot				60	-
prot			MDT	61	/
prot		bright		E8	Y
prot		bright	MDT	E9	Z
prot		dark		6C	%
prot		dark	MDT	6D	_
prot	skip			F0	0
prot	skip		MDT	F1	1
prot	skip	bright		F8	8
prot	skip	bright	MDT	F9	9
prot	skip	dark		7C	@
prot	skip	dark	MDT	7D	QUOTE

Execute Interface Block fields

Field name	COBOL PIC	Minimum release	Description
EIBAID	X(1)		Most recent AID character
EIBATT	X(1)		RU attach header flag
EIBCALEN	S9(4) COMP		Length of DFHCOMMAREA
EIBCOMPL	X(1)	1.6	RECEIVE command completion flag
EIBCONF	X(1)	1.6	LU6.2 comfirmation flag
EIBCPOSN	S9(4) COMP		Most recent cursor address
EIBDATE	S9(7) COMP-3		Task start date
EIBDS	X(8)		Most recent data set name
EIBEOC	X(1)		RU end-of-chain flag
EIBERR	X(1)	1.6	LU6.2 error flag
EIBERRCD	X(4)	1.6	LU6.2 error code
EIBFMH	X(1)		FMH flag
EIBFN	X(2)		Most recent CICS command code
EIBFREE	X(1)		Free facility flag
EIBNODAT	X(1)	1.6	LU6.2 no data flag
EIBRCODE	X(6)		CICS response code
EIBRECV	X(1)		RECEIVE command more-data flag
EIBREQID	X(8)		Interval control request-id
EIBRESP	X(4)	1.7	Exceptional condition code
EIBRESP2	X(4)	1.7	Exceptional condition extended code
EIBRSRCE	X(8)		Last resource (file, queue, etc.)
EIBSIG	X(1)	1.6	SIGNAL flag
EIBSYNC	X(1)		Syncpoint flag
EIBSYNRB	X(1)	1.6	Syncpoint rollback flag
EIBTASKN	S9(7) COMP-3		Task number
EIBTIME	S9(7) COMP-3		Task starting time
EIBTRMID	X(4)		Terminal-id
EIBTRNID	X(4)		Transaction-id

Index

In this index, I've omitted all leading special characters (like slashes and ampersands) from index entries. Thus, to find references to the ICCF /CANCEL command, look under CANCEL.

A command
  ICCF, 432
  ISPF, 402
  VM/CMS, 466
ABCODE option
  ABEND, 65
  ASSIGN, 73
ABEND command, 65-66
ABSTIME option
  ASKTIME, 71
  FORMATTIME, 102
ACCUM option
  SEND CONTROL, 189
  SEND MAP, 192
  SEND TEXT, 200
ADD command (VM/CMS), 449
ADDRESS command, 22, 67-70
ADDVOLUMES parameter (ALTER), 382
AID keys, 27-28
ALARM option
  SEND CONTROL, 188
  SEND MAP, 192
  SEND TEXT, 199
ALIGN command (ICCF), 420
ALL parameter (LISTCAT), 380
ALLOCATE command, 363
ALLOCATION parameter (LISTCAT), 380

ALTER command
  AMS, 382-383
  ICCF, 420
AMS
  under DOS/VSE, 364
  under ICCF, 365
  under MVS, 362
  under TSO, 363
  under VM/CMS, 365
AMS commands, coding rules for, 360-361
AMSERV command (VM/CMS), 433
APPLID option (ASSIGN), 73
arguments, CICS command, 64
ASIS option
  RECEIVE MAP, 165
  RECEIVE, 161
ASKIP parameter (DFHMDF), 50
ASKTIME command, 71-72
ASSEMBLE procedure (ICCF), 403
assembler statement, 39-40
ASSIGN command, 73-76
ASYNC command (ICCF), 403
ATTRB parameter (DFHMDF), 50
attribute bytes, 28-30, 36-38, 473
AUTOLIST mode (ISPF), 395
AUTONUM mode (ISPF), 395
AUTOPAGE option (SEND PAGE), 197

AUTOSAVE mode (ISPF), 395
AUXILIARY option (WRITEQ TS), 229

B command (ISPF), 402
BACKWARD command
    ICCF, 420
    VM/CMS, 449
base color terminal, 37
Base Locator for Linkage, 21-22
BIF DEEDIT command, 77
binary fullword, 64
binary halfword, 64
binary/hex conversion, 469
BLDINDEX command, 377-378
BLL cells, 21-22
BMS, 35-62
BMS macro instruction, coding rules, 39-40
BOTTOM command
    ICCF, 421
    VM/CMS, 449
BOUNDS command (ISPF), 396
browse option (ISPF), 394
browse transaction, temporary storage, 351
BRT parameter (DFHMDF), 50
BTRANS option (ASSIGN), 73
BUFFER option (RECEIVE), 161

C command
    ICCF, 432
    ISPF, 402
    VM/CMS, 466
CANCEL command
    CICS, 78-79
    ICCF, 403, 421
    ISPF, 397
    VM/CMS, 450
CANCEL option
    ABEND, 65
    HANDLE ABEND, 110
CAPS mode (ISPF), 395
CASE command (ICCF), 421
CATALOG parameter
    ALTER, 382
    BLDINDEX, 377
    DEFINE AIX, 373
    DEFINE CLUSTER, 369
    DEFINE PATH, 375
    DELETE command, 384
    LISTCAT, 379
CEBR transaction, 351
CECI transaction, 349-350
CEDA transaction, 333
CEDF transaction, 352

CEMT transaction, 340-341
CENTER command (ICCF), 421
CEOT transaction, 339
CESN transaction, 337
CHANGE command
    ICCF, 421
    ISPF, 397, 401
    VM/CMS, 433, 450
CHARACTER parameter (PRINT), 386
character string, 64
checklist
    program specification, 3
    structure chart, 14
    testing, 348
CISZ parameter (DEFINE CLUSTER), 369
CLEAR key, 27-28
CLOSE command (VM/CMS), 434
CMS command (VM/CMS), 450
CMSG transaction, 342-344
COBOL procedure (ICCF), 403
COBOL restrictions, 32-33
COLOR option (ASSIGN), 73
COLOR parameter
    DFHMDF, 50
    DFHMDI, 47
    DFHMSD, 43
COLUMN parameter (DFHMDI), 46
command-level interpreter, 349-350
COMMANDS command (VM/CMS), 434
commands, coding rules for
    CICS, 23, 64
    AMS, 360-361
COMMAREA option
    LINK, 124
    RETURN, 175
    XCTL, 232
comments (AMS), 361
common module, 14
Common System Area, 20
Common Work Area, 20
communication area, 20
    in pseudo-conversational program, 23-24
COMPARE command (VM/CMS), 434
compiler, 316
compiler options, 325
COMPLETE option (DUMP), 93
COMPRESS command (VM/CMS), 450
CONNECT command (ICCF), 404
CONTINU command (ICCF), 404
conversational program, 8
COPY command
    ISPF, 397
    VM/CMS, 451

COPY member, 3
COPY option (ISSUE), 119
COPYFILE command
   ICCF, 404
   VM/CMS, 434
COPYMEM command (ICCF), 404
COUNT command (VM/CMS), 451
COUNT parameter
   PRINT, 386
   REPRO, 388
CP command (VM/CMS), 433
CPYLIB procedure (ICCF), 404
CREATE command (ISPF), 397
CREATION parameter (LISTCAT), 380
CSA, 20
CSA option (ADDRESS), 67
CSPG transaction, 345
CSSF transaction, 338
CSSN transaction, 336
CTLCHAR option
   ISSUE, 119
   SEND, 185
CTRL parameter
   DFHMDI, 46
   DFHMSD, 42
CURSOR command (ICCF), 422
CURSOR option
   SEND CONTROL, 188
   SEND MAP, 192
   SEND TEXT, 200
cursor positioning, 28
CUSTINQ program, 280-293
CUSTMNT program, 262-279
customer inquiry program, 280-293
customer maintenance program, 262-279
CWA, 20
CWA option (ADDRESS), 67
CWALENG option (ASSIGN), 73

D command
   ICCF, 432
   ISPF, 402
   VM/CMS, 466
DATA option (FREEMAIN), 105
data types (CICS command), 64
data-area, 64
data-value, 64
DATAONLY option (SEND MAP), 192
DATASET option
   DELETE, 82
   ENDBR, 95

DATASET option (continued)
   READ, 139
   READNEXT, 144
   READPREV, 149
   RESETBR, 169
   REWRITE, 177
   STARTBR, 208
   UNLOCK, 218
   WRITE, 223
DATE option (FORMATTIME), 103
DATEFORM option (FORMATTIME), 103
DATESEP option (FORMATTIME), 103
DAYCOUNT option (FORMATTIME), 103
DAYOFMONTH option (FORMATTIME), 103
DAYOFWEEK option (FORMATTIME), 103
DCT option (DUMP), 94
DD statement (VSAM), 362
DDMMYY option (FORMATTIME), 103
deadlock, 31
debugging, 349-355
DEFINE ALTERNATEINDEX command, 372
DEFINE CLUSTER command, 367-371
DEFRESP option (SEND), 184
DELAY command, 80-81
DELETE command
   CICS, 82-86, 384-385
   ICCF, 422
   VM/CMS, 451
DELETEQ TD command, 87-88
DELETEQ TS command, 89-90
DELIM command (ICCF), 422
DEQ command, 91-92
design, program, 9-16
DEST option (SEND), 184
DESTCOUNT option (ASSIGN), 73
DESTID option (ASSIGN), 73
DESTIDLENG option (ASSIGN), 73
DETACH command (VM/CMS), 435
development procedure, 2
device code (LISTCAT), 380
DFHBMSCA, 28-29
DFHCOMMAREA, 20
DFHEITCL procedure, 320-321
DFHFCT macro, 331-332
DFHMAPS procedure, 318-319
DFHMDF macro, 49-56
DFHMDI macro, 45-48
DFHMSD macro instruction, 41-44
DFHPCT macro, 330
DFHPPT macro, 328-329
DIAL command (VM/CMS), 435

DISABLED condition
    DELETE, 83
    ENDBR, 95
    READ, 140
    READNEXT, 145
    READPREV, 150
    RESETBR, 170
    REWRITE, 177
    STARTBR, 209
    UNLOCK, 218
    WRITE, 224
DISCONN command (VM/CMS), 435
DISCONNECT option (ISSUE), 119
DISPC command (ICCF), 405
DISPLAY command (ICCF), 405
DLBL statement (VSAM), 364
DOWN command
    ICCF, 422
    VM/CMS, 451
DRK parameter (DFHMDF), 50
DSATTS parameter
    DFHMDI, 46
    DFHMSD, 43
DSIDERR condition
    DELETE, 83
    ENDBR, 95
    READ, 140
    READNEXT, 145
    READPREV, 150
    RESETBR, 170
    REWRITE, 177
    STARTBR, 209
    UNLOCK, 218
    WRITE, 224
dump, transaction, 353-355
DUMP command, 93-94
DUMP parameter (PRINT), 386
DUMPCODE option (DUMP), 93
DUP command (ICCF), 423
DUPKEY condition
    DELETE, 83
    READ, 140
    READNEXT, 145
    READPREV, 150
DUPLICAT command (VM/CMS), 452
DUPREC condition
    REWRITE, 177
    WRITE, 224

EBCDIC code table, 470-472
ECADDR option (WAIT EVENT), 219

ECHO command (ICCF), 405
ED macro (ICCF), 405
EDIT command (ICCF), 405
edit module, 30-31
edit option (ISPF), 395-402
EI option (TRACE), 215
EIB, 20, 474
EIB option (ADDRESS), 67
EIBAID, 27-28
EIBCALEN, 23-24
EIBDATE, 71
EIBRCODE, 27
EIBTIME, 71
END command
    ICCF, 406, 423
END-EXEC, 23
ENDBR command, 95-96
ENDDATA condition (RETRIEVE), 173
ENDFILE condition
    READNEXT, 145
    READPREV, 150
ENQ command, 97-99
ENQBUSY condition (ENQ), 98
ENTER command
    CICS, 100-101
    ICCF, 423
ENTRIES parameter (LISTCAT), 379
ENTRY option (LOAD), 126
entry-name parameter
    DELETE command, 384
    LISTCAT, 379
ENVDEFERR condition (RETRIEVE), 173
EQUAL option
    READ, 140
    RESETBR, 170
    STARTBR, 209
ERASE command (VM/CMS), 435
ERASE option
    SEND, 185
    SEND CONTROL, 188
    SEND MAP, 192
    SEND TEXT, 199
ERASE parameter (DELETE command), 384
ERASEAUP option
    ISSUE, 119
    SEND CONTROL, 188
    SEND MAP, 192
ERASEP command (ICCF), 406
ERRTERM option (ROUTE), 181
exceptional conditions, 25-27
EXEC CICS, 23

EXEC command
    ICCF, 406
    VM/CMS, 436
Execute Interface Block, 20, 474
execution diagnostics facility, 352
EXPAND command (VM/CMS), 452
EXPIRATION parameter (LISTCAT), 380
EXPIRED condition
    DELAY, 80
    POST, 133
EXTATT parameter
    DFHMDI, 46
    DFHMSD, 42-43
EXTDS option (ASSIGN), 73
extended attribute bytes, 37-38
extended color, 37
extended highlighting, 37
EXTERNALSORT parameter (BLDINDEX), 377

F command (VM/CMS), 466
FACILITY option (ASSIGN), 74
FCI option (ASSIGN), 74
FCT, 331-332
FCT option (DUMP), 94
FIELD option (BIF DEEDIT), 77
FILE command
    ICCF, 423
    VM/CMS, 452
File Control Table, 331-332
FILE parameter
    DEFINE AIX, 373
    DEFINE CLUSTER, 368
FILEDEF command (VM/CMS), 436-437
FILELIST command (VM/CMS), 437
FIND command
    ICCF, 424
    ISPF, 394, 398, 401
    VM/CMS, 452
FINDUP command (VM/CMS), 453
FLENGTH option
    DUMP, 93
    GETMAIN, 106
    LOAD, 126
FOR parameter
    DEFINE AIX, 373
    DEFINE CLUSTER, 368
    DEFINE PATH, 375
FORCE parameter (DELETE), 384
FORMAT command (ICCF), 424
FORMATTIME command, 102-104

FORMFEED option
    SEND CONTROL, 189
    SEND MAP, 192
    SEND TEXT, 200
FORWARD command
    ICCF, 424
    VM/CMS, 453
FREEKB option
    SEND CONTROL, 188
    SEND MAP, 192
    SEND TEXT, 200
FREEMAIN command, 105
FREESPACE parameter (DEFINE CLUSTER), 368
FROM option
    DUMP, 93
    ENTER, 100
    JOURNAL, 120
    REWRITE, 177
    SEND, 184
    SEND MAP, 191
    SEND TEXT, 199
    START, 206
    WRITE, 223
    WRITEQ TD, 227
    WRITEQ TS, 229
FROMADDRESS parameter
    PRINT, 386
    REPRO, 388
FROMKEY parameter
    PRINT, 386
    REPRO, 388
FROMNUMBER parameter
    PRINT, 386
    REPRO, 388
FRSET option
    SEND CONTROL, 188
    SEND MAP, 192
FSEDPF macro (ICCF), 406
FSET parameter (DFHMDF), 50
fullword, 64

GENERIC option
    DELETE, 82
    READ, 140
    RESETBR, 169
    STARTBR, 208
GET command (VM/CMS), 453
GETFILE command (ICCF), 424
GETINV program, 261
GETL procedure (ICCF), 406

GETMAIN command, 106-107
GETP procedure (ICCF), 407
getpage command (CSPG), 345
GETR procedure (ICCF), 407
GROUP command (ICCF), 407
GTEQ option
   READ, 140
   RESETBR, 170
   STARTBR, 209

halfword, 64
HANDLE ABEND command, 110-111
HANDLE AID command, 27-28, 112-113
HANDLE CONDITION command, 25-27, 114-115
HARDCOPY command (ICCF), 407
HC macro (ICCF), 408
HEADER option (SEND TEXT), 200
HEADER parameter (DFHMDI), 46
HELP command (VM/CMS), 437-438, 453
HEX command (ISPF), 394
HEX mode (ISPF), 395
HEX parameter (PRINT), 386
hex/binary conversion, 469
HEXTYPE command (VM/CMS), 454
hhmmss, 64
HILIGHT option (ASSIGN), 74
HILIGHT parameter
   DFHMDF, 50
   DFHMSD, 43
HIPO, 16
HISTORY parameter (LISTCAT), 380
HOLD option (LOAD), 126
HONEOM option
   SEND CONTROL, 189
   SEND MAP, 192
   SEND TEXT, 200
HT command (VM/CMS), 438

I command
   ICCF, 432
   ISPF, 402
   VM/CMS, 466
I/O module, 14
IC parameter (DFHMDF), 50
ICCF, 432
IDENTIFY command (VM/CMS), 438
IGNORE CONDITION command, 116-117
IGREQCD condition
   SEND CONTROL, 189
   SEND MAP, 193
   SEND TEXT, 201
ILLOGIC condition
   DELETE, 83

ILLOGIC condition (continued)
   ENDBR, 95
   READ, 140
   READNEXT, 145
   READPREV, 150
   RESETBR, 170
   REWRITE, 178
   STARTBR, 209
   UNLOCK, 218
   WRITE, 224
IMBED parameter (DEFINE CLUSTER), 368
INDATASET parameter
   BLDINDEX, 377
   PRINT, 386
   REPRO, 388
INDEXED parameter (DEFINE CLUSTER), 368
INDICATE command (VM/CMS), 438
INFILE parameter
   ALTER, 382
   BLDINDEX, 377
   PRINT, 386
   REPRO, 388
INITIAL parameter (DFHMDF), 50
INITIMG option (GETMAIN), 106
INPUT command
   ICCF, 408, 424
   VM/CMS, 454
INSERT command (ICCF), 408, 425
intensity attribute, 36
INTERNALSORT parameter (BLDINDEX), 377
INTERVAL option
   DELAY, 80
   POST, 132
   ROUTE, 180
   START, 205
INTO option
   READ, 139
   READNEXT, 144
   READPREV, 149
   READQ TD, 155
   READQ TS, 158
   RECEIVE, 161
   RECEIVE MAP, 165
   RETRIEVE, 172
inventory listing program
   SEND MAP, 306-314
   SEND TEXT, 300-305
   transient data, 294-299
inventory menu program, 236-242
INVERRTERM condition (ROUTE), 181
INVITE option (SEND), 184
INVLDC condition (ROUTE), 181
INVLST1 program, 294-299

INVLST2 program, 300-305
INVLST3 program, 306-314
INVMENU program, 236-242
INVMPSZ condition
    RECEIVE MAP, 165
    SEND MAP, 193
INVREQ condition
    ASSIGN, 75
    CANCEL, 78
    DELAY, 80
    DELETE, 83
    ENDBR, 95
    ENTER, 100
    POST, 133
    READNEXT, 145
    READPREV, 150
    READQ TS, 159
    RESETBR, 170
    RETRIEVE, 173
    RETURN, 175
    REWRITE, 178
    ROUTE, 181
    SEND CONTROL, 189
    SEND MAP, 193
    SEND PAGE, 197
    SEND TEXT, 201
    START, 206
    STARTBR, 209
    WAIT EVENT, 219
    WAIT JOURNAL, 221
    WRITE, 224
    WRITEQ TS, 230
INVTSREQ condition (RETRIEVE), 173
IOERR condition
    DELETE, 83
    ENDBR, 95
    JOURNAL, 121
    READ, 140
    READNEXT, 145
    READPREV, 150
    READQ TD, 156
    READQ TS, 159
    RESETBR, 170
    RETRIEVE, 173
    REWRITE, 178
    START, 206
    STARTBR, 209
    UNLOCK, 218
    WAIT JOURNAL, 221
    WRITE, 224
    WRITEQ TD, 227
    WRITEQ TS, 230
IPL command (VM/CMS), 439

ISCINVREQ condition
    CANCEL, 78
    DELETE, 83
    DELETEQ TD, 87
    DELETEQ TS, 89
    ENDBR, 95
    READ, 140
    READNEXT, 145
    READPREV, 150
    READQ TD, 156
    READQ TS, 159
    RESETBR, 170
    REWRITE, 178
    START, 206
    STARTBR, 209
    UNLOCK, 218
    WRITE, 224
    WRITEQ TD, 227
    WRITEQ TS, 230
ISPF, 392-402
ISSUE command, 118-119
ITEM option
    READQ TS, 158
    WRITEQ TS, 229
ITEMERR condition
    READQ TS, 159
    WRITEQ TS, 230

JCL procedures
    DOS/VSE, 322-323
    MVS, 318-321
JFILEID option
    JOURNAL, 120
    WAIT JOURNAL, 221
JIDERR condition
    JOURNAL, 121
    WAIT JOURNAL, 221
JOURNAL command, 120-122
JTYPEID option (JOURNAL), 120
JUSTFIRST option (SEND TEXT), 200
JUSTIFY command (ICCF), 425
JUSTIFY option (SEND TEXT), 200
JUSTIFY parameter (DFHMDI), 46
JUSTLAST option (SEND TEXT), 200

K command (ICCF), 432
KEYLENGTH option
    DELETE, 82
    READ, 139
    READNEXT, 145
    READPREV, 150

KEYLENGTH option (continued)
    RESETBR, 169
    STARTBR, 208
    WRITE, 223
KEYS parameter
    DEFINE AIX, 373
    DEFINE CLUSTER, 368

L40, L64, and L80 options
    SEND CONTROL, 189
    SEND MAP, 192
    SEND TEXT, 200
label, 64
LABEL option (HANDLE ABEND), 110
LADD command (ICCF), 425
LANG parameter (DFHMSD), 42
LAST option
    SEND, 184
    SEND CONTROL, 189
    SEND MAP, 192
    SEND TEXT, 200
LDC option (ROUTE), 181
LEFT command
    ICCF, 425
    VM/CMS, 454
LENGERR condition
    GETMAIN, 107
    JOURNAL, 121
    READ, 141
    READNEXT, 145
    READPREV, 150
    READQ TD, 156
    READQ TS, 159
    RECEIVE, 162
    RETRIEVE, 173
    REWRITE, 178
    WRITE, 224
    WRITEQ TD, 227
LENGTH option
    BIF DEEDIT, 77
    DEQ, 91
    DUMP, 93
    ENQ, 97
    GETMAIN, 106
    JOURNAL, 120
    LINK, 124
    LOAD, 126
    READ, 139
    READNEXT, 144
    READPREV, 149
    READQ TD, 155
    READQ TS, 158
    RECEIVE, 161

LENGTH option (continued)
    RETRIEVE, 172
    RETURN, 175
    REWRITE, 177
    SEND, 184
    SEND MAP, 191
    SEND TEXT, 199
    START, 206
    WRITE, 223
    WRITEQ TD, 227
    WRITEQ TS, 229
    XCTL, 232
LENGTH parameter (DFHMDF), 50
LEVEL parameter (LISTCAT), 379
LIBC command (ICCF), 408
LIBRARY command (ICCF), 408
LIBRC procedure (ICCF), 409
LIBRL procedure (ICCF), 409
LIBRP procedure (ICCF), 409
line commands (ISPF), 402
LINE parameter (DFHMDI), 46
LINK command
    CICS, 32-33, 124-125
    VM/CMS, 439
Linkage Section, 21-22
linkage-editor, 316
LIST command (ICCF), 409
LIST option (ROUTE), 180
LISTC command (ICCF), 409
LISTCAT command, 379-381
LISTFILE command (VM/CMS), 439
LISTP command (ICCF), 410
LISTX command (ICCF), 410
LOAD command, 126-129
LOAD procedure (ICCF), 410, 425
LOCATE command
    ISPF, 394, 398
    VM/CMS, 454
LOCNOT command (ICCF), 410
LOCUP command (ICCF), 426
LOGOFF command
    ICCF, 411
    VM/CMS, 439
LOGON command
    ICCF, 411
    VM/CMS, 440
LOWERCAS command (VM/CMS), 455

M command
    ICCF, 432
    ISPF, 402
    VM/CMS, 466
macro instruction, 39-40

MAIL command (ICCF), 411
MAIN option (WRITEQ TS), 229
map, 35, 39
MAP option
    RECEIVE MAP, 165
    SEND MAP, 191
MAPATTS parameter
    DFHMDI, 47
    DFHMSD, 43
MAPCOLUMN option (ASSIGN), 74
MAPFAIL condition, 28, 165
MAPHEIGHT option (ASSIGN), 74
MAPLINE option (ASSIGN), 74
MAPONLY option (SEND MAP), 192
mapset, 35, 39
MAPSET option
    RECEIVE MAP, 165
    SEND MAP, 191
MAPWIDTH option (ASSIGN), 74
MASK command (ISPF), 396
MASSINSERT option (WRITE), 224
Master terminal transaction, 340-341
MAXLENGTH option (RECEIVE), 161
MDT, 36
menu program, 236-242
message switching transaction, 342-344
MODE parameter (DFHMSD), 42
MODEL parameter
    DEFINE AIX, 373
    DEFINE CLUSTER, 368
    DEFINE PATH, 375
Modified Data Tag, 36
module name, 10-13
module number, 11, 14
module planning, 15-16
MONTHOFYEAR option (FORMATTIME), 103
MOVE command
    ISPF, 399
    VM/CMS, 455
MOVEFILE command (VM/CMS), 440
MSG command
    ICCF, 411
    VM/CMS, 440
msgterm command (CSPG), 345
multitasking, 18-19
MVLIB procedure (ICCF), 411

name
    in CICS command option, 64
    module, 10-13
name parameter (ALTER), 382
NAME parameter
    DEFINE AIX, 373

NAME parameter (continued)
    DEFINE CLUSTER, 368
    DEFINE PATH, 375
    LISTCAT, 380
NETNAME option (ASSIGN), 74
NEWNAME parameter (ALTER), 382
NEXT command
    ICCF, 426
    VM/CMS, 455
NEXT option (READQ TS), 158
NFIND command (VM/CMS), 455
NFINDUP command (VM/CMS), 456
NLEOM option
    ROUTE, 181
    SEND MAP, 192
    SEND TEXT, 200
NOCHECK option (START), 206
NOHANDLE option, 25-27
NOJBUFSP condition (JOURNAL), 121
NONINDEXED parameter (DEFINE CLUSTER),
    368
NONSPANNED parameter (DEFINE CLUSTER),
    368
NONUNIQUEKEY parameter (DEFINE AIX), 373
NORM parameter (DFHMDF), 50
NOSPACE condition
    REWRITE, 178
    WRITE, 224
    WRITEQ TD, 227
    WRITEQ TS, 230
NOSTG condition (GETMAIN), 107
NOSUSPEND option
    ENQ, 97
    GETMAIN, 106
    JOURNAL, 121
    READQ TD, 155
    WRITEQ TS, 229
NOTAUTH condition
    CANCEL, 78
    DELETE, 83
    DELETEQ TD, 87
    DELETEQ TS, 89
    ENDBR, 96
    JOURNAL, 121
    LINK, 124
    LOAD, 127
    READ, 141
    READNEXT, 145
    READPREV, 150
    READQ TD, 156
    READQ TS, 159
    RELEASE, 167
    RESETBR, 170

NOTAUTH condition (continued)
    RETRIEVE, 173
    RETURN, 175
    REWRITE, 178
    START, 206
    STARTBR, 209
    UNLOCK, 218
    WAIT JOURNAL, 222
    WRITE, 224
    WRITEQ TD, 228
    WRITEQ TS, 230
    XCTL, 232
NOTFND condition
    CANCEL, 79
    DELETE, 83
    READ, 141
    READNEXT, 146
    READPREV, 151
    RESETBR, 170
    RETRIEVE, 173
    STARTBR, 209
NOTOPEN condition
    DELETE, 83
    ENDBR, 96
    JOURNAL, 121
    READ, 141
    READNEXT, 146
    READPREV, 151
    READQ TD, 156
    RESETBR, 170
    REWRITE, 178
    STARTBR, 209
    UNLOCK, 218
    WAIT JOURNAL, 222
    WRITE, 224
    WRITEQ TD, 228
NOTREADY command (VM/CMS), 440
NOTRUNCATE option (RECEIVE), 161
NOTUSABLE parameter (LISTCAT), 380
NULLS mode (ISPF), 395
NUM parameter (DFHMDF), 50
NUMBER mode (ISPF), 395
number, module, 11, 14
NUMBERED parameter (DEFINE CLUSTER), 368
NUMERIC option (DELETE), 83
NUMITEMS option (READQ TS), 158
NUMTAB option (ASSIGN), 74

OFF option (TRACE), 215
ON option (TRACE), 215
Online resource definition, 333

OPCLASS option
    ASSIGN, 74
    ROUTE, 180
OPERKEYS option (ASSIGN), 74
OPERPURGE option (SEND PAGE), 197
OPID option (ASSIGN), 74
OPSECURITY option (ASSIGN), 74
options
    CICS command, 64
    translator and compiler, 325
order-entry program, 243-261
ORDRENT program, 243-261
OUTDATASET parameter
    BLDINDEX, 377
    REPRO, 388
OUTFILE parameter
    BLDINDEX, 377
    LISTCAT, 380
    REPRO, 388
OUTLINE option (ASSIGN), 74
OVERFLOW condition (SEND MAP), 193
overview, program, 3
OWNER parameter
    DEFINE AIX, 373
    DEFINE CLUSTER, 368

P command (VM/CMS), 466
PA key, 27-28
    ISPF, 393
    VM/CMS, 467
PACK mode (ISPF), 395
Page retrieval transaction, 345
PAGENUM option (ASSIGN), 74
PAGING option
    SEND CONTROL, 189
    SEND MAP, 192
    SEND TEXT, 200
parameters (AMS), 360-361
PATH command, 375-376
PATHENTRY parameter (DEFINE PATH), 375
PCT, 18, 330
PCT option (DUMP), 94
PEEK command (VM/CMS), 440
PF key, 27-28
    ISPF, 393
    VM/CMS, 467
PFXLENG option (JOURNAL), 120
PGMIDERR condition
    HANDLE ABEND, 110
    LINK, 124
    LOAD, 127

PGMIDERR condition (continued)
    RELEASE, 167
    XCTL, 232
PICIN parameter (DFHMDF), 50
PICOUT parameter (DFHMDF), 50
pointer-ref, 64
pointer-value, 64
POP HANDLE command, 130-131
POS parameter (DFHMDF), 50
POST command, 132-134
PPT, 18, 328-329
PPT option (DUMP), 94
PREFIX option (JOURNAL), 120
PRESERVE command (VM/CMS), 456
primary parameter
    DEFINE AIX, 373
    DEFINE CLUSTER, 368
print chart, 7
PRINT command
    AMS, 386-387
    VM/CMS, 441
PRINT macro (ICCF), 412
PRINT NOGEN, 39
PRINT option
    ISSUE, 119
    SEND CONTROL, 188
    SEND MAP, 192
    SEND TEXT, 200
Procedure Division, 23
Processing Program Table, 18, 328-329
program control, 32
Program Control Table, 18, 330
program design, 9-16
PROGRAM option
    DUMP, 94
    HANDLE ABEND, 110
    LINK, 124
    LOAD, 126
    RELEASE, 167
    XCTL, 232
program overview, 3
program specifications, 3-7
programs
    customer inquiry, 280-293
    customer maintenance, 262-279
    GETINV, 261
    inventory listing (SEND MAP), 306-314
    inventory listing (SEND TEXT), 300-305
    inventory listing (transient data), 294-299
    inventory menu, 236-242
    order entry, 243-261

programmed symbols, 38
PROT parameter (DFHMDF), 50
PROTECT command (ICCF), 412
PROTECT option (START), 206
protection attribute, 36
PS option (ASSIGN), 74
PSERV procedure (ICCF), 412
pseudo-conversational programming, 8, 23-24,
    31-32
pseudocode, 15-16
PUNCH command (VM/CMS), 441
PURGE command (ICCF), 413
PURGE MESSAGE command, 135-136
PURGE parameter (DELETE), 384
PURGEP command (ICCF), 413
PUSH HANDLE command, 137-138
PUT command (VM/CMS), 456
PUTD command (VM/CMS), 456

QBUSY condition (READQ TD), 156
QIDERR condition
    DELETEQ TD, 87
    DELETEQ TS, 89
    READQ TD, 156
    READQ TS, 159
    WRITEQ TD, 228
    WRITEQ TS, 230
QNAME option (ASSIGN), 74
QUERY command
    VM/CMS, 441-443, 457
QUEUE option,
    DELETEQ TD, 87
    DELETEQ TS, 89
    READQ TD, 155
    READQ TS, 158
    RETRIEVE, 172
    START, 206
    WRITEQ TD, 227
    WRITEQ TS, 229
QUIT command
    ICCF, 426
    VM/CMS, 457
QZERO condition (READQ TD), 156

R command (ISPF), 402
RBA option
    DELETE, 83
    READ, 140
    READNEXT, 145
    READPREV, 150
    RESETBR, 169

RBA option (continued)
    STARTBR, 209
    WRITE, 223
RDO, 330
RDR command (VM/CMS), 444
RDRLIST command (VM/CMS), 444
READ command, 139-143
READNEXT command, 144-148
READPREV command, 149-154
READQ TD command, 155-157
READQ TS command, 158-160
READY command (VM/CMS), 444
RECEIVE command
    CICS, 161-164
    VM/CMS, 444
RECEIVE MAP command, 165-166
RECORDSIZE parameter (DEFINE CLUSTER), 368
RECOVER command (VM/CMS), 457
RECOVERY mode (ISPF), 396
RELATE parameter (DEFINE AIX), 373
RELEASE command, 167-168
RELIST macro (ICCF), 413
REMOVEVOLUMES parameter (ALTER), 382
RENAME command
    ICCF, 413
    VM/CMS, 445
RENUM command (ICCF), 426
REPEAT command
    ICCF, 427
    VM/CMS, 457
REPLACE command
    ICCF, 413, 427
    ISPF, 399
REPLACE parameter (REPRO), 388
REPLICATE parameter (DEFINE CLUSTER), 368
REPRO command, 388-389
REQID option
    CANCEL, 78
    DELAY, 80
    ENDBR, 95
    JOURNAL, 120
    POST, 132
    READNEXT, 145
    READPREV, 150
    RESETBR, 170
    ROUTE, 181
    SEND CONTROL, 189
    SEND MAP, 192
    SEND TEXT, 200

REQID option (continued)
    START, 206
    STARTBR, 209
    WAIT JOURNAL, 221
RESET command
    ISPF, 399
    VM/CMS, 445
RESET option (HANDLE ABEND), 110
RESETBR command, 169-171
Resource Definition Online, 333
RESOURCE option
    DEQ, 91
    ENQ, 97
    ENTER, 100
RESP option, 25-27
RESTART option (ASSIGN), 74
RESTORE command (VM/CMS), 458
RETRIEVE command, 172-174
RETURN command, 32-33, 175-176
REWIND command (VM/CMS), 445
REWRITE command, 177-179
REWRITE option (WRITEQ TS), 229
RGTLEFT command (VM/CMS), 458
RIDFLD option
    DELETE, 82
    READ, 139
    READNEXT, 144
    READPREV, 149
    RESETBR, 169
    STARTBR, 208
    WRITE, 223
RIGHT command
    ICCF, 427
    VM/CMS, 458
ROLLBACK option (SYNCPOINT), 213
ROLLEDBACK condition (SYNCPOINT), 213
ROUTE command, 180-183
ROUTEP command (ICCF), 414
RRN option
    DELETE, 83
    READ, 140
    READNEXT, 145
    READPREV, 150
    RESETBR, 170
    STARTBR, 209
    WRITE, 224
RTEFAIL condition (ROUTE), 181
RTERMID option
    RETRIEVE, 172
    START, 206

RTESOME condition (ROUTE) 181
RTRANSID option
    RETRIEVE, 172
    START, 206
RUN command (ICCF), 414

SAVE command
    ICCF, 414, 427
    ISPF, 400
    VM/CMS, 458
SCALE command (VM/CMS), 466
SCHANGE command (VM/CMS), 459
SCREEN command (ICCF), 427
screen flow diagram, 6-7
screen layout, 5-6
SCRNHT option (ASSIGN), 74
SCRNWD option (ASSIGN), 75
scrolling (ISPF), 393
SDSERV procedure (ICCF), 414
SEARCH command (ICCF), 428
secondary parameter
    DEFINE AIX, 373
    DEFINE CLUSTER, 368
SEND command
    CICS, 184-187
    ICCF, 415
SEND CONTROL command, 188-190
SEND MAP command, 191-196
SEND PAGE command, 197-198
SEND TEXT command, 199-204
SENDFILE command (VM/CMS), 445
SET command
    ICCF, 415, 428
    VM/CMS, 446, 459-463
SET option
    GETMAIN, 106
    LOAD, 126
    POST, 132
    READ, 139
    READNEXT, 144
    READPREV, 149
    READQ TD, 155
    READQ TS, 158
    RECEIVE, 161
    RECEIVE MAP, 165
    RETRIEVE, 172
SETTIME command (ICCF), 416
SHAREOPTIONS parameter
    DEFINE AIX, 373
    DEFINE CLUSTER, 368-369
shift attribute, 36

SHIFT command
    ICCF, 428
    VM/CMS, 464
SHOW command (ICCF), 416-417, 429
Sign-off transaction, 338
Sign-on transaction, 336-337
SINGLE option (TRACE), 215
SIT option (DUMP), 94
SIZE parameter (DFHMDI), 46
SKIP command (ICCF), 417
SKIP parameter
    PRINT, 386
    REPRO, 388
SLEEP command (VM/CMS), 446
SORT command (VM/CMS), 446, 464
SORT procedure (ICCF), 417
SPANNED parameter (DEFINE CLUSTER), 368
specifications, program, 3-7
SPLIT command (ICCF), 429
SPOOL command (VM/CMS), 446-447
SQUEEZE command (ICCF), 417
SSERV procedure (ICCF), 418
START command, 205-207
STARTBR command, 208-210
STARTCODE option (ASSIGN), 75
STARTIO option
    JOURNAL, 121
    WAIT JOURNAL, 221
STATS mode (ISPF), 396
STATUSP command (ICCF), 418
storage, program, 20-22
storage dump, 353-355
STORAGE option (DUMP), 94
STORAGE parameter (DFHMSD), 42
STRFIELD option (SEND), 185
structure chart, 9-14
SUBALLOCATION parameter
    DEFINE AIX, 373
    DEFINE CLUSTER, 368
SUBMIT command (ISPF), 400
SUMRY command (ICCF), 418
SUSPEND command, 211-212
SWITCH command (ICCF), 418
symbolic cursor positioning, 28
symbolic map, 57-59
SYNC command (ICCF), 418
SYNCPOINT command, 213-214
SYSID option
    ASSIGN, 75
    CANCEL, 78
    DELETE, 83

SYSID option (continued)
DELETEQ TD, 87
DELETEQ TS, 89
ENDBR, 95
READ, 140
READNEXT, 145
READPREV, 150
READQ TD, 155
READQ TS, 158
RESETBR, 170
REWRITE, 177
START, 205
STARTBR, 209
UNLOCK, 218
WRITE, 223
WRITEQ TD, 227
WRITEQ TS, 229
SYSIDERR condition
CANCEL, 79
DELETE, 83
DELETEQ TD, 87
DELETEQ TS, 89
ENDBR, 96
READ, 141
READNEXT, 146
READPREV, 151
READQ TD, 156
READQ TS, 159
RESETBR, 170
REWRITE, 178
START, 206
STARTBR, 209
UNLOCK, 218
WRITE, 224
WRITEQ TD, 228
WRITEQ TS, 230

TA command (ICCF), 432
TABL command (VM/CMS), 466
TABLES option (DUMP), 94
TABS command (ISPF), 396
TABS mode (ISPF), 396
TABSET command (ICCF), 430
TAPE command (VM/CMS), 447
task, 18-19
TASK option (DUMP), 93
TC command (ICCF), 432
TCT option (DUMP), 94
TCTUA, 21
TCTUA option (ADDRESS), 67
TCTUALENG option (ASSIGN), 75
temporary storage browse transaction, 351

TERM parameter (DFHMSD), 42
TERMCODE option (ASSIGN), 75
TERMERR condition
RECEIVE, 162
SEND, 185
TERMID option
ISSUE, 119
START, 205
TERMIDERR condition
ISSUE, 119
START, 206
Terminal Control Table User Area, 21
TERMINAL option
SEND CONTROL, 189
SEND MAP, 192
SEND TEXT, 200
terminal status transaction, 339
testing, 348
TIME command (ICCF), 419
TIME option
DELAY, 80
FORMATTIME, 103
POST, 132
ROUTE, 180
START, 205
TIMESEP option (FORMATTIME), 103
TIOAPFX parameter (DFHMSD), 42
TITLE option (ROUTE), 181
TL command (ICCF), 432
TO parameter
DEFINE AIX, 373
DEFINE CLUSTER, 368
DEFINE PATH, 375
TOADDRESS parameter
PRINT, 386
REPRO, 388
TOKEY parameter
PRINT, 386
REPRO, 388
TONUMBER parameter
PRINT, 386
REPRO, 388
TOP command
ICCF, 430
VM/CMS, 464
TR command (ICCF), 432
TRACE command, 215-216
TRACEID option (ENTER), 100
TRAILER option (SEND TEXT), 200
TRAILER parameter (DFHMDI), 46
trans-id, 18
transaction, 18-19

transaction dump, 353-355
transaction identifier, 18
Transaction Work Area, 21
TRANSFER command (VM/CMS), 448
TRANSID option
    CANCEL, 78
    RETURN, 175
    START, 205, 206
translator, 316
translator options, 325
trigger field, 38
TS command (ICCF), 432
TSIOERR condition
    PURGE MESSAGE, 135
    SEND CONTROL, 189
    SEND MAP, 193
    SEND PAGE, 197
    SEND TEXT, 201
TWA, 21
TWA option (ADDRESS), 67
TWALENG option (ASSIGN), 75
TYPE command (VM/CMS), 448
type I commands (ICCF), 420-431
type II commands (ICCF), 420-431
type III commands (ICCF), 420,432
TYPE parameter (DFHMSD), 42

UNINHIBIT parameter (ALTER), 382
UNIQUE parameter
    DEFINE AIX, 373
    DEFINE CLUSTER, 368
UNIQUEKEY parameter (DEFINE AIX), 373
UNLOCK command, 217-218
UNPROT parameter (DFHMDF), 50
UP command
    ICCF, 430
    VM/CMS, 464
UPDATE option (READ), 140
UPDATE parameter (DEFINE PATH), 375
update technique, 31-32
UPGRADE parameter (DEFINE AIX), 373
UPPERCAS command (VM/CMS), 465
USER option (TRACE), 215
USERID option (ASSIGN), 75
USERS command (ICCF), 419

validation attribute, 37
VALIDATION option (ASSIGN), 75
VALIDN parameter

DFHMDF, 50
DFHMDI, 47
DFHMSD, 43
verb list, 11-13
VERIFY command (ICCF), 430
VIEW command (ICCF), 431
VM/CMS, 433-467
VOLUME parameter (LISTCAT), 380
VOLUMES parameter
    DEFINE AIX, 373
    DEFINE CLUSTER, 368
VSAM, 359-390, see also AMS
VS COBOL II, 22

WAIT EVENT command, 219-220
WAIT JOURNAL command, 221-222
WAIT option
    ISSUE, 119
    JOURNAL, 121
    RETRIEVE, 172
    SEND, 184
    SEND CONTROL, 189
    SEND MAP, 192
    SEND TEXT, 200
WORKFILES parameter (BLDINDEX), 377
Working-Storage Section, 20
WORKVOLUMES parameter (BLDINDEX), 377
WRITE command, 223-226
WRITEQ TD command, 227-228
WRITEQ TS command, 229-231

XCTL command, 32-33, 232-234
XEDIT command (VM/CMS), 449
XINIT parameter (DFHMDF), 50

YEAR option (FORMATTIME), 103
YYDDD option (FORMATTIME), 102
YYDDMM option (FORMATTIME), 103
YYMMDD option (FORMATTIME), 103

ZONE command (ICCF), 431

" command
    ICCF, 432
    VM/CMS, 466
& command (VM/CMS), 465
/ command (VM/CMS), 466
= command (VM/CMS), 465
? command (VM/CMS), 465

CICS for the
COBOL Programmer

Part 1: An Introductory Course

Doug Lowe

Part 1 of *CICS for the COBOL Programmer* teaches all the basics of CICS programming in a simple, down-to-earth way. In it, you'll learn:

- the critical concepts and terminology that relate to CICS programming

- how to use BMS macro instructions to create mapsets

- how to use the pseudo-conversational programming technique effectively, without compromising the readability of your program

- how to *design* a CICS program that's easy to code, test, debug, and maintain

- how to use a basic subset of CICS commands to control 3270 terminals, process VSAM files, and manage program execution

- how to handle exceptional conditions

- how to detect the use of PF keys, PA keys, and the clear key

- how to change 3270 attribute bytes and control the cursor's position

- why program efficiency is vital under CICS...and how to write programs that make the best use of your system's resources

- how to test CICS programs using top-down testing techniques

- how to debug CICS abends using CEDF or a transaction dump

Along the way, you'll see plenty of coding examples...for CICS commands, common COBOL routines, and BMS mapsets...that show you how each new CICS element works. With these solid examples and the clear explanations the text provides, you'll have no trouble understanding even the most complicated aspects of CICS programming.

2 reasons why this book works

1. To learn CICS programming, you have to grasp several complex concepts all at the same time. This book works because the author, Doug Lowe, carefully explains

how each of these concepts relates to the whole. In contrast, most CICS books (and courses) present each CICS element separately, without showing the vital relationships. No wonder so many people are baffled by CICS!

2. Although effective program design is critical to the success of any programmer, few CICS courses adequately deal with the subject. In fact, most of them don't say anything at all about design.

In contrast, this book presents an effective approach to CICS program design that lets you break your programs down into logical units that are easier to code, test, debug, and maintain. And that's the key to becoming a more productive CICS programmer.

Who this book is for

Whether you're a COBOL programmer new to the bewildering world of CICS or a CICS veteran, *CICS for the COBOL Programmer, Part 1* is for *you.*

CICS, Part 1, 10 chapters, 326 pages, **$25.00**

CICS for the
COBOL Programmer

Part 2: An Advanced Course

Doug Lowe

CICS for the COBOL Programmer, Part 2 is for the experienced CICS programmer who wants to become a master. It goes beyond the basics of CICS to teach you advanced feaures like:

- browse commands to process VSAM files sequentially

- VSAM alternate index processing

- temporary storage and transient data control

- interval control

- BMS page building and message routing

- DL/I data base processing

- advanced terminal features like color and extended highlighting

- terminal control (non-BMS)

- abend handling

- journal control

- storage control

When you finish this book, you'll not only know about a wide variety of advanced CICS features, but you'll also understand how those features work, how they relate, and how to select the advanced CICS features that are appropriate for any given programming situation. And that's the knowledge that will set you apart as a master CICS programmer.

CICS, Part 2, 11 chapters, 322 pages, $25.00

For trainers...

We've designed 2 products that make it easier for you to run courses based on our CICS books.

The *Instructor's Guide* gives you practical ideas to make your course more effective. To be specific, the Instructor's Guide gives you:

- content listings, behavioral objectives, and course suggestions by chapter for both of the CICS texts

- 4 lab problems—2 for Part 1 and 2 for Part 2—that require a student to write realistic CICS programs

- complete lab solutions—including a BMS mapset, a symbolic map, and the COBOL source program for each lab problem

- 8 tests—4 for Part 1 and 4 for Part 2—with fill-in, multiple-choice, and simple coding problems

- all the test answers, along with recommendations for scoring each test

- transparency masters for 242 illustrations from the texts

The *training minireel* is a 1600-BPI tape that can let you implement the lab problems easily. On it are the CICS table entries you need to set up the problems, the DOS and OS job streams you need to create the VSAM test files, and the complete lab solutions.

Both products can save you many hours of planning and preparation. Try them and see!

Instructor's Guide, 5 tabbed sections in a 3-ring binder, 421 pages, **$100**

Minireel, 19 source files, **$75**

JCL books from Mike Murach & Associates, Inc.

MVS JCL

MVS/370 • MVS/XA • JES2 • JES3   Doug Lowe

Anyone who's ever worked in an MVS shop knows that JCL is tough to master. You learn enough to get by...but then you stick to that. It's just too frustrating to try to learn something new from the IBM manuals. And too time-consuming to keep asking your co-workers for help...especially when you know they're limping along too.

That's why you need a copy of *MVS JCL*. It zeros in on the JCL you need for everyday jobs...so you can learn to code significant job streams in a hurry.

You'll learn how to compile, link-edit, and execute programs, process tape data sets, and manage QSAM, ISAM, BDAM, and VSAM files. Code JES2/JES3 control statements to manage job and program execution, data set allocation, and SYSOUT processing. Create and use JCL procedures. And much more.

But that's not all this book does. Beyond teaching you JCL, this book explains the basics of how MVS works so you can apply that understanding as you code JCL. You'll learn about the unique interrelationship between virtual storage and multiprogramming under MVS. You'll learn about data management: what data sets are and how data sets, volumes, and units are allocated. You'll learn about job management, including the crucial role played by JES2/JES3 as MVS processes jobs. And you'll learn about the components of a complete MVS system, including the role of system generation and initialization in tying the components together. That's the kind of perspective that's missing in other books and courses about MVS, even though it's background you must have if you want to bring MVS under your control.

MVS JCL, 16 chapters, 444 pages, $32.50

DOS/VSE JCL

Steve Eckols

The job control language for a DOS/VSE system can be overwhelming. There are more parameters that you would ever want to know about. And those parameters let you do more things than you would ever want to do. Of course, all those parameters are described in the IBM manuals...somewhere. But who has time to wade through pages and pages of details that don't seem to apply to your situation (although you can't ever be sure, because the manuals are so confusing)?

Certainly you don't. That's why you need *DOS/VSE JCL*. It doesn't try to teach every nuance of every parameter. Instead, it teaches you how to code the JCL for applications that occur every day in a VSE shop. You'll learn how to manage job and program execution, how to identify the files a program needs to use, and how to use cataloged procedures. You'll learn how to code POWER JECL statements to manage job scheduling and

output processing and how to use ICCF to manage POWER job processing. You'll learn how to process tape and DASD files. And you'll learn how to use language translators and the linkage-editor, maintain VSE libraries, and use three utility programs: sort/merge, DITTO, and AMS.

Whether you're a novice or an expert, this book will help you use your DOS/VSE system more effectively. If you're new to VSE, this book will get you started right, giving you the confidence you need to take charge of your system. If you're an experienced VSE user, this book will help you understand *why* you've been doing what you've been doing so you can do it better in the future.

DOS/VSE JCL, 18 chapters, 421 pages, $30.00

Order Form

Our Unlimited Guarantee

To our customers who order directly from us: You must be satisfied. Our books must work for you, or you can send them back for a full refund . . . no matter how many you buy, no matter how long you've had them.

Name & Title _____

Company (if company address) _____

Address_____

City, State, Zip _____

Phone number (including area code) _____ CREF1

Qty	Product code and title	Price
CICS		
_____ CREF	The CICS Programmer's Desk Reference	$32.50
_____ CIC1	CICS for the COBOL Programmer: Part 1	25.00
_____ CIC2	CICS for the COBOL Programmer: Part 2	25.00
_____ CCIG	CICS Instructor's Guide	100.00
_____ CCM	CICS Training Minireel	75.00
OS/MVS		
_____ MJCL	MVS JCL	$32.50
_____ TSO	MVS TSO	25.00
_____ MBAL	MVS Assembler Language	30.00
_____ OSUT	OS Utilities	15.00
_____ OSDB	OS Debugging for the COBOL Programmer	20.00
DOS/VSE		
_____ VJCL	DOS/VSE JCL	$30.00
_____ ICCF	DOS/VSE ICCF	25.00
_____ VBAL	DOS/VSE Assembler Language	30.00
VM/CMS		
_____ VMCC	VM/CMS: Commands and Concepts (available in January 1988)	$25.00

Qty	Product code and title	Price
VSAM		
_____ VSMX	VSAM: Access Method Services and Application Programming	$25.00
_____ VSAM	VSAM for the COBOL Programmer	15.00
Data Base Processing		
_____ IMS1	IMS for the COBOL Programmer Part 1: DL/I Data Base Processing	$30.00
_____ IMS2	IMS for the COBOL Programmer Part 2: Data Communications and MFS	30.00
COBOL Language Elements		
_____ SC1R	Structured ANS COBOL: Part 1	$25.00
_____ SC2R	Structured ANS COBOL: Part 2	25.00
_____ RW	Report Writer	13.50
COBOL Program Development		
_____ DDCP	How to Design and Develop COBOL Programs	$30.00
_____ CPHB	The COBOL Programmer's Handbook	20.00
System Development		
_____ DDBS	How to Design and Develop Business Systems	$20.00

☐ Bill me the appropriate price plus UPS shipping and handling (and sales tax in California) for each book ordered.

☐ Bill the appropriate book prices plus UPS shipping and handling (and sales tax in California) to my _____VISA _____MasterCard:

Card number_____

Valid thru (month/year)_____

Cardowner's signature _____

(not valid without signature)

☐ I want to **save** UPS shipping and handling charges. Here's my check or money order for $_____. California residents, please add 6% sales tax to your total. (Offer valid in the U.S. only.)

To order more quickly,

Call **toll-free** 1-800-221-5528

(Weekdays, 9 to 4 Pacific Std. Time)

In California, call 1-800-221-5527

Mike Murach & Associates, Inc.

4697 West Jacquelyn Avenue
Fresno, California 93722
(209) 275-3335

BUSINESS REPLY MAIL

FIRST CLASS   PERMIT NO. 3063   FRESNO, CA

POSTAGE WILL BE PAID BY ADDRESSEE

Mike Murach & Associates, Inc.

4697 West Jacquelyn Avenue
Fresno, CA 93722-9986

Comment form

Your opinions count

If you have comments, criticisms, or suggestions, I'm eager to get them. Your opinions today will affect our products of tomorrow. If you have questions, you can expect an answer within one week of the time we receive them. And if you discover any errors in this book, typographical or otherwise, please point them out so we can make corrections when the book is reprinted.

Thanks for your help.

Mike Murach
Fresno, California

Book title: The CICS Programmer's Desk Reference

_____
_____
_____
_____
_____
_____
_____
_____
_____
_____
_____
_____
_____
_____
_____
_____
_____
_____
_____

Name & Title _____
Company (if company address) _____
Address _____
City, State, Zip _____

Fold where indicated and tape shut.
No postage necessary if mailed in the U.S.

9813

9813

DATE DUE

ILL-1181195 5-18-79			
ILL 283-79 06-13-80			
ILL 364097 3/20/91			
MAY 31 '91			
JUL 31 '91			
APR 21 '92			
APR 22 '92			